BARRON'S

FOREIGN LANGUAGE GUIDES

FRENCH
Verbs

THIRD EDITION
by

Christopher Kendris
B.S., M.S., Columbia University
M.A., Ph.D., Northwestern University
Diplômé, Faculté des Lettres,
Université de Paris et Institut de Phonétique, Paris (en Sorbonne)

and

Theodore Kendris
Ph.D., Université Laval, Québec, Canada

A Valuable Supplemental Learning Tool

BARRON'S

*To St. Sophia Greek Orthodox Church
of Albany, New York, our parish
and
To the eternal memory of our beloved
YOLANDA KENDRIS,
who is always by our side
With love*

All inquiries should be addressed to:
Barron's Educational Series, Inc.
250 Wireless Boulevard
Hauppauge, New York 11788
www.barronseduc.com

Library of Congress Catalog Card No. 2010940164

ISBN: 978-0-7641-4608-4

PRINTED IN CHINA
9 8 7 6 5 4 3 2

Contents

About the Authors

Dr. Christopher Kendris has worked as an interpreter and translator of French for the U.S. State Department at the American Embassy in Paris. He earned his B.S. in the School of General Studies and his M.S. in the School of Library Service, both at Columbia University in the City of New York, where he held a New York State scholarship. He earned his M.A. and Ph.D. at Northwestern University in Evanston, Illinois, where he held a teaching assistantship and tutorial fellowship for four years. He also earned two diplomas with *Mention très Honorable* at the Université de Paris (en Sorbonne), Faculté des Lettres, École Supérieure de Préparation et de Perfectionnement des Professeurs de Français à l'Étranger, and at the Institut de Phonétique, Paris. His highly esteemed mentor was Dr. Bernard Weinberg, a teacher, author, scholar, friend, and professor of romance languages and literatures at the University of Chicago and Northwestern University in Evanston, Illinois.

In 1986, Dr. Kendris was one of ninety-five teachers in the United States to be awarded a Rockefeller Foundation Fellowship for Teachers of Foreign Languages in American High Schools. He has had forty years of teaching experience. Dr. Kendris has taught French and Spanish at the College of the University of Chicago as a visiting summer lecturer, as well as at Colby College, Duke University, Rutgers (the State University of New Jersey), the State University of New York at Albany, the Albany Academy of Albany, the Schenectady School District, and the Schenectady County Community College in Schenectady, New York. In the 1960s, he was Chairman of the Department of Foreign Languages at Farmingdale High School in Farmingdale, New York, where he was also a teacher of all levels of French and Spanish, and he prepared students for the New York State French and Spanish Regents exams, SAT exams, and AP tests. Dr. Kendris is the author of thirty-two secondary school and college books, workbooks, and other language guides of French and Spanish, some of which have been best sellers since 1970 all over the world, and all of which have been published by Barron's Educational Series. He also worked as cataloger of books at the U.S. Library of Congress in Washington, D.C. in the 1970s. Dr. Kendris is listed in *Contemporary Authors* and the *Directory of American Scholars*.

Dr. Theodore Kendris earned his B.A. in modern languages at Union College in Schenectady, New York, where he received the Thomas J. Judson Memorial Award for modern language study. He went on to earn his M.A. in French language and literature at Northwestern University in Evanston, Illinois, where he was a teaching assistant and senior teaching fellow. He earned his Ph.D. in French literature at l'Université Laval in Quebec City, where he studied the Middle Ages and Renaissance. While at Université Laval, he taught French writing skills as chargé de cours in the French as a Second Language program, and in 1997 he was awarded a doctoral scholarship by the Fondation de l'Université Laval. Dr. Kendris has also taught in the Department of English and Foreign Languages at the University of St. Francis in Joliet, Illinois, as well as at the Hazleton campus of Penn State University.

Dr. Kendris is the author of *Inglés completo: Repaso integral de gramática inglesa para hispanohablantes,* published by Barron's in 2008. He is also the coauthor of several language guides, including *Pronounce It Perfectly in French; French Vocabulary; 501 French Verbs, Sixth Edition;* and *501 Spanish Verbs, Seventh Edition*—all published by Barron's.

Abbreviations

adj. adjectif (adjective)	*n.* nom (noun)
adv. adverbe (adverb)	*obj.* objet (object)
ant. antérieure (anterior)	*p.* page
art. article	*pp.* pages
comp. computer	*part.* participe (participle)
cond. conditionnel (conditional)	*pl.* pluriel (plural)
def. défini (definite)	*plpf.* plus-que-parfait (pluperfect)
dir. direct	*pr.* or *prés.* présent (present)
e.g. for example	*prep.* préposition (preposition)
f. or *fem.* féminin (feminine)	*pron.* pronom (pronoun)
fam. familiar	*qqch* quelque chose (something)
fut. futur (future)	*qqn* quelqu'un (someone, somebody)
i.e. that is, that is to say	*refl.* reflexive
imp. imparfait (imperfect)	*s.* or *sing.* singulier (singular)
ind. indicatif (indicative)	*subj.* subjonctif (subjunctive)
inf. infinitif (infinitive)	*v.* verbe (verb)
m. or *masc.* masculin (masculine)	

Introduction

This new edition of *French Verbs* includes improvements to the existing text, additional new material, and offers an important feature—color as an aid to learning. In the front section of this book, rules regarding the use of verbs are made clearer by color highlights. In the body of the book, color takes the mystery out of conjugation. In all, the reader will find that color makes the entire book easier to use. Whatever facilitates learning enhances the ability to use what is learned. This pocket reference of over 300 commonly used French verbs for students, businesspeople, and travelers provides fingertip access to correct verb forms.

Verb conjugations are usually found scattered in French grammar books and they are difficult to find quickly when needed. Verbs have always been a major problem for students no matter what system or approach the teacher uses. You will master French verb forms if you study this book a few minutes every day, especially the pages before and after the alphabetical listing of the 301 verbs.

We compiled this book in order to help make your work easier and at the same time to teach you French verb forms systematically. It is a useful book because it provides a quick and easy way to find the full conjugation of many French verbs.

The verbs included here are arranged alphabetically by infinitive at the top of each page. The book contains many common verbs of high frequency, both reflexive and non-reflexive, which you need to know. It also contains many other frequently used verbs that are irregular in some way. On page 312 we give you an additional 1,000 French verbs that are conjugated in the same way as model verbs among the 301. If the verb you have in mind is not given, consult the list that begins on page 312. Our other book, *501 French verbs fully conjugated in all the tenses,* sixth edition, contains more than two hundred additional verbs and many new features, including a CD-ROM with practice exercises and answers explained.

The subject pronouns have been omitted from the conjugations in order to emphasize the verb forms. We give you the subject pronouns on page xxxix. Turn to that page now and become acquainted with them.

The first thing to do when you use this book is to become familiar with it from cover to cover—in particular, the front and back pages where you will find valuable and useful information to make your study easier and more enjoyable. Take a minute right now and turn to the table of contents at the beginning of this book as we guide you.

(a)   On page ix we explain which verbs are conjugated with *avoir* or *être* to form a compound tense. Study those pages and refer to them frequently until you master those verbs.

(b)   On page xiii we show you how to form a present participle regularly in French and we give you examples. We also give you the common irregular present participles on page xiv.

(c)   On page xiv we do the same for past participles. We give you the present and past participles of each verb at the top of the page where verb forms are given for a particular verb.

(d)   On page xv you will find the principal parts of some important verbs which, in French, are called *Les temps primitifs*. This is useful because if you know these you can easily form all the tenses and moods from them.

(e)   On pages xvi and xvii there are two tables showing the derivation of tenses of a typical verb conjugated with *avoir* and another conjugated with *être*. These are presented as in a picture so that you can see what tenses are derived from the principal parts.

(f)   On pages xviii and xix we give you a sample English verb conjugation so that you can get an idea of the way a verb is expressed in the English tenses. Many people do not know one tense from another because they have never learned the use of verb tenses in a systematic and organized way—not even in English! How can you know, for instance, that you need the conditional form of a verb in French when you want to say *"I would go* to the movies if . . ."* or the pluperfect tense in French if you want to say *"I had gone . . . "?* The sample English verb conjugation with the names of the tenses and their numerical ranking will help you distinguish one tense from another so that you will know what tense you need to express a verb in French.

(g)   On page xx we begin a summary of meanings and uses of French verb tenses and moods as related to English verb tenses and moods. That section is very important and useful because we separate the seven simple tenses from the seven compound tenses. We give you the name of each tense in French and English starting with the present indicative, which we call tense number 1, because it is the tense most frequently used. We assign a number to each tense name so that you can fix each one in your mind and associate the name and number in their logical order. We explain briefly what each tense is, when you use it, and we give examples using verbs in sentences in French and English.

(h) On page xxxv we give you a summary of all the fourteen tenses in French with English equivalents, which we have divided into the seven simple tenses and the seven compound tenses. After referring to that summary frequently, you will soon know that tense number 1 is the present indicative, tense number 2 is the imperfect indicative, and so on.

(i) On page xxxvi we show you how to form the seven simple tenses for regular verbs and here, again, we have assigned the same number to each tense name. We also explain how each compound tense is based on each simple tense in the table on page xxxvii and on page xxxviii. Try to see these two divisions as two frames, two pictures, with the seven simple tenses in one frame and the seven compound tenses in another frame. Place them side by side in your mind, and you will see how tense number 8 is related to tense number 1, tense number 9 to tense number 2, and so on. If you study the numerical arrangement of each of the seven simple tenses and associate the tense number with the tense name, you will find it very easy to learn the names of the seven compound tenses, how they rank numerically according to use, how they are formed, and when they are used. Spend at least ten minutes every day studying these preliminary pages to help you understand better the fourteen tenses in French.

Finally, in the back pages of this book there are useful indexes and an additional 1,000 French verbs that are conjugated like model verbs among the 301.

We sincerely hope that this book will be of some help to you in learning and using French verbs.

CHRISTOPHER KENDRIS
B.S., M.S., M.A., Ph.D.

THEODORE KENDRIS
B.A., M.A., Ph.D.

Verbs Conjugated with *avoir* or *être* to Form a Compound Tense

Most verbs use **avoir** as the helping verb in the **passé composé**. However, a number of verbs, in addition to reflexive verbs, use **être** as the helping verb. The most common ones are:

aller (to go)
arriver (to arrive)
descendre (to go down, come down)
devenir (to become)
entrer (to enter)
monter (to go up, come up)
mourir (to die)
naître (to be born)
partir (to leave)

passer (to go by, pass by)
rentrer (to go in again, to return home)
rester (to remain, stay)
retourner (to return, go back)
revenir (to come back)
sortir (to go out)
tomber (to fall)
venir (to come)

> TIP: Most French verbs are conjugated with *avoir* to form a compound tense. All reflexive verbs, such as *se laver,* are conjugated with *être*.

So, if you're having some trouble choosing your helping verb in the **passé composé**, just remember APEMAN, which will help you remember the French verbs we are dealing with in this unit. Most of the verbs in this list are intransitive and use **être** as a helping verb. As you will see below, a few of them sometimes take a direct object, in which case you should use **avoir**.

Here is a way to break down the verbs that use **être** as a helping verb into smaller groups. Note the general similarity in the type of action described by the verbs in each APEMAN group.

Aller/Venir-Devenir-Revenir
Passer/Rester
Entrer-Rentrer/Sortir
Monter/Descendre/Tomber
Arriver/Partir/Retourner
Naître/Mourir

Look at the acrostic formed by the first letter of each group (bottom of page ix). That's right: APEMAN! It's helpful to discuss the connections between the verbs in each of these groups. You may come up with a way that works better for you. This way of looking at the "être verbs" is not set in stone—or the Stone Age. It's a tool to help you organize your study. The best way to remember which verbs use être as a helping verb in the passé composé is to practice using them!

A
Aller/Venir-Devenir-Revenir

Aller and **venir** are used to talk about opposite movements.

EXAMPLES:
Marie est allée au supermarché.
Marie went to the supermarket.

Les Gosselin sont venus chez nous hier soir.
The Gosselins came to our home yesterday evening.

The verbs based on **venir** follow the same pattern in the passé composé.

EXAMPLES:
Ma mère est devenue pédiatre pour aider les enfants.
My mother became a pediatrician to help children.

Est-ce que Pierre est revenu de l'école?
Has Peter come back from school?

However, **prévenir** (to warn) uses **avoir** in the passé composé:

EXAMPLE:
J'ai prévenu ma soeur qu'on annonçait de la pluie.
I warned my sister that they were predicting rain.

P

Passer uses être as its auxiliary verb when it has no direct object.

EXAMPLE:
Jean-Claude est passé au bureau de sa directrice.
Jean-Claude went by his director's office.

But **passer** uses **avoir** when it is used transitively (that is, with a direct object).

EXAMPLE:
Elle m'a passé le sel. (direct object = le sel)
She passed me the salt. / She passed the salt to me.

Rester takes **être** as its auxiliary in the **passé composé**. While **passer** means "to pass by," **rester** means "to stay." Well, they're not quite opposites.

EXAMPLE:
Sabrina est restée à la maison parce qu'elle était malade.
Sabrina stayed at home because she was sick.

E
Entrer-Rentrer/Sortir
Entrer and **sortir** are antonyms. **Être** is the helping verb when you use **entrer** in the **passé composé**.

EXAMPLE:
Nous sommes entrés par la porte principale.
We came in by the main door.

When it has no direct object, **rentrer** (to go in again, to return home) also uses **être** as its helping verb in the **passé composé**.

EXAMPLE:
Anne et Marie sont rentrées à 23h.
Anne and Mary returned at 11 P.M.

But when **rentrer** takes a direct object, you should use **avoir** as the helping verb.

EXAMPLE:
Frédéric a rentré le chat avant de fermer la porte.
Fred brought the cat inside before closing the door.

Sortir is the antonym of **entrer**, and it also uses **être** as its helping verb in the **passé composé**.

EXAMPLE:
Jeanne est sortie avec ses amis.
Jean went out with her friends.

However, if **sortir** takes a direct object, you should use **avoir** as the helping verb.

EXAMPLE:
David a sorti son portefeuille pour chercher sa carte de crédit.
David took out his wallet to look for his credit card.

M
Monter/Descendre/Tomber

These three verbs are used to describe up or down movement. When **monter** and **descendre** are used intransitively (without a direct object), they use **être** as the helping verb.

EXAMPLES:
Elle est montée lentement.
She went up slowly.

Elle est descendue vite.
She came down quickly.

When they are used transitively (with a direct object), these verbs take **avoir** as the helping verb.

EXAMPLES:
Elle a monté l'escalier.
She went up the stairs.

Elle a descendu la valise.
She brought down the suitcase.

Tomber is almost always used intransitively and therefore usually takes **être** as its helping verb in the **passé composé**.

EXAMPLE:
Elle est tombée dans l'escalier.
She fell down the stairs.

A
Arriver/Partir/Retourner

This group of verbs is used for arrivals and departures. They take the helping verb **être** in the **passé composé**.

EXAMPLES:
Madeleine est arrivée.
Madeleine arrived.

Francine est partie.
Francine left.

Mes parents sont retournés.
My parents returned.

However, when **retourner** takes a direct object (meaning to turn over, to turn around), you should use **avoir** as the helping verb.

EXAMPLE:
Quand Jean a retourné la pierre, il a trouvé ses clés.
When John turned over the stone, he found his keys.

N
Naître/Mourir
Finally, we have **naître** and its antonym, **mourir**. Both verbs take the helping verb être in the passé composé.

EXAMPLES:
Ma tante est née en 1965.
My aunt was born in 1965.

Charles de Gaulle est mort en 1970.
Charles de Gaulle died in 1970.

Early modern humans created the cave paintings in the *grotte de Lascaux* (the Lascaux Cave) in Dordogne, in southwest France, over 17,000 years ago.

Formation of the Present and Past Participles in French

Formation of the present participle in French

The present participle is regularly formed in the following way. Take the "**nous**" form of the present indicative of the verb you have in mind, drop the ending **-ons** and add **-ant**. That ending is the equivalent to *-ing* in English. Examples:

chantons, chantant	**mangeons,** mangeant
finissons, finissant	**allons,** allant
vendons, vendant	**travaillons,** travaillant

Common irregular present participles

The three common irregular present participles are: **ayant** from **avoir**; **étant** from **être**; **sachant** from **savoir**.

Formation of the past participle in French

The past participle is regularly formed from the infinitive:

-er ending verbs, drop the **-er** and add **é**: **donner**, donné
-ir ending verbs, drop the **-ir** and add **i**: **finir**, fini
-re ending verbs, drop the **-re** and add **u**: **vendre**, vendu

Common irregular past participles

INFINITIVE	PAST PARTICIPLE	INFINITIVE	PAST PARTICIPLE
apprendre	**appris**	naître	**né**
asseoir	**assis**	offrir	**offert**
avoir	**eu**	ouvrir	**ouvert**
boire	**bu**	paraître	**paru**
comprendre	**compris**	permettre	**permis**
conduire	**conduit**	plaire	**plu**
connaître	**connu**	pleuvoir	**plu**
construire	**construit**	pouvoir	**pu**
courir	**couru**	prendre	**pris**
couvrir	**couvert**	promettre	**promis**
craindre	**craint**	recevoir	**reçu**
croire	**cru**	revenir	**revenu**
devenir	**devenu**	rire	**ri**
devoir	**dû, due**	savoir	**su**
dire	**dit**	suivre	**suivi**
écrire	**écrit**	taire	**tu**
être	**été**	tenir	**tenu**
faire	**fait**	valoir	**valu**
falloir	**fallu**	venir	**venu**
lire	**lu**	vivre	**vécu**
mettre	**mis**	voir	**vu**
mourir	**mort**	vouloir	**voulu**

Principal Parts of Some Important Verbs
(Les temps primitifs de quelques verbes importants)

The principal parts of a verb are very important to know because from them you can easily form all the tenses. See the following page where two tables are given, one showing the derivation of tenses of a verb conjugated with **avoir** and the other with **être**. Note that the headings at the top of each column are the same as the following headings:

INFINITIF	PARTICIPE PRÉSENT	PARTICIPE PASSÉ	PRÉSENT DE L'INDICATIF	PASSÉ SIMPLE
aller	allant	allé	je vais	j'allai
avoir	ayant	eu	j'ai	j'eus
battre	battant	battu	je bats	je battis
boire	buvant	bu	je bois	je bus
craindre	craignant	craint	je crains	je craignis
croire	croyant	cru	je crois	je crus
devoir	devant	dû, due	je dois	je dus
dire	disant	dit	je dis	je dis
écrire	écrivant	écrit	j'écris	j'écrivis
être	étant	été	je suis	je fus
faire	faisant	fait	je fais	je fis
lire	lisant	lu	je lis	je lus
mettre	mettant	mis	je mets	je mis
mourir	mourant	mort	je meurs	je mourus
naître	naissant	né	je nais	je naquis
ouvrir	ouvrant	ouvert	j'ouvre	j'ouvris
porter	portant	porté	je porte	je portai
pouvoir	pouvant	pu	je peux *or* je puis*	je pus
prendre	prenant	pris	je prends	je pris
recevoir	recevant	reçu	je reçois	je reçus
savoir	sachant	su	je sais	je sus
venir	venant	venu	je viens	je vins
vivre	vivant	vécu	je vis	je vécus
voir	voyant	vu	je vois	je vis
voler	volant	volé	je vole	je volai

*In the affirmative, it is most common to say "Je peux." In the inverted interrogative, you should say "Puis-je?"

Tables Showing Derivation of Tenses of Verbs Conjugated with *avoir* and *être*

Derivation of Tenses of Verbs Conjugated with *avoir*

INFINITIF	PARTICIPE PRÉSENT	PARTICIPE PASSÉ	PRÉSENT DE L'INDICATIF	PASSÉ SIMPLE
donner	**donnant**	**donné**	**je donne**	**je donnai**

FUTUR	IMPARFAIT DE L'INDICATIF	PASSÉ COMPOSÉ	PRÉSENT DE L'INDICATIF	PASSÉ SIMPLE
donnerai	donnais	**ai** donné	donne	donnai
donneras	donnais	**as** donné	donnes	donnas
donnera	donnait	**a** donné	donne	donna
donnerons	donnions	**avons** donné	donnons	donnâmes
donnerez	donniez	**avez** donné	donnez	donnâtes
donneront	donnaient	**ont** donné	donnent	donnèrent

CONDITIONNEL		PLUS-QUE-PARFAIT DE L'INDICATIF	IMPÉRATIF	IMPARFAIT DU SUBJONCTIF
donnerais		**avais** donné	donne	donnasse
donnerais		**avais** donné	donnons	donnasses
donnerait		**avait** donné	donnez	donnât
donnerions		**avions** donné		donnassions
donneriez		**aviez** donné		donnassiez
donneraient		**avaient** donné		donnassent

		PASSÉ ANTÉRIEUR	PRÉSENT DU SUBJONCTIF	
		eus donné	donne	
		eus donné	donnes	
		eut donné	donne	
		eûmes donné	donnions	
		eûtes donné	donniez	
		eurent donné	donnent	

FUTUR ANTÉRIEUR	CONDITIONNEL PASSÉ	PASSÉ DU SUBJONCTIF	PLUS-QUE-PARFAIT DU SUBJONCTIF
aurai donné	**aurais** donné	**aie** donné	**eusse** donné
auras donné	**aurais** donné	**aies** donné	**eusses** donné
aura donné	**aurait** donné	**ait** donné	**eût** donné
aurons donné	**aurions** donné	**ayons** donné	**eussions** donné
aurez donné	**auriez** donné	**ayez** donné	**eussiez** donné
auront donné	**auraient** donné	**aient** donné	**eussent** donné

Derivation of Tenses of Verbs Conjugated with *être*

INFINITIF	PARTICIPE PRÉSENT	PARTICIPE PASSÉ	PRÉSENT DE L'INDICATIF	PASSÉ SIMPLE
arriver	**arrivant**	**arrivé**	**j'arrive**	**j'arrivai**

FUTUR	IMPARFAIT DE L'INDICATIF	PASSÉ COMPOSÉ	PRÉSENT DE L'INDICATIF	PASSÉ SIMPLE
arriver**ai**	arriv**ais**	**suis** arrivé(e)	arrive	arriv**ai**
arriver**as**	arriv**ais**	**es** arrivé(e)	arrives	arriv**as**
arriver**a**	arriv**ait**	**est** arrivé(e)	arrive	arriv**a**
arriver**ons**	arriv**ions**	**sommes** arrivé(e)s	arriv**ons**	arriv**âmes**
arriver**ez**	arriv**iez**	**êtes** arrivé(e)(s)	arriv**ez**	arriv**âtes**
arriver**ont**	arriv**aient**	**sont** arrivé(e)s	arriv**ent**	arriv**èrent**

CONDITIONNEL		PLUS-QUE-PARFAIT DE L'INDICATIF	IMPÉRATIF	IMPARFAIT DU SUBJONCTIF
arriver**ais**		**étais** arrivé(e)	arrive	arriv**asse**
arriver**ais**		**étais** arrivé(e)	arriv**ons**	arriv**asses**
arriver**ait**		**était** arrivé(e)	arriv**ez**	arriv**ât**
arriver**ions**		**étions** arrivé(e)s		arriv**assions**
arriver**iez**		**étiez** arrivé(e)(s)		arriv**assiez**
arriver**aient**		**étaient** arrivé(e)s		arriv**assent**

	PASSÉ ANTÉRIEUR	PRÉSENT DU SUBJONCTIF
	fus arrivé(e)	arrive
	fus arrivé(e)	arrives
	fut arrivé(e)	arrive
	fûmes arrivé(e)s	arriv**ions**
	fûtes arrivé(e)(s)	arriv**iez**
	furent arrivé(e)s	arriv**ent**

FUTUR ANTÉRIEUR	CONDITIONNEL PASSÉ	PASSÉ DU SUBJONCTIF	PLUS-QUE-PARFAIT DU SUBJONCTIF
serai arrivé(e)	**serais** arrivé(e)	**sois** arrivé(e)	**fusse** arrivé(e)
seras arrivé(e)	**serais** arrivé(e)	**sois** arrivé(e)	**fusses** arrivé(e)
sera arrivé(e)	**serait** arrivé(e)	**soit** arrivé(e)	**fût** arrivé(e)
serons arrivé(e)s	**serions** arrivé(e)s	**soyons** arrivé(e)s	**fussions** arrivé(e)s
serez arrivé(e)(s)	**seriez** arrivé(e)(s)	**soyez** arrivé(e)(s)	**fussiez** arrivé(e)(s)
seront arrivé(e)s	**seraient** arrivé(e)s	**soient** arrivé(e)s	**fussent** arrivé(e)s

Sample English Verb Conjugation

INFINITIVE **to go—aller**
PRESENT PARTICIPLE going   *PAST PARTICIPLE* gone

Tense no.	The seven simple tenses
1 *Present Indicative*	I go, you go, he (she, it) goes; we go, you go, they go
	or: I do go, you do go, he (she, it) does go; we do go, you do go, they do go
	or: I am going, you are going, he (she, it) is going; we are going, you are going, they are going
2 *Imperfect Indicative*	I was going, you were going, he (she, it) was going; we were going, you were going, they were going
	or: I went, you went, he (she, it) went; we went, you went, they went
	or: I used to go, you used to go, he (she, it) used to go; we used to go, you used to go, he (she, it) used to go
3 *Passé Simple*	I went, you went, he (she, it) went; we went, you went, they went
	or: I did go, you did go, he (she, it) did go; we did go, you did go, they did go
4 *Future*	I shall (will) go, you will go, he (she, it) will go; we shall (will) go, you will go, they will go
5 *Conditional*	I would go, you would go, he (she, it) would go; we would go, you would go, they would go
6 *Present Subjunctive*	that I may go, that you may go, that he (she, it) may go; that we may go, that you may go, that they may go
7 *Imperfect Subjunctive*	that I might go, that you might go, that he (she, it) might go; that we might go, that you might go, that they might go

INFINITIVE **to go—aller**
PRESENT PARTICIPLE going   *PAST PARTICIPLE* gone

Tense no.	The seven compound tenses
8 *Passé Composé*	I have gone, you have gone, he (she, it) has gone; we have gone, you have gone, they have gone
or:	I went, you went, he (she, it) went; we went, you went, they went
or:	I did go, you did go, he (she, it) did go; we did go, you did go, they did go
9 *Pluperfect or Past Perfect Indicative*	I had gone, you had gone, he (she, it) had gone; we had gone, you had gone, they had gone
10 *Past Anterior*	I had gone, you had gone, he (she, it) had gone; we had gone, you had gone, they had gone
11 *Future Perfect or Future Anterior*	I shall (will) have gone, you will have gone, he (she, it) will have gone; we shall (will) have gone, you will have gone, they will have gone
12 *Conditional Perfect*	I would have gone, you would have gone, he (she, it) would have gone; we would have gone, you would have gone, they would have gone
13 *Past Subjunctive*	that I may have gone, that you may have gone, that he (she, it) may have gone; that we may have gone, that you may have gone, that they may have gone
14 *Pluperfect or Past Perfect Subjunctive*	that I might have gone, that you might have gone, that he (she, it) might have gone; that we might have gone, that you might have gone, that they might have gone
Imperative (Command)	Go! (sing.) Let's go! Go! (pl.)

A Summary of Meanings and Uses of French Verb Tenses and Moods as Related to English Verb Tenses and Moods

A verb is where the action is! A verb is a word that expresses an action (like *go, eat, write*) or a state of being (like *think, believe, be*). Tense means time. French and English verb tenses are divided into three main groups of time: past, present, and future. A verb tense shows if an action or state of being took place, is taking place, or will take place.

French and English verbs are also used in four moods (or modes). Mood has to do with the *way* a person regards an action or a state. For example, a person may merely make a statement or ask a question—this is the Indicative Mood, which we use most of the time in French and English. A person may say that he *would do* something if something else were possible or that he *would have done* something if something else had been possible—this is the Conditional Mood. A person may use a verb *in such a way* to indicate a wish, a fear, a regret, a supposition, or something of this sort—this is the Subjunctive Mood. The Subjunctive Mood is used in French much more than in English. A person may command that something be done—this is the Imperative Mood.

There are six tenses in English: Present, Past, Future, Present Perfect, Past Perfect, and Future Perfect. The first two are simple tenses. The other four are compound tenses and are based on the simple tenses. In French, however, there are fourteen tenses, seven of which are simple and seven of which are compound.

In the pages that follow, the tenses and moods are given in French and the equivalent name or names in English are given in parentheses. We have numbered each tense name for easy reference and recognition. Although some of the names given in English are not considered to be tenses (for there are only six), they are given for the purpose of identification as they are related to the French names. The comparison includes only the essential points you need to know about the meanings and uses of French verb tenses and moods as related to English usage.

We shall use examples to illustrate their meanings and uses. See page xxxvi for the formation of the seven simple tenses for regular verbs.

THE SEVEN SIMPLE TENSES

Tense No. 1   Le Présent de l'indicatif
**   (Present Indicative)**

This tense is used most of the time in French and English. It indicates:

(a) An action or a state of being at the present time.
   EXAMPLES:
   1. Je **vais** à l'école maintenant. I *am going* to school now.
   2. Je **pense**; donc, je **suis**. I *think;* therefore, I *am*.

(b) Habitual action.
   EXAMPLE:
   Je **vais** à la bibliothèque tous les jours.
   I *go* to the library every day. OR: I *do go* to the library every day.

(c) A general truth, something that is permanently true.
   EXAMPLES:
   1. Deux et deux **font** quatre. Two and two *are* four.
   2. Voir c'**est** croire. Seeing *is* believing.

(d) Vividness when talking or writing about past events. This is called
   the *historical present*.
   EXAMPLE:
   Marie-Antoinette **est** condamnée à mort. Elle **monte** dans la charrette
   et **est** en route pour la guillotine.
   Marie-Antoinette *is* condemned to die. She *goes* into the cart and
   is on her way to the guillotine.

(e) A near future.
   EXAMPLE:
   Il **arrive** demain. He *arrives* tomorrow.

(f) An action or state of being that occurred in the past and
   continues up to the present. In English, this tense is the Present
   Perfect, which is formed with the present tense of *to have* (*have*
   or *has*) plus the past participle of the verb you are using.
   EXAMPLES:
   1. Je **suis** ici depuis dix minutes.
      I *have been* here for ten minutes. (I am still here at present)
   2. Elle **est** malade depuis trois jours.
      She *has been* sick for three days. (She is still sick at present)
   3. J'**attends** l'autobus depuis dix minutes.
      I *have been waiting* for the bus for ten minutes.

NOTE: In this last example the formation of the English verb tense is slightly different from the other two examples in English. The present participle *(waiting)* is used instead of the past participle *(waited)*.

NOTE ALSO: For the formation of this tense for regular verbs see page xxxvi.

Tense No. 2   L'Imparfait de l'indicatif
            (Imperfect Indicative)

This is a past tense. It is used to indicate:

(a) An action that was going on in the past at the same time as another action.
    EXAMPLE:
    Il **lisait** pendant que j'**écrivais**. He *was reading* while I *was writing*.

(b) An action that was going on in the past when another action occurred.
    EXAMPLE:
    Il **lisait** quand je suis entré. He *was reading* when I came in.

(c) An action that a person did habitually in the past.
    EXAMPLE:
    Nous **allions** à la plage tous les jours. We *used to go* to the beach every day.
    OR:
    We *would go* to the beach every day.

(d) A description of a mental or physical condition in the past.
    EXAMPLES:
    (mental condition)   Il **était** triste quand je l'ai vu.
                            He *was* sad when I saw him.
    (physical condition)   Quand ma mère **était** jeune, elle **était** blonde.
                            When my mother *was* young, she *was* blond.

(e) An action or state of being that occurred in the past and *lasted for a certain length of time* prior to another past action. In English, it is usually translated as a pluperfect tense and is formed with *had been* plus the present participle of the verb you are using. It is like the special use of the **Présent de l'indicatif** described in the above section (Tense No. 1) in paragraph (f), except that the action or state of being no longer exists at present.

EXAMPLE:

J'**attendais** l'autobus depuis dix minutes quand il est arrivé.

I *had been waiting* for the bus for ten minutes when it arrived.

NOTE: For the formation of this tense for regular verbs see page xxxvi.

Tense No. 3   Le Passé simple
                 (Past Definite or Simple Past)

This past tense is not ordinarily used in conversational French or in
informal writing. It is a literary tense. It is used in formal writing, such as
history and literature. You should be able merely to recognize this tense
when you see it in your French readings. It should be noted that French
writers use the **Passé simple** less and less these days. The **Passé composé**
is taking its place in literature, except for **avoir** and **être**, which you must
know in this tense.

   EXAMPLES:

   (a) Il **alla** en Afrique. He *went* to Africa.
   (b) Il **voyagea** en Amérique. He *traveled* to America.
   (c) Elle **fut** heureuse. She *was* happy.
   (d) Elle **eut** un grand bonheur. She *had* great happiness.

   NOTE: For the formation of this tense for regular verbs see page xxxvi.

Tense No. 4   Le Futur
                 (Future)

In French and English this tense is used to express an action or a state of
being that will take place at some time in the future.

EXAMPLES:

(a) J'**irai** en France l'été prochain.
    I *shall go* to France next summer.

    OR:

    I *will go* to France next summer.

(b) J'y **penserai**.
    I *shall think* about it.
    OR:
    I *will think* about it.

(c) Je **partirai** dès qu'il arrivera.
    I *shall leave* as soon as he
    arrives.
(d) Je te **dirai** tout quand tu seras ici.
    I *shall tell* you all when you are
    here.

If the action of the verb you are using is not past or present and if future time is implied, the future tense is used when the clause begins with any of the following conjunctions: **aussitôt que** (as soon as), **dès que** (as soon as), **quand** (when), **lorsque** (when), and **tant que** (as long as).

NOTE: For the formation of this tense for regular verbs see page xxxvi.

Another way to express the future is **le Futur proche** (the Near Future). As one may guess, the **Futur proche** is used when talking about something that will take place in the near future. In French, the near future is formed by using **aller** with the infinitive of the verb that you want to use. In English, you use *to go* with the infinitive of the verb that you want to use.

EXAMPLES:

> Demain, je **vais acheter** un nouveau portable.
> Tomorrow I *am going to buy* a new cell phone.
> Nous **allons manger** en ville.
> We are *going to eat* downtown.

Tense No. 5   Le Conditionnel présent
                 (Conditional)

The Conditional is used in French and English to express:

(a) An action that you would do if something else were possible.
  EXAMPLE:
  Je **ferais** le travail si j'avais le temps.
  I *would do* the work if I had the time.

(b) A conditional desire. This is the Conditional of courtesy in French.
  EXAMPLES:
  J'**aimerais** du thé. I *would like* some tea.
  Je **voudrais** du café. I *would like* some coffee.

(c) An obligation or duty.
  EXAMPLE:
  Je **devrais** étudier pour l'examen. I *should* study for the examination.
  OR: I *ought* to study for the examination.

  NOTE (1): The French verb **devoir** plus the infinitive is used to express the idea of *should* when you mean *ought*.

  NOTE (2): When the Conditional of the verb **pouvoir** is used in French, it is translated into English as *could* or *would be able*.

EXAMPLE:

Je **pourrais** venir après le dîner. I *could come* after dinner.

OR: I *would be able* to come after dinner.

NOTE: For the formation of this tense for regular verbs see page xxxvi.

Tense No. 6   **Le Présent du subjonctif**
              (Present Subjunctive)

The Subjunctive is used in French much more than in English. It is disappearing in English, except for the following major uses:

(a) The Subjunctive is used in French and English to express a command.

EXAMPLE:

Soyez à l'heure! *Be* on time!

NOTE: In English, the form in the Subjunctive applies mainly to the verb *to be*. Also, note that all the verbs in French are not in the Subjunctive when expressing a command. See **L'impératif** on page xxxiv.

(b) The Subjunctive is commonly used in English to express a condition contrary to fact.

EXAMPLE:

If I *were* you, I would not do it.

NOTE: In French the Subjunctive is not used in this instance. Instead, the **Imparfait de l'indicatif** is used if what precedes is *si (if)*. Same example in French: Si j'**étais** vous, je ne le ferai pas.

(c) The Present Subjunctive is used in French and English after a verb that expresses some kind of insistence, preference, or suggestion.

EXAMPLES:

1. Je préfère qu'il **fasse** le travail maintenant.
   I prefer that *he do* the work now.
2. J'exige qu'il **soit** puni.
   I demand that *he be* punished.

(d) The Subjunctive is used in French after a verb that expresses doubt, fear, joy, sorrow, or some other emotion. Notice in the following examples that the Subjunctive is not used in English but it is in French.

EXAMPLES:

1. Je doute qu'il **vienne**.
   I doubt that he *is coming.* OR: I doubt that he *will come.*
2. J'ai peur qu'il ne **soit** malade. (expletive *ne* is required)
   I'm afraid that he *is* sick.
3. Je suis heureux qu'il **vienne**.
   I'm happy that he *is coming.*
4. Je regrette qu'il **soit** malade.
   I'm sorry that he *is* sick.

(e) The Present Subjunctive is used in French after certain conjunctions. Notice, however, that the Subjunctive is not always used in English.

EXAMPLES:

1. Je partirai **à moins qu'il ne vienne**.
   I shall leave unless he *comes.*
2. Je resterai **jusqu'à ce qu'il vienne**.
   I shall stay until he *comes.*
3. **Quoiqu'elle soit** belle, il ne l'aime pas.
   Although she *is* beautiful, he does not love her.
4. Je l'explique **pour qu'elle comprenne**.
   I'm explaining it *so that she may understand.*

(f) The Present Subjunctive is used in French after certain impersonal expressions that show a need, doubt, possibility or impossibility. Notice, however, that the Subjunctive is not always used in English in the following examples:

1. Il est urgent qu'il **vienne**.
   It is urgent that he *come.*
2. Il vaut mieux qu'il **vienne**.
   It is better that he *come.*
3. Il est possible qu'il **vienne**.
   It is possible that he *will come.*
4. Il est douteux qu'il **vienne**.
   It is doubtful that he *will come.*
5. Il est nécessaire qu'il **vienne**.
   It is necessary that he *come.* OR: He must come.
6. Il faut qu'il **vienne**.
   It is necessary that he *come.* OR: He must come.
7. Il est important que vous **fassiez** le travail.
   It is important that you *do* the work.
8. Il est indispensable qu'elle **fasse** le travail.
   It is required that she *do* the work.

NOTE: For the formation of this tense for regular verbs see pages xxxvi and xxxvii.

(g) The Subjunctive is used in French after a superlative that expresses an opinion. Those superlatives that take the Subjunctive are commonly: **le seul, la seule** (the only); **le premier, la première** (the first); **le dernier, la dernière** (the last); **le plus petit, la plus petite** (the smallest); **le plus grand, la plus grande** (the largest).

EXAMPLE:

À mon avis, Marie est **la seule** étudiante qui **comprenne** le subjonctif parfaitement.

In my opinion, Mary is the *only* student who *understands* the subjunctive perfectly.

Tense No. 7   L'Imparfait du subjonctif
              (Imperfect Subjunctive)

L'Imparfait du subjonctif is used for the same reasons as the **Présent du subjonctif**—that is, after certain verbs, conjunctions, and impersonal expressions that were used in examples above under the section, **le Présent du subjonctif**. The main difference between these two is the time of the action. If present, use the **Présent du subjonctif** (Tense No. 6). If the action is related to the past, the **Imparfait du subjonctif** (this tense) is used, provided that the action was *not* completed. If the action was completed, the **Plus-que-parfait du subjonctif** is used. See below under the section, **Plus-que-parfait du subjonctif** (Tense No. 14).

Since the Subjunctive Mood is troublesome in French and English, you may be pleased to know that this tense is rarely used in English. It is used in French, however, but only in formal writing and in literature. For that reason, you should merely be familiar with it so you can recognize it when you see it in your French readings. In conversational French and in informal writing, **l'Imparfait du subjonctif** is avoided. Use, instead, the **Présent du subjonctif**.

Notice that the **Imparfait du subjonctif** is used in French in both of the following examples, but is used in English only in the second example, (b):

EXAMPLES:
(a) Je voulais qu'il vint. I wanted him to come.
(action not completed; he did not come while I wanted him to come)

NOTE: The Subjunctive of **venir** is used because the verb that precedes is one that requires the Subjunctive *after* it—in this example it is **vouloir**. In conversational French and informal writing, the **Imparfait du subjonctif** is avoided. Use, instead, the **Présent du subjonctif**: Je voulais qu'il **vienne**.

(b) Je le lui expliquais **pour qu'elle le comprît**.

I was explaining it to her *so that she might understand it.* (action not completed; the understanding was not completed at the time of the explaining)

NOTE: The Subjunctive of **comprendre** is used because the conjunction that precedes is one that requires the Subjunctive *after* it—in this example it is **pour que.** In conversational French and informal writing, the **Imparfait du subjonctif** is avoided. Use, instead, the **Présent du subjonctif**: Je le lui expliquais pour qu'elle le **comprenne**.

NOTE: For the formation of this tense for regular verbs see page xxxvii.

THE SEVEN COMPOUND TENSES

Tense No. 8   Le Passé composé
(Past Indefinite or Compound Past)

This past tense is used in conversational French, correspondence, and other informal writing. The **Passé composé** is used more and more in literature these days and is taking the place of the **Passé simple** (Tense No. 3). It is a compound tense because it is formed with the **Présent de l'indicatif** (Tense No. 1) of *avoir* or *être* (depending on which of these two auxiliaries is required to form a compound tense) plus the past participle. See page ix for the distinction made between verbs conjugated with *avoir* or *être.*

EXAMPLES:

1. Il **est allé** à l'école. He *went* to school.
2. Il **est allé** à l'école. He *did go* to school.
3. Il **est allé** à l'école. He *has gone* to school.
4. J'**ai mangé** dans ce restaurant beaucoup de fois.
   I *have eaten* in this restaurant many times.

NOTE: In examples 3 and 4 in English the verb is formed with the Present tense of *to have (have* or *has)* plus the past participle of the verb you are using. In English, this form is called the Present Perfect.

5. J'**ai parlé** au garçon. I *spoke* to the boy. OR: I *have spoken* to the boy.
   OR: I *did speak* to the boy.

Tense No. 9 Le Plus-que-parfait de l'indicatif
(Pluperfect or Past Perfect Indicative)

In French and English this tense is used to express an action that happened in the past *before* another past action. Since it is used in relation to another past action, the other past action is expressed in either the **Passé composé** (Tense No. 8) or the **Imparfait de l'indicatif** (Tense No. 2) in French. This tense is used in formal writing and literature as well as in conversational French and informal writing. The correct use of this tense is strictly observed in French. In English, however, too often we neglect to use it correctly. It is a compound tense because it is formed with the **Imparfait de l'indicatif** of *avoir* or *être* (depending on which of these two auxiliaries is required to form a compound tense) plus the past participle. See page ix for the distinction made between verbs conjugated with *avoir* or *être*. In English, this tense is formed with the Past Tense of *to have* (had) plus the past participle of the verb you are using.

EXAMPLES:
(a) Je me suis rappelé que j'**avais oublié** de le lui dire.
I remembered that I *had forgotten* to tell (it to) him.

NOTE: It would be incorrect in English to say: I remembered that I *forgot* to tell him. The point here is that *first* I forgot; then, I remembered. Both actions are in the past. The action that occurred in the past *before* the other past action is in the Pluperfect. And in this example it is *I had forgotten* (**j'avais oublié**).

(b) J'**avais étudié** la leçon que le professeur a expliquée.
I *had studied* the lesson that the teacher explained.

NOTE: *First* I studied the lesson; then, the teacher explained it. Both actions are in the past. The action that occurred in the past *before* the other past action is in the Pluperfect. And in this example it is *I had studied* (**j'avais étudié**). If you say *J'ai étudié la leçon que le professeur avait expliquée*, you are saying that you *studied* the lesson that the teacher *had explained*. In other words, the teacher explained the lesson first and then you studied it.

(c) J'étais fatigué ce matin parce que je n'**avais** pas **dormi**.
I was tired this morning because I *had* not *slept*.

Tense No. 10   Le Passé antérieur
(Past Anterior)

This tense is similar to the **Plus-que-parfait de l'indicatif** (Tense No. 9). The main difference is that in French it is a literary tense; that is, it is used in formal writing, such as history and literature. More and more French writers today use the **Plus-que-parfait** instead of this tense. Generally speaking, the **Passé antérieur** is to the **Plus-que-parfait** what the **Passé simple** is to the **Passé composé**. The **Passé antérieur** is a compound tense. In French, it is formed with the **Passé simple** of *avoir* or *être* (depending on which of these two auxiliaries is required to form a compound tense) plus the past participle. In English, it is formed in the same way as the Pluperfect or Past Perfect. This tense is ordinarily introduced by conjunctions of time: **après que, aussitôt que, dès que, lorsque, quand**.

EXAMPLE:

> Quand il **eut mangé** tout, il partit. When he *had eaten* everything, he left.

NOTE: In conversational French and informal writing, the **Plus-que-parfait de l'indicatif** is used instead: Quand il **avait mangé** tout, il est parti. The translation into English is the same.

Tense No. 11   Le Futur antérieur
(Future Perfect or Future Anterior)

In French and English this tense is used to express an action that will happen in the future *before* another future action. Since it is used in relation to another future action, the other future action is expressed in the simple Future in French, but not always in the simple Future in English. In French, it is used in conversation and informal writing as well as in formal writing and in literature. It is a compound tense because it is formed with the **Futur** of *avoir* and *être* (depending on which of these two auxiliaries is required to form a compound tense) plus the past participle of the verb you are using. In English, it is formed by using *shall have* or *will have* plus the past participle of the verb you are using.

EXAMPLES:

(a) Elle arrivera demain et j'**aurai fini** le travail.
    She will arrive tomorrow and I *shall (will) have finished* the work.

NOTE: First, I shall finish the work; then, she will arrive. The action that will occur in the future *before* the other future action is in the **Futur antérieur**.

(b) Quand elle arrivera demain, j'**aurai fini** le travail.
   When she arrives tomorrow, I *shall (will) have finished* the work.

   NOTE: The idea of future time here is the same as in example (a).
   In English, the Present tense is used *(When she arrives . . .)*
   to express a near future. In French the **Futur** is used (**Quand elle
   arrivera . . .**) because **quand** precedes and the action will take place
   in the future. Study Tense No. 4 on page xxiii.

Tense No. 12   Le Conditionnel passé
(Conditional Perfect)

This is used in French and English to express an action that you *would
have done* if something else had been possible; that is, you would have
done something *on condition* that something else had been possible. It is
a compound tense because it is formed with the **Conditionnel présent** of
avoir or *être* plus the past participle of the verb you are using. In English,
it is formed by using *would have* plus the past participle. Observe the
difference between the following examples and the one given for the use
of the **Conditionnel présent**, which was explained and illustrated in
Tense No. 5.

EXAMPLES:
   (a) J'**aurais fait** le travail si j'avais étudié.
      I *would have done* the work if I had studied.
   (b) J'**aurais fait** le travail si j'avais eu le temps.
      I *would have done* the work if I had had the time.

> NOTE: Review the **Plus-que-parfait de l'indicatif**, which was explained
> above in Tense No. 9 in order to understand the use of *if I had studied*
> (**si j'avais étudié**) and *if I had had the time* (**si j'avais eu le temps**).

   NOTE FURTHER: The French verb **devoir** plus the infinitive is used to
   express the idea of *should* when you mean *ought to*. The past
   participle of **devoir** is **dû**. It is conjugated with *avoir*.

EXAMPLE:
   J'**aurais dû** étudier.
   I *should have* studied. OR: I *ought to have* studied.

Tense No. 13   Le Passé du subjonctif
(Past or Perfect Subjunctive)

This tense is used to express an action that took place in the past in relation
to the present time. It is like the **Passé composé**, except that the auxiliary
verb (*avoir* or *être*) is in the **Présent du subjonctif**. The Subjunctive is
used (as was noted in the previous sections of verb tenses in the
Subjunctive) because what precedes is a certain verb, a certain conjunction,
or a certain impersonal expression. The **Passé du subjonctif** is also used in
relation to a future time when another action will be completed. This tense
is rarely used in English. In French, however, this tense is used in formal
writing and in literature as well as in conversational French and informal
writing. It is a compound tense because it is formed with the **Présent du
subjonctif** of *avoir* or *être* as the auxiliary plus the past participle of the
verb you are using.

EXAMPLES:

(a) A past action in relation to the present

> Il est possible qu'elle **soit partie**.
> It is possible that she *may have left*. OR: It is possible that she *has left*.
> Je doute qu'il **ait fait** cela.
> I doubt that he *did* that.

(b) An action that will take place in the future

> J'insiste que vous **soyez rentré** avant dix heures.
> I insist that you *be back* before ten o'clock.

Tense No. 14   Le Plus-que-parfait du subjonctif
(Pluperfect or Past Perfect Subjunctive)

This tense is used for the same reasons as the **Imparfait du subjonctif**
(Tense No. 7)—that is, after certain verbs, conjunctions, and impersonal
expressions that were used in examples previously under **le Présent du
subjonctif**. The main difference between the **Imparfait du subjonctif**
and this tense is the time of the action in the past. If the action was *not*
completed, the **Imparfait du subjonctif** is used. If the action was
completed, this tense is used. It is rarely used in English. In French, it is
used only in formal writing and in literature. For that reason, you should
merely be familiar with it so you can recognize it in your readings in
French literature. In conversational French and in informal writing, this
tense is avoided. Use, instead, the **Passé du subjonctif** (Tense No. 13).

This is a compound tense. It is formed by using the **Imparfait du subjonctif** of *avoir* or *être* plus the past participle. This tense is like the **Plus-que-parfait de l'indicatif**, except that the auxiliary verb *(avoir or être)* is in the **Imparfait du subjonctif**. Review the uses of the Subjunctive mood in Tense No. 6.

EXAMPLES:

   (a) Il était possible qu'elle **fût partie**.

      It was possible that she *might have left*.

NOTE: Avoid this tense in conversational and informal French.
Use, instead, **le Passé du subjonctif**:
Il était possible qu'elle **soit partie**.

   (b) Je ne croyais pas qu'elle **eût dit** cela.

      I did not believe that she *had said* that.

NOTE: Avoid this tense in conversational and informal French.
Use, instead, **le Passé du subjonctif**:
Je ne croyais pas qu'elle **ait dit** cela.

   (c) Je n'ai pas cru qu'elle **eût dit** cela.

      I did not believe that she *had said* that.

NOTE FURTHER: The French verb **devoir** plus the infinitive is used to express the idea of *should* when you mean *ought*. The past participle of **devoir** is **dû**. It is conjugated with **avoir**.

   (d) J'ai craint que vous ne **fussiez tombé**.

      I was afraid that you *had fallen*.

NOTE: Avoid this tense in conversational and informal French.
Use, instead, **le Passé du subjonctif**:
J'ai craint que vous ne **soyez tombé**.

L'Impératif
(Imperative or Command)

The Imperative Mood is used in French and English to express a command or a request. It is also used to express an indirect request made in the third person, as in (e) and (f) below. In both languages it is formed by dropping the subject pronoun and using the present tense. There are a few exceptions in both languages when the **Présent du subjonctif** is used.

EXAMPLES:

(a) **Sortez!** Get out!

(b) **Entrez!** Come in!

(c) **Buvons!** Let's drink!

(d) **Soyez** à l'heure! *Be* on time (Subjunctive is used)

(e) Dieu le **veuille!** May God *grant* it! (Subjunctive is used)

(f) Qu'ils **mangent du** gâteau! Let them *eat* cake! (Subjunctive is used)

(g) **Asseyez-vous!** Sit down!

(h) **Levez-vous!** Get up!

(i) **Ne vous asseyez pas!** Don't sit down!

(j) **Ne vous levez pas!** Don't get up!

NOTE: The Imperative is not a tense. It is a mood.

NOTE FURTHER: If you use a reflexive verb in the Imperative, drop the subject pronoun but keep the reflexive pronoun. Example: **Lavez-vous!** Wash yourself! See also examples (g) through (j).

Summary of verb tenses and moods in French with English equivalents

	Les sept temps simples *The seven simple tenses*		Les sept temps composés *The seven compound tenses*
Tense No.	Tense Name	Tense No.	Tense Name
1	**Présent de l'indicatif** *Present indicative*	8	**Passé composé**
2	**Imparfait de l'indicatif** *Imperfect indicative*	9	**Plus-que-parfait de l'indicatif** *Pluperfect indicative*
3	**Passé simple** *Past definite or Simple past*	10	**Passé antérieur** *Past anterior*
4	**Futur** *Future*	11	**Futur antérieur** *Future perfect*
5	**Conditionnel** *Conditional*	12	**Conditionnel passé** *Conditional perfect*
6	**Présent du subjonctif** *Present subjunctive*	13	**Passé du subjonctif** *Past subjunctive*
7	**Imparfait du subjonctif** *Imperfect subjunctive*	14	**Plus-que-parfait du subjonctif** *Pluperfect subjunctive*

The imperative is not a tense; it is a mood.

Formation of the Tenses

In French there are seven simple tenses and seven compound tenses. A simple tense means that the verb form consists of one word. A compound tense is a verb form that consists of two words (the auxiliary verb and the past participle). The auxiliary verb is also called a helping verb and in French it is any of the seven simple tenses of **avoir** or **être**.

FORMATION OF THE SEVEN SIMPLE TENSES
FOR REGULAR VERBS

Tense No. 1   Présent de l'indicatif
(Present Indicative)

-er verbs: drop **-er** and add **e, es, e; ons, ez, ent**

-ir verbs: drop **-ir** and add **is, is, it; issons, issez, issent**

-re verbs: drop **-re** and add **s, s, -; ons, ez, ent**

Tense No. 2   Imparfait de l'indicatif
(Imperfect Indicative)

For **-er, -ir, -re** verbs, take the **"nous"** form in the present indicative of the verb you have in mind, drop the ending **-ons** and add: **ais, ais, ait; ions, iez, aient**

Tense No. 3   Passé simple
(Past Definite or Simple Past)

For all **-er** verbs, drop **-er** and add **ai, as, a; âmes, âtes, èrent**

For **-ir** and **-re** verbs, drop the ending of the infinitive and add **is, is, it; îmes, îtes, irent**

Tense No. 4   Futur
(Future)

Add the following endings to the whole infinitive, but for **-re** verbs drop **e** in **-re** before adding the future endings, which are: **ai, as, a; ons, ez, ont**

Tense No. 5   Conditionnel
(Conditional)

Add the following endings to the whole infinitive, but for **-re** verbs drop **e** in **-re** before adding the conditional endings, which are: **ais, ais, ait; ions, iez, aient**. Note that these endings are the same as those for the imperfect indicative (Tense No. 2).

Tense No. 6   Présent du subjonctif
(Present Subjunctive)

Drop **-ant** ending of the present participle of the verb you have in mind and add **e, es, e; ions, iez, ent**

You can also use the "**nous**" (or "**ils**") forms of the present indicative. The present participle is regularly formed by taking the "**nous**" form of the present indicative and dropping the **-ons** from the ending before adding **-ant**. See pages xiii through xiv for further details.

Tense No. 7   Imparfait du subjonctif
(Imperfect Subjunctive)

There is a shortcut to finding the forms of this difficult tense. Go straight to the 3rd person, singular, **passé simple** tense of the verb you have in mind. If the ending is **-a**, as in **parla** (**parler**), drop **-a** and add **-asse, -asses, -ât; -assions, -assiez, -assent**. If the ending is **-it**, as in **finit** (**finir**) or **vendit** (**vendre**), drop **-it** and add **-isse, -isses, -ît; -issions, -issiez, -issent**. If you find the ending **-ut**, as in many irregular **-re** verbs (**lire/lut**), drop **-ut** and add **-usse, -usses, -ût; -ussions, -ussiez, -ussent**. Note the accent mark (^) on **-ât, -ît,** and **-ût**.

FORMATION OF THE SEVEN COMPOUND TENSES

An Easy Way to Form the Seven Compound Tenses in French

avoir or être* in the following simple tenses	+	PLUS the past participle of the verb you have in mind**	=	EQUALS the following compound tenses

1. Présent de l'indicatif
2. Imparfait de l'indicatif
3. Passé simple
4. Futur
5. Conditionnel
6. Présent du subjonctif
7. Imparfait du subjonctif

8. Passé composé
9. Plus-que-parfait de l'indicatif
10. Passé antérieur
11. Futur antérieur
12. Conditionnel passé
13. Passé du subjonctif
14. Plus-que-parfait du subjonctif

*To know if **avoir** or **être** is required, see pages ix–xiii.
**To know how to form a past participle, see page xiv.

Each compound tense is based on each simple tense. The fourteen tenses given on page xxxv are arranged in a logical order, which is numerical. Here is how you form each of the seven compound tenses:

Tense number 8 is based on Tense number 1; in other words, you form the **passé composé** by using the auxiliary **avoir** or **être** (whichever is appropriate) in the **présent de l'indicatif** plus the past participle of the verb you have in mind. Examples: **j'ai parlé; je suis allé(e)**.

Tense number 9 is based on Tense number 2; in other words, you form the **plus-que-parfait de l'indicatif** by using the auxiliary **avoir** or **être** (whichever is appropriate) in the **imparfait de l'indicatif** plus the past participle of the verb you have in mind. Examples: **j'avais parlé; j'étais allé(e)**.

Tense number 10 is based on Tense number 3; in other words, you form the **passé antérieur** by using the auxiliary **avoir** or **être** (whichever is appropriate) in the **passé simple** plus the past participle of the verb you have in mind. Examples: **j'eus parlé; je fus allé(e)**.

Tense number 11 is based on Tense number 4; in other words, you form the **futur antérieur** by using the auxiliary **avoir** or **être** (whichever is appropriate) in the **futur** plus the past participle of the verb you have in mind. Examples: **j'aurai parlé; je serai allé(e)**.

Tense number 12 is based on Tense number 5; in other words, you form the **conditionnel passé** by using the auxiliary **avoir** or **être** (whichever is appropriate) in the **conditionnel** plus the past participle of the verb you have in mind. Examples: **j'aurais parlé; je serais allé(e)**.

Tense number 13 is based on Tense number 6; in other words, you form the **passé du subjonctif** by using the auxiliary **avoir** or **être** (whichever is appropriate) in the **présent du subjonctif** plus the past participle of the verb you have in mind. Examples: **que j'aie parlé; que je sois allé(e)**. This tense is like the **passé composé** (Tense number 8), except that the auxiliary verb **avoir** or **être** is in the present subjunctive.

Tense number 14 is based on Tense number 7; in other words, you form the **plus-que-parfait du subjonctif** by using the auxiliary **avoir** or **être** (whichever is appropriate) in the **imparfait du subjonctif** plus the past participle of the verb you have in mind. Examples: **que j'eusse parlé; que je fusse allé(e)**.

If you ever expect to know or even recognize the meaning of any of the seven compound tenses, or to know how to form them, you certainly have to know **avoir** and **être** in the seven simple tenses. If you do not, you cannot form the seven compound tenses—and they are the easiest to form. This is one perfect example to illustrate that learning French verb forms is a cumulative experience because in order to know the seven compound tenses, you must first know the forms of **avoir** and **être** in the seven simple tenses. They are found on pages 31 and 119 in this book.

To know which verbs are conjugated with **avoir** or **être** to form the seven compound tenses, see page ix. To understand the uses of the seven simple tenses, see pages xxi–xxviii. To understand the uses of the seven compound tenses, see pages xxviii–xxxiii. To know the translation of all fourteen tenses into English, see pages xviii–xix.

Subject Pronouns

(a) The subject pronouns for all verb forms on the following pages have been omitted in order to emphasize the verb forms, which is what this book is all about. See the box that follows if you need to review the subject pronouns in French.

(b) You realize, of course, that when you use a verb form in the Imperative (Command) you do not use the subject pronoun with it, as is also done in English. Example: **Parlez!** *Speak!* If you use a reflexive verb in the Imperative, drop the subject pronoun but keep the reflexive pronoun. Example: **Lavez-vous!** *Wash yourself!*

Subject Pronouns

singular	*plural*
je *or* **j'**	**nous**
tu	**vous**
il, elle, on	**ils, elles**

Regular -er verb   to accept

The Seven Simple Tenses		The Seven Compound Tenses	
Singular	Plural	Singular	Plural

1 présent de l'indicatif

accepte	acceptons		
acceptes	acceptez		
accepte	acceptent		

8 passé composé

ai accepté	avons accepté
as accepté	avez accepté
a accepté	ont accepté

2 imparfait de l'indicatif

acceptais	acceptions
acceptais	acceptiez
acceptait	acceptaient

9 plus-que-parfait de l'indicatif

avais accepté	avions accepté
avais accepté	aviez accepté
avait accepté	avaient accepté

3 passé simple

acceptai	acceptâmes
acceptas	acceptâtes
accepta	acceptèrent

10 passé antérieur

eus accepté	eûmes accepté
eus accepté	eûtes accepté
eut accepté	eurent accepté

4 futur

accepterai	accepterons
accepteras	accepterez
acceptera	accepteront

11 futur antérieur

aurai accepté	aurons accepté
auras accepté	aurez accepté
aura accepté	auront accepté

5 conditionnel

accepterais	accepterions
accepterais	accepteriez
accepterait	accepteraient

12 conditionnel passé

aurais accepté	aurions accepté
aurais accepté	auriez accepté
aurait accepté	auraient accepté

6 présent du subjonctif

accepte	acceptions
acceptes	acceptiez
accepte	acceptent

13 passé du subjonctif

aie accepté	ayons accepté
aies accepté	ayez accepté
ait accepté	aient accepté

7 imparfait du subjonctif

acceptasse	acceptassions
acceptasses	acceptassiez
acceptât	acceptassent

14 plus-que-parfait du subjonctif

eusse accepté	eussions accepté
eusses accepté	eussiez accepté
eût accepté	eussent accepté

Impératif
accepte
acceptons
acceptez

Michel a accepté de travailler dimanche prochain.   Michael agreed to work next Sunday.

Acceptez-vous les cartes bancaires?   Do you accept credit cards?

acceptable   acceptable, satisfactory
une acceptation   acceptance
accepter une invitation   to accept an invitation
accepter de faire qqch   to agree to do something

accompagner   Part. pr. **accompagnant**   Part. passé **accompagné**

to accompany

Regular -er verb

The Seven Simple Tenses		The Seven Compound Tenses	
Singular	Plural	Singular	Plural
1 présent de l'indicatif		**8 passé composé**	
accompagne	**accompagnons**	**ai accompagné**	**avons accompagné**
accompagnes	**accompagnez**	**as accompagné**	**avez accompagné**
accompagne	**accompagnent**	**a accompagné**	**ont accompagné**
2 imparfait de l'indicatif		**9 plus-que-parfait de l'indicatif**	
accompagnais	**accompagnions**	**avais accompagné**	**avions accompagné**
accompagnais	**accompagniez**	**avais accompagné**	**aviez accompagné**
accompagnait	**accompagnaient**	**avait accompagné**	**avaient accompagné**
3 passé simple		**10 passé antérieur**	
accompagnai	**accompagnâmes**	**eus accompagné**	**eûmes accompagné**
accompagnas	**accompagnâtes**	**eus accompagné**	**eûtes accompagné**
accompagna	**accompagnèrent**	**eut accompagné**	**eurent accompagné**
4 futur		**11 futur antérieur**	
accompagnerai	**accompagnerons**	**aurai accompagné**	**aurons accompagné**
accompagneras	**accompagnerez**	**auras accompagné**	**aurez accompagné**
accompagnera	**accompagneront**	**aura accompagné**	**auront accompagné**
5 conditionnel		**12 conditionnel passé**	
accompagnerais	**accompagnerions**	**aurais accompagné**	**aurions accompagné**
accompagnerais	**accompagneriez**	**aurais accompagné**	**auriez accompagné**
accompagnerait	**accompagneraient**	**aurait accompagné**	**auraient accompagné**
6 présent du subjonctif		**13 passé du subjonctif**	
accompagne	**accompagnions**	**aie accompagné**	**ayons accompagné**
accompagnes	**accompagniez**	**aies accompagné**	**ayez accompagné**
accompagne	**accompagnent**	**ait accompagné**	**aient accompagné**
7 imparfait du subjonctif		**14 plus-que-parfait du subjonctif**	
accompagnasse	**accompagnassions**	**eusse accompagné**	**eussions accompagné**
accompagnasses	**accompagnassiez**	**eusses accompagné**	**eussiez accompagné**
accompagnât	**accompagnassent**	**eût accompagné**	**eussent accompagné**

Impératif
accompagne
accompagnons
accompagnez

Hier après-midi Monsieur Durand a accompagné ses étudiants au musée.
Yesterday afternoon, Mr. Durand accompanied his students to the museum.

une compagnie   company, theatrical troupe
raccompagner quelqu'un   to see someone out, see someone off
un animal de compagnie (animal domestique)   a pet
s'accompagner de   to be accompanied by
un accompagnement   accompanying, accompaniment (music)
un accompagnateur, une accompagnatrice   accompanist (music)
un compagnon, une compagne   companion

2

Irregular verb   to greet, welcome

The Seven Simple Tenses		The Seven Compound Tenses	
Singular	Plural	Singular	Plural
1 présent de l'indicatif		8 passé composé	
accueille	**accueillons**	**ai accueilli**	**avons accueilli**
accueilles	**accueillez**	**as accueilli**	**avez accueilli**
accueille	**accueillent**	**a accueilli**	**ont accueilli**
2 imparfait de l'indicatif		9 plus-que-parfait de l'indicatif	
accueillais	**accueillions**	**avais accueilli**	**avions accueilli**
accueillais	**accueilliez**	**avais accueilli**	**aviez accueilli**
accueillait	**accueillaient**	**avait accueilli**	**avaient accueilli**
3 passé simple		10 passé antérieur	
accueillis	**accueillîmes**	**eus accueilli**	**eûmes accueilli**
accueillis	**accueillîtes**	**eus accueilli**	**eûtes accueilli**
accueillit	**accueillirent**	**eut accueilli**	**eurent accueilli**
4 futur		11 futur antérieur	
accueillerai	**accueillerons**	**aurai accueilli**	**aurons accueilli**
accueilleras	**accueillerez**	**auras accueilli**	**aurez accueilli**
accueillera	**accueilleront**	**aura accueilli**	**auront accueilli**
5 conditionnel		12 conditionnel passé	
accueillerais	**accueillerions**	**aurais accueilli**	**aurions accueilli**
accueillerais	**accueilleriez**	**aurais accueilli**	**auriez accueilli**
accueillerait	**accueilleraient**	**aurait accueilli**	**auraient accueilli**
6 présent du subjonctif		13 passé du subjonctif	
accueille	**accueillions**	**aie accueilli**	**ayons accueilli**
accueilles	**accueilliez**	**aies accueilli**	**ayez accueilli**
accueille	**accueillent**	**ait accueilli**	**aient accueilli**
7 imparfait du subjonctif		14 plus-que-parfait du subjonctif	
accueillisse	**accueillissions**	**eusse accueilli**	**eussions accueilli**
accueillisses	**accueillissiez**	**eusses accueilli**	**eussiez accueilli**
accueillît	**accueillissent**	**eût accueilli**	**eussent accueilli**

	Impératif
	accueille
	accueillons
	accueillez

Chaque fois que je rends visite à mes grands-parents, ils m'accueillent chaleureusement.   Each time that I visit my grandparents, they welcome me warmly.

accueillir chaleureusement   to give a warm welcome
accueillir froidement   to give a cool reception
faire bon accueil   to give a warm welcome
un accueil   welcome, reception; **un accueil chaleureux**   warm welcome
accueillant, accueillante   hospitable

For other words and expressions related to this verb, see **cueillir**.

3

acheter

Part. pr. **achetant**   Part. passé **acheté**

to buy, to purchase

Regular -er verb endings: spelling change:
e changes to è before syllable with mute e.

The Seven Simple Tenses		The Seven Compound Tenses	
Singular	Plural	Singular	Plural
1 présent de l'indicatif		**8 passé composé**	
achète	achetons	ai acheté	avons acheté
achètes	achetez	as acheté	avez acheté
achète	achètent	a acheté	ont acheté
2 imparfait de l'indicatif		**9 plus-que-parfait de l'indicatif**	
achetais	achetions	avais acheté	avions acheté
achetais	achetiez	avais acheté	aviez acheté
achetait	achetaient	avait acheté	avaient acheté
3 passé simple		**10 passé antérieur**	
achetai	achetâmes	eus acheté	eûmes acheté
achetas	achetâtes	eus acheté	eûtes acheté
acheta	achetèrent	eut acheté	eurent acheté
4 futur		**11 futur antérieur**	
achèterai	achèterons	aurai acheté	aurons acheté
achèteras	achèterez	auras acheté	aurez acheté
achètera	achèteront	aura acheté	auront acheté
5 conditionnel		**12 conditionnel passé**	
achèterais	achèterions	aurais acheté	aurions acheté
achèterais	achèteriez	aurais acheté	auriez acheté
achèterait	achèteraient	aurait acheté	auraient acheté
6 présent du subjonctif		**13 passé du subjonctif**	
achète	achetions	aie acheté	ayons acheté
achètes	achetiez	aies acheté	ayez acheté
achète	achètent	ait acheté	aient acheté
7 imparfait du subjonctif		**14 plus-que-parfait du subjonctif**	
achetasse	achetassions	eusse acheté	eussions acheté
achetasses	achetassiez	eusses acheté	eussiez acheté
achetât	achetassent	eût acheté	eussent acheté

	Impératif	
achète	achetons	achetez

L'amitié ne s'achète pas.   Friendship cannot be bought.
Achetons une nouvelle voiture!   Let's buy a new car!

un achat en ligne   online purchase
un achat électronique   electronic purchase (Internet)
un achat   purchase; acheter qqch à qqn   to buy something from someone
un acheteur, une acheteuse   buyer, purchaser
achetable   purchasable; racheter   to ransom; to buy back
acheter comptant   to buy in cash; acheter à crédit   to buy on credit

Irregular verb   to admit

The Seven Simple Tenses		The Seven Compound Tenses	
Singular	Plural	Singular	Plural
1 présent de l'indicatif		8 passé composé	
admets	admettons	ai admis	avons admis
admets	admettez	as admis	avez admis
admet	admettent	a admis	ont admis
2 imparfait de l'indicatif		9 plus-que-parfait de l'indicatif	
admettais	admettions	avais admis	avions admis
admettais	admettiez	avais admis	aviez admis
admettait	admettaient	avait admis	avaient admis
3 passé simple		10 passé antérieur	
admis	admîmes	eus admis	eûmes admis
admis	admîtes	eus admis	eûtes admis
admit	admirent	eut admis	eurent admis
4 futur		11 futur antérieur	
admettrai	admettrons	aurai admis	aurons admis
admettras	admettrez	auras admis	aurez admis
admettra	admettront	aura admis	auront admis
5 conditionnel		12 conditionnel passé	
admettrais	admettrions	aurais admis	aurions admis
admettrais	admettriez	aurais admis	auriez admis
admettrait	admettraient	aurait admis	auraient admis
6 présent du subjonctif		13 passé du subjonctif	
admette	admettions	aie admis	ayons admis
admettes	admettiez	aies admis	ayez admis
admette	admettent	ait admis	aient admis
7 imparfait du subjonctif		14 plus-que-parfait du subjonctif	
admisse	admissions	eusse admis	eussions admis
admisses	admissiez	eusses admis	eussiez admis
admît	admissent	eût admis	eussent admis

Impératif
admets   admettons   admettez

Je connais un homme qui n'admet pas toujours ses fautes.   I know a man who does not always admit his transgressions.

C'est une idée folle, je l'admets.   It's a crazy idea, I admit it.

l'admissibilité *f.*   acceptability
se faire admettre dans un club   to be admitted to a club
admissible   acceptable
admis, admise   admitted, accepted
une admission   admission, admittance
C'est chose admise que . . .   It's generally admitted that . . .

See also mettre, permettre, promettre, remettre, and soumettre.

admirer	Part. pr. **admirant**	Part. passé **admiré**

to admire

Regular -er verb

The Seven Simple Tenses		The Seven Compound Tenses	
Singular	Plural	Singular	Plural
1 présent de l'indicatif		**8 passé composé**	
admire	admirons	ai admiré	avons admiré
admires	admirez	as admiré	avez admiré
admire	admirent	a admiré	ont admiré
2 imparfait de l'indicatif		**9 plus-que-parfait de l'indicatif**	
admirais	admirions	avais admiré	avions admiré
admirais	admiriez	avais admiré	aviez admiré
admirait	admiraient	avait admiré	avaient admiré
3 passé simple		**10 passé antérieur**	
admirai	admirâmes	eus admiré	eûmes admiré
admiras	admirâtes	eus admiré	eûtes admiré
admira	admirèrent	eut admiré	eurent admiré
4 futur		**11 futur antérieur**	
admirerai	admirerons	aurai admiré	aurons admiré
admireras	admirerez	auras admiré	aurez admiré
admirera	admireront	aura admiré	auront admiré
5 conditionnel		**12 conditionnel passé**	
admirerais	admirerions	aurais admiré	aurions admiré
admirerais	admireriez	aurais admiré	auriez admiré
admirerait	admireraient	aurait admiré	auraient admiré
6 présent du subjonctif		**13 passé du subjonctif**	
admire	admirions	aie admiré	ayons admiré
admires	admiriez	aies admiré	ayez admiré
admire	admirent	ait admiré	aient admiré
7 imparfait du subjonctif		**14 plus-que-parfait du subjonctif**	
admirasse	admirassions	eusse admiré	eussions admiré
admirasses	admirassiez	eusses admiré	eussiez admiré
admirât	admirassent	eût admiré	eussent admiré

Impératif
admire
admirons
admirez

Quelle personne admirez-vous le plus?   Which person do you admire the most?

admirablement   admirably, wonderfully
être en admiration devant   to be filled with admiration for
une admiration   admiration, wonder
admirativement   admiringly
admiratif, admirative   admiring
un admirateur, une admiratrice   admirer

Regular -er verb   to worship, to adore

The Seven Simple Tenses		The Seven Compound Tenses	
Singular	Plural	Singular	Plural
1 présent de l'indicatif		8 passé composé	
adore	adorons	ai adoré	avons adoré
adores	adorez	as adoré	avez adoré
adore	adorent	a adoré	ont adoré
2 imparfait de l'indicatif		9 plus-que-parfait de l'indicatif	
adorais	adorions	avais adoré	avions adoré
adorais	adoriez	avais adoré	aviez adoré
adorait	adoraient	avait adoré	avaient adoré
3 passé simple		10 passé antérieur	
adorai	adorâmes	eus adoré	eûmes adoré
adoras	adorâtes	eus adoré	eûtes adoré
adora	adorèrent	eut adoré	eurent adoré
4 futur		11 futur antérieur	
adorerai	adorerons	aurai adoré	aurons adoré
adoreras	adorerez	auras adoré	aurez adoré
adorera	adoreront	aura adoré	auront adoré
5 conditionnel		12 conditionnel passé	
adorerais	adorerions	aurais adoré	aurions adoré
adorerais	adoreriez	aurais adoré	auriez adoré
adorerait	adoreraient	aurait adoré	auraient adoré
6 présent du subjonctif		13 passé du subjonctif	
adore	adorions	aie adoré	ayons adoré
adores	adoriez	aies adoré	ayez adoré
adore	adorent	ait adoré	aient adoré
7 imparfait du subjonctif		14 plus-que-parfait du subjonctif	
adorasse	adorassions	eusse adoré	eussions adoré
adorasses	adorassiez	eusses adoré	eussiez adoré
adorât	adorassent	eût adoré	eussent adoré
		Impératif	
		adore	
		adorons	
		adorez	

Laure adore sa nièce.   Laura adores her niece.
Madeleine est une fille adorable. Elle adore écouter la musique québécoise.
Madeleine is an adorable girl. She adores listening to Québécois music.

adorable adorable, charming, delightful
une adoration adoration, worship
adorablement adorably
un adorateur, une adoratrice adorer, worshipper
dorer to gild

7

to be the matter, to be a question of   Reflexive regular -ir verb

The Seven Simple Tenses	The Seven Compound Tenses
Singular	Singular
1 présent de l'indicatif **il s'agit**	8 passé composé **il s'est agi**
2 imparfait de l'indicatif **il s'agissait**	9 plus-que-parfait de l'indicatif **il s'était agi**
3 passé simple **il s'agit**	10 passé antérieur **il se fut agi**
4 futur **il s'agira**	11 futur antérieur **il se sera agi**
5 conditionnel **il s'agirait**	12 conditionnel passé **il se serait agi**
6 présent du subjonctif **qu'il s'agisse**	13 passé du subjonctif **qu'il se soit agi**
7 imparfait du subjonctif **qu'il s'agît**	14 plus-que-parfait du subjonctif **qu'il se fût agi**

Impératif
—

Hier, le petit Michel est entré dans la maison en pleurant.
—De quoi s'agit-il?! s'exclame sa mère.
—Il s'agit . . . il s'agit . . . de mon vélo. Quelqu'un a volé mon vélo!

s'agir de   to have to do with, to be a matter of
De quoi s'agit-il?   What's the matter? What's up?
Voici ce dont il s'agit.   This is what it's about.
Il s'agit de mon vélo.   It's about my bike.

Note: This verb is impersonal and is used primarily in the tenses given above.

8

Part. pr. **aidant**   Part. passé **aidé**   **aider**

Regular -er verb   to aid, to help, to assist

The Seven Simple Tenses		The Seven Compound Tenses	
Singular	Plural	Singular	Plural
1 présent de l'indicatif		**8 passé composé**	
aide	aidons	ai aidé	avons aidé
aides	aidez	as aidé	avez aidé
aide	aident	a aidé	ont aidé
2 imparfait de l'indicatif		**9 plus-que-parfait de l'indicatif**	
aidais	aidions	avais aidé	avions aidé
aidais	aidiez	avais aidé	aviez aidé
aidait	aidaient	avait aidé	avaient aidé
3 passé simple		**10 passé antérieur**	
aidai	aidâmes	eus aidé	eûmes aidé
aidas	aidâtes	eus aidé	eûtes aidé
aida	aidèrent	eut aidé	eurent aidé
4 futur		**11 futur antérieur**	
aiderai	aiderons	aurai aidé	aurons aidé
aideras	aiderez	auras aidé	aurez aidé
aidera	aideront	aura aidé	auront aidé
5 conditionnel		**12 conditionnel passé**	
aiderais	aiderions	aurais aidé	aurions aidé
aiderais	aideriez	aurais aidé	auriez aidé
aiderait	aideraient	aurait aidé	auraient aidé
6 présent du subjonctif		**13 passé du subjonctif**	
aide	aidions	aie aidé	ayons aidé
aides	aidiez	aies aidé	ayez aidé
aide	aident	ait aidé	aient aidé
7 imparfait du subjonctif		**14 plus-que-parfait du subjonctif**	
aidasse	aidassions	eusse aidé	eussions aidé
aidasses	aidassiez	eusses aidé	eussiez aidé
aidât	aidassent	eût aidé	eussent aidé
		Impératif	
		aide	
		aidons	
		aidez	

Tous les soirs Daniel aide Matthieu, son petit frère, à faire sa leçon de mathématiques.   Every evening Daniel helps his little brother Matthew do his math lesson.

un aide-mémoire   handbook, memory aid
À l'aide tout de suite!   Get help right away!
aider qqn à faire qqch   to help someone do something
s'aider   to help oneself; to help each other
une aide   aid, assistance, help; à l'aide de   with the help of
Aide-toi et le ciel t'aidera.   Heaven helps those who help themselves.

aimer

Part. pr. **aimant**   Part. passé **aimé**

to love, to like

Regular -er verb

The Seven Simple Tenses		The Seven Compound Tenses	
Singular	Plural	Singular	Plural
1 présent de l'indicatif		**8 passé composé**	
aime	aimons	ai aimé	avons aimé
aimes	aimez	as aimé	avez aimé
aime	aiment	a aimé	ont aimé
2 imparfait de l'indicatif		**9 plus-que-parfait de l'indicatif**	
aimais	aimions	avais aimé	avions aimé
aimais	aimiez	avais aimé	aviez aimé
aimait	aimaient	avait aimé	avaient aimé
3 passé simple		**10 passé antérieur**	
aimai	aimâmes	eus aimé	eûmes aimé
aimas	aimâtes	eus aimé	eûtes aimé
aima	aimèrent	eut aimé	eurent aimé
4 futur		**11 futur antérieur**	
aimerai	aimerons	aurai aimé	aurons aimé
aimeras	aimerez	auras aimé	aurez aimé
aimera	aimeront	aura aimé	auront aimé
5 conditionnel		**12 conditionnel passé**	
aimerais	aimerions	aurais aimé	aurions aimé
aimerais	aimeriez	aurais aimé	auriez aimé
aimerait	aimeraient	aurait aimé	auraient aimé
6 présent du subjonctif		**13 passé du subjonctif**	
aime	aimions	aie aimé	ayons aimé
aimes	aimiez	aies aimé	ayez aimé
aime	aiment	ait aimé	aient aimé
7 imparfait du subjonctif		**14 plus-que-parfait du subjonctif**	
aimasse	aimassions	eusse aimé	eussions aimé
aimasses	aimassiez	eusses aimé	eussiez aimé
aimât	aimassent	eût aimé	eussent aimé

	Impératif	
aime	aimons	aimez

Je n'aime pas les ascenseurs. J'aime mieux monter l'escalier.   I don't like elevators. I prefer to walk up the stairs.

J'aimerais acheter quelques pâtisseries.   I would like to buy some pastries.

amour *m.*   love; une chanson d'amour   love song (song of love)
aimer bien qqn   to like somebody
aimer (à) faire qqch   to enjoy doing something
aimer mieux   to prefer, to like better
aimable   friendly, amiable, pleasant
un amant, une amante   a lover; amoureux, amoureuse de   in love with;
   tomber amoureux, amoureuse   to fall in love

Part. pr. **ajoutant**   Part. passé **ajouté**   **ajouter**

Regular **-er** verb   to add

The Seven Simple Tenses		The Seven Compound Tenses	
Singular	Plural	Singular	Plural
1 présent de l'indicatif		8 passé composé	
ajoute	ajoutons	ai ajouté	avons ajouté
ajoutes	ajoutez	as ajouté	avez ajouté
ajoute	ajoutent	a ajouté	ont ajouté
2 imparfait de l'indicatif		9 plus-que-parfait de l'indicatif	
ajoutais	ajoutions	avais ajouté	avions ajouté
ajoutais	ajoutiez	avais ajouté	aviez ajouté
ajoutait	ajoutaient	avait ajouté	avaient ajouté
3 passé simple		10 passé antérieur	
ajoutai	ajoutâmes	eus ajouté	eûmes ajouté
ajoutas	ajoutâtes	eus ajouté	eûtes ajouté
ajouta	ajoutèrent	eut ajouté	eurent ajouté
4 futur		11 futur antérieur	
ajouterai	ajouterons	aurai ajouté	aurons ajouté
ajouteras	ajouterez	auras ajouté	aurez ajouté
ajoutera	ajouteront	aura ajouté	auront ajouté
5 conditionnel		12 conditionnel passé	
ajouterais	ajouterions	aurais ajouté	aurions ajouté
ajouterais	ajouteriez	aurais ajouté	auriez ajouté
ajouterait	ajouteraient	aurait ajouté	auraient ajouté
6 présent du subjonctif		13 passé du subjonctif	
ajoute	ajoutions	aie ajouté	ayons ajouté
ajoutes	ajoutiez	aies ajouté	ayez ajouté
ajoute	ajoutent	ait ajouté	aient ajouté
7 imparfait du subjonctif		14 plus-que-parfait du subjonctif	
ajoutasse	ajoutassions	eusse ajouté	eussions ajouté
ajoutasses	ajoutassiez	eusses ajouté	eussiez ajouté
ajoutât	ajoutassent	eût ajouté	eussent ajouté

Impératif
ajoute
ajoutons
ajoutez

     Une gousse d'ail ajoute du goût à votre ragoût.   A clove of garlic adds taste to your stew.

rajouter to add (something) more
un rajout addition
un ajout addition, additive
ajouter foi à to add credence to, to give credence to
jouter to tilt, to joust; to dispute, to fight
une joute contest, tournament

aller	Part. pr. allant	Part. passé allé(e)(s)
to go		Irregular verb

The Seven Simple Tenses		The Seven Compound Tenses	
Singular	Plural	Singular	Plural

1 présent de l'indicatif		8 passé composé	
vais	allons	suis allé(e)	sommes allé(e)s
vas	allez	es allé(e)	êtes allé(e)(s)
va	vont	est allé(e)	sont allé(e)s

2 imparfait de l'indicatif		9 plus-que-parfait de l'indicatif	
allais	allions	étais allé(e)	étions allé(e)s
allais	alliez	étais allé(e)	étiez allé(e)(s)
allait	allaient	était allé(e)	étaient allé(e)s

3 passé simple		10 passé antérieur	
allai	allâmes	fus allé(e)	fûmes allé(e)s
allas	allâtes	fus allé(e)	fûtes allé(e)(s)
alla	allèrent	fut allé(e)	furent allé(e)s

4 futur		11 futur antérieur	
irai	irons	serai allé(e)	serons allé(e)s
iras	irez	seras allé(e)	serez allé(e)(s)
ira	iront	sera allé(e)	seront allé(e)s

5 conditionnel		12 conditionnel passé	
irais	irions	serais allé(e)	serions allé(e)s
irais	iriez	serais allé(e)	seriez allé(e)(s)
irait	iraient	serait allé(e)	seraient allé(e)s

6 présent du subjonctif		13 passé du subjonctif	
aille	allions	sois allé(e)	soyons allé(e)s
ailles	alliez	sois allé(e)	soyez allé(e)(s)
aille	aillent	soit allé(e)	soient allé(e)s

7 imparfait du subjonctif		14 plus-que-parfait du subjonctif	
allasse	allassions	fusse allé(e)	fussions allé(e)s
allasses	allassiez	fusses allé(e)	fussiez allé(e)(s)
allât	allassent	fût allé(e)	fussent allé(e)s

	Impératif	
va	allons	allez

Comment allez-vous?   How are you?
Je vais bien, merci.   I am fine, thank you.
Je vais mal.   I am not well.

aller chercher   to go get
aller à la pêche   to go fishing
aller à la rencontre de quelqu'un   to go to go to meet someone
aller à pied   to walk, to go on foot
aller au fond des choses   to get to the bottom of things
Ça va?   Is everything O.K.?   Oui, ça va!   Yes, everything is O.K.!

Aller is often used to express the future (instead of Tense No. 4): Nous allons dîner
   en ville.   We are going to have dinner downtown.

12

Reflexive irregular verb   to go away

The Seven Simple Tenses		The Seven Compound Tenses	
Singular	Plural	Singular	Plural
1 présent de l'indicatif		8 passé composé	
m'en vais	**nous en allons**	**m'en suis allé(e)**	**nous en sommes allé(e)s**
t'en vas	**vous en allez**	**t'en es allé(e)**	**vous en êtes allé(e)(s)**
s'en va	**s'en vont**	**s'en est allé(e)**	**s'en sont allé(e)s**
2 imparfait de l'indicatif		9 plus-que-parfait de l'indicatif	
m'en allais	**nous en allions**	**m'en étais allé(e)**	**nous en étions allé(e)s**
t'en allais	**vous en alliez**	**t'en étais allé(e)**	**vous en étiez allé(e)(s)**
s'en allait	**s'en allaient**	**s'en était allé(e)**	**s'en étaient allé(e)s**
3 passé simple		10 passé antérieur	
m'en allai	**nous en allâmes**	**m'en fus allé(e)**	**nous en fûmes allé(e)s**
t'en allas	**vous en allâtes**	**t'en fus allé(e)**	**vous en fûtes allé(e)(s)**
s'en alla	**s'en allèrent**	**s'en fut allé(e)**	**s'en furent allé(e)s**
4 futur		11 futur antérieur	
m'en irai	**nous en irons**	**m'en serai allé(e)**	**nous en serons allé(e)s**
t'en iras	**vous en irez**	**t'en seras allé(e)**	**vous en serez allé(e)(s)**
s'en ira	**s'en iront**	**s'en sera allé(e)**	**s'en seront allé(e)s**
5 conditionnel		12 conditionnel passé	
m'en irais	**nous en irions**	**m'en serais allé(e)**	**nous en serions allé(e)s**
t'en irais	**vous en iriez**	**t'en serais allé(e)**	**vous en seriez allé(e)(s)**
s'en irait	**s'en iraient**	**s'en serait allé(e)**	**s'en seraient allé(e)s**
6 présent du subjonctif		13 passé du subjonctif	
m'en aille	**nous en allions**	**m'en sois allé(e)**	**nous en soyons allé(e)s**
t'en ailles	**vous en alliez**	**t'en sois allé(e)**	**vous en soyez allé(e)(s)**
s'en aille	**s'en aillent**	**s'en soit allé(e)**	**s'en soient allé(e)s**
7 imparfait du subjonctif		14 plus-que-parfait du subjonctif	
m'en allasse	**nous en allassions**	**m'en fusse allé(e)**	**nous en fussions allé(e)s**
t'en allasses	**vous en allassiez**	**t'en fusses allé(e)**	**vous en fussiez allé(e)(s)**
s'en allât	**s'en allassent**	**s'en fût allé(e)**	**s'en fussent allé(e)s**

Impératif
**va-t'en; ne t'en va pas   allons-nous-en; ne nous en allons pas
allez-vous-en; ne vous en allez pas**

This verb also has the following idiomatic meanings: to move away (from one residence to another), to die, to pass away, to steal away.

   Monsieur et Madame Moreau n'habitent plus ici. Ils s'en sont allés.   Mr. and Mrs. Moreau don't live here anymore. They went away.
   Madame Morel est gravement malade; elle s'en va.   Mrs. Morel is gravely ill; she's dying.
   Le cambrioleur s'en est allé furtivement.   The burglar went away stealthily.

13

to bring, to lead

Regular -er verb endings: spelling change:
e changes to è before syllable with mute e.

The Seven Simple Tenses		The Seven Compound Tenses	
Singular	Plural	Singular	Plural
1　présent de l'indicatif		8　passé composé	
amène	amenons	ai amené	avons amené
amènes	amenez	as amené	avez amené
amène	amènent	a amené	ont amené
2　imparfait de l'indicatif		9　plus-que-parfait de l'indicatif	
amenais	amenions	avais amené	avions amené
amenais	ameniez	avais amené	aviez amené
amenait	amenaient	avait amené	avaient amené
3　passé simple		10　passé antérieur	
amenai	amenâmes	eus amené	eûmes amené
amenas	amenâtes	eus amené	eûtes amené
amena	amenèrent	eut amené	eurent amené
4　futur		11　futur antérieur	
amènerai	amènerons	aurai amené	aurons amené
amèneras	amènerez	auras amené	aurez amené
amènera	amèneront	aura amené	auront amené
5　conditionnel		12　conditionnel passé	
amènerais	amènerions	aurais amené	aurions amené
amènerais	amèneriez	aurais amené	auriez amené
amènerait	amèneraient	aurait amené	auraient amené
6　présent du subjonctif		13　passé du subjonctif	
amène	amenions	aie amené	ayons amené
amènes	ameniez	aies amené	ayez amené
amène	amènent	ait amené	aient amené
7　imparfait du subjonctif		14　plus-que-parfait du subjonctif	
amenasse	amenassions	eusse amené	eussions amené
amenasses	amenassiez	eusses amené	eussiez amené
amenât	amenassent	eût amené	eussent amené

Impératif
amène
amenons
amenez

Aujourd'hui ma mère a amené ma petite soeur chez le dentiste. Quand elles sont entrées chez lui, le dentiste leur a demandé:—Quel bon vent vous amène ici??

amener une conversation　to direct, lead a conversation
amène　pleasant, agreeable; des propos peu amènes　unkind words
Qu'est-ce qui vous amène ici?　What brings you here?

See also **emmener** and **mener**.

14

Regular -er verb | to amuse, to entertain

The Seven Simple Tenses | The Seven Compound Tenses

Singular	Plural	Singular	Plural
1 présent de l'indicatif		**8 passé composé**	
amuse	amusons	ai amusé	avons amusé
amuses	amusez	as amusé	avez amusé
amuse	amusent	a amusé	ont amusé
2 imparfait de l'indicatif		**9 plus-que-parfait de l'indicatif**	
amusais	amusions	avais amusé	avions amusé
amusais	amusiez	avais amusé	aviez amusé
amusait	amusaient	avait amusé	avaient amusé
3 passé simple		**10 passé antérieur**	
amusai	amusâmes	eus amusé	eûmes amusé
amusas	amusâtes	eus amusé	eûtes amusé
amusa	amusèrent	eut amusé	eurent amusé
4 futur		**11 futur antérieur**	
amuserai	amuserons	aurai amusé	aurons amusé
amuseras	amuserez	auras amusé	aurez amusé
amusera	amuseront	aura amusé	auront amusé
5 conditionnel		**12 conditionnel passé**	
amuserais	amuserions	aurais amusé	aurions amusé
amuserais	amuseriez	aurais amusé	auriez amusé
amuserait	amuseraient	aurait amusé	auraient amusé
6 présent du subjonctif		**13 passé du subjonctif**	
amuse	amusions	aie amusé	ayons amusé
amuses	amusiez	aies amusé	ayez amusé
amuse	amusent	ait amusé	aient amusé
7 imparfait du subjonctif		**14 plus-que-parfait du subjonctif**	
amusasse	amusassions	eusse amusé	eussions amusé
amusasses	amusassiez	eusses amusé	eussiez amusé
amusât	amusassent	eût amusé	eussent amusé

Impératif
amuse
amusons
amusez

Cet acteur sait bien jouer son rôle. Il amuse les spectateurs. C'est un comédien accompli. Il est amusant, n'est-ce pas?

amusant, amusante amusing
un amuseur amuser, entertainer
un amuse-bouche, un amuse-gueule tidbit, snack
une amusette diversion, pastime, idle pleasure
un amusement amusement, entertainment
Tes remarques ne m'amusent pas. Your remarks don't amuse me.

See also s'amuser.

| s'amuser | Part. pr. s'amusant | Part. passé amusé(e)(s) |

s'amuser Part. pr. **s'amusant** Part. passé **amusé(e)(s)**

to have a good time, to amuse oneself, Reflexive regular -er verb
to enjoy oneself

The Seven Simple Tenses		The Seven Compound Tenses	
Singular	Plural	Singular	Plural
1 présent de l'indicatif		8 passé composé	
m'amuse	nous amusons	me suis amusé(e)	nous sommes amusé(e)s
t'amuses	vous amusez	t'es amusé(e)	vous êtes amusé(e)(s)
s'amuse	s'amusent	s'est amusé(e)	se sont amusé(e)s
2 imparfait de l'indicatif		9 plus-que-parfait de l'indicatif	
m'amusais	nous amusions	m'étais amusé(e)	nous étions amusé(e)s
t'amusais	vous amusiez	t'étais amusé(e)	vous étiez amusé(e)(s)
s'amusait	s'amusaient	s'était amusé(e)	s'étaient amusé(e)s
3 passé simple		10 passé antérieur	
m'amusai	nous amusâmes	me fus amusé(e)	nous fûmes amusé(e)s
t'amusas	vous amusâtes	te fus amusé(e)	vous fûtes amusé(e)(s)
s'amusa	s'amusèrent	se fut amusé(e)	se furent amusé(e)s
4 futur		11 futur antérieur	
m'amuserai	nous amuserons	me serai amusé(e)	nous serons amusé(e)s
t'amuseras	vous amuserez	te seras amusé(e)	vous serez amusé(e)(s)
s'amusera	s'amuseront	se sera amusé(e)	se seront amusé(e)s
5 conditionnel		12 conditionnel passé	
m'amuserais	nous amuserions	me serais amusé(e)	nous serions amusé(e)s
t'amuserais	vous amuseriez	te serais amusé(e)	vous seriez amusé(e)(s)
s'amuserait	s'amuseraient	se serait amusé(e)	se seraient amusé(e)s
6 présent du subjonctif		13 passé du subjonctif	
m'amuse	nous amusions	me sois amusé(e)	nous soyons amusé(e)s
t'amuses	vous amusiez	te sois amusé(e)	vous soyez amusé(e)(s)
s'amuse	s'amusent	se soit amusé(e)	se soient amusé(e)s
7 imparfait du subjonctif		14 plus-que-parfait du subjonctif	
m'amusasse	nous amusassions	me fusse amusé(e)	nous fussions amusé(e)s
t'amusasses	vous amusassiez	te fusses amusé(e)	vous fussiez amusé(e)(s)
s'amusât	s'amusassent	se fût amusé(e)	se fussent amusé(e)s

Impératif
amuse-toi; ne t'amuse pas
amusons-nous; ne nous amusons pas
amusez-vous; ne vous amusez pas

Est-ce que vous vous amusez dans la classe de français? Do you enjoy yourself
in French class?

Je m'amuse beaucoup dans cette classe. I enjoy myself a great deal in this class.
Je me suis bien amusé au cinéma. I had a great time at the movies.
Amuse-toi bien! Have a great time!

s'amuser à + inf. to enjoy oneself + pres. part.
s'amuser de to make fun of
s'amuser avec to play with

16 See also amuser.

Regular -er verb endings: spelling change: to call, to name, to appeal
l becomes ll before syllable with a mute e.

The Seven Simple Tenses		The Seven Compound Tenses	
Singular	Plural	Singular	Plural
1 présent de l'indicatif		**8 passé composé**	
appelle	**appelons**	**ai appelé**	**avons appelé**
appelles	**appelez**	**as appelé**	**avez appelé**
appelle	**appellent**	**a appelé**	**ont appelé**
2 imparfait de l'indicatif		**9 plus-que-parfait de l'indicatif**	
appelais	**appelions**	**avais appelé**	**avions appelé**
appelais	**appeliez**	**avais appelé**	**aviez appelé**
appelait	**appelaient**	**avait appelé**	**avaient appelé**
3 passé simple		**10 passé antérieur**	
appelai	**appelâmes**	**eus appelé**	**eûmes appelé**
appelas	**appelâtes**	**eus appelé**	**eûtes appelé**
appela	**appelèrent**	**eut appelé**	**eurent appelé**
4 futur		**11 futur antérieur**	
appellerai	**appellerons**	**aurai appelé**	**aurons appelé**
appelleras	**appellerez**	**auras appelé**	**aurez appelé**
appellera	**appelleront**	**aura appelé**	**auront appelé**
5 conditionnel		**12 conditionnel passé**	
appellerais	**appellerions**	**aurais appelé**	**aurions appelé**
appellerais	**appelleriez**	**aurais appelé**	**auriez appelé**
appellerait	**appelleraient**	**aurait appelé**	**auraient appelé**
6 présent du subjonctif		**13 passé du subjonctif**	
appelle	**appelions**	**aie appelé**	**ayons appelé**
appelles	**appeliez**	**aies appelé**	**ayez appelé**
appelle	**appellent**	**ait appelé**	**aient appelé**
7 imparfait du subjonctif		**14 plus-que-parfait du subjonctif**	
appelasse	**appelassions**	**eusse appelé**	**eussions appelé**
appelasses	**appelassiez**	**eusses appelé**	**eussiez appelé**
appelât	**appelassent**	**eût appelé**	**eussent appelé**
		Impératif	
		appelle	
		appelons	
		appelez	

Appelez un taxi, s'il vous plaît.   Call a taxi, please.

appellation *f.* contrôlée   French government approval of the quality of a wine
  or cheese
une appellation   appellation; un appel   appeal, summons
en appeler à qqn   to appeal to someone
rappeler   to call back, to remind, to recall
un appel   call; appel téléphonique   telephone call; faire l'appel   to call the roll

s'appeler   Part. pr. **s'appelant**   Part. passé **appelé(e)(s)**

to be named, to call oneself	Reflexive verb; regular -er verb endings: spelling change: l becomes ll before syllable with a mute e

The Seven Simple Tenses	The Seven Compound Tenses

Singular	Plural	Singular	Plural
1 présent de l'indicatif		8 passé composé	
m'appelle	**nous appelons**	**me suis appelé(e)**	**nous sommes appelé(e)s**
t'appelles	**vous appelez**	**t'es appelé(e)**	**vous êtes appelé(e)(s)**
s'appelle	**s'appellent**	**s'est appelé(e)**	**se sont appelé(e)s**
2 imparfait de l'indicatif		9 plus-que-parfait de l'indicatif	
m'appelais	**nous appelions**	**m'étais appelé(e)**	**nous étions appelé(e)s**
t'appelais	**vous appeliez**	**t'étais appelé(e)**	**vous étiez appelé(e)(s)**
s'appelait	**s'appelaient**	**s'était appelé(e)**	**s'étaient appelé(e)s**
3 passé simple		10 passé antérieur	
m'appelai	**nous appelâmes**	**me fus appelé(e)**	**nous fûmes appelé(e)s**
t'appelas	**vous appelâtes**	**te fus appelé(e)**	**vous fûtes appelé(e)(s)**
s'appela	**s'appelèrent**	**se fut appelé(e)**	**se furent appelé(e)s**
4 futur		11 futur antérieur	
m'appellerai	**nous appellerons**	**me serai appelé(e)**	**nous serons appelé(e)s**
t'appelleras	**vous appellerez**	**te seras appelé(e)**	**vous serez appelé(e)(s)**
s'appellera	**s'appelleront**	**se sera appelé(e)**	**se seront appelé(e)s**
5 conditionnel		12 conditionnel passé	
m'appellerais	**nous appellerions**	**me serais appelé(e)**	**nous serions appelé(e)s**
t'appellerais	**vous appelleriez**	**te serais appelé(e)**	**vous seriez appelé(e)(s)**
s'appellerait	**s'appelleraient**	**se serait appelé(e)**	**se seraient appelé(e)s**
6 présent du subjonctif		13 passé du subjonctif	
m'appelle	**nous appelions**	**me sois appelé(e)**	**nous soyons appelé(e)s**
t'appelles	**vous appeliez**	**te sois appelé(e)**	**vous soyez appelé(e)(s)**
s'appelle	**s'appellent**	**se soit appelé(e)**	**se soient appelé(e)s**
7 imparfait du subjonctif		14 plus-que-parfait du subjonctif	
m'appelasse	**nous appelassions**	**me fusse appelé(e)**	**nous fussions appelé(e)s**
t'appelasses	**vous appelassiez**	**te fusses appelé(e)**	**vous fussiez appelé(e)(s)**
s'appelât	**s'appelassent**	**se fût appelé(e)**	**se fussent appelé(e)s**

Impératif
appelle-toi; ne t'appelle pas
appelons-nous; ne nous appelons pas
appelez-vous; ne vous appelez pas

—Bonjour, mon enfant. Comment t'appelles-tu?
—Je m'appelle Henri.
—As-tu des frères et des soeurs?
—Oui, j'ai deux frères et trois soeurs. Ils s'appellent Joseph, Bernard, Thérèse, Paulette, et Andrée.

Permettez-moi de me présenter. Je m'appelle . . .   Please allow me to introduce myself. My name is . . .

For other words and expressions related to this verb, see **appeler, rappeler,** and **se rappeler.**

Regular -er verb   to bring, tò bear

The Seven Simple Tenses		The Seven Compound Tenses	
Singular	Plural	Singular	Plural
1 présent de l'indicatif		8 passé composé	
apporte	**apportons**	**ai apporté**	**avons apporté**
apportes	**apportez**	**as apporté**	**avez apporté**
apporte	**apportent**	**a apporté**	**ont apporté**
2 imparfait de l'indicatif		9 plus-que-parfait de l'indicatif	
apportais	**apportions**	**avais apporté**	**avions apporté**
apportais	**apportiez**	**avais apporté**	**aviez apporté**
apportait	**apportaient**	**avait apporté**	**avaient apporté**
3 passé simple		10 passé antérieur	
apportai	**apportâmes**	**eus apporté**	**eûmes apporté**
apportas	**apportâtes**	**eus apporté**	**eûtes apporté**
apporta	**apportèrent**	**eut apporté**	**eurent apporté**
4 futur		11 futur antérieur	
apporterai	**apporterons**	**aurai apporté**	**aurons apporté**
apporteras	**apporterez**	**auras apporté**	**aurez apporté**
apportera	**apporteront**	**aura apporté**	**auront apporté**
5 conditionnel		12 conditionnel passé	
apporterais	**apporterions**	**aurais apporté**	**aurions apporté**
apporterais	**apporteriez**	**aurais apporté**	**auriez apporté**
apporterait	**apporteraient**	**aurait apporté**	**auraient apporté**
6 présent du subjonctif		13 passé du subjonctif	
apporte	**apportions**	**aie apporté**	**ayons apporté**
apportes	**apportiez**	**aies apporté**	**ayez apporté**
apporte	**apportent**	**ait apporté**	**aient apporté**
7 imparfait du subjonctif		14 plus-que-parfait du subjonctif	
apportasse	**apportassions**	**eusse apporté**	**eussions apporté**
apportasses	**apportassiez**	**eusses apporté**	**eussiez apporté**
apportât	**apportassent**	**eût apporté**	**eussent apporté**
		Impératif	
		apporte	
		apportons	
		apportez	

Hier soir, j'ai dîné dans un restaurant français. Quand le garçon m'a apporté mon repas, je lui ai dit: —**Apportez-moi du pain, aussi, s'il vous plaît.**   Yesterday evening, I had dinner in a French restaurant. When the server brought me my meal, I said to him: —Bring me some bread, too, please.

un apport something brought; **un apport dotal** wife's dowry
un apporteur a person who brings something (usually news); **un apporteur de bonnes nouvelles** bearer of good news

See also **porter**.

apprendre	Part. pr. **apprenant**	Part. passé **appris**

to learn

Irregular verb

The Seven Simple Tenses		The Seven Compound Tenses	
Singular	Plural	Singular	Plural
1 présent de l'indicatif		8 passé composé	
apprends	apprenons	ai appris	avons appris
apprends	apprenez	as appris	avez appris
apprend	apprennent	a appris	ont appris
2 imparfait de l'indicatif		9 plus-que-parfait de l'indicatif	
apprenais	apprenions	avais appris	avions appris
apprenais	appreniez	avais appris	aviez appris
apprenait	apprenaient	avait appris	avaient appris
3 passé simple		10 passé antérieur	
appris	apprîmes	eus appris	eûmes appris
appris	apprîtes	eus appris	eûtes appris
apprit	apprirent	eut appris	eurent appris
4 futur		11 futur antérieur	
apprendrai	apprendrons	aurai appris	aurons appris
apprendras	apprendrez	auras appris	aurez appris
apprendra	apprendront	aura appris	auront appris
5 conditionnel		12 conditionnel passé	
apprendrais	apprendrions	aurais appris	aurions appris
apprendrais	apprendriez	aurais appris	auriez appris
apprendrait	apprendraient	aurait appris	auraient appris
6 présent du subjonctif		13 passé du subjonctif	
apprenne	apprenions	aie appris	ayons appris
apprennes	appreniez	aies appris	ayez appris
apprenne	apprennent	ait appris	aient appris
7 imparfait du subjonctif		14 plus-que-parfait du subjonctif	
apprisse	apprissions	eusse appris	eussions appris
apprisses	apprissiez	eusses appris	eussiez appris
apprît	apprissent	eût appris	eussent appris

Impératif
apprends
apprenons
apprenez

À l'école j'apprends à lire en français. In school, I'm learning to read in French.

Robert, apprends ce poème par cœur pour demain. Robert, learn this poem by heart (memorize this poem) for tomorrow.

David m'a appris à réparer ma voiture. David taught me to fix my car.

apprendre par cœur to memorize
apprendre à qqn à faire qqch to teach somebody to do something
apprendre qqch à qqn to inform someone of something; to teach someone something
apprendre à faire qqch to learn to do something

See also comprendre, prendre, and reprendre.

20

Regular -er verb endings: spelling change: retain the   to arrange
ge before a or o to keep the soft g sound of the verb.

The Seven Simple Tenses		The Seven Compound Tenses	
Singular	Plural	Singular	Plural
1 présent de l'indicatif		**8 passé composé**	
arrange	**arrangeons**	**ai arrangé**	**avons arrangé**
arranges	**arrangez**	**as arrangé**	**avez arrangé**
arrange	**arrangent**	**a arrangé**	**ont arrangé**
2 imparfait de l'indicatif		**9 plus-que-parfait de l'indicatif**	
arrangeais	**arrangions**	**avais arrangé**	**avions arrangé**
arrangeais	**arrangiez**	**avais arrangé**	**aviez arrangé**
arrangeait	**arrangeaient**	**avait arrangé**	**avaient arrangé**
3 passé simple		**10 passé antérieur**	
arrangeai	**arrangeâmes**	**eus arrangé**	**eûmes arrangé**
arrangeas	**arrangeâtes**	**eus arrangé**	**eûtes arrangé**
arrangea	**arrangèrent**	**eut arrangé**	**eurent arrangé**
4 futur		**11 futur antérieur**	
arrangerai	**arrangerons**	**aurai arrangé**	**aurons arrangé**
arrangeras	**arrangerez**	**auras arrangé**	**aurez arrangé**
arrangera	**arrangeront**	**aura arrangé**	**auront arrangé**
5 conditionnel		**12 conditionnel passé**	
arrangerais	**arrangerions**	**aurais arrangé**	**aurions arrangé**
arrangerais	**arrangeriez**	**aurais arrangé**	**auriez arrangé**
arrangerait	**arrangeraient**	**aurait arrangé**	**auraient arrangé**
6 présent du subjonctif		**13 passé du subjonctif**	
arrange	**arrangions**	**aie arrangé**	**ayons arrangé**
arranges	**arrangiez**	**aies arrangé**	**ayez arrangé**
arrange	**arrangent**	**ait arrangé**	**aient arrangé**
7 imparfait du subjonctif		**14 plus-que-parfait du subjonctif**	
arrangeasse	**arrangeassions**	**eusse arrangé**	**eussions arrangé**
arrangeasses	**arrangeassiez**	**eusses arrangé**	**eussiez arrangé**
arrangeât	**arrangeassent**	**eût arrangé**	**eussent arrangé**
		Impératif	
		arrange	
		arrangeons	
		arrangez	

arranger qqch   to arrange, contrive something
arranger l'affaire   to straighten out a matter
arranger qqn   to accommodate, suit someone; **Ça m'arrange bien.**   That suits me
   fine.   **Ça s'arrangera.**   It will turn out all right.
s'arranger   to come to an agreement

arrêter

Part. pr. **arrêtant** Part. passé **arrêté**

to arrest, to stop (someone or something)

Regular -er verb

The Seven Simple Tenses		The Seven Compound Tenses	
Singular	Plural	Singular	Plural
1 présent de l'indicatif		**8 passé composé**	
arrête	arrêtons	ai arrêté	avons arrêté
arrêtes	arrêtez	as arrêté	avez arrêté
arrête	arrêtent	a arrêté	ont arrêté
2 imparfait de l'indicatif		**9 plus-que-parfait de l'indicatif**	
arrêtais	arrêtions	avais arrêté	avions arrêté
arrêtais	arrêtiez	avais arrêté	aviez arrêté
arrêtait	arrêtaient	avait arrêté	avaient arrêté
3 passé simple		**10 passé antérieur**	
arrêtai	arrêtâmes	eus arrêté	eûmes arrêté
arrêtas	arrêtâtes	eus arrêté	eûtes arrêté
arrêta	arrêtèrent	eut arrêté	eurent arrêté
4 futur		**11 futur antérieur**	
arrêterai	arrêterons	aurai arrêté	aurons arrêté
arrêteras	arrêterez	auras arrêté	aurez arrêté
arrêtera	arrêteront	aura arrêté	auront arrêté
5 conditionnel		**12 conditionnel passé**	
arrêterais	arrêterions	aurais arrêté	aurions arrêté
arrêterais	arrêteriez	aurais arrêté	auriez arrêté
arrêterait	arrêteraient	aurait arrêté	auraient arrêté
6 présent du subjonctif		**13 passé du subjonctif**	
arrête	arrêtions	aie arrêté	ayons arrêté
arrêtes	arrêtiez	aies arrêté	ayez arrêté
arrête	arrêtent	ait arrêté	aient arrêté
7 imparfait du subjonctif		**14 plus-que-parfait du subjonctif**	
arrêtasse	arrêtassions	eusse arrêté	eussions arrêté
arrêtasses	arrêtassiez	eusses arrêté	eussiez arrêté
arrêtât	arrêtassent	eût arrêté	eussent arrêté
		Impératif	
		arrête	
		arrêtons	
		arrêtez	

L'agent de police a arrêté les voitures pour laisser les piétons traverser la rue.
Il a crié:—Arrêtez! Arrêtez!   The police officer stopped the cars to let the
pedestrians cross the street. He shouted: —Stop! Stop!

un arrêt   halt, stop, arrest
arrêt d'autobus   bus stop
un arrêté ministériel   decree
arrêter qqn de faire qqch   to stop someone from doing something
une arrestation   arrest, apprehension; être en état d'arrestation   to be under arrest
arrêter un jour   to set a date; arrêter un marché   to make a deal

22   See also s'arrêter.

Reflexive regular -er verb   to stop (oneself, itself), to pause

The Seven Simple Tenses		The Seven Compound Tenses	
Singular	Plural	Singular	Plural
1 présent de l'indicatif		**8 passé composé**	
m'arrête	nous arrêtons	me suis arrêté(e)	nous sommes arrêté(e)s
t'arrêtes	vous arrêtez	t'es arrêté(e)	vous êtes arrêté(e)(s)
s'arrête	s'arrêtent	s'est arrêté(e)	se sont arrêté(e)s
2 imparfait de l'indicatif		**9 plus-que-parfait de l'indicatif**	
m'arrêtais	nous arrêtions	m'étais arrêté(e)	nous étions arrêté(e)s
t'arrêtais	vous arrêtiez	t'étais arrêté(e)	vous étiez arrêté(e)(s)
s'arrêtait	s'arrêtaient	s'était arrêté(e)	s'étaient arrêté(e)s
3 passé simple		**10 passé antérieur**	
m'arrêtai	nous arrêtâmes	me fus arrêté(e)	nous fûmes arrêté(e)s
t'arrêtas	vous arrêtâtes	te fus arrêté(e)	vous fûtes arrêté(e)(s)
s'arrêta	s'arrêtèrent	se fut arrêté(e)	se furent arrêté(e)s
4 futur		**11 futur antérieur**	
m'arrêterai	nous arrêterons	me serai arrêté(e)	nous serons arrêté(e)s
t'arrêteras	vous arrêterez	te seras arrêté(e)	vous serez arrêté(e)(s)
s'arrêtera	s'arrêteront	se sera arrêté(e)	se seront arrêté(e)s
5 conditionnel		**12 conditionnel passé**	
m'arrêterais	nous arrêterions	me serais arrêté(e)	nous serions arrêté(e)s
t'arrêterais	vous arrêteriez	te serais arrêté(e)	vous seriez arrêté(e)(s)
s'arrêterait	s'arrêteraient	se serait arrêté(e)	se seraient arrêté(e)s
6 présent du subjonctif		**13 passé du subjonctif**	
m'arrête	nous arrêtions	me sois arrêté(e)	nous soyons arrêté(e)s
t'arrêtes	vous arrêtiez	te sois arrêté(e)	vous soyez arrêté(e)(s)
s'arrête	s'arrêtent	se soit arrêté(e)	se soient arrêté(e)s
7 imparfait du subjonctif		**14 plus-que-parfait du subjonctif**	
m'arrêtasse	nous arrêtassions	me fusse arrêté(e)	nous fussions arrêté(e)s
t'arrêtasses	vous arrêtassiez	te fusses arrêté(e)	vous fussiez arrêté(e)(s)
s'arrêtât	s'arrêtassent	se fût arrêté(e)	se fussent arrêté(e)s

Impératif
arrête-toi; ne t'arrête pas
arrêtons-nous; ne nous arrêtons pas
arrêtez-vous; ne vous arrêtez pas

Madame Dumont s'est arrêtée devant une pâtisserie pour acheter une belle tarte aux cerises. Deux autres dames se sont arrêtées derrière elle et les trois sont entrées dans le magasin.

s'arrêter de faire qqch   to desist from doing something
sans s'arrêter   without stopping

For other words and expressions related to this verb, see **arrêter**.

to arrive, to happen   Regular -er verb

The Seven Simple Tenses		The Seven Compound Tenses	
Singular	Plural	Singular	Plural
1 présent de l'indicatif		**8 passé composé**	
arrive	arrivons	suis arrivé(e)	sommes arrivé(e)s
arrives	arrivez	es arrivé(e)	êtes arrivé(e)(s)
arrive	arrivent	est arrivé(e)	sont arrivé(e)s
2 imparfait de l'indicatif		**9 plus-que-parfait de l'indicatif**	
arrivais	arrivions	étais arrivé(e)	étions arrivé(e)s
arrivais	arriviez	étais arrivé(e)	étiez arrivé(e)(s)
arrivait	arrivaient	était arrivé(e)	étaient arrivé(e)s
3 passé simple		**10 passé antérieur**	
arrivai	arrivâmes	fus arrivé(e)	fûmes arrivé(e)s
arrivas	arrivâtes	fus arrivé(e)	fûtes arrivé(e)(s)
arriva	arrivèrent	fut arrivé(e)	furent arrivé(e)s
4 futur		**11 futur antérieur**	
arriverai	arriverons	serai arrivé(e)	serons arrivé(e)s
arriveras	arriverez	seras arrivé(e)	serez arrivé(e)(s)
arrivera	arriveront	sera arrivé(e)	seront arrivé(e)s
5 conditionnel		**12 conditionnel passé**	
arriverais	arriverions	serais arrivé(e)	serions arrivé(e)s
arriverais	arriveriez	serais arrivé(e)	seriez arrivé(e)(s)
arriverait	arriveraient	serait arrivé(e)	seraient arrivé(e)s
6 présent du subjonctif		**13 passé du subjonctif**	
arrive	arrivions	sois arrivé(e)	soyons arrivé(e)s
arrives	arriviez	sois arrivé(e)	soyez arrivé(e)(s)
arrive	arrivent	soit arrivé(e)	soient arrivé(e)s
7 imparfait du subjonctif		**14 plus-que-parfait du subjonctif**	
arrivasse	arrivassions	fusse arrivé(e)	fussions arrivé(e)s
arrivasses	arrivassiez	fusses arrivé(e)	fussiez arrivé(e)(s)
arrivât	arrivassent	fût arrivé(e)	fussent arrivé(e)s

Impératif
arrive
arrivons
arrivez

À quelle heure est-ce que l'avion arrive à Paris?   At what time does the plane arrive in Paris?

Le train pour Québec arrivera à 15h22.   The train to Québec will arrive at 3:22 P.M.

Qu'est-ce qui arrive?   What's happening? What's going on?

Qu'est-ce qui est arrivé?   What happened?

Quoi qu'il arrive . . .   Come what may . . .

J'arrive!   I'm coming!

arriver à faire qqch   to succeed in + pres. part.; to manage to do something

arriver à   to happen to; Cela n'arrive qu'à moi!   It's just my luck! That would happen to me!

Reflexive irregular verb   to sit down

The Seven Simple Tenses		The Seven Compound Tenses	
Singular	Plural	Singular	Plural
1 présent de l'indicatif		**8 passé composé**	
m'assieds	nous asseyons	me suis assis(e)	nous sommes assis(es)
t'assieds	vous asseyez	t'es assis(e)	vous êtes assis(e)(es)
s'assied	s'asseyent	s'est assis(e)	se sont assis(es)
2 imparfait de l'indicatif		**9 plus-que-parfait de l'indicatif**	
m'asseyais	nous asseyions	m'étais assis(e)	nous étions assis(es)
t'asseyais	vous asseyiez	t'étais assis(e)	vous étiez assis(e)(es)
s'asseyait	s'asseyaient	s'était assis(e)	s'étaient assis(es)
3 passé simple		**10 passé antérieur**	
m'assis	nous assîmes	me fus assis(e)	nous fûmes assis(es)
t'assis	vous assîtes	te fus assis(e)	vous fûtes assis(e)(es)
s'assit	s'assirent	se fut assis(e)	se furent assis(es)
4 futur		**11 futur antérieur**	
m'assiérai	nous assiérons	me serai assis(e)	nous serons assis(es)
t'assiéras	vous assiérez	te seras assis(e)	vous serez assis(e)(es)
s'assiéra	s'assiéront	se sera assis(e)	se seront assis(es)
5 conditionnel		**12 conditionnel passé**	
m'assiérais	nous assiérions	me serais assis(e)	nous serions assis(es)
t'assiérais	vous assiériez	te serais assis(e)	vous seriez assis(e)(es)
s'assiérait	s'assiéraient	se serait assis(e)	se seraient assis(es)
6 présent du subjonctif		**13 passé du subjonctif**	
m'asseye	nous asseyions	me sois assis(e)	nous soyons assis(es)
t'asseyes	vous asseyiez	te sois assis(e)	vous soyez assis(e)(es)
s'asseye	s'asseyent	se soit assis(e)	se soient assis(es)
7 imparfait du subjonctif		**14 plus-que-parfait du subjonctif**	
m'assisse	nous assissions	me fusse assis(e)	nous fussions assis(es)
t'assisses	vous assissiez	te fusses assis(e)	vous fussiez assis(e)(es)
s'assît	s'assissent	se fût assis(e)	se fussent assis(es)

Impératif
assieds-toi; ne t'assieds pas
asseyons-nous; ne nous asseyons pas
asseyez-vous; ne vous asseyez pas

Quand je voyage en train, je m'assieds toujours près d'une fenêtre. When I travel by train, I always sit by a window.
Puis-je m'asseoir ici? May I sit down here?
Certainement—asseyez-vous. Certainly—sit down.

asseoir qqn to seat someone
rasseoir to seat again, to reseat, se rasseoir to sit down again

assister
Part. pr. assistant   **Part. passé assisté**

to assist (at), to be present (at), to attend   Regular -er verb

The Seven Simple Tenses		The Seven Compound Tenses	
Singular	Plural	Singular	Plural
1 présent de l'indicatif		**8 passé composé**	
assiste	assistons	ai assisté	avons assisté
assistes	assistez	as assisté	avez assisté
assiste	assistent	a assisté	ont assisté
2 imparfait de l'indicatif		**9 plus-que-parfait de l'indicatif**	
assistais	assistions	avais assisté	avions assisté
assistais	assistiez	avais assisté	aviez assisté
assistait	assistaient	avait assisté	avaient assisté
3 passé simple		**10 passé antérieur**	
assistai	assistâmes	eus assisté	eûmes assisté
assistas	assistâtes	eus assisté	eûtes assisté
assista	assistèrent	eut assisté	eurent assisté
4 futur		**11 futur antérieur**	
assisterai	assisterons	aurai assisté	aurons assisté
assisteras	assisterez	auras assisté	aurez assisté
assistera	assisteront	aura assisté	auront assisté
5 conditionnel		**12 conditionnel passé**	
assisterais	assisterions	aurais assisté	aurions assisté
assisterais	assisteriez	aurais assisté	auriez assisté
assisterait	assisteraient	aurait assisté	auraient assisté
6 présent du subjonctif		**13 passé du subjonctif**	
assiste	assistions	aie assisté	ayons assisté
assistes	assistiez	aies assisté	ayez assisté
assiste	assistent	ait assisté	aient assisté
7 imparfait du subjonctif		**14 plus-que-parfait du subjonctif**	
assistasse	assistassions	eusse assisté	eussions assisté
assistasses	assistassiez	eusses assisté	eussiez assisté
assistât	assistassent	eût assisté	eussent assisté
		Impératif	
		assiste	
		assistons	
		assistez	

Lundi prochain j'assisterai à une conférence de presse.   Next Monday, I will attend a press conference.

assistance *f.*   assistance, help; attendance; audience
assister à   to be present at, to attend
les assistants   those present; spectators
les services de l'Assistance publique   health and social security services

| Part. pr. s'assurant | | Part. passé assuré(e)(s) | | s'assurer |

Reflexive regular -er verb   to make sure, to assure oneself, to insure oneself

The Seven Simple Tenses		The Seven Compound Tenses	
Singular	Plural	Singular	Plural
1 présent de l'indicatif		8 passé composé	
m'assure	nous assurons	me suis assuré(e)	nous sommes assuré(e)s
t'assures	vous assurez	t'es assuré(e)	vous êtes assuré(e)(s)
s'assure	s'assurent	s'est assuré(e)	se sont assuré(e)s
2 imparfait de l'indicatif		9 plus-que-parfait de l'indicatif	
m'assurais	nous assurions	m'étais assuré(e)	nous étions assuré(e)s
t'assurais	vous assuriez	t'étais assuré(e)	vous étiez assuré(e)(s)
s'assurait	s'assuraient	s'était assuré(e)	s'étaient assuré(e)s
3 passé simple		10 passé antérieur	
m'assurai	nous assurâmes	me fus assuré(e)	nous fûmes assuré(e)s
t'assuras	vous assurâtes	te fus assuré(e)	vous fûtes assuré(e)(s)
s'assura	s'assurèrent	se fut assuré(e)	se furent assuré(e)s
4 futur		11 futur antérieur	
m'assurerai	nous assurerons	me serai assuré(e)	nous serons assuré(e)s
t'assureras	vous assurerez	te seras assuré(e)	vous serez assuré(e)(s)
s'assurera	s'assureront	se sera assuré(e)	se seront assuré(e)s
5 conditionnel		12 conditionnel passé	
m'assurerais	nous assurerions	me serais assuré(e)	nous serions assuré(e)s
t'assurerais	vous assureriez	te serais assuré(e)	vous seriez assuré(e)(s)
s'assurerait	s'assureraient	se serait assuré(e)	se seraient assuré(e)s
6 présent du subjonctif		13 passé du subjonctif	
m'assure	nous assurions	me sois assuré(e)	nous soyons assuré(e)s
t'assures	vous assuriez	te sois assuré(e)	vous soyez assuré(e)(s)
s'assure	s'assurent	se soit assuré(e)	se soient assuré(e)s
7 imparfait du subjonctif		14 plus-que-parfait du subjonctif	
m'assurasse	nous assurassions	me fusse assuré(e)	nous fussions assuré(e)s
t'assurasses	vous assurassiez	te fusses assuré(e)	vous fussiez assuré(e)(s)
s'assurât	s'assurassent	se fût assuré(e)	se fussent assuré(e)s

Impératif
assure-toi; ne t'assure pas
assurons-nous; ne nous assurons pas
assurez-vous; ne vous assurez pas

Pour s'assurer que la porte était bien fermée, Madame Lafontaine l'a fermée à clef. Puis elle a fermé toutes les fenêtres pour avoir de l'assurance et un sentiment de sécurité.

Assurément, elle a raison. Il y a des cambrioleurs dans le voisinage.

assurément   assuredly
assurance f.   assurance, insurance
s'assurer de la protection de qqn   to secure someone's protection
l'assurance-vie f.   life insurance, life assurance

attendre	Part. pr. **attendant**	Part. passé **attendu**

to wait, to wait for, to expect   Regular -re verb

The Seven Simple Tenses		The Seven Compound Tenses	
Singular	Plural	Singular	Plural
1 présent de l'indicatif		8 passé composé	
attends	**attendons**	**ai attendu**	**avons attendu**
attends	**attendez**	**as attendu**	**avez attendu**
attend	**attendent**	**a attendu**	**ont attendu**
2 imparfait de l'indicatif		9 plus-que-parfait de l'indicatif	
attendais	**attendions**	**avais attendu**	**avions attendu**
attendais	**attendiez**	**avais attendu**	**aviez attendu**
attendait	**attendaient**	**avait attendu**	**avaient attendu**
3 passé simple		10 passé antérieur	
attendis	**attendîmes**	**eus attendu**	**eûmes attendu**
attendis	**attendîtes**	**eus attendu**	**eûtes attendu**
attendit	**attendirent**	**eut attendu**	**eurent attendu**
4 futur		11 futur antérieur	
attendrai	**attendrons**	**aurai attendu**	**aurons attendu**
attendras	**attendrez**	**auras attendu**	**aurez attendu**
attendra	**attendront**	**aura attendu**	**auront attendu**
5 conditionnel		12 conditionnel passé	
attendrais	**attendrions**	**aurais attendu**	**aurions attendu**
attendrais	**attendriez**	**aurais attendu**	**auriez attendu**
attendrait	**attendraient**	**aurait attendu**	**auraient attendu**
6 présent du subjonctif		13 passé du subjonctif	
attende	**attendions**	**aie attendu**	**ayons attendu**
attendes	**attendiez**	**aies attendu**	**ayez attendu**
attende	**attendent**	**ait attendu**	**aient attendu**
7 imparfait du subjonctif		14 plus-que-parfait du subjonctif	
attendisse	**attendissions**	**eusse attendu**	**eussions attendu**
attendisses	**attendissiez**	**eusses attendu**	**eussiez attendu**
attendît	**attendissent**	**eût attendu**	**eussent attendu**
		Impératif	
		attends	
		attendons	
		attendez	

faire attendre qqch à qqn   to make someone wait for something; to keep someone waiting for something
en attendant   meanwhile, in the meantime
Cela peut attendre!   It can wait!
s'attendre à   to expect; **s'attendre à ce que + subjunctive**   to expect that, to anticipate
J'attends l'autobus depuis vingt minutes!   I have been waiting for the bus for 20 minutes!
Georges ne s'attendait pas à gagner.   George wasn't expecting to win.

28

Regular -er verb   to catch

The Seven Simple Tenses | | The Seven Compound Tenses | |
Singular	Plural	Singular	Plural
1 présent de l'indicatif		8 passé composé	
attrape	**attrapons**	**ai attrapé**	**avons attrapé**
attrapes	**attrapez**	**as attrapé**	**avez attrapé**
attrape	**attrapent**	**a attrapé**	**ont attrapé**
2 imparfait de l'indicatif		9 plus-que-parfait de l'indicatif	
attrapais	**attrapions**	**avais attrapé**	**avions attrapé**
attrapais	**attrapiez**	**avais attrapé**	**aviez attrapé**
attrapait	**attrapaient**	**avait attrapé**	**avaient attrapé**
3 passé simple		10 passé antérieur	
attrapai	**attrapâmes**	**eus attrapé**	**eûmes attrapé**
attrapas	**attrapâtes**	**eus attrapé**	**eûtes attrapé**
attrapa	**attrapèrent**	**eut attrapé**	**eurent attrapé**
4 futur		11 futur antérieur	
attraperai	**attraperons**	**aurai attrapé**	**aurons attrapé**
attraperas	**attraperez**	**auras attrapé**	**aurez attrapé**
attrapera	**attraperont**	**aura attrapé**	**auront attrapé**
5 conditionnel		12 conditionnel passé	
attraperais	**attraperions**	**aurais attrapé**	**aurions attrapé**
attraperais	**attraperiez**	**aurais attrapé**	**auriez attrapé**
attraperait	**attraperaient**	**aurait attrapé**	**auraient attrapé**
6 présent du subjonctif		13 passé du subjonctif	
attrape	**attrapions**	**aie attrapé**	**ayons attrapé**
attrapes	**attrapiez**	**aies attrapé**	**ayez attrapé**
attrape	**attrapent**	**ait attrapé**	**aient attrapé**
7 imparfait du subjonctif		14 plus-que-parfait du subjonctif	
attrapasse	**attrapassions**	**eusse attrapé**	**eussions attrapé**
attrapasses	**attrapassiez**	**eusses attrapé**	**eussiez attrapé**
attrapât	**attrapassent**	**eût attrapé**	**eussent attrapé**

Impératif
attrape
attrapons
attrapez

Il fait froid. Mets ton manteau ou tu attraperas un rhume.   It's cold outside.
Put on your coat or you will catch cold.
   —**Je n'ai pas le temps maintenant, maman—je dois attraper l'autobus.**   I
don't have the time now, Mother—I have to catch the bus.

attraper un rhume   to catch cold
attraper qqn à qqch   to catch someone at something (to surprise)
s'attraper   to be catching, infectious
une attrape   trick
un attrape-mouche   flypaper (sticky paper to catch flies)

avancer	Part. pr. avançant	Part. passé avancé

to advance, to go forward	Regular -er verb endings: spelling change: c changes to ç before a or o to keep s sound.

The Seven Simple Tenses | The Seven Compound Tenses

Singular	Plural	Singular	Plural
1 présent de l'indicatif		**8 passé composé**	
avance	avançons	ai avancé	avons avancé
avances	avancez	as avancé	avez avancé
avance	avancent	a avancé	ont avancé
2 imparfait de l'indicatif		**9 plus-que-parfait de l'indicatif**	
avançais	avancions	avais avancé	avions avancé
avançais	avanciez	avais avancé	aviez avancé
avançait	avançaient	avait avancé	avaient avancé
3 passé simple		**10 passé antérieur**	
avançai	avançâmes	eus avancé	eûmes avancé
avanças	avançâtes	eus avancé	eûtes avancé
avança	avancèrent	eut avancé	eurent avancé
4 futur		**11 futur antérieur**	
avancerai	avancerons	aurai avancé	aurons avancé
avanceras	avancerez	auras avancé	aurez avancé
avancera	avanceront	aura avancé	auront avancé
5 conditionnel		**12 conditionnel passé**	
avancerais	avancerions	aurais avancé	aurions avancé
avancerais	avanceriez	aurais avancé	auriez avancé
avancerait	avanceraient	aurait avancé	auraient avancé
6 présent du subjonctif		**13 passé du subjonctif**	
avance	avancions	aie avancé	ayons avancé
avances	avanciez	aies avancé	ayez avancé
avance	avancent	ait avancé	aient avancé
7 imparfait du subjonctif		**14 plus-que-parfait du subjonctif**	
avançasse	avançassions	eusse avancé	eussions avancé
avançasses	avançassiez	eusses avancé	eussiez avancé
avançât	avançassent	eût avancé	eussent avancé

	Impératif	
avance	avançons	avancez

une avance   advance, progress
à l'avance, d'avance   in advance, beforehand
arriver en avance   to arrive early
s'avancer   to advance (oneself)
l'avant   m. front
devancer   to arrive ahead
Ta montre avance.   Your watch is fast.
avancer une théorie   to promote a theory
Comment avance le travail?   How is the work coming along?

Irregular verb   to have

The Seven Simple Tenses		The Seven Compound Tenses	
Singular	Plural	Singular	Plural
1 présent de l'indicatif		8 passé composé	
ai	**avons**	**ai eu**	**avons eu**
as	**avez**	**as eu**	**avez eu**
a	**ont**	**a eu**	**ont eu**
2 imparfait de l'indicatif		9 plus-que-parfait de l'indicatif	
avais	**avions**	**avais eu**	**avions eu**
avais	**aviez**	**avais eu**	**aviez eu**
avait	**avaient**	**avait eu**	**avaient eu**
3 passé simple		10 passé antérieur	
eus	**eûmes**	**eus eu**	**eûmes eu**
eus	**eûtes**	**eus eu**	**eûtes eu**
eut	**eurent**	**eut eu**	**eurent eu**
4 futur		11 futur antérieur	
aurai	**aurons**	**aurai eu**	**aurons eu**
auras	**aurez**	**auras eu**	**aurez eu**
aura	**auront**	**aura eu**	**auront eu**
5 conditionnel		12 conditionnel passé	
aurais	**aurions**	**aurais eu**	**aurions eu**
aurais	**auriez**	**aurais eu**	**auriez eu**
aurait	**auraient**	**aurait eu**	**auraient eu**
6 présent du subjonctif		13 passé du subjonctif	
aie	**ayons**	**aie eu**	**ayons eu**
aies	**ayez**	**aies eu**	**ayez eu**
ait	**aient**	**ait eu**	**aient eu**
7 imparfait du subjonctif		14 plus-que-parfait du subjonctif	
eusse	**eussions**	**eusse eu**	**eussions eu**
eusses	**eussiez**	**eusses eu**	**eussiez eu**
eût	**eussent**	**eût eu**	**eussent eu**
		Impératif	
		aie	
		ayons	
		ayez	

avoir . . . ans   to be . . . years old
avoir à + inf.   to have to, to be obliged to + inf.
avoir besoin de   to need, to have need of
avoir chaud   to be (feel) warm (persons)
avoir froid   to be (feel) cold (persons)
avoir mal à la gorge   to have a sore throat
avoir sommeil   to be (feel) sleepy

avoir qqch à faire   to have
   something to do
avoir de la chance   to be lucky
avoir faim   to be hungry
avoir soif   to be thirsty
Il y a . . .   There is . . . / There
   are . . .

balayer	Part. pr. **balayant**	Part. passé **balayé**
to sweep	Regular -er verb endings: spelling change: -ayer verbs may change y to i in front of a mute e or may keep y.	

The Seven Simple Tenses		The Seven Compound Tenses	
Singular	Plural	Singular	Plural

1 présent de l'indicatif

		8 passé composé	
balaye	balayons	ai balayé	avons balayé
balayes	balayez	as balayé	avez balayé
balaye	balayent	a balayé	ont balayé

2 imparfait de l'indicatif

		9 plus-que-parfait de l'indicatif	
balayais	balayions	avais balayé	avions balayé
balayais	balayiez	avais balayé	aviez balayé
balayait	balayaient	avait balayé	avaient balayé

3 passé simple

		10 passé antérieur	
balayai	balayâmes	eus balayé	eûmes balayé
balayas	balayâtes	eus balayé	eûtes balayé
balaya	balayèrent	eut balayé	eurent balayé

4 futur

		11 futur antérieur	
balayerai	balayerons	aurai balayé	aurons balayé
balayeras	balayerez	auras balayé	aurez balayé
balayera	balayeront	aura balayé	auront balayé

5 conditionnel

		12 conditionnel passé	
balayerais	balayerions	aurais balayé	aurions balayé
balayerais	balayeriez	aurais balayé	auriez balayé
balayerait	balayeraient	aurait balayé	auraient balayé

6 présent du subjonctif

		13 passé du subjonctif	
balaye	balayions	aie balayé	ayons balayé
balayes	balayiez	aies balayé	ayez balayé
balaye	balayent	ait balayé	aient balayé

7 imparfait du subjonctif

		14 plus-que-parfait du subjonctif	
balayasse	balayassions	eusse balayé	eussions balayé
balayasses	balayassiez	eusses balayé	eussiez balayé
balayât	balayassent	eût balayé	eussent balayé

	Impératif
	balaye
	balayons
	balayez

—Marie, as-tu balayé les chambres?

—Non, madame.

—Et pourquoi pas?

—Parce que je n'ai pas de balai, je n'ai pas de balayette, et je ne suis pas balayeuse. Voilà pourquoi!

un balai broom; une balayette small broom; un balayeur, une balayeuse sweeper

un balai d'essuie-glace windshield wiper blade

Regular -ir verb   to build, to construct

The Seven Simple Tenses		The Seven Compound Tenses	
Singular	Plural	Singular	Plural
1 présent de l'indicatif		8 passé composé	
bâtis	bâtissons	ai bâti	avons bâti
bâtis	bâtissez	as bâti	avez bâti
bâtit	bâtissent	a bâti	ont bâti
2 imparfait de l'indicatif		9 plus-que-parfait de l'indicatif	
bâtissais	bâtissions	avais bâti	avions bâti
bâtissais	bâtissiez	avais bâti	aviez bâti
bâtissait	bâtissaient	avait bâti	avaient bâti
3 passé simple		10 passé antérieur	
bâtis	bâtîmes	eus bâti	eûmes bâti
bâtis	bâtîtes	eus bâti	eûtes bâti
bâtit	bâtirent	eut bâti	eurent bâti
4 futur		11 futur antérieur	
bâtirai	bâtirons	aurai bâti	aurons bâti
bâtiras	bâtirez	auras bâti	aurez bâti
bâtira	bâtiront	aura bâti	auront bâti
5 conditionnel		12 conditionnel passé	
bâtirais	bâtirions	aurais bâti	aurions bâti
bâtirais	bâtiriez	aurais bâti	auriez bâti
bâtirait	bâtiraient	aurait bâti	auraient bâti
6 présent du subjonctif		13 passé du subjonctif	
bâtisse	bâtissions	aie bâti	ayons bâti
bâtisses	bâtissiez	aies bâti	ayez bâti
bâtisse	bâtissent	ait bâti	aient bâti
7 imparfait du subjonctif		14 plus-que-parfait du subjonctif	
bâtisse	bâtissions	eusse bâti	eussions bâti
bâtisses	bâtissiez	eusses bâti	eussiez bâti
bâtît	bâtissent	eût bâti	eussent bâti
		Impératif	
		bâtis	
		bâtissons	
		bâtissez	

un bâtiment   building, edifice, ship; un bâtisseur   builder
bâtir   to baste (sewing term; when basting food, use **arroser**);
    du fil à bâtir   basting thread
rebâtir   to rebuild
bâtir des châteaux en Espagne   to build castles in the air
bâtir sur le sable   to build on sand
bien bâti, bien bâtie   well built

battre	Part. pr. **battant**	Part. passé **battu**
to beat, to hit, to strike		Irregular verb in 1s, 2s, 3s present indicative

The Seven Simple Tenses		The Seven Compound Tenses	
Singular	Plural	Singular	Plural
1 présent de l'indicatif		8 passé composé	
bats	**battons**	**ai battu**	**avons battu**
bats	**battez**	**as battu**	**avez battu**
bat	**battent**	**a battu**	**ont battu**
2 imparfait de l'indicatif		9 plus-que-parfait de l'indicatif	
battais	**battions**	**avais battu**	**avions battu**
battais	**battiez**	**avais battu**	**aviez battu**
battait	**battaient**	**avait battu**	**avaient battu**
3 passé simple		10 passé antérieur	
battis	**battîmes**	**eus battu**	**eûmes battu**
battis	**battîtes**	**eus battu**	**eûtes battu**
battit	**battirent**	**eut battu**	**eurent battu**
4 futur		11 futur antérieur	
battrai	**battrons**	**aurai battu**	**aurons battu**
battras	**battrez**	**auras battu**	**aurez battu**
battra	**battront**	**aura battu**	**auront battu**
5 conditionnel		12 conditionnel passé	
battrais	**battrions**	**aurais battu**	**aurions battu**
battrais	**battriez**	**aurais battu**	**auriez battu**
battrait	**battraient**	**aurait battu**	**auraient battu**
6 présent du subjonctif		13 passé du subjonctif	
batte	**battions**	**aie battu**	**ayons battu**
battes	**battiez**	**aies battu**	**ayez battu**
batte	**battent**	**ait battu**	**aient battu**
7 imparfait du subjonctif		14 plus-que-parfait du subjonctif	
battisse	**battissions**	**eusse battu**	**eussions battu**
battisses	**battissiez**	**eusses battu**	**eussiez battu**
battît	**battissent**	**eût battu**	**eussent battu**

	Impératif	
bats	battons	battez

Il faut battre le fer quand il est chaud.   You have to strike while the iron is hot.

battre des mains   to clap, to applaud
battre la campagne   to scour the countryside
le battant   leaf, flap (of a table)
une porte à deux battants   double door
une batte   bat, beater
le battement   banging (of a door); throbbing, flutter, beating
un batteur   whisk, beater
le battage   beating

Part. pr. **se battant**   Part. passé **battu(e)(s)**   **se battre**

Reflexive irregular verb in 1s, 2s, 3s present indicative   to fight

The Seven Simple Tenses		The Seven Compound Tenses	
Singular	Plural	Singular	Plural
1 présent de l'indicatif		8 passé composé	
me bats	nous battons	me suis battu(e)	nous sommes battu(e)s
te bats	vous battez	t'es battu(e)	vous êtes battu(e)(s)
se bat	se battent	s'est battu(e)	se sont battu(e)s
2 imparfait de l'indicatif		9 plus-que-parfait de l'indicatif	
me battais	nous battions	m'étais battu(e)	nous étions battu(e)s
te battais	vous battiez	t'étais battu(e)	vous étiez battu(e)(s)
se battait	se battaient	s'était battu(e)	s'étaient battu(e)s
3 passé simple		10 passé antérieur	
me battis	nous battîmes	me fus battu(e)	nous fûmes battu(e)s
te battis	vous battîtes	te fus battu(e)	vous fûtes battu(e)(s)
se battit	se battirent	se fut battu(e)	se furent battu(e)s
4 futur		11 futur antérieur	
me battrai	nous battrons	me serai battu(e)	nous serons battu(e)s
te battras	vous battrez	te seras battu(e)	vous serez battu(e)(s)
se battra	se battront	se sera battu(e)	se seront battu(e)s
5 conditionnel		12 conditionnel passé	
me battrais	nous battrions	me serais battu(e)	nous serions battu(e)s
te battrais	vous battriez	te serais battu(e)	vous seriez battu(e)(s)
se battrait	se battraient	se serait battu(e)	se seraient battu(e)s
6 présent du subjonctif		13 passé du subjonctif	
me batte	nous battions	me sois battu(e)	nous soyons battu(e)s
te battes	vous battiez	te sois battu(e)	vous soyez battu(e)(s)
se batte	se battent	se soit battu(e)	se soient battu(e)s
7 imparfait du subjonctif		14 plus-que-parfait du subjonctif	
me battisse	nous battissions	me fusse battu(e)	nous fussions battu(e)s
te battisses	vous battissiez	te fusses battu(e)	vous fussiez battu(e)(s)
se battît	se battissent	se fût battu(e)	se fussent battu(e)s

Impératif
bats-toi; ne te bats pas
battons-nous; ne nous battons pas
battez-vous; ne vous battez pas

   Nos voisins se battent toujours. La dernière fois ils se sont battus à coups de poings. Il y a toujours un grand combat chez eux.   Our neighbors are always fighting. The last time, they had a fistfight. There is always a big fight at their place.

For other words and expressions related to this verb, see battre.

bavarder	Part. pr. **bavardant**	Part. passé **bavardé**

to chat, to chatter, to babble, to gossip

Regular -er verb

The Seven Simple Tenses		The Seven Compound Tenses	
Singular	Plural	Singular	Plural
1 présent de l'indicatif		8 passé composé	
bavarde	**bavardons**	**ai bavardé**	**avons bavardé**
bavardes	**bavardez**	**as bavardé**	**avez bavardé**
bavarde	**bavardent**	**a bavardé**	**ont bavardé**
2 imparfait de l'indicatif		9 plus-que-parfait de l'indicatif	
bavardais	**bavardions**	**avais bavardé**	**avions bavardé**
bavardais	**bavardiez**	**avais bavardé**	**aviez bavardé**
bavardait	**bavardaient**	**avait bavardé**	**avaient bavardé**
3 passé simple		10 passé antérieur	
bavardai	**bavardâmes**	**eus bavardé**	**eûmes bavardé**
bavardas	**bavardâtes**	**eus bavardé**	**eûtes bavardé**
bavarda	**bavardèrent**	**eut bavardé**	**eurent bavardé**
4 futur		11 futur antérieur	
bavarderai	**bavarderons**	**aurai bavardé**	**aurons bavardé**
bavarderas	**bavarderez**	**auras bavardé**	**aurez bavardé**
bavardera	**bavarderont**	**aura bavardé**	**auront bavardé**
5 conditionnel		12 conditionnel passé	
bavarderais	**bavarderions**	**aurais bavardé**	**aurions bavardé**
bavarderais	**bavarderiez**	**aurais bavardé**	**auriez bavardé**
bavarderait	**bavarderaient**	**aurait bavardé**	**auraient bavardé**
6 présent du subjonctif		13 passé du subjonctif	
bavarde	**bavardions**	**aie bavardé**	**ayons bavardé**
bavardes	**bavardiez**	**aies bavardé**	**ayez bavardé**
bavarde	**bavardent**	**ait bavardé**	**aient bavardé**
7 imparfait du subjonctif		14 plus-que-parfait du subjonctif	
bavardasse	**bavardassions**	**eusse bavardé**	**eussions bavardé**
bavardasses	**bavardassiez**	**eusses bavardé**	**eussiez bavardé**
bavardât	**bavardassent**	**eût bavardé**	**eussent bavardé**

	Impératif	
	bavarde	
	bavardons	
	bavardez	

Aimez-vous les personnes qui bavardent tout le temps? Je connais un homme qui est bavard. Sa femme est bavarde aussi. Do you like people who gossip all the time? I know a man who is talkative. His wife is talkative too.

le bavardage chitchat, chattering, talkativeness
bavard, bavarde talkative, loquacious, garrulous
perdre son temps à bavarder to waste one's time babbling

la bave drool, dribble
baver to drool
le clavardage chat (Internet, Québec); combination of **le clavier** (keyboard) and **le bavardage**
clavarder to chat (Internet, Québec)

Part. pr. blessant		Part. passé blessé	**blesser**
Regular -er verb		to harm, to hurt, to injure, to wound, to offend	

The Seven Simple Tenses		The Seven Compound Tenses	
Singular	Plural	Singular	Plural
1 présent de l'indicatif		8 passé composé	
blesse	blessons	ai blessé	avons blessé
blesses	blessez	as blessé	avez blessé
blesse	blessent	a blessé	ont blessé
2 imparfait de l'indicatif		9 plus-que-parfait de l'indicatif	
blessais	blessions	avais blessé	avions blessé
blessais	blessiez	avais blessé	aviez blessé
blessait	blessaient	avait blessé	avaient blessé
3 passé simple		10 passé antérieur	
blessai	blessâmes	eus blessé	eûmes blessé
blessas	blessâtes	eus blessé	eûtes blessé
blessa	blessèrent	eut blessé	eurent blessé
4 futur		11 futur antérieur	
blesserai	blesserons	aurai blessé	aurons blessé
blesseras	blesserez	auras blessé	aurez blessé
blessera	blesseront	aura blessé	auront blessé
5 conditionnel		12 conditionnel passé	
blesserais	blesserions	aurais blessé	aurions blessé
blesserais	blesseriez	aurais blessé	auriez blessé
blesserait	blesseraient	aurait blessé	auraient blessé
6 présent du subjonctif		13 passé du subjonctif	
blesse	blessions	aie blessé	ayons blessé
blesses	blessiez	aies blessé	ayez blessé
blesse	blessent	ait blessé	aient blessé
7 imparfait du subjonctif		14 plus-que-parfait du subjonctif	
blessasse	blessassions	eusse blessé	eussions blessé
blessasses	blessassiez	eusses blessé	eussiez blessé
blessât	blessassent	eût blessé	eussent blessé
		Impératif	
		blesse	
		blessons	
		blessez	

Ma soeur jouait au foot et le ballon l'a blessée au visage. C'était une blessure grave.   My sister was playing soccer and the ball injured her face. It was a serious injury.

blesser à mort   to wound mortally
une blessure   wound, injury
une parole blessante   a cutting word
être blessé à la jambe (au bras)   to be injured in the leg (in the arm)

See also **se blesser**. Do not confuse **blesser** with **bénir**, which means *to bless*.

se blesser	Part. pr. se blessant	Part. passé blessé(e)(s)

to hurt oneself, to injure oneself, to wound oneself

Reflexive regular -er verb

The Seven Simple Tenses		The Seven Compound Tenses	
Singular	Plural	Singular	Plural
1 présent de l'indicatif		**8 passé composé**	
me blesse	nous blessons	me suis blessé(e)	nous sommes blessé(e)s
te blesses	vous blessez	t'es blessé(e)	vous êtes blessé(e)(s)
se blesse	se blessent	s'est blessé(e)	se sont blessé(e)s
2 imparfait de l'indicatif		**9 plus-que-parfait de l'indicatif**	
me blessais	nous blessions	m'étais blessé(e)	nous étions blessé(e)s
te blessais	vous blessiez	t'étais blessé(e)	vous étiez blessé(e)(s)
se blessait	se blessaient	s'était blessé(e)	s'étaient blessé(e)s
3 passé simple		**10 passé antérieur**	
me blessai	nous blessâmes	me fus blessé(e)	nous fûmes blessé(e)s
te blessas	vous blessâtes	te fus blessé(e)	vous fûtes blessé(e)(s)
se blessa	se blessèrent	se fut blessé(e)	se furent blessé(e)s
4 futur		**11 futur antérieur**	
me blesserai	nous blesserons	me serai blessé(e)	nous serons blessé(e)s
te blesseras	vous blesserez	te seras blessé(e)	vous serez blessé(e)(s)
se blessera	se blesseront	se sera blessé(e)	se seront blessé(e)s
5 conditionnel		**12 conditionnel passé**	
me blesserais	nous blesserions	me serais blessé(e)	nous serions blessé(e)s
te blesserais	vous blesseriez	te serais blessé(e)	vous seriez blessé(e)(s)
se blesserait	se blesseraient	se serait blessé(e)	se seraient blessé(e)s
6 présent du subjonctif		**13 passé du subjonctif**	
me blesse	nous blessions	me sois blessé(e)	nous soyons blessé(e)s
te blesses	vous blessiez	te sois blessé(e)	vous soyez blessé(e)(s)
se blesse	se blessent	se soit blessé(e)	se soient blessé(e)s
7 imparfait du subjonctif		**14 plus-que-parfait du subjonctif**	
me blessasse	nous blessassions	me fusse blessé(e)	nous fussions blessé(e)s
te blessasses	vous blessassiez	te fusses blessé(e)	vous fussiez blessé(e)(s)
se blessât	se blessassent	se fût blessé(e)	se fussent blessé(e)s

Impératif
blesse-toi; ne te blesse pas
blessons-nous; ne nous blessons pas
blessez-vous; ne vous blessez pas

Madame Leblanc est tombée dans la rue et elle s'est blessée au genou. C'était une blessure légère, heureusement. Mrs. Leblanc fell down in the street and hurt her knee. Fortunately, it was a minor injury.

se blesser de   to take offense at
se blesser pour un rien   to be easily offended

For other words and expressions related to this verb, see blesser. Do not confuse blesser and se blesser with bénir, which means *to bless*.

Part. pr. **buvant**   Part. passé **bu**   **boire**

Irregular verb   to drink

The Seven Simple Tenses		The Seven Compound Tenses	
Singular	Plural	Singular	Plural
1 présent de l'indicatif		8 passé composé	
bois	**buvons**	**ai bu**	**avons bu**
bois	**buvez**	**as bu**	**avez bu**
boit	**boivent**	**a bu**	**ont bu**
2 imparfait de l'indicatif		9 plus-que-parfait de l'indicatif	
buvais	**buvions**	**avais bu**	**avions bu**
buvais	**buviez**	**avais bu**	**aviez bu**
buvait	**buvaient**	**avait bu**	**avaient bu**
3 passé simple		10 passé antérieur	
bus	**bûmes**	**eus bu**	**eûmes bu**
bus	**bûtes**	**eus bu**	**eûtes bu**
but	**burent**	**eut bu**	**eurent bu**
4 futur		11 futur antérieur	
boirai	**boirons**	**aurai bu**	**aurons bu**
boiras	**boirez**	**auras bu**	**aurez bu**
boira	**boiront**	**aura bu**	**auront bu**
5 conditionnel		12 conditionnel passé	
boirais	**boirions**	**aurais bu**	**aurions bu**
boirais	**boiriez**	**aurais bu**	**auriez bu**
boirait	**boiraient**	**aurait bu**	**auraient bu**
6 présent du subjonctif		13 passé du subjonctif	
boive	**buvions**	**aie bu**	**ayons bu**
boives	**buviez**	**aies bu**	**ayez bu**
boive	**boivent**	**ait bu**	**aient bu**
7 imparfait du subjonctif		14 plus-que-parfait du subjonctif	
busse	**bussions**	**eusse bu**	**eussions bu**
busses	**bussiez**	**eusses bu**	**eussiez bu**
bût	**bussent**	**eût bu**	**eussent bu**
		Impératif	
		bois **buvons** **buvez**	

—Michel, as-tu bu ton lait?   Michael, have you drunk your milk?
—Non, maman, je ne l'ai pas bu.   No, Mother, I did not drink it.
—Bois-le tout de suite, je te dis.   Drink it right away, I'm telling you.
boire à la santé de qqn   to drink to someone's health
une boisson   drink; boisson gazeuse   carbonated drink
un buveur, une buveuse   drinker; une buvette   bar
un buvard   ink blotter; boire un coup   to have a drink

brosser   Part. pr. **brossant**   Part. passé **brossé**

to brush   Regular -er verb

The Seven Simple Tenses		The Seven Compound Tenses	
Singular	Plural	Singular	Plural
1 présent de l'indicatif		8 passé composé	
brosse	brossons	ai brossé	avons brossé
brosses	brossez	as brossé	avez brossé
brosse	brossent	a brossé	ont brossé
2 imparfait de l'indicatif		9 plus-que-parfait de l'indicatif	
brossais	brossions	avais brossé	avions brossé
brossais	brossiez	avais brossé	aviez brossé
brossait	brossaient	avait brossé	avaient brossé
3 passé simple		10 passé antérieur	
brossai	brossâmes	eus brossé	eûmes brossé
brossas	brossâtes	eus brossé	eûtes brossé
brossa	brossèrent	eut brossé	eurent brossé
4 futur		11 futur antérieur	
brosserai	brosserons	aurai brossé	aurons brossé
brosseras	brosserez	auras brossé	aurez brossé
brossera	brosseront	aura brossé	auront brossé
5 conditionnel		12 conditionnel passé	
brosserais	brosserions	aurais brossé	aurions brossé
brosserais	brosseriez	aurais brossé	auriez brossé
brosserait	brosseraient	aurait brossé	auraient brossé
6 présent du subjonctif		13 passé du subjonctif	
brosse	brossions	aie brossé	ayons brossé
brosses	brossiez	aies brossé	ayez brossé
brosse	brossent	ait brossé	aient brossé
7 imparfait du subjonctif		14 plus-que-parfait du subjonctif	
brossasse	brossassions	eusse brossé	eussions brossé
brossasses	brossassiez	eusses brossé	eussiez brossé
brossât	brossassent	eût brossé	eussent brossé

Impératif
brosse   brossons   brossez

—Henriette, as-tu brossé tes souliers?   Henrietta, have you brushed your shoes?
—Non, maman, je ne les ai pas brossés.   No, Mother, I haven't brushed them.
—Et pourquoi pas, ma petite?   And why not, my dear?
—Parce que je n'ai pas de brosse.   Because I don't have a brush.

une brosse brush; **brosse à chaussures** shoebrush; **brosse à dents** toothbrush;
    brosse à ongles nailbrush
donner un coup de brosse to brush
le brossage brushing

See also se brosser.

40

Part. pr. se brossant Part. passé brossé(e)(s) **se brosser**

Reflexive regular -er verb to brush oneself

The Seven Simple Tenses		The Seven Compound Tenses	
Singular	Plural	Singular	Plural

1 présent de l'indicatif

me brosse	nous brossons
te brosses	vous brossez
se brosse	se brossent

8 passé composé

me suis brossé(e)	nous sommes brossé(e)s
t'es brossé(e)	vous êtes brossé(e)(s)
s'est brossé(e)	se sont brossé(e)s

2 imparfait de l'indicatif

me brossais	nous brossions
te brossais	vous brossiez
se brossait	se brossaient

9 plus-que-parfait de l'indicatif

m'étais brossé(e)	nous étions brossé(e)s
t'étais brossé(e)	vous étiez brossé(e)(s)
s'était brossé(e)	s'étaient brossé(e)s

3 passé simple

me brossai	nous brossâmes
te brossas	vous brossâtes
se brossa	se brossèrent

10 passé antérieur

me fus brossé(e)	nous fûmes brossé(e)s
te fus brossé(e)	vous fûtes brossé(e)(s)
se fut brossé(e)	se furent brossé(e)s

4 futur

me brosserai	nous brosserons
te brosseras	vous brosserez
se brossera	se brosseront

11 futur antérieur

me serai brossé(e)	nous serons brossé(e)s
te seras brossé(e)	vous serez brossé(e)(s)
se sera brossé(e)	se seront brossé(e)s

5 conditionnel

me brosserais	nous brosserions
te brosserais	vous brosseriez
se brosserait	se brosseraient

12 conditionnel passé

me serais brossé(e)	nous serions brossé(e)s
te serais brossé(e)	vous seriez brossé(e)(s)
se serait brossé(e)	se seraient brossé(e)s

6 présent du subjonctif

me brosse	nous brossions
te brosses	vous brossiez
se brosse	se brossent

13 passé du subjonctif

me sois brossé(e)	nous soyons brossé(e)s
te sois brossé(e)	vous soyez brossé(e)(s)
se soit brossé(e)	se soient brossé(e)s

7 imparfait du subjonctif

me brossasse	nous brossassions
te brossasses	vous brossassiez
se brossât	se brossassent

14 plus-que-parfait du subjonctif

me fusse brossé(e)	nous fussions brossé(e)s
te fusses brossé(e)	vous fussiez brossé(e)(s)
se fût brossé(e)	se fussent brossé(e)s

Impératif
brosse-toi; ne te brosse pas
brossons-nous; ne nous brossons pas
brossez-vous; ne vous brossez pas

—Tina Marie, est-ce que tu t'es brossée?
—Non, maman, je ne me suis pas brossée.
—Et pourquoi pas? Brosse-toi vite!
—Parce que je n'ai pas de brosse à habits, je n'ai pas de brosse à cheveux, je n'ai pas de brosse à chaussures. Je n'ai aucune brosse. Je n'ai pas de brosse à dents, non plus.
—Quelle fille!

se brosser les dents, les cheveux, etc. to brush one's teeth, hair, etc.

For other words and expressions related to this verb, see brosser.

brûler

Part. pr. **brûlant** Part. passé **brûlé**

to burn

Regular **-er** verb

The Seven Simple Tenses		The Seven Compound Tenses	
Singular	Plural	Singular	Plural
1 présent de l'indicatif		**8 passé composé**	
brûle	**brûlons**	**ai brûlé**	**avons brûlé**
brûles	**brûlez**	**as brûlé**	**avez brûlé**
brûle	**brûlent**	**a brûlé**	**ont brûlé**
2 imparfait de l'indicatif		**9 plus-que-parfait de l'indicatif**	
brûlais	**brûlions**	**avais brûlé**	**avions brûlé**
brûlais	**brûliez**	**avais brûlé**	**aviez brûlé**
brûlait	**brûlaient**	**avait brûlé**	**avaient brûlé**
3 passé simple		**10 passé antérieur**	
brûlai	**brûlâmes**	**eus brûlé**	**eûmes brûlé**
brûlas	**brûlâtes**	**eus brûlé**	**eûtes brûlé**
brûla	**brûlèrent**	**eut brûlé**	**eurent brûlé**
4 futur		**11 futur antérieur**	
brûlerai	**brûlerons**	**aurai brûlé**	**aurons brûlé**
brûleras	**brûlerez**	**auras brûlé**	**aurez brûlé**
brûlera	**brûleront**	**aura brûlé**	**auront brûlé**
5 conditionnel		**12 conditionnel passé**	
brûlerais	**brûlerions**	**aurais brûlé**	**aurions brûlé**
brûlerais	**brûleriez**	**aurais brûlé**	**auriez brûlé**
brûlerait	**brûleraient**	**aurait brûlé**	**auraient brûlé**
6 présent du subjonctif		**13 passé du subjonctif**	
brûle	**brûlions**	**aie brûlé**	**ayons brûlé**
brûles	**brûliez**	**aies brûlé**	**ayez brûlé**
brûle	**brûlent**	**ait brûlé**	**aient brûlé**
7 imparfait du subjonctif		**14 plus-que-parfait du subjonctif**	
brûlasse	**brûlassions**	**eusse brûlé**	**eussions brûlé**
brûlasses	**brûlassiez**	**eusses brûlé**	**eussiez brûlé**
brûlât	**brûlassent**	**eût brûlé**	**eussent brûlé**

Impératif
brûle
brûlons
brûlez

—Joséphine, avez-vous brûlé les vieux papiers que je vous ai donnés?
Josephine, did you burn the old papers that I gave you?

—Oui, madame, et je me suis brûlée. J'ai une brûlure aux doigts. Yes,
ma'am, and I just burned myself. I burned my fingers. (I have a burn on my fingers.)

une **brûlure** burn
un **brûleur** burner, roaster
brûler d'amour to be madly in love
brûler de faire qqch to be eager to do
something

brûler un feu rouge to pass through a
red traffic light
une **crème brûlée** a crème brûlée
(dessert)
Note: The Académie française now
allows brûler and related words to be
spelled without the circumflex accent:
bruler, une brulure, etc.

42

Regular -er verb   to hide

The Seven Simple Tenses		The Seven Compound Tenses	
Singular	Plural	Singular	Plural
1 présent de l'indicatif		8 passé composé	
cache	cachons	ai caché	avons caché
caches	cachez	as caché	avez caché
cache	cachent	a caché	ont caché
2 imparfait de l'indicatif		9 plus-que-parfait de l'indicatif	
cachais	cachions	avais caché	avions caché
cachais	cachiez	avais caché	aviez caché
cachait	cachaient	avait caché	avaient caché
3 passé simple		10 passé antérieur	
cachai	cachâmes	eus caché	eûmes caché
cachas	cachâtes	eus caché	eûtes caché
cacha	cachèrent	eut caché	eurent caché
4 futur		11 futur antérieur	
cacherai	cacherons	aurai caché	aurons caché
cacheras	cacherez	auras caché	aurez caché
cachera	cacheront	aura caché	auront caché
5 conditionnel		12 conditionnel passé	
cacherais	cacherions	aurais caché	aurions caché
cacherais	cacheriez	aurais caché	auriez caché
cacherait	cacheraient	aurait caché	auraient caché
6 présent du subjonctif		13 passé du subjonctif	
cache	cachions	aie caché	ayons caché
caches	cachiez	aies caché	ayez caché
cache	cachent	ait caché	aient caché
7 imparfait du subjonctif		14 plus-que-parfait du subjonctif	
cachasse	cachassions	eusse caché	eussions caché
cachasses	cachassiez	eusses caché	eussiez caché
cachât	cachassent	eût caché	eussent caché

	Impératif	
cache	cachons	cachez

—Pierre, qu'est-ce que tu as caché derrière toi?
—Rien, papa.
—Ne me dis pas ça. Tu caches quelque chose.
—Voilà, papa, c'est un petit chat que j'ai trouvé dans le parc.

une cache, une cachette   hiding place
la cache   cache (computer)
un cachet   seal, mark, tablet (pill)
un cachetage   sealing

cacher qqch à qqn   to hide
    something from someone
cacheter   to seal up
le cache-cache   hide-and-seek
le vin cacheté   vintage wine

See also se **cacher**.

to hide oneself

Reflexive regular -er verb

The Seven Simple Tenses		The Seven Compound Tenses	
Singular	Plural	Singular	Plural
1 présent de l'indicatif		**8 passé composé**	
me cache	nous cachons	me suis caché(e)	nous sommes caché(e)s
te caches	vous cachez	t'es caché(e)	vous êtes caché(e)(s)
se cache	se cachent	s'est caché(e)	se sont caché(e)s
2 imparfait de l'indicatif		**9 plus-que-parfait de l'indicatif**	
me cachais	nous cachions	m'étais caché(e)	nous étions caché(e)s
te cachais	vous cachiez	t'étais caché(e)	vous étiez caché(e)(s)
se cachait	se cachaient	s'était caché(e)	s'étaient caché(e)s
3 passé simple		**10 passé antérieur**	
me cachai	nous cachâmes	me fus caché(e)	nous fûmes caché(e)s
te cachas	vous cachâtes	te fus caché(e)	vous fûtes caché(e)(s)
se cacha	se cachèrent	se fut caché(e)	se furent caché(e)s
4 futur		**11 futur antérieur**	
me cacherai	nous cacherons	me serai caché(e)	nous serons caché(e)s
te cacheras	vous cacherez	te seras caché(e)	vous serez caché(e)(s)
se cachera	se cacheront	se sera caché(e)	se seront caché(e)s
5 conditionnel		**12 conditionnel passé**	
me cacherais	nous cacherions	me serais caché(e)	nous serions caché(e)s
te cacherais	vous cacheriez	te serais caché(e)	vous seriez caché(e)(s)
se cacherait	se cacheraient	se serait caché(e)	se seraient caché(e)s
6 présent du subjonctif		**13 passé du subjonctif**	
me cache	nous cachions	me sois caché(e)	nous soyons caché(e)s
te caches	vous cachiez	te sois caché(e)	vous soyez caché(e)(s)
se cache	se cachent	se soit caché(e)	se soient caché(e)s
7 imparfait du subjonctif		**14 plus-que-parfait du subjonctif**	
me cachasse	nous cachassions	me fusse caché(e)	nous fussions caché(e)s
te cachasses	vous cachassiez	te fusses caché(e)	vous fussiez caché(e)(s)
se cachât	se cachassent	se fût caché(e)	se fussent caché(e)s

Impératif
cache-toi; ne te cache pas
cachons-nous; ne nous cachons pas
cachez-vous; ne vous cachez pas

Mon chien Coco se chache souvent sous mon lit. La semaine dernière il s'est caché sous le chapeau de mon père. Il aime jouer à cache-cache.   My dog Coco often hides under my bed. Last week he hid under my father's hat. He loves to play hide-and-seek.

se cacher de qqn   to hide from someone   un cachot   cell, prison

See also cacher.

Regular -er verb   to break

The Seven Simple Tenses		The Seven Compound Tenses	
Singular	Plural	Singular	Plural
1 présent de l'indicatif		8 passé composé	
casse	cassons	ai cassé	avons cassé
casses	cassez	as cassé	avez cassé
casse	cassent	a cassé	ont cassé
2 imparfait de l'indicatif		9 plus-que-parfait de l'indicatif	
cassais	cassions	avais cassé	avions cassé
cassais	cassiez	avais cassé	aviez cassé
cassait	cassaient	avait cassé	avaient cassé
3 passé simple		10 passé antérieur	
cassai	cassâmes	eus cassé	eûmes cassé
cassas	cassâtes	eus cassé	eûtes cassé
cassa	cassèrent	eut cassé	eurent cassé
4 futur		11 futur antérieur	
casserai	casserons	aurai cassé	aurons cassé
casseras	casserez	auras cassé	aurez cassé
cassera	casseront	aura cassé	auront cassé
5 conditionnel		12 conditionnel passé	
casserais	casserions	aurais cassé	aurions cassé
casserais	casseriez	aurais cassé	auriez cassé
casserait	casseraient	aurait cassé	auraient cassé
6 présent du subjonctif		13 passé du subjonctif	
casse	cassions	aie cassé	ayons cassé
casses	cassiez	aies cassé	ayez cassé
casse	cassent	ait cassé	aient cassé
7 imparfait du subjonctif		14 plus-que-parfait du subjonctif	
cassasse	cassassions	eusse cassé	eussions cassé
cassasses	cassassiez	eusses cassé	eussiez cassé
cassât	cassassent	eût cassé	eussent cassé

Impératif
casse
cassons
cassez

—Jean, c'est toi qui as cassé mon joli vase?   John, is it you who broke my pretty vase?
    —Non, maman, c'est Mathilde.   No, Mother, it was Mathilda.
    —Mathilde, c'est toi qui as cassé mon joli vase?   Mathilda, is it you who broke my pretty vase?
    —Non, maman, c'est Jean.   No, Mother, it was John.
    —Quels enfants!   What children!

une casse breakage, damage	casser la croûte to have a snack
un casse-croûte snack	un casse-pieds a bore, a pain in the neck
un casse-noisettes, un casse-noix nutcracker	un casse-tête puzzle
	concasser to crush (cereal, stones) 45

See also se casser.

to break (a part of one's body,   Reflexive regular -er verb
e.g., leg, arm, nose)

The Seven Simple Tenses		The Seven Compound Tenses	
Singular	Plural	Singular	Plural
1 présent de l'indicatif		8 passé composé	
me casse	nous cassons	me suis cassé(e)	nous sommes cassé(e)s
te casses	vous cassez	t'es cassé(e)	vous êtes cassé(e)(s)
se casse	se cassent	s'est cassé(e)	se sont cassé(e)s
2 imparfait de l'indicatif		9 plus-que-parfait de l'indicatif	
me cassais	nous cassions	m'étais cassé(e)	nous étions cassé(e)s
te cassais	vous cassiez	t'étais cassé(e)	vous étiez cassé(e)(s)
se cassait	se cassaient	s'était cassé(e)	s'étaient cassé(e)s
3 passé simple		10 passé antérieur	
me cassai	nous cassâmes	me fus cassé(e)	nous fûmes cassé(e)s
te cassas	vous cassâtes	te fus cassé(e)	vous fûtes cassé(e)(s)
se cassa	se cassèrent	se fut cassé(e)	se furent cassé(e)s
4 futur		11 futur antérieur	
me casserai	nous casserons	me serai cassé(e)	nous serons cassé(e)s
te casseras	vous casserez	te seras cassé(e)	vous serez cassé(e)(s)
se cassera	se casseront	se sera cassé(e)	se seront cassé(e)s
5 conditionnel		12 conditionnel passé	
me casserais	nous casserions	me serais cassé(e)	nous serions cassé(e)s
te casserais	vous casseriez	te serais cassé(e)	vous seriez cassé(e)(s)
se casserait	se casseraient	se serait cassé(e)	se seraient cassé(e)s
6 présent du subjonctif		13 passé du subjonctif	
me casse	nous cassions	me sois cassé(e)	nous soyons cassé(e)s
te casses	vous cassiez	te sois cassé(e)	vous soyez cassé(e)(s)
se casse	se cassent	se soit cassé(e)	se soient cassé(e)s
7 imparfait du subjonctif		14 plus-que-parfait du subjonctif	
me cassasse	nous cassassions	me fusse cassé(e)	nous fussions cassé(e)s
te cassasses	vous cassassiez	te fusses cassé(e)	vous fussiez cassé(e)(s)
se cassât	se cassassent	se fût cassé(e)	se fussent cassé(e)s

Impératif
casse-toi . . .; ne te casse pas . . .
cassons-nous . . .; ne nous cassons pas . . .
cassez-vous . . .; ne vous cassez pas . . .

Pendant les vacances d'hiver, nous sommes allés faire du ski dans les montagnes. Mon père s'est cassé le bras, ma mère s'est cassé la jambe, et moi, je me suis cassé le pied.   During winter vacation we went skiing in the mountains. My father broke his arm, my mother broke her leg, and I broke my foot.

se casser la tête to rack one's brains	casser la tête à qqn to annoy someone
se casser le nez to find nobody answering the door	un casse-cou daredevil, reckless person

See also casser.

Part. pr. **causant**   Part. passé **causé**   **causer**

Regular -er verb   to cause, to chat

The Seven Simple Tenses		The Seven Compound Tenses	
Singular	Plural	Singular	Plural
1 présent de l'indicatif		8 passé composé	
cause	**causons**	**ai causé**	**avons causé**
causes	**causez**	**as causé**	**avez causé**
cause	**causent**	**a causé**	**ont causé**
2 imparfait de l'indicatif		9 plus-que-parfait de l'indicatif	
causais	**causions**	**avais causé**	**avions causé**
causais	**causiez**	**avais causé**	**aviez causé**
causait	**causaient**	**avait causé**	**avaient causé**
3 passé simple		10 passé antérieur	
causai	**causâmes**	**eus causé**	**eûmes causé**
causas	**causâtes**	**eus causé**	**eûtes causé**
causa	**causèrent**	**eut causé**	**eurent causé**
4 futur		11 futur antérieur	
causerai	**causerons**	**aurai causé**	**aurons causé**
causeras	**causerez**	**auras causé**	**aurez causé**
causera	**causeront**	**aura causé**	**auront causé**
5 conditionnel		12 conditionnel passé	
causerais	**causerions**	**aurais causé**	**aurions causé**
causerais	**causeriez**	**aurais causé**	**auriez causé**
causerait	**causeraient**	**aurait causé**	**auraient causé**
6 présent du subjonctif		13 passé du subjonctif	
cause	**causions**	**aie causé**	**ayons causé**
causes	**causiez**	**aies causé**	**ayez causé**
cause	**causent**	**ait causé**	**aient causé**
7 imparfait du subjonctif		14 plus-que-parfait du subjonctif	
causasse	**causassions**	**eusse causé**	**eussions causé**
causasses	**causassiez**	**eusses causé**	**eussiez causé**
causât	**causassent**	**eût causé**	**eussent causé**

Impératif
cause
causons
causez

Quand je voyage, j'aime beaucoup causer avec les passagers. Est-ce que vous causez avec vos voisins dans la salle de classe? En français, bien sûr! Je connais un garçon qui n'est pas très causant.

causant, causante talkative
causatif, causative causative
une cause cause, reason
causer de la pluie et du beau temps
to chat about the weather

une cause célèbre famous trial
une causerie chat, informal talk
causeur, causeuse talkative
une causeuse love seat
causer de la peine à qqn to hurt
someone

céder	Part. pr. **cédant**	Part. passé **cédé**

to yield, to cede

Regular -er verb endings: spelling change:
e changes to è before syllable with mute e.

The Seven Simple Tenses		The Seven Compound Tenses	
Singular	Plural	Singular	Plural

1 présent de l'indicatif		8 passé composé	
cède	**cédons**	ai cédé	avons cédé
cèdes	**cédez**	as cédé	avez cédé
cède	**cèdent**	a cédé	ont cédé

2 imparfait de l'indicatif		9 plus-que-parfait de l'indicatif	
cédais	cédions	avais cédé	avions cédé
cédais	cédiez	avais cédé	aviez cédé
cédait	cédaient	avait cédé	avaient cédé

3 passé simple		10 passé antérieur	
cédai	cédâmes	eus cédé	eûmes cédé
cédas	cédâtes	eus cédé	eûtes cédé
céda	cédèrent	eut cédé	eurent cédé

4 futur		11 futur antérieur	
céderai	céderons	aurai cédé	aurons cédé
céderas	céderez	auras cédé	aurez cédé
cédera	céderont	aura cédé	auront cédé

5 conditionnel		12 conditionnel passé	
céderais	céderions	aurais cédé	aurions cédé
céderais	céderiez	aurais cédé	auriez cédé
céderait	céderaient	aurait cédé	auraient cédé

6 présent du subjonctif		13 passé du subjonctif	
cède	**cédions**	aie cédé	ayons cédé
cèdes	**cédiez**	aies cédé	ayez cédé
cède	**cèdent**	ait cédé	aient cédé

7 imparfait du subjonctif		14 plus-que-parfait du subjonctif	
cédasse	cédassions	eusse cédé	eussions cédé
cédasses	cédassiez	eusses cédé	eussiez cédé
cédât	cédassent	eût cédé	eussent cédé

Impératif
cède
cédons
cédez

Dans l'autobus, j'ai cédé ma place à une personne âgée.   On the bus, I gave up my seat for an elderly person.

céder à   to give up, give in, yield to
accéder à   to accede to, to comply with
concéder à   to concede to, to grant
céder le pas à qqn   to give way to someone

céder par faiblesse   to give in out of weakness
céder à la tentation   to give in to temptation

Note: The Académie française now allows the accent grave (`) in the future (je cèderai, tu cèderas, etc.) and conditional (je cèderais, tu cèderais, etc.) of this verb.

Regular -er verb   to cease

The Seven Simple Tenses		The Seven Compound Tenses	
Singular	Plural	Singular	Plural
1 présent de l'indicatif		**8 passé composé**	
cesse	cessons	ai cessé	avons cessé
cesses	cessez	as cessé	avez cessé
cesse	cessent	a cessé	ont cessé
2 imparfait de l'indicatif		**9 plus-que-parfait de l'indicatif**	
cessais	cessions	avais cessé	avions cessé
cessais	cessiez	avais cessé	aviez cessé
cessait	cessaient	avait cessé	avaient cessé
3 passé simple		**10 passé antérieur**	
cessai	cessâmes	eus cessé	eûmes cessé
cessas	cessâtes	eus cessé	eûtes cessé
cessa	cessèrent	eut cessé	eurent cessé
4 futur		**11 futur antérieur**	
cesserai	cesserons	aurai cessé	aurons cessé
cesseras	cesserez	auras cessé	aurez cessé
cessera	cesseront	aura cessé	auront cessé
5 conditionnel		**12 conditionnel passé**	
cesserais	cesserions	aurais cessé	aurions cessé
cesserais	cesseriez	aurais cessé	auriez cessé
cesserait	cesseraient	aurait cessé	auraient cessé
6 présent du subjonctif		**13 passé du subjonctif**	
cesse	cessions	aie cessé	ayons cessé
cesses	cessiez	aies cessé	ayez cessé
cesse	cessent	ait cessé	aient cessé
7 imparfait du subjonctif		**14 plus-que-parfait du subjonctif**	
cessasse	cessassions	eusse cessé	eussions cessé
cessasses	cessassiez	eusses cessé	eussiez cessé
cessât	cessassent	eût cessé	eussent cessé

Impératif
cesse
cessons
cessez

Il n'a pas cessé de neiger depuis hier.   It has not stopped snowing since yesterday.

sans cesse   constantly, without ceasing
une cesse   cease, ceasing
cesser de se voir   to stop seeing each other
cesser le feu   to cease fire
un cessez-le-feu   cease-fire

cesser de faire qqch   to stop doing something

to change | Regular -er verb endings: spelling change: retain the ge before a or o to keep the soft g sound of the verb.

The Seven Simple Tenses		The Seven Compound Tenses	
Singular	Plural	Singular	Plural

1 présent de l'indicatif		8 passé composé	
change	changeons	ai changé	avons changé
changes	changez	as changé	avez changé
change	changent	a changé	ont changé

2 imparfait de l'indicatif		9 plus-que-parfait de l'indicatif	
changeais	changions	avais changé	avions changé
changeais	changiez	avais changé	aviez changé
changeait	changeaient	avait changé	avaient changé

3 passé simple		10 passé antérieur	
changeai	changeâmes	eus changé	eûmes changé
changeas	changeâtes	eus changé	eûtes changé
changea	changèrent	eut changé	eurent changé

4 futur		11 futur antérieur	
changerai	changerons	aurai changé	aurons changé
changeras	changerez	auras changé	aurez changé
changera	changeront	aura changé	auront changé

5 conditionnel		12 conditionnel passé	
changerais	changerions	aurais changé	aurions changé
changerais	changeriez	aurais changé	auriez changé
changerait	changeraient	aurait changé	auraient changé

6 présent du subjonctif		13 passé du subjonctif	
change	changions	aie changé	ayons changé
changes	changiez	aies changé	ayez changé
change	changent	ait changé	aient changé

7 imparfait du subjonctif		14 plus-que-parfait du subjonctif	
changeasse	changeassions	eusse changé	eussions changé
changeasses	changeassiez	eusses changé	eussiez changé
changeât	changeassent	eût changé	eussent changé

Impératif
change
changeons
changez

---

changer d'avis   to change one's mind
changer de route   to take another road
un changement soudain   a sudden change
changer de l'argent   to exchange some money
le bureau de change   money exchange desk (office)

changer de train (d'avion)   to change trains (planes)
changer de vêtements   to change clothes
échanger   to exchange
Plus ça change, plus c'est la même chose!   The more things change, the more they remain the same!

Regular -er verb   to sing

The Seven Simple Tenses		The Seven Compound Tenses	
Singular	Plural	Singular	Plural
1 présent de l'indicatif		8 passé composé	
chante	**chantons**	**ai chanté**	**avons chanté**
chantes	**chantez**	**as chanté**	**avez chanté**
chante	**chantent**	**a chanté**	**ont chanté**
2 imparfait de l'indicatif		9 plus-que-parfait de l'indicatif	
chantais	**chantions**	**avais chanté**	**avions chanté**
chantais	**chantiez**	**avais chanté**	**aviez chanté**
chantait	**chantaient**	**avait chanté**	**avaient chanté**
3 passé simple		10 passé antérieur	
chantai	**chantâmes**	**eus chanté**	**eûmes chanté**
chantas	**chantâtes**	**eus chanté**	**eûtes chanté**
chanta	**chantèrent**	**eut chanté**	**eurent chanté**
4 futur		11 futur antérieur	
chanterai	**chanterons**	**aurai chanté**	**aurons chanté**
chanteras	**chanterez**	**auras chanté**	**aurez chanté**
chantera	**chanteront**	**aura chanté**	**auront chanté**
5 conditionnel		12 conditionnel passé	
chanterais	**chanterions**	**aurais chanté**	**aurions chanté**
chanterais	**chanteriez**	**aurais chanté**	**auriez chanté**
chanterait	**chanteraient**	**aurait chanté**	**auraient chanté**
6 présent du subjonctif		13 passé du subjonctif	
chante	**chantions**	**aie chanté**	**ayons chanté**
chantes	**chantiez**	**aies chanté**	**ayez chanté**
chante	**chantent**	**ait chanté**	**aient chanté**
7 imparfait du subjonctif		14 plus-que-parfait du subjonctif	
chantasse	**chantassions**	**eusse chanté**	**eussions chanté**
chantasses	**chantassiez**	**eusses chanté**	**eussiez chanté**
chantât	**chantassent**	**eût chanté**	**eussent chanté**

Impératif
chante
chantons
chantez

Madame Chanteclaire aime bien chanter en jouant du piano. Tous les matins elle chante dans la salle de bains et quelquefois elle chante quand elle dort. Elle donne des leçons de chant.

une chanson song
C'est une autre chanson! That's another story!
une chanson d'amour love song
Si ça vous chante . . . If you are in the mood for it . . .
une chanson de geste epic poem

un chant carol, chant, singing
le chantage blackmail
un chanteur, une chanteuse singer
enchanter to enchant
faire chanter qqn to blackmail someone

charger	Part. pr. **chargeant**	Part. passé **chargé**

to burden, to charge, to load	Regular -er verb endings: spelling change: retain the ge before a or o to keep the soft g sound of the verb.

The Seven Simple Tenses	The Seven Compound Tenses

Singular	Plural	Singular	Plural

1 présent de l'indicatif

charge	chargeons
charges	chargez
charge	chargent

8 passé composé

ai chargé	avons chargé
as chargé	avez chargé
a chargé	ont chargé

2 imparfait de l'indicatif

chargeais	chargions
chargeais	chargiez
chargeait	chargeaient

9 plus-que-parfait de l'indicatif

avais chargé	avions chargé
avais chargé	aviez chargé
avait chargé	avaient chargé

3 passé simple

chargeai	chargeâmes
chargeas	chargeâtes
chargea	chargèrent

10 passé antérieur

eus chargé	eûmes chargé
eus chargé	eûtes chargé
eut chargé	eurent chargé

4 futur

chargerai	chargerons
chargeras	chargerez
chargera	chargeront

11 futur antérieur

aurai chargé	aurons chargé
auras chargé	aurez chargé
aura chargé	auront chargé

5 conditionnel

chargerais	chargerions
chargerais	chargeriez
chargerait	chargeraient

12 conditionnel passé

aurais chargé	aurions chargé
aurais chargé	auriez chargé
aurait chargé	auraient chargé

6 présent du subjonctif

charge	chargions
charges	chargiez
charge	chargent

13 passé du subjonctif

aie chargé	ayons chargé
aies chargé	ayez chargé
ait chargé	aient chargé

7 imparfait du subjonctif

chargeasse	chargeassions
chargeasses	chargeassiez
chargeât	chargeassent

14 plus-que-parfait du subjonctif

eusse chargé	eussions chargé
eusses chargé	eussiez chargé
eût chargé	eussent chargé

Impératif
charge
chargeons
chargez

---

une charge   a load, burden
chargé d'impôts   heavily taxed
un chargé d'affaires   envoy
Je m'en charge.   I'll take care of it.
télécharger   to download (computer)
un chargeur de batterie   battery charger
décharger   to unload

charger de malédictions   to curse
charger de louanges   to overwhelm
with praises

52

Part. pr. **chassant**	Part. passé **chassé**		**chasser**

Regular -er verb | to hunt, to pursue, to chase, to drive out

The Seven Simple Tenses | The Seven Compound Tenses

Singular	Plural	Singular	Plural
1 présent de l'indicatif		8 passé composé	
chasse	chassons	ai chassé	avons chassé
chasses	chassez	as chassé	avez chassé
chasse	chassent	a chassé	ont chassé
2 imparfait de l'indicatif		9 plus-que-parfait de l'indicatif	
chassais	chassions	avais chassé	avions chassé
chassais	chassiez	avais chassé	aviez chassé
chassait	chassaient	avait chassé	avaient chassé
3 passé simple		10 passé antérieur	
chassai	chassâmes	eus chassé	eûmes chassé
chassas	chassâtes	eus chassé	eûtes chassé
chassa	chassèrent	eut chassé	eurent chassé
4 futur		11 futur antérieur	
chasserai	chasserons	aurai chassé	aurons chassé
chasseras	chasserez	auras chassé	aurez chassé
chassera	chasseront	aura chassé	auront chassé
5 conditionnel		12 conditionnel passé	
chasserais	chasserions	aurais chassé	aurions chassé
chasserais	chasseriez	aurais chassé	auriez chassé
chasserait	chasseraient	aurait chassé	auraient chassé
6 présent du subjonctif		13 passé du subjonctif	
chasse	chassions	aie chassé	ayons chassé
chasses	chassiez	aies chassé	ayez chassé
chasse	chassent	ait chassé	aient chassé
7 imparfait du subjonctif		14 plus-que-parfait du subjonctif	
chassasse	chassassions	eusse chassé	eussions chassé
chassasses	chassassiez	eusses chassé	eussiez chassé
chassât	chassassent	eût chassé	eussent chassé

Impératif
chasse
chassons
chassez

pourchasser to chase, pursue	un chasse-mouches fly swatter
un chasse-neige snow plow	tirer la chasse d'eau to flush the toilet

Proverb: **Je chasse toujours les arcs-en-ciel.** I'm always chasing rainbows.

Pronounce out loud this tongue twister as fast as you can:
Le chasseur, sachant chasser sans son chien, chassera.
(The hunter, knowing how to hunt without his dog, will hunt.)

Sachant is the pres. part. of **savoir**.

chercher	Part. pr. **cherchant**	Part. passé **cherché**
to look for, to search, to seek		Regular -er verb

The Seven Simple Tenses		The Seven Compound Tenses	
Singular	Plural	Singular	Plural
1 présent de l'indicatif		8 passé composé	
cherche	cherchons	ai cherché	avons cherché
cherches	cherchez	as cherché	avez cherché
cherche	cherchent	a cherché	ont cherché
2 imparfait de l'indicatif		9 plus-que-parfait de l'indicatif	
cherchais	cherchions	avais cherché	avions cherché
cherchais	cherchiez	avais cherché	aviez cherché
cherchait	cherchaient	avait cherché	avaient cherché
3 passé simple		10 passé antérieur	
cherchai	cherchâmes	eus cherché	eûmes cherché
cherchas	cherchâtes	eus cherché	eûtes cherché
chercha	cherchèrent	eut cherché	eurent cherché
4 futur		11 futur antérieur	
chercherai	chercherons	aurai cherché	aurons cherché
chercheras	chercherez	auras cherché	aurez cherché
cherchera	chercheront	aura cherché	auront cherché
5 conditionnel		12 conditionnel passé	
chercherais	chercherions	aurais cherché	aurions cherché
chercherais	chercheriez	aurais cherché	auriez cherché
chercherait	chercheraient	aurait cherché	auraient cherché
6 présent du subjonctif		13 passé du subjonctif	
cherche	cherchions	aie cherché	ayons cherché
cherches	cherchiez	aies cherché	ayez cherché
cherche	cherchent	ait cherché	aient cherché
7 imparfait du subjonctif		14 plus-que-parfait du subjonctif	
cherchasse	cherchassions	eusse cherché	eussions cherché
cherchasses	cherchassiez	eusses cherché	eussiez cherché
cherchât	cherchassent	eût cherché	eussent cherché

	Impératif	
cherche	cherchons	cherchez

—Monsieur, monsieur, j'ai perdu mon livre de français. J'ai cherché partout et je n'arrive pas à le trouver.

—Continue à chercher parce que demain je donnerai un examen.

se chercher to look for one another
chercheur seeker, investigator
aller chercher to go and get
chercher à to attempt to, try to
aller chercher qqn ou qqch to go get someone or something
un moteur de recherche search engine (Internet)

Je vais envoyer chercher le médecin.
I am going to send for the doctor.
rechercher to investigate, to seek, to look for again
faire des travaux de recherches to carry out research work
envoyer chercher to send for

| Regular -ir verb | | to choose, to select, to pick | |

The Seven Simple Tenses | | The Seven Compound Tenses | |

Singular	Plural	Singular	Plural
1 présent de l'indicatif		**8 passé composé**	
choisis	choisissons	ai choisi	avons choisi
choisis	choisissez	as choisi	avez choisi
choisit	choisissent	a choisi	ont choisi
2 imparfait de l'indicatif		**9 plus-que-parfait de l'indicatif**	
choisissais	choisissions	avais choisi	avions choisi
choisissais	choisissiez	avais choisi	aviez choisi
choisissait	choisissaient	avait choisi	avaient choisi
3 passé simple		**10 passé antérieur**	
choisis	choisîmes	eus choisi	eûmes choisi
choisis	choisîtes	eus choisi	eûtes choisi
choisit	choisirent	eut choisi	eurent choisi
4 futur		**11 futur antérieur**	
choisirai	choisirons	aurai choisi	aurons choisi
choisiras	choisirez	auras choisi	aurez choisi
choisira	choisiront	aura choisi	auront choisi
5 conditionnel		**12 conditionnel passé**	
choisirais	choisirions	aurais choisi	aurions choisi
choisirais	choisiriez	aurais choisi	auriez choisi
choisirait	choisiraient	aurait choisi	auraient choisi
6 présent du subjonctif		**13 passé du subjonctif**	
choisisse	choisissions	aie choisi	ayons choisi
choisisses	choisissiez	aies choisi	ayez choisi
choisisse	choisissent	ait choisi	aient choisi
7 imparfait du subjonctif		**14 plus-que-parfait du subjonctif**	
choisisse	choisissions	eusse choisi	eussions choisi
choisisses	choisissiez	eusses choisi	eussiez choisi
choisît	choisissent	eût choisi	eussent choisi

Impératif
choisis
choisissons
choisissez

---

un choix   choice
faire choix de   to make choice of
l'embarras du choix   too much to choose from
faire un bon choix   to make a good choice
faire un mauvais choix   to make a bad choice
au choix   optional, elective
Il faut savoir choisir ses amis.   You must know how to choose your friends.
Il n'y a pas grand choix.   There's not much choice.

commander

Part. pr. **commandant**   Part. passé **commandé**

to command, to order

Regular -er verb

The Seven Simple Tenses		The Seven Compound Tenses	
Singular	Plural	Singular	Plural
1 présent de l'indicatif		**8 passé composé**	
commande	commandons	ai commandé	avons commandé
commandes	commandez	as commandé	avez commandé
commande	commandent	a commandé	ont commandé
2 imparfait de l'indicatif		**9 plus-que-parfait de l'indicatif**	
commandais	commandions	avais commandé	avions commandé
commandais	commandiez	avais commandé	aviez commandé
commandait	commandaient	avait commandé	avaient commandé
3 passé simple		**10 passé antérieur**	
commandai	commandâmes	eus commandé	eûmes commandé
commandas	commandâtes	eus commandé	eûtes commandé
commanda	commandèrent	eut commandé	eurent commandé
4 futur		**11 futur antérieur**	
commanderai	commanderons	aurai commandé	aurons commandé
commanderas	commanderez	auras commandé	aurez commandé
commandera	commanderont	aura commandé	auront commandé
5 conditionnel		**12 conditionnel passé**	
commanderais	commanderions	aurais commandé	aurions commandé
commanderais	commanderiez	aurais commandé	auriez commandé
commanderait	commanderaient	aurait commandé	auraient commandé
6 présent du subjonctif		**13 passé du subjonctif**	
commande	commandions	aie commandé	ayons commandé
commandes	commandiez	aies commandé	ayez commandé
commande	commandent	ait commandé	aient commandé
7 imparfait du subjonctif		**14 plus-que-parfait du subjonctif**	
commandasse	commandassions	eusse commandé	eussions commandé
commandasses	commandassiez	eusses commandé	eussiez commandé
commandât	commandassent	eût commandé	eussent commandé

Impératif
commande
commandons
commandez

Hier soir mes amis et moi avons dîné dans un restaurant chinois. Nous avons commandé beaucoup de choses intéressantes.

un commandant   commanding officer
une commande   an order
commander à qqn de faire qqch   to order someone to do something
recommander   to recommend; recommander à qqn de faire qqch   to advise someone to do something
décommander un rendez-vous   to cancel a date, an appointment

Part. pr. **commençant**   Part. passé **commencé**   **commencer**

Regular -er verb endings: spelling change: to begin, to start, to commence
c changes to ç before a or o to keep s sound.

The Seven Simple Tenses		The Seven Compound Tenses	
Singular	Plural	Singular	Plural
1 présent de l'indicatif		8 passé composé	
commence	commençons	ai commencé	avons commencé
commences	commencez	as commencé	avez commencé
commence	commencent	a commencé	ont commencé
2 imparfait de l'indicatif		9 plus-que-parfait de l'indicatif	
commençais	commencions	avais commencé	avions commencé
commençais	commenciez	avais commencé	aviez commencé
commençait	commençaient	avait commencé	avaient commencé
3 passé simple		10 passé antérieur	
commençai	commençâmes	eus commencé	eûmes commencé
commenças	commençâtes	eus commencé	eûtes commencé
commença	commencèrent	eut commencé	eurent commencé
4 futur		11 futur antérieur	
commencerai	commencerons	aurai commencé	aurons commencé
commenceras	commencerez	auras commencé	aurez commencé
commencera	commenceront	aura commencé	auront commencé
5 conditionnel		12 conditionnel passé	
commencerais	commencerions	aurais commencé	aurions commencé
commencerais	commenceriez	aurais commencé	auriez commencé
commencerait	commenceraient	aurait commencé	auraient commencé
6 présent du subjonctif		13 passé du subjonctif	
commence	commencions	aie commencé	ayons commencé
commences	commenciez	aies commencé	ayez commencé
commence	commencent	ait commencé	aient commencé
7 imparfait du subjonctif		14 plus-que-parfait du subjonctif	
commençasse	commençassions	eusse commencé	eussions commencé
commençasses	commençassiez	eusses commencé	eussiez commencé
commençât	commençassent	eût commencé	eussent commencé

Impératif
commence   commençons   commencez

Dépêche-toi! Le film commence à midi!   Hurry up! The movie starts at noon!
Commençons au commencement.   Let's begin at the beginning.
Nous commençons à nous inquiéter parce que Marie-Ève n'est pas encore revenue.   We are beginning to worry because Marie-Eve hasn't come back yet.

commencer à + inf.   to begin + inf.   pour commencer   to begin with
le commencement   the beginning   commencer par   to begin by
au commencement   in the beginning   recommencer à   to begin again + inf.
du commencement à la fin   from
  beginning to end

57

comprendre	Part. pr. **comprenant**	Part. passé **compris**

to understand   Irregular verb

The Seven Simple Tenses		The Seven Compound Tenses	
Singular	Plural	Singular	Plural
1 présent de l'indicatif		**8 passé composé**	
comprends	comprenons	ai compris	avons compris
comprends	comprenez	as compris	avez compris
comprend	comprennent	a compris	ont compris
2 imparfait de l'indicatif		**9 plus-que-parfait de l'indicatif**	
comprenais	comprenions	avais compris	avions compris
comprenais	compreniez	avais compris	aviez compris
comprenait	comprenaient	avait compris	avaient compris
3 passé simple		**10 passé antérieur**	
compris	comprîmes	eus compris	eûmes compris
compris	comprîtes	eus compris	eûtes compris
comprit	comprirent	eut compris	eurent compris
4 futur		**11 futur antérieur**	
comprendrai	comprendrons	aurai compris	aurons compris
comprendras	comprendrez	auras compris	aurez compris
comprendra	comprendront	aura compris	auront compris
5 conditionnel		**12 conditionnel passé**	
comprendrais	comprendrions	aurais compris	aurions compris
comprendrais	comprendriez	aurais compris	auriez compris
comprendrait	comprendraient	aurait compris	auraient compris
6 présent du subjonctif		**13 passé du subjonctif**	
comprenne	comprenions	aie compris	ayons compris
comprennes	compreniez	aies compris	ayez compris
comprenne	comprennent	ait compris	aient compris
7 imparfait du subjonctif		**14 plus-que-parfait du subjonctif**	
comprisse	comprissions	eusse compris	eussions compris
comprisses	comprissiez	eusses compris	eussiez compris
comprît	comprissent	eût compris	eussent compris

Impératif
comprends
comprenons
comprenez

Je ne comprends jamais la prof de biologie. Je n'ai pas compris la leçon d'hier,
je ne comprends pas la leçon d'aujourd'hui, et je ne comprendrai jamais rien!
I never understand the biology professor. I didn't understand the lesson yesterday,
I don't understand today's lesson, and I'll never understand anything!

faire comprendre à qqn que . . . to
make it clear to someone that . . .
la compréhension comprehension,
understanding
Ça se comprend. Of course; That is
understood.

y compris included, including
service compris, y compris le service
service included (no tip necessary)

See also **apprendre, prendre,
reprendre,** and **surprendre.**

Regular -er verb   to count, to intend, to expect to

The Seven Simple Tenses		The Seven Compound Tenses	
Singular	Plural	Singular	Plural
1 présent de l'indicatif		**8 passé composé**	
compte	comptons	ai compté	avons compté
comptes	comptez	as compté	avez compté
compte	comptent	a compté	ont compté
2 imparfait de l'indicatif		**9 plus-que-parfait de l'indicatif**	
comptais	comptions	avais compté	avions compté
comptais	comptiez	avais compté	aviez compté
comptait	comptaient	avait compté	avaient compté
3 passé simple		**10 passé antérieur**	
comptai	comptâmes	eus compté	eûmes compté
comptas	comptâtes	eus compté	eûtes compté
compta	comptèrent	eut compté	eurent compté
4 futur		**11 futur antérieur**	
compterai	compterons	aurai compté	aurons compté
compteras	compterez	auras compté	aurez compté
comptera	compteront	aura compté	auront compté
5 conditionnel		**12 conditionnel passé**	
compterais	compterions	aurais compté	aurions compté
compterais	compteriez	aurais compté	auriez compté
compterait	compteraient	aurait compté	auraient compté
6 présent du subjonctif		**13 passé du subjonctif**	
compte	comptions	aie compté	ayons compté
comptes	comptiez	aies compté	ayez compté
compte	comptent	ait compté	aient compté
7 imparfait du subjonctif		**14 plus-que-parfait du subjonctif**	
comptasse	comptassions	eusse compté	eussions compté
comptasses	comptassiez	eusses compté	eussiez compté
comptât	comptassent	eût compté	eussent compté

	Impératif
	compte
	comptons
	comptez

Je compte aller en France l'été prochain avec ma femme pour voir nos amis français. I intend to go to France next summer with my wife to see our French friends.

la comptabilité bookkeeping	compter sur to count (rely) on; **Puis-je y**
comptable accountable	compter? Can I depend on it?
le comptage accounting	escompter to discount; un escompte discount
payer comptant to pay cash	donner sans compter to give generously
compter faire qqch to expect	sans compter . . . say nothing of . . .
to do something	le comptoir counter (in a store)

59

to lead, to drive, to conduct, to manage   Irregular verb

The Seven Simple Tenses		The Seven Compound Tenses	
Singular	Plural	Singular	Plural
1 présent de l'indicatif		8 passé composé	
conduis	**conduisons**	**ai conduit**	**avons conduit**
conduis	**conduisez**	**as conduit**	**avez conduit**
conduit	**conduisent**	**a conduit**	**ont conduit**
2 imparfait de l'indicatif		9 plus-que-parfait de l'indicatif	
conduisais	**conduisions**	**avais conduit**	**avions conduit**
conduisais	**conduisiez**	**avais conduit**	**aviez conduit**
conduisait	**conduisaient**	**avait conduit**	**avaient conduit**
3 passé simple		10 passé antérieur	
conduisis	**conduisîmes**	**eus conduit**	**eûmes conduit**
conduisis	**conduisîtes**	**eus conduit**	**eûtes conduit**
conduisit	**conduisirent**	**eut conduit**	**eurent conduit**
4 futur		11 futur antérieur	
conduirai	**conduirons**	**aurai conduit**	**aurons conduit**
conduiras	**conduirez**	**auras conduit**	**aurez conduit**
conduira	**conduiront**	**aura conduit**	**auront conduit**
5 conditionnel		12 conditionnel passé	
conduirais	**conduirions**	**aurais conduit**	**aurions conduit**
conduirais	**conduiriez**	**aurais conduit**	**auriez conduit**
conduirait	**conduiraient**	**aurait conduit**	**auraient conduit**
6 présent du subjonctif		13 passé du subjonctif	
conduise	**conduisions**	**aie conduit**	**ayons conduit**
conduises	**conduisiez**	**aies conduit**	**ayez conduit**
conduise	**conduisent**	**ait conduit**	**aient conduit**
7 imparfait du subjonctif		14 plus-que-parfait du subjonctif	
conduisisse	**conduisissions**	**eusse conduit**	**eussions conduit**
conduisisses	**conduisissiez**	**eusses conduit**	**eussiez conduit**
conduisît	**conduisissent**	**eût conduit**	**eussent conduit**

Impératif
     conduis   **conduisons**   **conduisez**

—Savez-vous conduire?
—Oui, je sais conduire. Je conduis une voiture, je dirige un orchestre, et hier j'ai conduit quelqu'un à la gare. Attendez, je vais vous conduire à la porte.
—Merci. Vous êtes très aimable.

un conducteur, une conductrice driver	**conduire une voiture** to drive a car
la conduite conduct, behavior	**se conduire** to conduct (behave)
induire to induce	oneself
induire en to lead into	**un permis de conduire** driver's license
	enduire to coat, spread

See also **introduire**, **produire**, and **traduire**.

60

Part. pr. **connaissant**   Part. passé **connu**   **connaître**

Irregular verb   to know, to be acquainted with,
                                            to make the acquaintance of

The Seven Simple Tenses | The Seven Compound Tenses

Singular	Plural	Singular	Plural
1 présent de l'indicatif		**8 passé composé**	
connais	connaissons	ai connu	avons connu
connais	connaissez	as connu	avez connu
connaît	connaissent	a connu	ont connu
2 imparfait de l'indicatif		**9 plus-que-parfait de l'indicatif**	
connaissais	connaissions	avais connu	avions connu
connaissais	connaissiez	avais connu	aviez connu
connaissait	connaissaient	avait connu	avaient connu
3 passé simple		**10 passé antérieur**	
connus	connûmes	eus connu	eûmes connu
connus	connûtes	eus connu	eûtes connu
connut	connurent	eut connu	eurent connu
4 futur		**11 futur antérieur**	
connaîtrai	connaîtrons	aurai connu	aurons connu
connaîtras	connaîtrez	auras connu	aurez connu
connaîtra	connaîtront	aura connu	auront connu
5 conditionnel		**12 conditionnel passé**	
connaîtrais	connaîtrions	aurais connu	aurions connu
connaîtrais	connaîtriez	aurais connu	auriez connu
connaîtrait	connaîtraient	aurait connu	auraient connu
6 présent du subjonctif		**13 passé du subjonctif**	
connaisse	connaissions	aie connu	ayons connu
connaisses	connaissiez	aies connu	ayez connu
connaisse	connaissent	ait connu	aient connu
7 imparfait du subjonctif		**14 plus-que-parfait du subjonctif**	
connusse	connussions	eusse connu	eussions connu
connusses	connussiez	eusses connu	eussiez connu
connût	connussent	eût connu	eussent connu

Impératif
connais
connaissons
connaissez

—Connaissez-vous quelqu'un qui puisse m'aider? Je suis touriste et je ne connais pas cette ville.
—Non, je ne connais personne. Je suis touriste aussi.
—Voulez-vous aller prendre un café? Nous pouvons faire connaissance.

la connaissance   knowledge, understanding, acquaintance
connaisseur, connaisseuse   expert
se connaître   to know each other, to know oneself
faire connaissance   to get acquainted
à ma connaissance   as far as I know

construire   Part. pr. **construisant**   Part. passé **construit**

to construct, to build   Irregular verb

The Seven Simple Tenses		The Seven Compound Tenses	
Singular	Plural	Singular	Plural
1 présent de l'indicatif		8 passé composé	
construis	construisons	ai construit	avons construit
construis	construisez	as construit	avez construit
construit	construisent	a construit	ont construit
2 imparfait de l'indicatif		9 plus-que-parfait de l'indicatif	
construisais	construisions	avais construit	avions construit
construisais	construisiez	avais construit	aviez construit
construisait	construisaient	avait construit	avaient construit
3 passé simple		10 passé antérieur	
construisis	construisîmes	eus construit	eûmes construit
construisis	construisîtes	eus construit	eûtes construit
construisit	construisirent	eut construit	eurent construit
4 futur		11 futur antérieur	
construirai	construirons	aurai construit	aurons construit
construiras	construirez	auras construit	aurez construit
construira	construiront	aura construit	auront construit
5 conditionnel		12 conditionnel passé	
construirais	construirions	aurais construit	aurions construit
construirais	construiriez	aurais construit	auriez construit
construirait	construiraient	aurait construit	auraient construit
6 présent du subjonctif		13 passé du subjonctif	
construise	construisions	aie construit	ayons construit
construises	construisiez	aies construit	ayez construit
construise	construisent	ait construit	aient construit
7 imparfait du subjonctif		14 plus-que-parfait du subjonctif	
construisisse	construisissions	eusse construit	eussions construit
construisisses	construisissiez	eusses construit	eussiez construit
construisît	construisissent	eût construit	eussent construit

Impératif
construis
construisons
construisez

—Je vois que vous êtes en train de construire quelque chose. Qu'est-ce que vous construisez?

—Je construis une tour comme la Tour Eiffel. Aimez-vous ce bateau que j'ai construit?

un constructeur   a manufacturer, builder, constructor
une construction   construction, building
reconstruire   to reconstruct, to rebuild
en construction   under construction

Part. pr. **contant**		Part. passé **conté**	**conter**
Regular -er verb			to relate, to narrate

The Seven Simple Tenses		The Seven Compound Tenses	
Singular	Plural	Singular	Plural

1 présent de l'indicatif		8 passé composé	
conte	contons	ai conté	avons conté
contes	contez	as conté	avez conté
conte	content	a conté	ont conté

2 imparfait de l'indicatif		9 plus-que-parfait de l'indicatif	
contais	contions	avais conté	avions conté
contais	contiez	avais conté	aviez conté
contait	contaient	avait conté	avaient conté

3 passé simple		10 passé antérieur	
contai	contâmes	eus conté	eûmes conté
contas	contâtes	eus conté	eûtes conté
conta	contèrent	eut conté	eurent conté

4 futur		11 futur antérieur	
conterai	conterons	aurai conté	aurons conté
conteras	conterez	auras conté	aurez conté
contera	conteront	aura conté	auront conté

5 conditionnel		12 conditionnel passé	
conterais	conterions	aurais conté	aurions conté
conterais	conteriez	aurais conté	auriez conté
conterait	conteraient	aurait conté	auraient conté

6 présent du subjonctif		13 passé du subjonctif	
conte	contions	aie conté	ayons conté
contes	contiez	aies conté	ayez conté
conte	content	ait conté	aient conté

7 imparfait du subjonctif		14 plus-que-parfait du subjonctif	
contasse	contassions	eusse conté	eussions conté
contasses	contassiez	eusses conté	eussiez conté
contât	contassent	eût conté	eussent conté

Impératif
conte
contons
contez

Notre professeur de français nous conte toujours des histoires intéressantes.
Son conte favori est *Un coeur simple* de Flaubert.

un conte   a story, tale
un conte de fées   fairy tale
un conte à dormir debout   cock-and-bull story
un conteur, une conteuse   writer of short stories

See also raconter.

continuer

Part. pr. **continuant** Part. passé **continué**

to continue | Regular **-er** verb

The Seven Simple Tenses	The Seven Compound Tenses

Singular	Plural	Singular	Plural
1 présent de l'indicatif		**8 passé composé**	
continue	continuons	ai continué	avons continué
continues	continuez	as continué	avez continué
continue	continuent	a continué	ont continué
2 imparfait de l'indicatif		**9 plus-que-parfait de l'indicatif**	
continuais	continuions	avais continué	avions continué
continuais	continuiez	avais continué	aviez continué
continuait	continuaient	avait continué	avaient continué
3 passé simple		**10 passé antérieur**	
continuai	continuâmes	eus continué	eûmes continué
continuas	continuâtes	eus continué	eûtes continué
continua	continuèrent	eut continué	eurent continué
4 futur		**11 futur antérieur**	
continuerai	continuerons	aurai continué	aurons continué
continueras	continuerez	auras continué	aurez continué
continuera	continueront	aura continué	auront continué
5 conditionnel		**12 conditionnel passé**	
continuerais	continuerions	aurais continué	aurions continué
continuerais	continueriez	aurais continué	auriez continué
continuerait	continueraient	aurait continué	auraient continué
6 présent du subjonctif		**13 passé du subjonctif**	
continue	continuions	aie continué	ayons continué
continues	continuiez	aies continué	ayez continué
continue	continuent	ait continué	aient continué
7 imparfait du subjonctif		**14 plus-que-parfait du subjonctif**	
continuasse	continuassions	eusse continué	eussions continué
continuasses	continuassiez	eusses continué	eussiez continué
continuât	continuassent	eût continué	eussent continué

	Impératif
	continue
	continuons
	continuez

—Allez-vous continuer à étudier le français l'année prochaine?
—Certainement. Je compte étudier cette belle langue continuellement.

la continuation continuation	continuer à + inf. to continue + inf.
continuel, continuelle continual	continuer de + inf. to continue (persist) in
continuellement continually	Cet ivrogne continue de boire. This
	drunkard persists in drinking (habit).

Part. pr. **corrigeant**	Part. passé **corrigé**	**corriger**

Regular -er verb endings: spelling change: retain the **to correct**
ge before a or o to keep the soft g sound of the verb.

The Seven Simple Tenses		The Seven Compound Tenses	
Singular	Plural	Singular	Plural
1 présent de l'indicatif		**8 passé composé**	
corrige	corrigeons	ai corrigé	avons corrigé
corriges	corrigez	as corrigé	avez corrigé
corrige	corrigent	a corrigé	ont corrigé
2 imparfait de l'indicatif		**9 plus-que-parfait de l'indicatif**	
corrigeais	corrigions	avais corrigé	avions corrigé
corrigeais	corrigiez	avais corrigé	aviez corrigé
corrigeait	corrigeaient	avait corrigé	avaient corrigé
3 passé simple		**10 passé antérieur**	
corrigeai	corrigeâmes	eus corrigé	eûmes corrigé
corrigeas	corrigeâtes	eus corrigé	eûtes corrigé
corrigea	corrigèrent	eut corrigé	eurent corrigé
4 futur		**11 futur antérieur**	
corrigerai	corrigerons	aurai corrigé	aurons corrigé
corrigeras	corrigerez	auras corrigé	aurez corrigé
corrigera	corrigeront	aura corrigé	auront corrigé
5 conditionnel		**12 conditionnel passé**	
corrigerais	corrigerions	aurais corrigé	aurions corrigé
corrigerais	corrigeriez	aurais corrigé	auriez corrigé
corrigerait	corrigeraient	aurait corrigé	auraient corrigé
6 présent du subjonctif		**13 passé du subjonctif**	
corrige	corrigions	aie corrigé	ayons corrigé
corriges	corrigiez	aies corrigé	ayez corrigé
corrige	corrigent	ait corrigé	aient corrigé
7 imparfait du subjonctif		**14 plus-que-parfait du subjonctif**	
corrigeasse	corrigeassions	eusse corrigé	eussions corrigé
corrigeasses	corrigeassiez	eusses corrigé	eussiez corrigé
corrigeât	corrigeassent	eût corrigé	eussent corrigé

	Impératif
	corrige
	corrigeons
	corrigez

Dans la classe de français nous corrigeons toujours nos devoirs en classe.
La prof de français écrit les corrections au tableau.

une correction correction; **recorriger** to correct again
corriger qqn de to correct someone of
se corriger de to correct one's ways
corrigible corrigible; **incorrigible** incorrigible
incorrectement inaccurately, incorrectly
la correction automatique automatic correction (comp.)
un correcteur, une correctrice proofreader

se coucher Part. pr. **se couchant** Part. passé **couché(e)(s)**

to go to bed, to lie down Reflexive regular -er verb

The Seven Simple Tenses		The Seven Compound Tenses	
Singular	Plural	Singular	Plural
1 présent de l'indicatif		8 passé composé	
me couche	**nous couchons**	**me suis couché(e)**	**nous sommes couché(e)s**
te couches	**vous couchez**	**t'es couché(e)**	**vous êtes couché(e)(s)**
se couche	**se couchent**	**s'est couché(e)**	**se sont couché(e)s**
2 imparfait de l'indicatif		9 plus-que-parfait de l'indicatif	
me couchais	**nous couchions**	**m'étais couché(e)**	**nous étions couché(e)s**
te couchais	**vous conchiez**	**t'étais couché(e)**	**vous étiez couché(e)(s)**
se couchait	**se couchaient**	**s'était couché(e)**	**s'étaient couché(e)s**
3 passé simple		10 passé antérieur	
me couchai	**nous couchâmes**	**me fus couché(e)**	**nous fûmes couché(e)s**
te couchas	**vous couchâtes**	**te fus couché(e)**	**vous fûtes couché(e)(s)**
se coucha	**se couchèrent**	**se fut couché(e)**	**se furent couché(e)s**
4 futur		11 futur antérieur	
me coucherai	**nous coucherons**	**me serai couché(e)**	**nous serons couché(e)s**
te coucheras	**vous coucherez**	**te seras couché(e)**	**vous serez couché(e)(s)**
se couchera	**se coucheront**	**se sera couché(e)**	**se seront couché(e)s**
5 conditionnel		12 conditionnel passé	
me coucherais	**nous coucherions**	**me serais couché(e)**	**nous serions couché(e)s**
te coucherais	**vous coucheriez**	**te serais couché(e)**	**vous seriez couché(e)(s)**
se coucherait	**se coucheraient**	**se serait couché(e)**	**se seraient couché(e)s**
6 présent du subjonctif		13 passé du subjonctif	
me couche	**nous couchions**	**me sois couché(e)**	**nous soyons couché(e)s**
te couches	**vous couchiez**	**te sois couché(e)**	**vous soyez couché(e)(s)**
se couche	**se couchent**	**se soit couché(e)**	**se soient couché(e)s**
7 imparfait du subjonctif		14 plus-que-parfait du subjonctif	
me couchasse	**nous couchassions**	**me fusse couché(e)**	**nous fussions couché(e)s**
te couchasses	**vous couchassiez**	**te fusses couché(e)**	**vous fussiez couché(e)(s)**
se couchât	**se couchassent**	**se fût couché(e)**	**se fussent couché(e)s**

Impératif
couche-toi; ne te couche pas
couchons-nous; ne nous couchons pas
couchez-vous; ne vous couchez pas

—**Couche-toi, Hélène! Il est minuit. Hier soir tu t'es couchée tard.** Go to bed, Helen! It's midnight. Last night you went to bed late.

le coucher du soleil sunset
une couche a layer
une couchette bunk, cot
Le soleil se couche. The sun is setting.
un sac de couchage sleeping bag
un couche-tard night owl, someone who stays up late

se recoucher to go back to bed
se coucher tôt to go to bed early
Comme on fait son lit on se couche! You've made your bed; now lie in it!

Regular -er verb | to cut, to switch off

The Seven Simple Tenses		The Seven Compound Tenses	
Singular	Plural	Singular	Plural
1 présent de l'indicatif		8 passé composé	
coupe	coupons	ai coupé	avons coupé
coupes	coupez	as coupé	avez coupé
coupe	coupent	a coupé	ont coupé
2 imparfait de l'indicatif		9 plus-que-parfait de l'indicatif	
coupais	coupions	avais coupé	avions coupé
coupais	coupiez	avais coupé	aviez coupé
coupait	coupaient	avait coupé	avaient coupé
3 passé simple		10 passé antérieur	
coupai	coupâmes	eus coupé	eûmes coupé
coupas	coupâtes	eus coupé	eûtes coupé
coupa	coupèrent	eut coupé	eurent coupé
4 futur		11 futur antérieur	
couperai	couperons	aurai coupé	aurons coupé
couperas	couperez	auras coupé	aurez coupé
coupera	couperont	aura coupé	auront coupé
5 conditionnel		12 conditionnel passé	
couperais	couperions	aurais coupé	aurions coupé
couperais	couperiez	aurais coupé	auriez coupé
couperait	couperaient	aurait coupé	auraient coupé
6 présent du subjonctif		13 passé du subjonctif	
coupe	coupions	aie coupé	ayons coupé
coupes	coupiez	aies coupé	ayez coupé
coupe	coupent	ait coupé	aient coupé
7 imparfait du subjonctif		14 plus-que-parfait du subjonctif	
coupasse	coupassions	eusse coupé	eussions coupé
coupasses	coupassiez	eusses coupé	eussiez coupé
coupât	coupassent	eût coupé	eussent coupé

Impératif
coupe
coupons
coupez

Ce morceau de pain est trop grand. Je vais le couper en deux.

un coupon coupon
une coupure cut, gash, crack
couper les cheveux en quatre to split hairs
se faire couper les cheveux to have
  one's hair cut
Aïe! Je me suis coupé le doigt!
  Ouch! I cut my finger!

découper to cut out
entrecouper to interrupt
couper la fièvre . to reduce a fever
une coupe de cheveux haircut
une coupe au rasoir razor cut
une coupe croisée crosscut

courir	Part. pr. **courant**	Part. passé **couru**

to run, to race | Irregular verb

The Seven Simple Tenses		The Seven Compound Tenses	
Singular	Plural	Singular	Plural

1 présent de l'indicatif		8 passé composé	
cours	courons	ai couru	avons couru
cours	courez	as couru	avez couru
court	courent	a couru	ont couru

2 imparfait de l'indicatif		9 plus-que-parfait de l'indicatif	
courais	courions	avais couru	avions couru
courais	couriez	avais couru	aviez couru
courait	couraient	avait couru	avaient couru

3 passé simple		10 passé antérieur	
courus	courûmes	eus couru	eûmes couru
courus	courûtes	eus couru	eûtes couru
courut	coururent	eut couru	eurent couru

4 futur		11 futur antérieur	
courrai	courrons	aurai couru	aurons couru
courras	courrez	auras couru	aurez couru
courra	courront	aura couru	auront couru

5 conditionnel		12 conditionnel passé	
courrais	courrions	aurais couru	aurions couru
courrais	courriez	aurais couru	auriez couru
courrait	courraient	aurait couru	auraient couru

6 présent du subjonctif		13 passé du subjonctif	
coure	courions	aie couru	ayons couru
coures	couriez	aies couru	ayez couru
coure	courent	ait couru	aient couru

7 imparfait du subjonctif		14 plus-que-parfait du subjonctif	
courusse	courussions	eusse couru	eussions couru
courusses	courussiez	eusses couru	eussiez couru
courût	courussent	eût couru	eussent couru

	Impératif
	cours
	courons
	courez

Les enfants sont toujours prêts à courir. Quand on est jeune on court sans se fatiguer. Michel a couru de la maison jusqu'à l'école.   Children are always ready to run. When you're young (one is young), you run (one runs) without getting tired. Michael ran from home to school.

le courrier courier, messenger, mail
un coureur runner
faire courir un bruit to spread a rumor
courir une course to run a race
courir le monde to roam all over the world

accourir vers to come running toward
courir les rues to run about the streets
par le temps qui court these days, nowadays
parcourir to go through, to travel through, to cover (distance)

Part. pr. **coûtant**   Part. passé **coûté**   **coûter**

Regular -er verb; impersonal   to cost

The Seven Simple Tenses | The Seven Compound Tenses

Singular	Plural	Singular	Plural
1 présent de l'indicatif		8 passé composé	
il coûte	**ils coûtent**	**il a coûté**	**ils ont coûté**
2 imparfait de l'indicatif		9 plus-que-parfait de l'indicatif	
il coûtait	**ils coûtaient**	**il avait coûté**	**ils avaient coûté**
3 passé simple		10 passé antérieur	
il coûta	**ils coûtèrent**	**il eut coûté**	**ils eurent coûté**
4 futur		11 futur antérieur	
il coûtera	**ils coûteront**	**il aura coûté**	**ils auront coûté**
5 conditionnel		12 conditionnel passé	
il coûterait	**ils coûteraient**	**il aurait coûté**	**ils auraient coûté**
6 présent du subjonctif		13 passé du subjonctif	
qu'il coûte	**qu'ils coûtent**	**qu'il ait coûté**	**qu'ils aient coûté**
7 imparfait du subjonctif		14 plus-que-parfait du subjonctif	
qu'il coûtât	**qu'ils coûtassent**	**qu'il eût coûté**	**qu'ils eussent coûté**

Impératif
—

—**Combien coûte cette table?**   How much does this table cost?
—**Elle coûte mille euros.**   It costs one thousand euros.
—**Et combien coûte ce lit?**   And how much does this bed cost?
—**Il coûte mille euros aussi.**   It costs one thousand euros too.
—**Ils coûtent joliment cher!**   They cost a pretty penny! (They are very expensive!)

coûteusement   expensively, dearly
coûte que coûte   at any cost
coûteux, coûteuse   costly, expensive
Cela coûte joliment cher.   That costs a pretty penny.
coûter cher, coûter peu   to be expensive, inexpensive
coûter à qqn   to cost someone;
   Cela lui en a coûté la vie.   That cost him his life.
coûter les yeux de la tête   to be very expensive

This verb is generally regarded as impersonal and is used primarily in the third person singular and plural.

couvrir

Part. pr. couvrant   **Part. passé couvert**

to cover

Irregular verb

The Seven Simple Tenses		The Seven Compound Tenses	
Singular	Plural	Singular	Plural
1 présent de l'indicatif		**8 passé composé**	
couvre	couvrons	ai couvert	avons couvert
couvres	couvrez	as couvert	avez couvert
couvre	couvrent	a couvert	ont couvert
2 imparfait de l'indicatif		**9 plus-que-parfait de l'indicatif**	
couvrais	couvrions	avais couvert	avions couvert
couvrais	couvriez	avais couvert	aviez couvert
couvrait	couvraient	avait couvert	avaient couvert
3 passé simple		**10 passé antérieur**	
couvris	couvrîmes	eus couvert	eûmes couvert
couvris	couvrîtes	eus couvert	eûtes couvert
couvrit	couvrirent	eut couvert	eurent couvert
4 futur		**11 futur antérieur**	
couvrirai	couvrirons	aurai couvert	aurons couvert
couvriras	couvrirez	auras couvert	aurez couvert
couvrira	couvriront	aura couvert	auront couvert
5 conditionnel		**12 conditionnel passé**	
couvrirais	couvririons	aurais couvert	aurions couvert
couvrirais	couvririez	aurais couvert	auriez couvert
couvrirait	couvriraient	aurait couvert	auraient couvert
6 présent du subjonctif		**13 passé du subjonctif**	
couvre	couvrions	aie couvert	ayons couvert
couvres	couvriez	aies couvert	ayez couvert
couvre	couvrent	ait couvert	aient couvert
7 imparfait du subjonctif		**14 plus-que-parfait du subjonctif**	
couvrisse	couvrissions	eusse couvert	eussions couvert
couvrisses	couvrissiez	eusses couvert	eussiez couvert
couvrît	couvrissent	eût couvert	eussent couvert

Impératif
couvre
couvrons
couvrez

Madame Champlain a couvert le lit d'un couvre-lit.   Mrs. Champlain covered the bed with a bedspread.

Dans ce cours nous couvrirons l'histoire du monde, de l'an mil jusqu'à présent. In this course we will cover the history of the world, from the year one thousand to the present.

un couvert place setting (spoon, knife, fork, etc.)	**Le temps se couvre.** The sky is overcast.
acheter des couverts to buy cutlery	**découvrir** to discover, disclose, uncover
mettre le couvert to lay the table	**se couvrir** to cover oneself, to put on one's hat
une couverture blanket	**le couvre-feu** curfew
70 See also **découvrir**.	**un couvre-lit** bedspread (des couvre-lits)

Irregular verb   to fear, to be afraid

The Seven Simple Tenses		The Seven Compound Tenses	
Singular	Plural	Singular	Plural
1 présent de l'indicatif		8 passé composé	
crains	craignons	ai craint	avons craint
crains	craignez	as craint	avez craint
craint	craignent	a craint	ont craint
2 imparfait de l'indicatif		9 plus-que-parfait de l'indicatif	
craignais	craignions	avais craint	avions craint
craignais	craigniez	avais craint	aviez craint
craignait	craignaient	avait craint	avaient craint
3 passé simple		10 passé antérieur	
craignis	craignîmes	eus craint	eûmes craint
craignis	craignîtes	eus craint	eûtes craint
craignit	craignirent	eut craint	eurent craint
4 futur		11 futur antérieur	
craindrai	craindrons	aurai craint	aurons craint
craindras	craindrez	auras craint	aurez craint
craindra	craindront	aura craint	auront craint
5 conditionnel		12 conditionnel passé	
craindrais	craindrions	aurais craint	aurions craint
craindrais	craindriez	aurais craint	auriez craint
craindrait	craindraient	aurait craint	auraient craint
6 présent du subjonctif		13 passé du subjonctif	
craigne	craignions	aie craint	ayons craint
craignes	craigniez	aies craint	ayez craint
craigne	craignent	ait craint	aient craint
7 imparfait du subjonctif		14 plus-que-parfait du subjonctif	
craignisse	craignissions	eusse craint	eussions craint
craignisses	craignissiez	eusses craint	eussiez craint
craignît	craignissent	eût craint	eussent craint

Impératif
crains
craignons
craignez

Le petit garçon craint de traverser le parc pendant la nuit. Il a raison parce que c'est dangereux. Il a des craintes.   The boy is afraid to cross the park at night. He's right because it's dangerous. He has fears.

une crainte fear, dread	craintif, craintive fearful
craindre pour sa vie to be in fear of one's life	craintivement fearfully
sans crainte fearless	
avec crainte fearfully	
de crainte que + subj. for fear that, for fear of	

crier	Part. pr. **criant**	Part. passé **crié**

to shout, to cry out

Regular **-er** verb

The Seven Simple Tenses		The Seven Compound Tenses	
Singular	Plural	Singular	Plural
1 présent de l'indicatif		8 passé composé	
crie	**crions**	**ai crié**	**avons crié**
cries	**criez**	**as crié**	**avez crié**
crie	**crient**	**a crié**	**ont crié**
2 imparfait de l'indicatif		9 plus-que-parfait de l'indicatif	
criais	**criions**	**avais crié**	**avions crié**
criais	**criiez**	**avais crié**	**aviez crié**
criait	**criaient**	**avait crié**	**avaient crié**
3 passé simple		10 passé antérieur	
criai	**criâmes**	**eus crié**	**eûmes crié**
crias	**criâtes**	**eus crié**	**eûtes crié**
cria	**crièrent**	**eut crié**	**eurent crié**
4 futur		11 futur antérieur	
crierai	**crierons**	**aurai crié**	**aurons crié**
crieras	**crierez**	**auras crié**	**aurez crié**
criera	**crieront**	**aura crié**	**auront crié**
5 conditionnel		12 conditionnel passé	
crierais	**crierions**	**aurais crié**	**aurions crié**
crierais	**crieriez**	**aurais crié**	**auriez crié**
crierait	**crieraient**	**aurait crié**	**auraient crié**
6 présent du subjonctif		13 passé du subjonctif	
crie	**criions**	**aie crié**	**ayons crié**
cries	**criiez**	**aies crié**	**ayez crié**
crie	**crient**	**ait crié**	**aient crié**
7 imparfait du subjonctif		14 plus-que-parfait du subjonctif	
criasse	**criassions**	**eusse crié**	**eussions crié**
criasses	**criassiez**	**eusses crié**	**eussiez crié**
criât	**criassent**	**eût crié**	**eussent crié**

Impératif
crie
crions
criez

Pour attraper l'autobus qui était en train de partir, Monsieur Duval a crié à **tue-tête.**   To catch the bus that was about to leave, Mr. Duval shouted at the top of his lungs.

un cri a shout, a cry	**un criailleur, une criailleuse** nagger
pousser un cri to utter a cry	**un criard, une criarde** someone who
crier à tue-tête to shout one's head off	constantly shouts, nags, scolds;
un crieur hawker	screecher
un crieur de journaux newsboy	**une couleur criarde** a piercing (loud)
	color

Irregular verb   to believe

The Seven Simple Tenses		The Seven Compound Tenses	
Singular	Plural	Singular	Plural
1 présent de l'indicatif		**8 passé composé**	
crois	**croyons**	**ai cru**	**avons cru**
crois	**croyez**	**as cru**	**avez cru**
croit	**croient**	**a cru**	**ont cru**
2 imparfait de l'indicatif		**9 plus-que-parfait de l'indicatif**	
croyais	**croyions**	**avais cru**	**avions cru**
croyais	**croyiez**	**avais cru**	**aviez cru**
croyait	**croyaient**	**avait cru**	**avaient cru**
3 passé simple		**10 passé antérieur**	
crus	**crûmes**	**eus cru**	**eûmes cru**
crus	**crûtes**	**eus cru**	**eûtes cru**
crut	**crurent**	**eut cru**	**eurent cru**
4 futur		**11 futur antérieur**	
croirai	**croirons**	**aurai cru**	**aurons cru**
croiras	**croirez**	**auras cru**	**aurez cru**
croira	**croiront**	**aura cru**	**auront cru**
5 conditionnel		**12 conditionnel passé**	
croirais	**croirions**	**aurais cru**	**aurions cru**
croirais	**croiriez**	**aurais cru**	**auriez cru**
croirait	**croiraient**	**aurait cru**	**auraient cru**
6 présent du subjonctif		**13 passé du subjonctif**	
croie	**croyions**	**aie cru**	**ayons cru**
croies	**croyiez**	**aies cru**	**ayez cru**
croie	**croient**	**ait cru**	**aient cru**
7 imparfait du subjonctif		**14 plus-que-parfait du subjonctif**	
crusse	**crussions**	**eusse cru**	**eussions cru**
crusses	**crussiez**	**eusses cru**	**eussiez cru**
crût	**crussent**	**eût cru**	**eussent cru**

Impératif
crois
croyons
croyez

Est-ce que vous croyez tout ce que vous entendez? Avez-vous cru l'histoire que je vous ai racontée? Do you believe everything that you hear? Did you believe the story that I told you?

Croyez-m'en! Take my word for it!
se croire to think oneself; to consider oneself
Paul se croit beau. Paul thinks himself handsome.
croyable believable
Je crois que oui. I think so.
Je crois que non. I don't think so.

incroyable unbelievable
croire à qqch to believe in something
croire en qqn to believe in someone

cueillir   Part. pr. cueillant   Part. passé cueilli

to gather, to pick   Irregular verb

The Seven Simple Tenses		The Seven Compound Tenses	
Singular	Plural	Singular	Plural
1 présent de l'indicatif		8 passé composé	
cueille	cueillons	ai cueilli	avons cueilli
cueilles	cueillez	as cueilli	avez cueilli
cueille	cueillent	a cueilli	ont cueilli
2 imparfait de l'indicatif		9 plus-que-parfait de l'indicatif	
cueillais	cueillions	avais cueilli	avions cueilli
cueillais	cueilliez	avais cueilli	aviez cueilli
cueillait	cueillaient	avait cueilli	avaient cueilli
3 passé simple		10 passé antérieur	
cueillis	cueillîmes	eus cueilli	eûmes cueilli
cueillis	cueillîtes	eus cueilli	eûtes cueilli
cueillit	cueillirent	eut cueilli	eurent cueilli
4 futur		11 futur antérieur	
cueillerai	cueillerons	aurai cueilli	aurons cueilli
cueilleras	cueillerez	auras cueilli	aurez cueilli
cueillera	cueilleront	aura cueilli	auront ceuilli
5 conditionnel		12 conditionnel passé	
cueillerais	cueillerions	aurais cueilli	aurions cueilli
cueillerais	cueilleriez	aurais cueilli	auriez cueilli
cueillerait	cueilleraient	aurait cueilli	auraient cueilli
6 présent du subjonctif		13 passé du subjonctif	
cueille	cueillions	aie cueilli	ayons cueilli
cueilles	cueilliez	aies cueilli	ayez cueilli
cueille	cueillent	ait cueilli	aient cueilli
7 imparfait du subjonctif		14 plus-que-parfait du subjonctif	
cueillisse	cueillissions	eusse cueilli	eussions cueilli
cueillisses	cueillissiez	eusses cueilli	eussiez cueilli
cueillît	cueillissent	eût cueilli	eussent cueilli

	Impératif
	cueille
	cueillons
	cueillez

Je vois que tu **cueilles** des fleurs. As-tu **cueilli** toutes les fleurs qui sont dans ce vase?   I see that you are picking flowers. Did you pick all the flowers that are in this vase?

un cueilleur, une cueilleuse   gatherer, picker
la cueillaison, la cueillette   gathering, picking
un cueilloir   basket for picking fruit; instrument for picking fruit on high branches
Cueillez, cueillez votre jeunesse (Ronsard: Make the most of your youth.)— Seize the day (Horace: *Carpe diem*).

For other words related to this verb, see accueillir.

Irregular verb   to cook

The Seven Simple Tenses		The Seven Compound Tenses	
Singular	Plural	Singular	Plural
1 présent de l'indicatif		8 passé composé	
cuis	cuisons	ai cuit	avons cuit
cuis	cuisez	as cuit	avez cuit
cuit	cuisent	a cuit	ont cuit
2 imparfait de l'indicatif		9 plus-que-parfait de l'indicatif	
cuisais	cuisions	avais cuit	avions cuit
cuisais	cuisiez	avais cuit	aviez cuit
cuisait	cuisaient	avait cuit	avaient cuit
3 passé simple		10 passé antérieur	
cuisis	cuisîmes	eus cuit	eûmes cuit
cuisis	cuisîtes	eus cuit	eûtes cuit
cuisit	cuisirent	eut cuit	eurent cuit
4 futur		11 futur antérieur	
cuirai	cuirons	aurai cuit	aurons cuit
cuiras	cuirez	auras cuit	aurez cuit
cuira	cuiront	aura cuit	auront cuit
5 conditionnel		12 . conditionnel passé	
cuirais	cuirions	aurais cuit	aurions cuit
cuirais	cuiriez	aurais cuit	auriez cuit
cuirait	cuiraient	aurait cuit	auraient cuit
6 présent du subjonctif		13 passé du subjonctif	
cuise	cuisions	aie cuit	ayons cuit
cuises	cuisiez	aies cuit	ayez cuit
cuise	cuisent	ait cuit	aient cuit
7 imparfait du subjonctif		14 plus-que-parfait du subjonctif	
cuisisse	cuisissions	eusse cuit	eussions cuit
cuisisses	cuisissiez	eusses cuit	eussiez cuit
cuisît	cuisissent	eût cuit	eussent cuit

	Impératif
	cuis
	cuisons
	cuisez

Qui a **cuit** ce morceau de viande? C'est dégoûtant! Il est trop **cuit**. Ne savez-vous pas faire **cuire** un bon morceau de viande? Vous n'êtes pas bon cuisinier.
Who cooked this piece of meat? It's disgusting! It's overdone. Don't you know how to cook a good cut of meat? You're not a good cook.

la cuisine kitchen	**une cuisinière** kitchen range (stove)
cuisinier, cuisinière cook	**un cuiseur** pressure cooker
faire cuire à la poêle to pan fry	**trop cuit** overcooked, overdone
Il est cuit. He's done for; His goose	**la cuisson** cooking (time)
is cooked.	**bien cuit** well done

danser   Part. pr. **dansant**   Part. passé **dansé**

to dance   Regular -er verb

The Seven Simple Tenses		The Seven Compound Tenses	
Singular	Plural	Singular	Plural
1 présent de l'indicatif		8 passé composé	
danse	dansons	ai dansé	avons dansé
danses	dansez	as dansé	avez dansé
danse	dansent	a dansé	ont dansé
2 imparfait de l'indicatif		9 plus-que-parfait de l'indicatif	
dansais	dansions	avais dansé	avions dansé
dansais	dansiez	avais dansé	aviez dansé
dansait	dansaient	avait dansé	avaient dansé
3 passé simple		10 passé antérieur	
dansai	dansâmes	eus dansé	eûmes dansé
dansas	dansâtes	eus dansé	eûtes dansé
dansa	dansèrent	eut dansé	eurent dansé
4 futur		11 futur antérieur	
danserai	danserons	aurai dansé	aurons dansé
danseras	danserez	auras dansé	aurez dansé
dansera	danseront	aura dansé	auront dansé
5 conditionnel		12 conditionnel passé	
danserais	danserions	aurais dansé	aurions dansé
danserais	danseriez	aurais dansé	auriez dansé
danserait	danseraient	aurait dansé	auraient dansé
6 présent du subjonctif		13 passé du subjonctif	
danse	dansions	aie dansé	ayons dansé
danses	dansiez	aies dansé	ayez dansé
danse	dansent	ait dansé	aient dansé
7 imparfait du subjonctif		14 plus-que-parfait du subjonctif	
dansasse	dansassions	eusse dansé	eussions dansé
dansasses	dansassiez	eusses dansé	eussiez dansé
dansât	dansassent	eût dansé	eussent dansé

	Impératif	
danse	dansons	dansez

René: **Veux-tu danser avec moi?**
Renée: **Je ne sais pas danser.**
René: **Je suis bon danseur. Je vais t'apprendre à danser. Viens! Dansons!**

danser de joie to dance for joy
une soirée dansante evening dancing
  party
un thé dansant tea dance
  (usually 5 o'clock)

un danseur, une danseuse dancer
une danse dance; **un bal** ball
  (dance)
Le chat parti, les souris dansent.
  When the cat's away the mice
  will play.

Irregular verb   to discover, to uncover

The Seven Simple Tenses		The Seven Compound Tenses	
Singular	Plural	Singular	Plural
1 présent de l'indicatif		8 passé composé	
découvre	**découvrons**	**ai découvert**	**avons découvert**
découvres	**découvrez**	**as découvert**	**avez découvert**
découvre	**découvrent**	**a découvert**	**ont découvert**
2 imparfait de l'indicatif		9 plus-que-parfait de l'indicatif	
découvrais	**découvrions**	**avais découvert**	**avions découvert**
découvrais	**découvriez**	**avais découvert**	**aviez découvert**
découvrait	**découvraient**	**avait découvert**	**avaient découvert**
3 passé simple		10 passé antérieur	
découvris	**découvrîmes**	**eus découvert**	**eûmes découvert**
découvris	**découvrîtes**	**eus découvert**	**eûtes découvert**
découvrit	**découvrirent**	**eut découvert**	**eurent découvert**
4 futur		11 futur antérieur	
découvrirai	**découvrirons**	**aurai découvert**	**aurons découvert**
découvriras	**découvrirez**	**auras découvert**	**aurez découvert**
découvrira	**découvriront**	**aura découvert**	**auront découvert**
5 conditionnel		12 conditionnel passé	
découvrirais	**découvririons**	**aurais découvert**	**aurions découvert**
découvrirais	**découvririez**	**aurais découvert**	**auriez découvert**
découvrirait	**découvriraient**	**aurait découvert**	**auraient découvert**
6 présent du subjonctif		13 passé du subjonctif	
découvre	**découvrions**	**aie découvert**	**ayons découvert**
découvres	**découvriez**	**aies découvert**	**ayez découvert**
découvre	**découvrent**	**ait découvert**	**aient découvert**
7 imparfait du subjonctif		14 plus-que-parfait du subjonctif	
découvrisse	**découvrissions**	**eusse découvert**	**eussions découvert**
découvrisses	**découvrissiez**	**eusses découvert**	**eussiez découvert**
découvrît	**découvrissent**	**eût découvert**	**eussent découvert**

Impératif
découvre   **découvrons**   **découvrez**

Ce matin j'ai couvert ce panier de fruits et maintenant il est découvert. Qui l'a découvert?

un découvreur   discoverer
une découverte   a discovery, invention
se découvrir   to take off one's clothes; to take off one's hat
aller à la découverte   to explore
Découvrir saint Pierre pour couvrir saint Paul.   To rob Peter to pay Paul.

See also **couvrir**.

décrire	Part. pr. **décrivant**	Part. passé **décrit**
to describe		Irregular verb

The Seven Simple Tenses		The Seven Compound Tenses	
Singular	Plural	Singular	Plural

1 présent de l'indicatif		8 passé composé	
décris	décrivons	ai décrit	avons décrit
décris	décrivez	as décrit	avez décrit
décrit	décrivent	a décrit	ont décrit

2 imparfait de l'indicatif		9 plus-que-parfait de l'indicatif	
décrivais	décrivions	avais décrit	avions décrit
décrivais	décriviez	avais décrit	aviez décrit
décrivait	décrivaient	avait décrit	avaient décrit

3 passé simple		10 passé antérieur	
décrivis	décrivîmes	eus décrit	eûmes décrit
décrivis	décrivîtes	eus décrit	eûtes décrit
décrivit	décrivirent	eut décrit	eurent décrit

4 futur		11 futur antérieur	
décrirai	décrirons	aurai décrit	aurons décrit
décriras	décrirez	auras décrit	aurez décrit
décrira	décriront	aura décrit	auront décrit

5 conditionnel		12 conditionnel passé	
décrirais	décririons	aurais décrit	aurions décrit
décrirais	décririez	aurais décrit	auriez décrit
décrirait	décriraient	aurait décrit	auraient décrit

6 présent du subjonctif		13 passé du subjonctif	
décrive	décrivions	aie décrit	ayons décrit
décrives	décriviez	aies décrit	ayez décrit
décrive	décrivent	ait décrit	aient décrit

7 imparfait du subjonctif		14 plus-que-parfait du subjonctif	
décrivisse	décrivissions	eusse décrit	eussions décrit
décrivisses	décrivissiez	eusses décrit	eussiez décrit
décrivît	décrivissent	eût décrit	eussent décrit

Impératif
décris
décrivons
décrivez

Quel beau paysage! Je le décrirai dans une lettre à mon ami. Je ferai une description en détail.

une description description	**proscrire** to proscribe
écrire to write	**prescrire** to prescribe, stipulate
indescriptible indescribable	**une prescription** prescription (law); **une ordonnance** prescription (medical)

See also écrire.

Regular -re verb   to defend, to forbid, to prohibit

The Seven Simple Tenses		The Seven Compound Tenses	
Singular	Plural	Singular	Plural
1 présent de l'indicatif		**8 passé composé**	
défends	défendons	ai défendu	avons défendu
défends	défendez	as défendu	avez défendu
défend	défendent	a défendu	ont défendu
2 imparfait de l'indicatif		**9 plus-que-parfait de l'indicatif**	
défendais	défendions	avais défendu	avions défendu
défendais	défendiez	avais défendu	aviez défendu
défendait	défendaient	avait défendu	avaient défendu
3 passé simple		**10 passé antérieur**	
défendis	défendîmes	eus défendu	eûmes défendu
défendis	défendîtes	eus défendu	eûtes défendu
défendit	défendirent	eut défendu	eurent défendu
4 futur		**11 futur antérieur**	
défendrai	défendrons	aurai défendu	aurons défendu
défendras	défendrez	auras défendu	aurez défendu
défendra	défendront	aura défendu	auront défendu
5 conditionnel		**12 conditionnel passé**	
défendrais	défendrions	aurais défendu	aurions défendu
défendrais	défendriez	aurais défendu	auriez défendu
défendrait	défendraient	aurait défendu	auraient défendu
6 présent du subjonctif		**13 passé du subjonctif**	
défende	défendions	aie défendu	ayons défendu
défendes	défendiez	aies défendu	ayez défendu
défende	défendent	ait défendu	aient défendu
7 imparfait du subjonctif		**14 plus-que-parfait du subjonctif**	
défendisse	défendissions	eusse défendu	eussions défendu
défendisses	défendissiez	eusses défendu	eussiez défendu
défendît	défendissent	eût défendu	eussent défendu

Impératif
défends
défendons
défendez

Le père: **Je te défends de fumer. C'est une mauvaise habitude.**
Le fils: **Alors, pourquoi fumes-tu, papa?**

une défense defense
Défense de . . . No . . . allowed
Défense d'entrer No entry/Keep Out
Défense de fumer No smoking
défendable justifiable
défendre qqch à qqn to forbid
  someone something

se défendre to defend oneself
défensif, défensive defensive
défensivement defensively
se défendre d'avoir fait qqch to deny
  having done something

79

déjeuner   Part. pr. **déjeunant**   Part. passé **déjeuné**

to lunch, to have lunch, breakfast

Regular **-er** verb

The Seven Simple Tenses		The Seven Compound Tenses	
Singular	Plural	Singular	Plural
1 présent de l'indicatif		8 passé composé	
déjeune	déjeunons	ai déjeuné	avons déjeuné
déjeunes	déjeunez	as déjeuné	avez déjeuné
déjeune	déjeunent	a déjeuné	ont déjeuné
2 imparfait de l'indicatif		9 plus-que-parfait de l'indicatif	
déjeunais	déjeunions	avais déjeuné	avions déjeuné
déjeunais	déjeuniez	avais déjeuné	aviez déjeuné
déjeunait	déjeunaient	avait déjeuné	avaient déjeuné
3 passé simple		10 passé antérieur	
déjeunai	déjeunâmes	eus déjeuné	eûmes déjeuné
déjeunas	déjeunâtes	eus déjeuné	eûtes déjeuné
déjeuna	déjeunèrent	eut déjeuné	eurent déjeuné
4 futur		11 futur antérieur	
déjeunerai	déjeunerons	aurai déjeuné	aurons déjeuné
déjeuneras	déjeunerez	auras déjeuné	aurez déjeuné
déjeunera	déjeuneront	aura déjeuné	auront déjeuné
5 conditionnel		12 conditionnel passé	
déjeunerais	déjeunerions	aurais déjeuné	aurions déjeuné
déjeunerais	déjeuneriez	aurais déjeuné	auriez déjeuné
déjeunerait	déjeuneraient	aurait déjeuné	auraient déjeuné
6 présent du subjonctif		13 passé du subjonctif	
déjeune	déjeunions	aie déjeuné	ayons déjeuné
déjeunes	déjeuniez	aies déjeuné	ayez déjeuné
déjeune	déjeunent	ait déjeuné	aient déjeuné
7 imparfait du subjonctif		14 plus-que-parfait du subjonctif	
déjeunasse	déjeunassions	eusse déjeuné	eussions déjeuné
déjeunasses	déjeunassiez	eusses déjeuné	eussiez déjeuné
déjeunât	déjeunassent	eût déjeuné	eussent déjeuné

	Impératif
	déjeune
	déjeunons
	déjeunez

Tous les matins je me lève et je prends mon petit déjeuner à sept heures et demie. A midi je déjeune avec mes camarades à l'école. Avec qui déjeunez-vous?

le déjeuner lunch	rompre le jeûne to break one's fast
le petit déjeuner breakfast	un jour de jeûne a day of fasting
jeûner to fast	déjeuner sur l'herbe to have a picnic
le jeûne fast, fasting	lunch (on the grass)

Note: The French tend to say **le petit déjeuner** (breakfast), **le déjeuner** (lunch), and **le dîner** (evening meal) or **le souper** (late evening snack). However, in some French-speaking regions such as Québec, the meals one eats during the day are **le déjeuner** (breakfast), **le dîner** (lunch), and **le souper** (supper).

Regular -er verb   to ask (for), to request

The Seven Simple Tenses		The Seven Compound Tenses	
Singular	Plural	Singular	Plural
1 présent de l'indicatif		**8 passé composé**	
demande	demandons	ai demandé	avons demandé
demandes	demandez	as demandé	avez demandé
demande	demandent	a demandé	ont demandé
2 imparfait de l'indicatif		**9 plus-que-parfait de l'indicatif**	
demandais	demandions	avais demandé	avions demandé
demandais	demandiez	avais demandé	aviez demandé
demandait	demandaient	avait demandé	avaient demandé
3 passé simple		**10 passé antérieur**	
demandai	demandâmes	eus demandé	eûmes demandé
demandas	demandâtes	eus demandé	eûtes demandé
demanda	demandèrent	eut demandé	eurent demandé
4 futur		**11 futur antérieur**	
demanderai	demanderons	aurai demandé	aurons demandé
demanderas	demanderez	auras demandé	aurez demandé
demandera	demanderont	aura demandé	auront demandé
5 conditionnel		**12 conditionnel passé**	
demanderais	demanderions	aurais demandé	aurions demandé
demanderais	demanderiez	aurais demandé	auriez demandé
demanderait	demanderaient	aurait demandé	auraient demandé
6 présent du subjonctif		**13 passé du subjonctif**	
demande	demandions	aie demandé	ayons demandé
demandes	demandiez	aies demandé	ayez demandé
demande	demandent	ait demandé	aient demandé
7 imparfait du subjonctif		**14 plus-que-parfait du subjonctif**	
demandasse	demandassions	eusse demandé	eussions demandé
demandasses	demandassiez	eusses demandé	eussiez demandé
demandât	demandassent	eût demandé	eussent demandé

Impératif
demande
demandons
demandez

J'ai demandé à une dame où s'arrête l'autobus. Elle m'a répondu: —Je ne sais pas, monsieur. Demandez à l'agent de police.

une demande a request	**mander** to send word by letter
une demande d'emploi job application	**un mandat** mandate; **un mandat-lettre**
sur demande on request, on application	letter money order; **un mandat-poste**
faire une demande de to apply for	postal money order
se demander to wonder	

demeurer   Part. pr. **demeurant**   Part. passé **demeuré**

to reside, to live, to remain, to stay   Regular -er verb

The Seven Simple Tenses		The Seven Compound Tenses	
Singular	Plural	Singular	Plural
1 présent de l'indicatif		8 passé composé	
demeure	**demeurons**	**ai demeuré**	**avons demeuré**
demeures	**demeurez**	**as demeuré**	**avez demeuré**
demeure	**demeurent**	**a demeuré**	**ont demeuré**
2 imparfait de l'indicatif		9 plus-que-parfait de l'indicatif	
demeurais	**demeurions**	**avais demeuré**	**avions demeuré**
demeurais	**demeuriez**	**avais demeuré**	**aviez demeuré**
demeurait	**demeuraient**	**avait demeuré**	**avaient demeuré**
3 passé simple		10 passé antérieur	
demeurai	**demeurâmes**	**eus demeuré**	**eûmes demeuré**
demeuras	**demeurâtes**	**eus demeuré**	**eûtes demeuré**
demeura	**demeurèrent**	**eut demeuré**	**eurent demeuré**
4 futur		11 futur antérieur	
demeurerai	**demeurerons**	**aurai demeuré**	**aurons demeuré**
demeureras	**demeurerez**	**auras demeuré**	**aurez demeuré**
demeurera	**demeureront**	**aura demeuré**	**auront demeuré**
5 conditionnel		12 conditionnel passé	
demeurerais	**demeurerions**	**aurais demeuré**	**aurions demeuré**
demeurerais	**demeureriez**	**aurais demeuré**	**auriez demeuré**
demeurerait	**demeureraient**	**aurait demeuré**	**auraient demeuré**
6 présent du subjonctif		13 passé du subjonctif	
demeure	**demeurions**	**aie demeuré**	**ayons demeuré**
demeures	**demeuriez**	**aies demeuré**	**ayez demeuré**
demeure	**demeurent**	**ait demeuré**	**aient demeuré**
7 imparfait du subjonctif		14 plus-que-parfait du subjonctif	
demeurasse	**demeurassions**	**eusse demeuré**	**eussions demeuré**
demeurasses	**demeurassiez**	**eusses demeuré**	**eussiez demeuré**
demeurât	**demeurassent**	**eût demeuré**	**eussent demeuré**
		Impératif	
		demeure	
		demeurons	
		demeurez	

—Oú demeurez-vous?

—Je demeure dans un appartement, rue des Jardins.

une demeure dwelling, residence	**demeurer à un hôtel** to stay at a hotel
au demeurant after all	**une mise en demeure** injunction
demeurer couché to stay in bed	**demeurer fidèle** to remain faithful
demeurer court to stop short	

Note: When **demeurer** means "to remain" or "to stay," the auxiliary verb is être.
Marcel est demeuré muet devant les accusations. Marcel remained silent
in the face of the charges.

82

Reflexive regular -er verb   to hurry, to hasten

The Seven Simple Tenses		The Seven Compound Tenses	
Singular	Plural	Singular	Plural
1 présent de l'indicatif		**8 passé composé**	
me dépêche	nous dépêchons	me suis dépêché(e)	nous sommes dépêché(e)s
te dépêches	vous dépêchez	t'es dépêché(e)	vous êtes dépêché(e)(s)
se dépêche	se dépêchent	s'est dépêché(e)	se sont dépêché(e)s
2 imparfait de l'indicatif		**9 plus-que-parfait de l'indicatif**	
me dépêchais	nous dépêchions	m'étais dépêché(e)	nous étions dépêché(e)s
te dépêchais	vous dépêchiez	t'étais dépêché(e)	vous étiez dépêché(e)(s)
se dépêchait	se dépêchaient	s'était dépêché(e)	s'étaient dépêché(e)s
3 passé simple		**10 passé antérieur**	
me dépêchai	nous dépêchâmes	me fus dépêché(e)	nous fûmes dépêché(e)s
te dépêchas	vous dépêchâtes	te fus dépêché(e)	vous fûtes dépêché(e)(s)
se dépêcha	se dépêchèrent	se fut dépêché(e)	se furent dépêché(e)s
4 futur		**11 futur antérieur**	
me dépêcherai	nous dépêcherons	me serai dépêché(e)	nous serons dépêché(e)s
te dépêcheras	vous dépêcherez	te seras dépêché(e)	vous serez dépêché(e)(s)
se dépêchera	se dépêcheront	se sera dépêché(e)	se seront dépêché(e)s
5 conditionnel		**12 conditionnel passé**	
me dépêcherais	nous dépêcherions	me serais dépêché(e)	nous serions dépêché(e)s
te dépêcherais	vous dépêcheriez	te serais dépêché(e)	vous seriez dépêché(e)(s)
se dépêcherait	se dépêcheraient	se serait dépêché(e)	se seraient dépêché(e)s
6 présent du subjonctif		**13 passé du subjonctif**	
me dépêche	nous dépêchions	me sois dépêché(e)	nous soyons dépêché(e)s
te dépêches	vous dépêchiez	te sois dépêché(e)	vous soyez dépêché(e)(s)
se dépêche	se dépêchent	se soit dépêché(e)	se soient dépêché(e)s
7 imparfait du subjonctif		**14 plus-que-parfait du subjonctif**	
me dépêchasse	nous dépêchassions	me fusse dépêché(e)	nous fussions dépêché(e)s
te dépêchasses	vous dépêchassiez	te fusses dépêché(e)	vous fussiez dépêché(e)(s)
se dépêchât	se dépêchassent	se fût dépêché(e)	se fussent dépêché(e)s

Impératif
dépêche-toi; ne te dépêche pas
dépêchons-nous; ne nous dépêchons pas
dépêchez-vous; ne vous dépêchez pas

En me dépêchant pour attraper l'autobus, je suis tombé et je me suis fait mal
au genou. Je me dépêchais de venir chez vous pour vous dire quelque chose de
très important.

une dépêche a telegram,	**se dépêcher de faire quelque chose** to hurry
a dispatch	to do something
dépêcher to dispatch	**Je me dépêche de finir mon travail.** I am
Dépêche-toi! Hurry up!	hurrying to finish my work.

83

to spend (money)   Regular -er verb

The Seven Simple Tenses		The Seven Compound Tenses	
Singular	Plural	Singular	Plural
1 présent de l'indicatif		8 passé composé	
dépense	dépensons	ai dépensé	avons dépensé
dépenses	dépensez	as dépensé	avez dépensé
dépense	dépensent	a dépensé	ont dépensé
2 imparfait de l'indicatif		9 plus-que-parfait de l'indicatif	
dépensais	dépensions	avais dépensé	avions dépensé
dépensais	dépensiez	avais dépensé	aviez dépensé
dépensait	dépensaient	avait dépensé	avaient dépensé
3 passé simple		10 passé antérieur	
dépensai	dépensâmes	eus dépensé	eûmes dépensé
dépensas	dépensâtes	eus dépensé	eûtes dépensé
dépensa	dépensèrent	eut dépensé	eurent dépensé
4 futur		11 futur antérieur	
dépenserai	dépenserons	aurai dépensé	aurons dépensé
dépenseras	dépenserez	auras dépensé	aurez dépensé
dépensera	dépenseront	aura dépensé	auront dépensé
5 conditionnel		12 conditionnel passé	
dépenserais	dépenserions	aurais dépensé	aurions dépensé
dépenserais	dépenseriez	aurais dépensé	auriez dépensé
dépenserait	dépenseraient	aurait dépensé	auraient dépensé
6 présent du subjonctif		13 passé du subjonctif	
dépense	dépensions	aie dépensé	ayons dépensé
dépenses	dépensiez	aies dépensé	ayez dépensé
dépense	dépensent	ait dépensé	aient dépensé
7 imparfait du subjonctif		14 plus-que-parfait du subjonctif	
dépensasse	dépensassions	eusse dépensé	eussions dépensé
dépensasses	dépensassiez	eusses dépensé	eussiez dépensé
dépensât	dépensassent	eût dépensé	eussent dépensé
		Impératif	
		dépense	
		dépensons	
		dépensez	

Mon père m'a dit que je dépense sottement. Je lui ai répondu que je n'ai rien dépensé cette semaine.

dépensier, dépensière   extravagant, unthrifty, spendthrift
dépenser sottement   to spend money foolishly
aux dépens de quelqu'un   at someone's expense
les dépenses du ménage   household expenses

Regular **-er** verb endings: spelling change: retain the   to disturb, to derange
ge before **a** or **o** to keep the soft g sound of the verb.

The Seven Simple Tenses		The Seven Compound Tenses	
Singular	Plural	Singular	Plural
1 présent de l'indicatif		8 passé composé	
dérange	**dérangeons**	**ai dérangé**	**avons dérangé**
déranges	**dérangez**	**as dérangé**	**avez dérangé**
dérange	**dérangent**	**a dérangé**	**ont dérangé**
2 imparfait de l'indicatif		9 plus-que-parfait de l'indicatif	
dérangeais	**dérangions**	**avais dérangé**	**avions dérangé**
dérangeais	**dérangiez**	**avais dérangé**	**aviez dérangé**
dérangeait	**dérangeaient**	**avait dérangé**	**avaient dérangé**
3 passé simple		10 passé antérieur	
dérangeai	**dérangeâmes**	**eus dérangé**	**eûmes dérangé**
dérangeas	**dérangeâtes**	**eus dérangé**	**eûtes dérangé**
dérangea	**dérangèrent**	**eut dérangé**	**eurent dérangé**
4 futur		11 futur antérieur	
dérangerai	**dérangerons**	**aurai dérangé**	**aurons dérangé**
dérangeras	**dérangerez**	**auras dérangé**	**aurez dérangé**
dérangera	**dérangeront**	**aura dérangé**	**auront dérangé**
5 conditionnel		12 conditionnel passé	
dérangerais	**dérangerions**	**aurais dérangé**	**aurions dérangé**
dérangerais	**dérangeriez**	**aurais dérangé**	**auriez dérangé**
dérangerait	**dérangeraient**	**aurait dérangé**	**auraient dérangé**
6 présent du subjonctif		13 passé du subjonctif	
dérange	**dérangions**	**aie dérangé**	**ayons dérangé**
déranges	**dérangiez**	**aies dérangé**	**ayez dérangé**
dérange	**dérangent**	**ait dérangé**	**aient dérangé**
7 imparfait du subjonctif		14 plus-que-parfait du subjonctif	
dérangeasse	**dérangeassions**	**eusse dérangé**	**eussions dérangé**
dérangeasses	**dérangeassiez**	**eusses dérangé**	**eussiez dérangé**
dérangeât	**dérangeassent**	**eût dérangé**	**eussent dérangé**

	Impératif	
dérange	**dérangeons**	**dérangez**

Le professeur:	**Entrez!**
L'élève:	**Excusez-moi, monsieur. Est-ce que je vous dérange?**
Le professeur:	**Non, tu ne me déranges pas. Qu'est-ce que tu veux?**
L'élève:	**Je veux savoir si nous avons un jour de congé demain.**

dérangé, dérangée upset, out of order, broken down
une personne dérangée a deranged person
un dérangement disarrangement, disorder, inconvenience
se déranger to inconvenience oneself
Je vous en prie, ne vous dérangez pas! I beg you (please), don't trouble yourself!
Ne pas déranger Do not disturb

descendre   Part. pr. **descendant**   Part. passé **descendu(e)(s)**

to go down, to descend, to take down, to bring down   Regular -re verb

The Seven Simple Tenses		The Seven Compound Tenses	
Singular	Plural	Singular	Plural
1 présent de l'indicatif		8 passé composé	
descends	**descendons**	**suis descendu(e)**	**sommes descendu(e)s**
descends	**descendez**	**es descendu(e)**	**êtes descendu(e)(s)**
descend	**descendent**	**est descendu(e)**	**sont descendu(e)s**
2 imparfait de l'indicatif		9 plus-que-parfait de l'indicatif	
descendais	**descendions**	**étais descendu(e)**	**étions descendu(e)s**
descendais	**descendiez**	**étais descendu(e)**	**étiez descendu(e)(s)**
descendait	**descendaient**	**était descendu(e)**	**étaient descendu(e)s**
3 passé simple		10 passé antérieur	
descendis	**descendîmes**	**fus descendu(e)**	**fûmes descendu(e)s**
descendis	**descendîtes**	**fus descendu(e)**	**fûtes descendu(e)(s)**
descendit	**descendirent**	**fut descendu(e)**	**furent descendu(e)s**
4 futur		11 futur antérieur	
descendrai	**descendrons**	**serai descendu(e)**	**serons descendu(e)s**
descendras	**descendrez**	**seras descendu(e)**	**serez descendu(e)(s)**
descendra	**descendront**	**sera descendu(e)**	**seront descendu(e)s**
5 conditionnel		12 conditionnel passé	
descendrais	**descendrions**	**serais descendu(e)**	**serions descendu(e)s**
descendrais	**descendriez**	**serais descendu(e)**	**seriez descendu(e)(s)**
descendrait	**descendraient**	**serait descendu(e)**	**seraient descendu(e)s**
6 présent du subjonctif		13 passé du subjonctif	
descende	**descendions**	**sois descendu(e)**	**soyons descendu(e)s**
descendes	**descendiez**	**sois descendu(e)**	**soyez descendu(e)(s)**
descende	**descendent**	**soit descendu(e)**	**soient descendu(e)s**
7 imparfait du subjonctif		14 plus-que-parfait du subjonctif	
descendisse	**descendissions**	**fusse descendu(e)**	**fussions descendu(e)s**
descendisses	**descendissiez**	**fusses descendu(e)**	**fussiez descendu(e)(s)**
descendît	**descendissent**	**fût descendu(e)**	**fussent descendu(e)s**
		Impératif	
		descends	
		descendons	
		descendez	

This verb is conjugated with avoir when it has a direct object.

Examples: **J'ai descendu l'escalier.** I went down the stairs.
              J'ai descendu les valises. I brought down the suitcases.

BUT: **Elle est descendue vite.** She came down quickly.

descendre à un hôtel to stop (stay over) at a hotel
descendre le store to pull down the window shade

See also monter.

Regular -er verb   to desire

The Seven Simple Tenses		The Seven Compound Tenses	
Singular	Plural	Singular	Plural
1 présent de l'indicatif		8 passé composé	
désire	désirons	ai désiré	avons désiré
désires	désirez	as désiré	avez désiré
désire	désirent	a désiré	ont désiré
2 imparfait de l'indicatif		9 plus-que-parfait de l'indicatif	
désirais	désirions	avais désiré	avions désiré
désirais	désiriez	avais désiré	aviez désiré
désirait	désiraient	avait désiré	avaient désiré
3 passé simple		10 passé antérieur	
désirai	désirâmes	eus désiré	eûmes désiré
désiras	désirâtes	eus désiré	eûtes désiré
désira	désirèrent	eut désiré	eurent désiré
4 futur		11 futur antérieur	
désirerai	désirerons	aurai désiré	aurons désiré
désireras	désirerez	auras désiré	aurez désiré
désirera	désireront	aura désiré	auront désiré
5 conditionnel		12 conditionnel passé	
désirerais	désirerions	aurais désiré	aurions désiré
désirerais	désireriez	aurais désiré	auriez désiré
désirerait	désireraient	aurait désiré	auraient désiré
6 présent du subjonctif		13 passé du subjonctif	
désire	désirions	aie désiré	ayons désiré
désires	désiriez	aies désiré	ayez désiré
désire	désirent	ait désiré	aient désiré
7 imparfait du subjonctif		14 plus-que-parfait du subjonctif	
désirasse	désirassions	eusse désiré	eussions désiré
désirasses	désirassiez	eusses désiré	eussiez désiré
désirât	désirassent	eût désiré	eussent désiré
		Impératif	
		désire	
		désirons	
		désirez	

La vendeuse: **Bonjour, monsieur. Vous désirez?**
Le client: **Je désire acheter une cravate.**
La vendeuse: **Bien, monsieur. Vous pouvez choisir. Voici toutes nos cravates.**

un désir desire, wish	**un désir de plaire** a desire to please
désirable desirable	**laisser à désirer** to leave much to be desired
la désirabilité desirability	**Je désire changer de l'argent.**
désireux, désireuse desirous	I would like to exchange some money.
indésirable undesirable	

détester

Part. pr. **détestant** Part. passé **détesté**

to detest, to dislike, to hate

Regular **-er** verb

The Seven Simple Tenses		The Seven Compound Tenses	
Singular	Plural	Singular	Plural
1 présent de l'indicatif		8 passé composé	
déteste	détestons	ai détesté	avons détesté
détestes	détestez	as détesté	avez détesté
déteste	détestent	a détesté	ont détesté
2 imparfait de l'indicatif		9 plus-que-parfait de l'indicatif	
détestais	détestions	avais détesté	avions détesté
détestais	détestiez	avais détesté	aviez détesté
détestait	détestaient	avait détesté	avaient détesté
3 passé simple		10 passé antérieur	
détestai	détestâmes	eus détesté	eûmes détesté
détestas	détestâtes	eus détesté	eûtes détesté
détesta	détestèrent	eut détesté	eurent détesté
4 futur		11 futur antérieur	
détesterai	détesterons	aurai détesté	aurons détesté
détesteras	détesterez	auras détesté	aurez détesté
détestera	détesteront	aura détesté	auront détesté
5 conditionnel		12 conditionnel passé	
détesterais	détesterions	aurais détesté	aurions détesté
détesterais	détesteriez	aurais détesté	auriez détesté
détesterait	détesteraient	aurait détesté	auraient détesté
6 présent du subjonctif		13 passé du subjonctif	
déteste	détestions	aie détesté	ayons détesté
détestes	détestiez	aies détesté	ayez détesté
déteste	détestent	ait détesté	aient détesté
7 imparfait du subjonctif		14 plus-que-parfait du subjonctif	
détestasse	détestassions	eusse détesté	eussions détesté
détestasses	détestassiez	eusses détesté	eussiez détesté
détestât	détestassent	eût détesté	eussent détesté
		Impératif	
		déteste	
		détestons	
		détestez	

Je déteste la médiocrité, je déteste le mensonge, et je déteste la calomnie.
Ce sont des choses détestables.

détestable	loathsome, hateful	Je déteste attendre.	I hate waiting.
détestablement	detestably	d'une manière détestable	in a detestable way

Irregular verb   to destroy

The Seven Simple Tenses		The Seven Compound Tenses	
Singular	Plural	Singular	Plural

1 présent de l'indicatif

détruis	détruisons	
détruis	détruisez	
détruit	détruisent	

8 passé composé

ai détruit	avons détruit
as détruit	avez détruit
a détruit	ont détruit

2 imparfait de l'indicatif

détruisais	détruisions
détruisais	détruisiez
détruisait	détruisaient

9 plus-que-parfait de l'indicatif

avais détruit	avions détruit
avais détruit	aviez détruit
avait détruit	avaient détruit

3 passé simple

détruisis	détruisîmes
détruisis	détruisîtes
détruisit	détruisirent

10 passé antérieur

eus détruit	eûmes détruit
eus détruit	eûtes détruit
eut détruit	eurent détruit

4 futur

détruirai	détruirons
détruiras	détruirez
détruira	détruiront

11 futur antérieur

aurai détruit	aurons détruit
auras détruit	aurez détruit
aura détruit	auront détruit

5 conditionnel

détruirais	détruirions
détruirais	détruiriez
détruirait	détruiraient

12 conditionnel passé

aurais détruit	aurions détruit
aurais détruit	auriez détruit
aurait détruit	auraient détruit

6 présent du subjonctif

détruise	détruisions
détruises	détruisiez
détruise	détruisent

13 passé du subjonctif

aie détruit	ayons détruit
aies détruit	ayez détruit
ait détruit	aient détruit

7 imparfait du subjonctif

détruisisse	détruisissions
détruisisses	détruisissiez
détruisît	détruisissent

14 plus-que-parfait du subjonctif

eusse détruit	eussions détruit
eusses détruit	eussiez détruit
eût détruit	eussent détruit

Impératif
détruis
détruisons
détruisez

---

la destruction destruction
destructif, destructive destructive
la destructivité destructiveness
destructible destructible
se détruire to destroy (to do away with) oneself

destructeur, destructrice *adj.*
  destructive; *n.* destroyer
Les drogues ont détruit sa vie.
  Drugs destroyed his/her life.

devenir Part. pr. **devenant** Part. passé **devenu(e)(s)**

to become   Irregular verb

The Seven Simple Tenses		The Seven Compound Tenses	
Singular	Plural	Singular	Plural
1 présent de l'indicatif		8 passé composé	
deviens	devenons	suis devenu(e)	sommes devenu(e)s
deviens	devenez	es devenu(e)	êtes devenu(e)(s)
devient	deviennent	est devenu(e)	sont devenu(e)s
2 imparfait de l'indicatif		9 plus-que-parfait de l'indicatif	
devenais	devenions	étais devenu(e)	étions devenu(e)s
devenais	deveniez	étais devenu(e)	étiez devenu(e)s
devenait	devenaient	était devenu(e)	étaient devenu(e)s
3 passé simple		10 passé antérieur	
devins	devînmes	fus devenu(e)	fûmes devenu(e)s
devins	devîntes	fus devenu(e)	fûtes devenu(e)(s)
devint	devinrent	fut devenu(e)	furent devenu(e)s
4 futur		11 futur antérieur	
deviendrai	deviendrons	serai devenu(e)	serons devenu(e)s
deviendras	deviendrez	seras devenu(e)	serez devenu(e)(s)
deviendra	deviendront	sera devenu(e)	seront devenu(e)s
5 conditionnel		12 conditionnel passé	
deviendrais	deviendrions	serais devenu(e)	serions devenu(e)s
deviendrais	deviendriez	serais devenu(e)	seriez devenu(e)(s)
deviendrait	deviendraient	serait devenu(e)	seraient devenu(e)s
6 présent du subjonctif		13 passé du subjonctif	
devienne	devenions	sois devenu(e)	soyons devenu(e)s
deviennes	deveniez	sois devenu(e)	soyez devenu(e)(s)
devienne	deviennent	soit devenu(e)	soient devenu(e)s
7 imparfait du subjonctif		14 plus-que-parfait du subjonctif	
devinsse	devinssions	fusse devenu(e)	fussions devenu(e)s
devinsses	devinssiez	fusses devenu(e)	fussiez devenu(e)(s)
devînt	devinssent	fût devenu(e)	fussent devenu(e)s
		Impératif	
		deviens	
		devenons	
		devenez	

J'ai entendu dire que Claudette est devenue docteur. Et vous, qu'est-ce que vous voulez devenir? I heard that Claudette became a doctor. And you, what do you want to become?

devenir fou, devenir folle to go mad, crazy
Qu'est devenue votre sœur? What has become of your sister?

See also **revenir, se souvenir,** and **venir.**

Irregular verb   to have to, must, ought, owe, should

The Seven Simple Tenses		The Seven Compound Tenses	
Singular	Plural	Singular	Plural
1 présent de l'indicatif		8 passé composé	
dois	devons	ai dû	avons dû
dois	devez	as dû	avez dû
doit	doivent	a dû	ont dû
2 imparfait de l'indicatif		9 plus-que-parfait de l'indicatif	
devais	devions	avais dû	avions dû
devais	deviez	avais dû	aviez dû
devait	devaient	avait dû	avaient dû
3 passé simple		10 passé antérieur	
dus	dûmes	eus dû	eûmes dû
dus	dûtes	eus dû	eûtes dû
dut	durent	eut dû	eurent dû
4 futur		11 futur antérieur	
devrai	devrons	aurai dû	aurons dû
devras	devrez	auras dû	aurez dû
devra	devront	aura dû	auront dû
5 conditionnel		12 conditionnel passé	
devrais	devrions	aurais dû	aurions dû
devrais	devriez	aurais dû	auriez dû
devrait	devraient	aurait dû	auraient dû
6 présent du subjonctif		13 passé du subjonctif	
doive	devions	aie dû	ayons dû
doives	deviez	aies dû	ayez dû
doive	doivent	ait dû	aient dû
7 imparfait du subjonctif		14 plus-que-parfait du subjonctif	
dusse	dussions	eusse dû	eussions dû
dusses	dussiez	eusses dû	eussiez dû
dût	dussent	eût dû	eussent dû

Impératif
dois
devons
devez

Combien je vous dois?   How much do I owe you?
Vous me devez cent euros.   You owe me 100 euros.
Avant quelle heure dois-je quitter la chambre?   Before what time must I leave (check out of) the room?

Vous auriez dû venir.   You should have come.
le devoir   duty, obligation
les devoirs   homework
Cette grosse somme d'argent est due lundi.
   This large sum of money is due on Monday.

Mon ami doit arriver demain.
   My friend is (due) to arrive tomorrow.
faire ses devoirs   to do one's homework

dîner	Part. pr. **dînant**	Part. passé **dîné**

to dine, to have dinner

Regular -er verb

The Seven Simple Tenses		The Seven Compound Tenses	
Singular	Plural	Singular	Plural
1 présent de l'indicatif		8 passé composé	
dîne	dînons	ai dîné	avons dîné
dînes	dînez	as dîné	avez dîné
dîne	dînent	a dîné	ont dîné
2 imparfait de l'indicatif		9 plus-que-parfait de l'indicatif	
dînais	dînions	avais dîné	avions dîné
dînais	dîniez	avais dîné	aviez dîné
dînait	dînaient	avait dîné	avaient dîné
3 passé simple		10 passé antérieur	
dînai	dînâmes	eus dîné	eûmes dîné
dînas	dînâtes	eus dîné	eûtes dîné
dîna	dînèrent	eut dîné	eurent dîné
4 futur		11 futur antérieur	
dînerai	dînerons	aurai dîné	aurons dîné
dîneras	dînerez	auras dîné	aurez dîné
dînera	dîneront	aura dîné	auront dîné
5 conditionnel		12 conditionnel passé	
dînerais	dînerions	aurais dîné	aurions dîné
dînerais	dîneriez	aurais dîné	auriez dîné
dînerait	dîneraient	aurait dîné	auraient dîné
6 présent du subjonctif		13 passé du subjonctif	
dîne	dînions	aie dîné	ayons dîné
dînes	dîniez	aies dîné	ayez dîné
dîne	dînent	ait dîné	aient dîné
7 imparfait du subjonctif		14 plus-que-parfait du subjonctif	
dînasse	dînassions	eusse dîné	eussions dîné
dînasses	dînassiez	eusses dîné	eussiez dîné
dînât	dînassent	eût dîné	eussent dîné

Impératif
dîne
dînons
dînez

Lundi j'ai dîné chez des amis. Mardi tu as dîné chez moi. Mercredi nous avons dîné chez Pierre. J'aurais dû dîner seul.

le dîner dinner	un dîneur diner
une dînette child's dinner party	donner un dîner to give a dinner
l'heure du dîner dinner time	dîner en ville to dine out
j'aurais dû I should have	J'aurais dû dîner. I should have had dinner.

Try reading aloud this play on sounds (the letter **d**) as fast as you can:

Denis a dîné du dos d'un dindon dodu.

Dennis dined on (ate) the back of a plump turkey.

Note: The Académie française now allows **dîner** and related words to be spelled without the circumflex accent (^): **diner**.

Part. pr. **disant**　　　Part. passé **dit**　　　**dire**

Irregular verb　　　　　　　　　　　　　to say, to tell

The Seven Simple Tenses		The Seven Compound Tenses	
Singular	Plural	Singular	Plural
1 présent de l'indicatif		8 passé composé	
dis	**disons**	**ai dit**	**avons dit**
dis	**dites**	**as dit**	**avez dit**
dit	**disent**	**a dit**	**ont dit**
2 imparfait de l'indicatif		9 plus-que-parfait de l'indicatif	
disais	**disions**	**avais dit**	**avions dit**
disais	**disiez**	**avais dit**	**aviez dit**
disait	**disaient**	**avait dit**	**avaient dit**
3 passé simple		10 passé antérieur	
dis	**dîmes**	**eus dit**	**eûmes dit**
dis	**dîtes**	**eus dit**	**eûtes dit**
dit	**dirent**	**eut dit**	**eurent dit**
4 futur		11 futur antérieur	
dirai	**dirons**	**aurai dit**	**aurons dit**
diras	**direz**	**auras dit**	**aurez dit**
dira	**diront**	**aura dit**	**auront dit**
5 conditionnel		12 conditionnel passé	
dirais	**dirions**	**aurais dit**	**aurions dit**
dirais	**diriez**	**aurais dit**	**auriez dit**
dirait	**diraient**	**aurait dit**	**auraient dit**
6 présent du subjonctif		13 passé du subjonctif	
dise	**disions**	**aie dit**	**ayons dit**
dises	**disiez**	**aies dit**	**ayez dit**
dise	**disent**	**ait dit**	**aient dit**
7 imparfait du subjonctif		14 plus-que-parfait du subjonctif	
disse	**dissions**	**eusse dit**	**eussions dit**
disses	**dissiez**	**eusses dit**	**eussiez dit**
dît	**dissent**	**eût dit**	**eussent dit**
		Impératif	
		dis	
		disons	
		dites	

Cela va sans dire.　That goes without saying.
Cela me dit qqch.　That rings a bell.

c'est-à-dire that is, that is to say	**Que voulez-vous dire?** What do you mean?
entendre dire que to hear it said that	**Comment dit-on** *je vous aime* **en anglais?** How does one say *I love you* in English?
vouloir dire to mean	**contredire** to contradict
dire du bien de to speak well of	**aussitôt dit, aussitôt fait** no sooner said than done

donner	Part. pr. donnant	Part. passé donné
to give		Regular -er verb

The Seven Simple Tenses		The Seven Compound Tenses	
Singular	Plural	Singular	Plural
1 présent de l'indicatif		**8 passé composé**	
donne	donnons	ai donné	avons donné
donnes	donnez	as donné	avez donné
donne	donnent	a donné	ont donné
2 imparfait de l'indicatif		**9 plus-que-parfait de l'indicatif**	
donnais	donnions	avais donné	avions donné
donnais	donniez	avais donné	aviez donné
donnait	donnaient	avait donné	avaient donné
3 passé simple		**10 passé antérieur**	
donnai	donnâmes	eus donné	eûmes donné
donnas	donnâtes	eus donné	eûtes donné
donna	donnèrent	eut donné	eurent donné
4 futur		**11 futur antérieur**	
donnerai	donnerons	aurai donné	aurons donné
donneras	donnerez	auras donné	aurez donné
donnera	donneront	aura donné	auront donné
5 conditionnel		**12 conditionnel passé**	
donnerais	donnerions	aurais donné	aurions donné
donnerais	donneriez	aurais donné	auriez donné
donnerait	donneraient	aurait donné	auraient donné
6 présent du subjonctif		**13 passé du subjonctif**	
donne	donnions	aie donné	ayons donné
donnes	donniez	aies donné	ayez donné
donne	donnent	ait donné	aient donné
7 imparfait du subjonctif		**14 plus-que-parfait du subjonctif**	
donnasse	donnassions	eusse donné	eussions donné
donnasses	donnassiez	eusses donné	eussiez donné
donnât	donnassent	eût donné	eussent donné

	Impératif
	donne
	donnons
	donnez

Ce qui est donné est donné. What is given is given. (Never take back what you have given.)

La façon de donner vaut mieux que ce qu'on donne. (Corneille) The way you give is worth more than what you give.

donner rendez-vous à qqn to make an appointment (a date) with someone
donner sur to look out upon: La salle à manger donne sur un joli jardin. The dining room looks out upon (faces) a pretty garden.

donner congé à to grant leave to
abandonner to abandon; **ordonner** to order; **pardonner** to pardon
donner à manger à qqn to give someone something to eat
une base de données database (computer)

Irregular verb   to sleep

The Seven Simple Tenses		The Seven Compound Tenses	
Singular	Plural	Singular	Plural
1 présent de l'indicatif		**8 passé composé**	
dors	**dormons**	**ai dormi**	**avons dormi**
dors	**dormez**	**as dormi**	**avez dormi**
dort	**dorment**	**a dormi**	**ont dormi**
2 imparfait de l'indicatif		**9 plus-que-parfait de l'indicatif**	
dormais	**dormions**	**avais dormi**	**avions dormi**
dormais	**dormiez**	**avais dormi**	**aviez dormi**
dormait	**dormaient**	**avait dormi**	**avaient dormi**
3 passé simple		**10 passé antérieur**	
dormis	**dormîmes**	**eus dormi**	**eûmes dormi**
dormis	**dormîtes**	**eus dormi**	**eûtes dormi**
dormit	**dormirent**	**eut dormi**	**eurent dormi**
4 futur		**11 futur antérieur**	
dormirai	**dormirons**	**aurai dormi**	**aurons dormi**
dormiras	**dormirez**	**auras dormi**	**aurez dormi**
dormira	**dormiront**	**aura dormi**	**auront dormi**
5 conditionnel		**12 conditionnel passé**	
dormirais	**dormirions**	**aurais dormi**	**aurions dormi**
dormirais	**dormiriez**	**aurais dormi**	**auriez dormi**
dormirait	**dormiraient**	**aurait dormi**	**auraient dormi**
6 présent du subjonctif		**13 passé du subjonctif**	
dorme	**dormions**	**aie dormi**	**ayons dormi**
dormes	**dormiez**	**aies dormi**	**ayez dormi**
dorme	**dorment**	**ait dormi**	**aient dormi**
7 imparfait du subjonctif		**14 plus-que-parfait du subjonctif**	
dormisse	**dormissions**	**eusse dormi**	**eussions dormi**
dormisses	**dormissiez**	**eusses dormi**	**eussiez dormi**
dormît	**dormissent**	**eût dormi**	**eussent dormi**

Impératif
dors
dormons
dormez

---

dormir toute la nuit   to sleep through the night
parler en dormant   to talk in one's sleep
empêcher de dormir   to keep from sleeping
la dormition   dormition (falling asleep)
le dortoir   dormitory
dormir à la belle étoile   to sleep outdoors
dormir sur les deux oreilles   to sleep soundly

endormir   to put to sleep
s'endormir   to fall asleep
     (helping verb **être**)
As-tu bien dormi, chéri(e)?
     Did you sleep well, darling?

95

douter	Part. pr. **doutant**	Part. passé **douté**

to doubt   Regular -er verb

The Seven Simple Tenses	The Seven Compound Tenses

Singular	Plural	Singular	Plural
1 présent de l'indicatif		8 passé composé	
doute	doutons	ai douté	avons douté
doutes	doutez	as douté	avez douté
doute	doutent	a douté	ont douté
2 imparfait de l'indicatif		9 plus-que-parfait de l'indicatif	
doutais	doutions	avais douté	avions douté
doutais	doutiez	avais douté	aviez douté
doutait	doutaient	avait douté	avaient douté
3 passé simple		10 passé antérieur	
doutai	doutâmes	eus douté	eûmes douté
doutas	doutâtes	eus douté	eûtes douté
douta	doutèrent	eut douté	eurent douté
4 futur		11 futur antérieur	
douterai	douterons	aurai douté	aurons douté
douteras	douterez	auras douté	aurez douté
doutera	douteront	aura douté	auront douté
5 conditionnel		12 conditionnel passé	
douterais	douterions	aurais douté	aurions douté
douterais	douteriez	aurais douté	auriez douté
douterait	douteraient	aurait douté	auraient douté
6 présent du subjonctif		13 passé du subjonctif	
doute	doutions	aie douté	ayons douté
doutes	doutiez	aies douté	ayez douté
doute	doutent	ait douté	aient douté
7 imparfait du subjonctif		14 plus-que-parfait du subjonctif	
doutasse	doutassions	eusse douté	eussions douté
doutasses	doutassiez	eusses douté	eussiez douté
doutât	doutassent	eût douté	eussent douté

Impératif
doute
doutons
doutez

Je doute que cet homme soit coupable. Il n'y a pas de doute qu'il est innocent.
I doubt that this man is guilty. There is no doubt that he is innocent.

le doute doubt	ne douter de rien to doubt nothing,
sans doute no doubt	to be too credulous
sans aucun doute undoubtedly	ne se douter de rien to suspect nothing
d'un air de doute dubiously	se douter de to suspect
redouter to dread, to fear	douteux, douteuse doubtful

Part. pr. **écoutant**   Part. passé **écouté**   **écouter**

Regular -er verb   to listen (to)

The Seven Simple Tenses		The Seven Compound Tenses	
Singular	Plural	Singular	Plural
1 présent de l'indicatif		8 passé composé	
écoute	écoutons	ai écouté	avons écouté
écoutes	écoutez	as écouté	avez écouté
écoute	écoutent	a écouté	ont écouté
2 imparfait de l'indicatif		9 plus-que-parfait de l'indicatif	
écoutais	écoutions	avais écouté	avions écouté
écoutais	écoutiez	avais écouté	aviez écouté
écoutait	écoutaient	avait écouté	avaient écouté
3 passé simple		10 passé antérieur	
écoutai	écoutâmes	eus écouté	eûmes écouté
écoutas	écoutâtes	eus écouté	eûtes écouté
écouta	écoutèrent	eut écouté	eurent écouté
4 futur		11 futur antérieur	
écouterai	écouterons	aurai écouté	aurons écouté
écouteras	écouterez	auras écouté	aurez écouté
écoutera	écouteront	aura écouté	auront écouté
5 conditionnel		12 conditionnel passé	
écouterais	écouterions	aurais écouté	aurions écouté
écouterais	écouteriez	aurais écouté	auriez écouté
écouterait	écouteraient	aurait écouté	auraient écouté
6 présent du subjonctif		13 passé du subjonctif	
écoute	écoutions	aie écouté	ayons écouté
écoutes	écoutiez	aies écouté	ayez écouté
écoute	écoutent	ait écouté	aient écouté
7 imparfait du subjonctif		14 plus-que-parfait du subjonctif	
écoutasse	écoutassions	eusse écouté	eussions écouté
écoutasses	écoutassiez	eusses écouté	eussiez écouté
écoutât	écoutassent	eût écouté	eussent écouté

Impératif
écoute
écoutons
écoutez

Écoutez-moi.   Listen to me.
Je vous écoute.   I'm listening to you.

aimer à s'écouter parler   to love to hear one's own voice
un écouteur   telephone receiver (ear piece)
être à l'écoute   to be listening in
n'écouter personne   not to heed anyone
savoir écouter   to be a good listener
écouter aux portes   to eavesdrop, to listen secretly

to write   Irregular verb

The Seven Simple Tenses		The Seven Compound Tenses	
Singular	Plural	Singular	Plural
1 présent de l'indicatif		8 passé composé	
écris	écrivons	ai écrit	avons écrit
écris	écrivez	as écrit	avez écrit
écrit	écrivent	a écrit	ont écrit
2 imparfait de l'indicatif		9 plus-que-parfait de l'indicatif	
écrivais	écrivions	avais écrit	avions écrit
écrivais	écriviez	avais écrit	aviez écrit
écrivait	écrivaient	avait écrit	avaient écrit
3 passé simple		10 passé antérieur	
écrivis	écrivîmes	eus écrit	eûmes écrit
écrivis	écrivîtes	eus écrit	eûtes écrit
écrivit	écrivirent	eut écrit	eurent écrit
4 futur		11 futur antérieur	
écrirai	écrirons	aurai écrit	aurons écrit
écriras	écrirez	auras écrit	aurez écrit
écrira	écriront	aura écrit	auront écrit
5 conditionnel		12 conditionnel passé	
écrirais	écririons	aurais écrit	aurions écrit
écrirais	écririez	aurais écrit	auriez écrit
écrirait	écriraient	aurait écrit	auraient écrit
6 présent du subjonctif		13 passé du subjonctif	
écrive	écrivions	aie écrit	ayons écrit
écrives	écriviez	aies écrit	ayez écrit
écrive	écrivent	ait écrit	aient écrit
7 imparfait du subjonctif		14 plus-que-parfait du subjonctif	
écrivisse	écrivissions	eusse écrit	eussions écrit
écrivisses	écrivissiez	eusses écrit	eussiez écrit
écrivît	écrivissent	eût écrit	eussent écrit

Impératif
écris
écrivons
écrivez

Jean: **As-tu écrit ta composition pour la classe de français?**   Did you write your composition for French class?

Jacques: **Non, je ne l'ai pas écrite.**   No, I didn't write it.

Jean: **Écris-la tout de suite!**   Write it right away!

un écrivain writer; **une femme écrivain** woman writer; **une écrivaine** (Québec) female writer
écriture *f.* handwriting, writing

écrire un petit mot à qqn to write a note to someone
par écrit in writing

See also **décrire**.

to frighten

Regular -er verb endings: spelling change: -ayer verbs
may change y to i in front of a mute e or may keep y.

The Seven Simple Tenses		The Seven Compound Tenses	
Singular	Plural	Singular	Plural
1 présent de l'indicatif		8 passé composé	
effraye	effrayons	ai effrayé	avons effrayé
effrayes	effrayez	as effrayé	avez effrayé
effraye	effrayent	a effrayé	ont effrayé
2 imparfait de l'indicatif		9 plus-que-parfait de l'indicatif	
effrayais	effrayions	avais effrayé	avions effrayé
effrayais	effrayiez	avais effrayé	aviez effrayé
effrayait	effrayaient	avait effrayé	avaient effrayé
3 passé simple		10 passé antérieur	
effrayai	effrayâmes	eus effrayé	eûmes effrayé
effrayas	effrayâtes	eus effrayé	eûtes effrayé
effraya	effrayèrent	eut effrayé	eurent effrayé
4 futur		11 futur antérieur	
effrayerai	effrayerons	aurai effrayé	aurons effrayé
effrayeras	effrayerez	auras effrayé	aurez effrayé
effrayera	effrayeront	aura effrayé	auront effrayé
5 conditionnel		12 conditionnel passé	
effrayerais	effrayerions	aurais effrayé	aurions effrayé
effrayerais	effrayeriez	aurais effrayé	auriez effrayé
effrayerait	effrayeraient	aurait effrayé	auraient effrayé
6 présent du subjonctif		13 passé du subjonctif	
effraye	effrayions	aie effrayé	ayons effrayé
effrayes	effrayiez	aies effrayé	ayez effrayé
effraye	effrayent	ait effrayé	aient effrayé
7 imparfait du subjonctif		14 plus-que-parfait du subjonctif	
effrayasse	effrayassions	eusse effrayé	eussions effrayé
effrayasses	effrayassiez	eusses effrayé	eussiez effrayé
effrayât	effrayassent	eût effrayé	eussent effrayé

Impératif
effraye
effrayons
effrayez

Le tigre a effrayé l'enfant. L'enfant a effrayé le singe. Le singe effrayera le
bébé. C'est effrayant!

effrayant, effrayante frightful, awful   effroyable dreadful, fearful
effrayé, effrayée frightened   effroyablement dreadfully, fearfully

égayer   Part. pr. égayant   Part. passé égayé

to amuse, to cheer up, to enliven, to entertain	Regular -er verb endings: spelling change: -ayer verbs may change y to i in front of a mute e or may keep y.

The Seven Simple Tenses		The Seven Compound Tenses	
Singular	Plural	Singular	Plural
1 présent de l'indicatif		**8 · passé composé**	
égaye	égayons	ai égayé	avons égayé
égayes	égayez	as égayé	avez égayé
égaye	égayent	a égayé	ont égayé
2 imparfait de l'indicatif		**9 plus-que-parfait de l'indicatif**	
égayais	égayions	avais égayé	avions égayé
égayais	égayiez	avais égayé	aviez égayé
égayait	égayaient	avait égayé	avaient égayé
3 passé simple		**10 passé antérieur**	
égayai	égayâmes	eus égayé	eûmes égayé
égayas	égayâtes	eus égayé	eûtes égayé
égaya	égayèrent	eut égayé	eurent égayé
4 futur		**11 futur antérieur**	
égayerai	égayerons	aurai égayé	aurons égayé
égayeras	égayerez	auras égayé	aurez égayé
égayera	égayeront	aura égayé	auront égayé
5 conditionnel		**12 conditionnel passé**	
égayerais	égayerions	aurais égayé	aurions égayé
égayerais	égayeriez	aurais égayé	auriez égayé
égayerait	égayeraient	aurait égayé	auraient égayé
6 présent du subjonctif		**13 passé du subjonctif**	
égaye	égayions	aie égayé	ayons égayé
égayes	égayiez	aies égayé	ayez égayé
égaye	égayent	ait égayé	aient égayé
7 imparfait du subjonctif		**14 plus-que-parfait du subjonctif**	
égayasse	égayassions	eusse égayé	eussions égayé
égayasses	égayassiez	eusses égayé	eussiez égayé
égayât	égayassent	eût égayé	eussent égayé

	Impératif
	égaye
	égayons
	égayez

égayant, égayante   lively
s'égayer aux dépens de   to make fun of
gai, gaie   gay, cheerful, merry
gaiement   gaily, cheerfully

Regular -er verb   to kiss, to embrace

The Seven Simple Tenses		The Seven Compound Tenses	
Singular	Plural	Singular	Plural

1 présent de l'indicatif

embrasse	**embrassons**		
embrasses	**embrassez**		
embrasse	**embrassent**		

8 passé composé

ai embrassé	**avons embrassé**		
as embrassé	**avez embrassé**		
a embrassé	**ont embrassé**		

2 imparfait de l'indicatif

embrassais	**embrassions**
embrassais	**embrassiez**
embrassait	**embrassaient**

9 plus-que-parfait de l'indicatif

avais embrassé	**avions embrassé**
avais embrassé	**aviez embrassé**
avait embrassé	**avaient embrassé**

3 passé simple

embrassai	**embrassâmes**
embrassas	**embrassâtes**
embrassa	**embrassèrent**

10 passé antérieur

eus embrassé	**eûmes embrassé**
eus embrassé	**eûtes embrassé**
eut embrassé	**eurent embrassé**

4 futur

embrasserai	**embrasserons**
embrasseras	**embrasserez**
embrassera	**embrasseront**

11 futur antérieur

aurai embrassé	**aurons embrassé**
auras embrassé	**aurez embrassé**
aura embrassé	**auront embrassé**

5 conditionnel

embrasserais	**embrasserions**
embrasserais	**embrasseriez**
embrasserait	**embrasseraient**

12 conditionnel passé

aurais embrassé	**aurions embrassé**
aurais embrassé	**auriez embrassé**
aurait embrassé	**auraient embrassé**

6 présent du subjonctif

embrasse	**embrassions**
embrasses	**embrassiez**
embrasse	**embrassent**

13 passé du subjonctif

aie embrassé	**ayons embrassé**
aies embrassé	**ayez embrassé**
ait embrassé	**aient embrassé**

7 imparfait du subjonctif

embrassasse	**embrassassions**
embrassasses	**embrassassiez**
embrassât	**embrassassent**

14 plus-que-parfait du subjonctif

eusse embrassé	**eussions embrassé**
eusses embrassé	**eussiez embrassé**
eût embrassé	**eussent embrassé**

Impératif
embrasse
embrassons
embrassez

—Embrasse-moi. Je t'aime. Ne me laisse pas.
—Je t'embrasse. Je t'aime aussi. Je ne te laisse pas. Embrassons-nous.

le bras   arm
un embrassement   embracement, embrace
s'embrasser   to embrace each other, to hug each other

emmener

Part. pr. emmenant   **Part. passé emmené**

to lead, to lead away,
to take away (persons)

Regular -er verb endings: spelling change:
e changes to è before syllable with mute e.

The Seven Simple Tenses		The Seven Compound Tenses	
Singular	Plural	Singular	Plural
1 présent de l'indicatif		**8 passé composé**	
emmène	emmenons	ai emmené	avons emmené
emmènes	emmenez	as emmené	avez emmené
emmène	emmènent	a emmené	ont emmené
2 imparfait de l'indicatif		**9 plus-que-parfait de l'indicatif**	
emmenais	emmenions	avais emmené	avions emmené
emmenais	emmeniez	avais emmené	aviez emmené
emmenait	emmenaient	avait emmené	avaient emmené
3 passé simple		**10 passé antérieur**	
emmenai	emmenâmes	eus emmené	eûmes emmené
emmenas	emmenâtes	eus emmené	eûtes emmené
emmena	emmenèrent	eut emmené	eurent emmené
4 futur		**11 futur antérieur**	
emmènerai	emmènerons	aurai emmené	aurons emmené
emmèneras	emmènerez	auras emmené	aurez emmené
emmènera	emmèneront	aura emmené	auront emmené
5 conditionnel		**12 conditionnel passé**	
emmènerais	emmènerions	aurais emmené	aurions emmené
emmènerais	emmèneriez	aurais emmené	auriez emmené
emmènerait	emmèneraient	aurait emmené	auraient emmené
6 présent du subjonctif		**13 passé du subjonctif**	
emmène	emmenions	aie emmené	ayons emmené
emmènes	emmeniez	aies emmené	ayez emmené
emmène	emmènent	ait emmené	aient emmené
7 imparfait du subjonctif		**14 plus-que-parfait du subjonctif**	
emmenasse	emmenassions	eusse emmené	eussions emmené
emmenasses	emmenassiez	eusses emmené	eussiez emmené
emmenât	emmenassent	eût emmené	eussent emmené
		Impératif	
		emmène	
		emmenons	
		emmenez	

Quand j'emmène une personne d'un lieu dans un autre, je mène cette personne avec moi. Mon père nous emmènera au cinéma lundi prochain. Samedi dernier il nous a emmenés au théâtre.

Le train m'a emmené à Paris.   The train took me to Paris.
Un agent de police a emmené l'assassin.   A policeman took away the assassin.

See also mener.

Part. pr. **empêchant**   Part. passé **empêché**   **empêcher**

Regular -er verb   to hinder, to prevent

The Seven Simple Tenses		The Seven Compound Tenses	
Singular	Plural	Singular	Plural
1 présent de l'indicatif		**8 passé composé**	
empêche	empêchons	ai empêché	avons empêché
empêches	empêchez	as empêché	avez empêché
empêche	empêchent	a empêché	ont empêché
2 imparfait de l'indicatif		**9 plus-que-parfait de l'indicatif**	
empêchais	empêchions	avais empêché	avions empêché
empêchais	empêchiez	avais empêché	aviez empêché
empêchait	empêchaient	avait empêché	avaient empêché
3 passé simple		**10 passé antérieur**	
empêchai	empêchâmes	eus empêché	eûmes empêché
empêchas	empêchâtes	eus empêché	eûtes empêché
empêcha	empêchèrent	eut empêché	eurent empêché
4 futur		**11 futur antérieur**	
empêcherai	empêcherons	aurai empêché	aurons empêché
empêcheras	empêcherez	auras empêché	aurez empêché
empêchera	empêcheront	aura empêché	auront empêché
5 conditionnel		**12 conditionnel passé**	
empêcherais	empêcherions	aurais empêché	aurions empêché
empêcherais	empêcheriez	aurais empêché	auriez empêché
empêcherait	empêcheraient	aurait empêché	auraient empêché
6 présent du subjonctif		**13 passé du subjonctif**	
empêche	empêchions	aie empêché	ayons empêché
empêches	empêchiez	aies empêché	ayez empêché
empêche	empêchent	ait empêché	aient empêché
7 imparfait du subjonctif		**14 plus-que-parfait du subjonctif**	
empêchasse	empêchassions	eusse empêché	eussions empêché
empêchasses	empêchassiez	eusses empêché	eussiez empêché
empêchât	empêchassent	eût empêché	eussent empêché

Impératif
empêche
empêchons
empêchez

Georgette a empêché son frère de finir ses devoirs parce qu'elle regardait la télé en même temps. Le bruit était un vrai empêchement.

un empêchement   impediment, hindrance
en cas d'empêchement   in case of prevention
empêcher qqn de faire qqch   to prevent someone from doing something
empêcher d'entrer   to keep from entering
s'empêcher de faire qqch   to refrain from doing something

to use, to employ | Regular -er verb endings: spelling change: -oyer verbs must change y to **i** in front of a mute **e**.

The Seven Simple Tenses		The Seven Compound Tenses	
Singular	Plural	Singular	Plural
1 présent de l'indicatif		**8 passé composé**	
emploie	employons	ai employé	avons employé
emploies	employez	as employé	avez employé
emploie	emploient	a employé	ont employé
2 imparfait de l'indicatif		**9 plus-que-parfait de l'indicatif**	
employais	employions	avais employé	avions employé
employais	employiez	avais employé	aviez employé
employait	employaient	avait employé	avaient employé
3 passé simple		**10 passé antérieur**	
employai	employâmes	eus employé	eûmes employé
employas	employâtes	eus employé	eûtes employé
employa	employèrent	eut employé	eurent employé
4 futur		**11 futur antérieur**	
emploierai	emploierons	aurai employé	aurons employé
emploieras	emploierez	auras employé	aurez employé
emploiera	emploieront	aura employé	auront employé
5 conditionnel		**12 conditionnel passé**	
emploierais	emploierions	aurais employé	aurions employé
emploierais	emploieriez	aurais employé	auriez employé
emploierait	emploieraient	aurait employé	auraient employé
6 présent du subjonctif		**13 passé du subjonctif**	
emploie	employions	aie employé	ayons employé
emploies	employiez	aies employé	ayez employé
emploie	emploient	ait employé	aient employé
7 imparfait du subjonctif		**14 plus-que-parfait du subjonctif**	
employasse	employassions	eusse employé	eussions employé
employasses	employassiez	eusses employé	eussiez employé
employât	employassent	eût employé	eussent employé

Impératif
emploie
employons
employez

---

un employé, une employée   employee
un employeur, une employeuse   employer
sans emploi   jobless
un emploi   employment
une demande d'emploi   job application

s'employer à faire qqch   to occupy oneself doing something
employer son temps   to spend one's time

Regular -er verb   to borrow

The Seven Simple Tenses		The Seven Compound Tenses	
Singular	Plural	Singular	Plural
1 présent de l'indicatif		8 passé composé	
emprunte	**empruntons**	**ai emprunté**	**avons emprunté**
empruntes	**empruntez**	**as emprunté**	**avez emprunté**
emprunte	**empruntent**	**a emprunté**	**ont emprunté**
2 imparfait de l'indicatif		9 plus-que-parfait de l'indicatif	
empruntais	**empruntions**	**avais emprunté**	**avions emprunté**
empruntais	**empruntiez**	**avais emprunté**	**aviez emprunté**
empruntait	**empruntaient**	**avait emprunté**	**avaient emprunté**
3 passé simple		10 passé antérieur	
empruntai	**empruntâmes**	**eus emprunté**	**eûmes emprunté**
empruntas	**empruntâtes**	**eus emprunté**	**eûtes emprunté**
emprunta	**empruntèrent**	**eut emprunté**	**eurent emprunté**
4 futur		11 futur antérieur	
emprunterai	**emprunterons**	**aurai emprunté**	**aurons emprunté**
emprunteras	**emprunterez**	**auras emprunté**	**aurez emprunté**
empruntera	**emprunteront**	**aura emprunté**	**auront emprunté**
5 conditionnel		12 conditionnel passé	
emprunterais	**emprunterions**	**aurais emprunté**	**aurions emprunté**
emprunterais	**emprunteriez**	**aurais emprunté**	**auriez emprunté**
emprunterait	**emprunteraient**	**aurait emprunté**	**auraient emprunté**
6 présent du subjonctif		13 passé du subjonctif	
emprunte	**empruntions**	**aie emprunté**	**ayons emprunté**
empruntes	**empruntiez**	**aies emprunté**	**ayez emprunté**
emprunte	**empruntent**	**ait emprunté**	**aient emprunté**
7 imparfait du subjonctif		14 plus-que-parfait du subjonctif	
empruntasse	**empruntassions**	**eusse emprunté**	**eussions emprunté**
empruntasses	**empruntassiez**	**eusses emprunté**	**eussiez emprunté**
empruntât	**empruntassent**	**eût emprunté**	**eussent emprunté**

Impératif
emprunte
empruntons
empruntez

---

emprunteur, emprunteuse   a person who makes a habit of borrowing
un emprunt   loan, borrowing
emprunter qqch à qqn   to borrow something from someone
   Monsieur Leblanc a emprunté de l'argent à mon père.   Mr. Leblanc borrowed
   some money from my father.

Note: Don't confuse **emprunter** with **prêter** (to lend)

enlever	Part. pr. **enlevant**	Part. passé **enlevé**

to carry away, to take away, to remove	Regular -er verb endings: spelling change: e changes to è before syllable with mute e.

The Seven Simple Tenses		The Seven Compound Tenses	
Singular	Plural	Singular	Plural

1 présent de l'indicatif		8 passé composé	
enlève	enlevons	ai enlevé	avons enlevé
enlèves	enlevez	as enlevé	avez enlevé
enlève	enlèvent	a enlevé	ont enlevé

2 imparfait de l'indicatif		9 plus-que-parfait de l'indicatif	
enlevais	enlevions	avais enlevé	avions enlevé
enlevais	enleviez	avais enlevé	aviez enlevé
enlevait	enlevaient	avait enlevé	avaient enlevé

3 passé simple		10 passé antérieur	
enlevai	enlevâmes	eus enlevé	eûmes enlevé
enlevas	enlevâtes	eus enlevé	eûtes enlevé
enleva	enlevèrent	eut enlevé	eurent enlevé

4 futur		11 futur antérieur	
enlèverai	enlèverons	aurai enlevé	aurons enlevé
enlèveras	enlèverez	auras enlevé	aurez enlevé
enlèvera	enlèveront	aura enlevé	auront enlevé

5 conditionnel		12 conditionnel passé	
enlèverais	enlèverions	aurais enlevé	aurions enlevé
enlèverais	enlèveriez	aurais enlevé	auriez enlevé
enlèverait	enlèveraient	aurait enlevé	auraient enlevé

6 présent du subjonctif		13 passé du subjonctif	
enlève	enlevions	aie enlevé	ayons enlevé
enlèves	enleviez	aies enlevé	ayez enlevé
enlève	enlèvent	ait enlevé	aient enlevé

7 imparfait du subjonctif		14 plus-que-parfait du subjonctif	
enlevasse	enlevassions	eusse enlevé	eussions enlevé
enlevasses	enlevassiez	eusses enlevé	eussiez enlevé
enlevât	enlevassent	eût enlevé	eussent enlevé

	Impératif
	enlève
	enlevons
	enlevez

Madame Dubac est entrée dans sa maison. Elle a enlevé son chapeau, son manteau et ses gants. Puis, elle est allée directement au salon pour enlever une chaise et la mettre dans la salle à manger. Après cela, elle a enlevé les ordures.

enlever les ordures   to take the garbage out
un enlèvement   lifting, carrying off, removal
enlèvement d'un enfant   baby snatching, kidnapping
un enlevage   spurt (sports)

Regular -er verb endings: spelling change: -uyer   **to bore, to annoy, to weary**
verbs must change y to i in front of mute e.

The Seven Simple Tenses		The Seven Compound Tenses	
Singular	Plural	Singular	Plural
1 présent de l'indicatif		8 passé composé	
ennuie	ennuyons	ai ennuyé	avons ennuyé
ennuies	ennuyez	as ennuyé	avez ennuyé
ennuie	ennuient	a ennuyé	ont ennuyé
2 imparfait de l'indicatif		9 plus-que-parfait de l'indicatif	
ennuyais	ennuyions	avais ennuyé	avions ennuyé
ennuyais	ennuyiez	avais ennuyé	aviez ennuyé
ennuyait	ennuyaient	avait ennuyé	avaient ennuyé
3 passé simple		10 passé antérieur	
ennuyai	ennuyâmes	eus ennuyé	eûmes ennuyé
ennuyas	ennuyâtes	eus ennuyé	eûtes ennuyé
ennuya	ennuyèrent	eut ennuyé	eurent ennuyé
4 futur		11 futur antérieur	
ennuierai	ennuierons	aurai ennuyé	aurons ennuyé
ennuieras	ennuierez	auras ennuyé	aurez ennuyé
ennuiera	ennuieront	aura ennuyé	auront ennuyé
5 conditionnel		12 conditionnel passé	
ennuierais	ennuierions	aurais ennuyé	aurions ennuyé
ennuierais	ennuieriez	aurais ennuyé	auriez ennuyé
ennuierait	ennuieraient	aurait ennuyé	auraient ennuyé
6 présent du subjonctif		13 passé du subjonctif	
ennuie	ennuyions	aie ennuyé	ayons ennuyé
ennuies	ennuyiez	aies ennuyé	ayez ennuyé
ennuie	ennuient	ait ennuyé	aient ennuyé
7 imparfait du subjonctif		14 plus-que-parfait du subjonctif	
ennuyasse	ennuyassions	eusse ennuyé	eussions ennuyé
ennuyasses	ennuyassiez	eusses ennuyé	eussiez ennuyé
ennuyât	ennuyassent	eût ennuyé	eussent ennuyé
		Impératif	
		ennuie	
		ennuyons	
		ennuyez	

—Est-ce que je vous ennuie?   Am I boring you?
—Oui, vous m'ennuyez. Allez-vous en!   Yes, you're boring me. Go away!

un ennui weariness, boredom, ennui	**mourir d'ennui** to be bored to tears
des ennuis worries, troubles	**s'ennuyer** to become bored, to get bored
ennuyeux, ennuyeuse boring	**Quel ennui!** What a nuisance!

enseigner	Part. pr. **enseignant**	Part. passé **enseigné**

to teach

The Seven Simple Tenses		The Seven Compound Tenses	
Singular	Plural	Singular	Plural
1 présent de l'indicatif		8 passé composé	
enseigne	**enseignons**	**ai enseigné**	**avons enseigné**
enseignes	**enseignez**	**as enseigné**	**avez enseigné**
enseigne	**enseignent**	**a enseigné**	**ont enseigné**
2 imparfait de l'indicatif		9 plus-que-parfait de l'indicatif	
enseignais	**enseignions**	**avais enseigné**	**avions enseigné**
enseignais	**enseigniez**	**avais enseigné**	**aviez enseigné**
enseignait	**enseignaient**	**avait enseigné**	**avaient enseigné**
3 passé simple		10 passé antérieur	
enseignai	**enseignâmes**	**eus enseigné**	**eûmes enseigné**
enseignas	**enseignâtes**	**eus enseigné**	**eûtes enseigné**
enseigna	**enseignèrent**	**eut enseigné**	**eurent enseigné**
4 futur		11 futur antérieur	
enseignerai	**enseignerons**	**aurai enseigné**	**aurons enseigné**
enseigneras	**enseignerez**	**auras enseigné**	**aurez enseigné**
enseignera	**enseigneront**	**aura enseigné**	**auront enseigné**
5 conditionnel		12 conditionnel passé	
enseignerais	**enseignerions**	**aurais enseigné**	**aurions enseigné**
enseignerais	**enseigneriez**	**aurais enseigné**	**auriez enseigné**
enseignerait	**enseigneraient**	**aurait enseigné**	**auraient enseigné**
6 présent du subjonctif		13 passé du subjonctif	
enseigne	**enseignions**	**aie enseigné**	**ayons enseigné**
enseignes	**enseigniez**	**aies enseigné**	**ayez enseigné**
enseigne	**enseignent**	**ait enseigné**	**aient enseigné**
7 imparfait du subjonctif		14 plus-que-parfait du subjonctif	
enseignasse	**enseignassions**	**eusse enseigné**	**eussions enseigné**
enseignasses	**enseignassiez**	**eusses enseigné**	**eussiez enseigné**
enseignât	**enseignassent**	**eût enseigné**	**eussent enseigné**
		Impératif	
		enseigne	
		enseignons	
		enseignez	

J'enseigne aux élèves à lire en français. L'enseignement est une profession.

enseigner qqch à qqn   to teach something to someone
une enseigne   sign
l'enseignement *m.*   teaching
l'enseignement *m.* **à distance**   distance education
renseigner qqn de qqch   to inform someone about something
se renseigner   to get information, to inquire
un renseignement, des renseignements   information

Regular **-re** verb   to hear, to understand

The Seven Simple Tenses | | The Seven Compound Tenses

Singular	Plural	Singular	Plural
1 présent de l'indicatif		**8 passé composé**	
entends	entendons	ai entendu	avons entendu
entends	entendez	as entendu	avez entendu
entend	entendent	a entendu	ont entendu
2 imparfait de l'indicatif		**9 plus-que-parfait de l'indicatif**	
entendais	entendions	avais entendu	avions entendu
entendais	entendiez	avais entendu	aviez entendu
entendait	entendaient	avait entendu	avaient entendu
3 passé simple		**10 passé antérieur**	
entendis	entendîmes	eus entendu	eûmes entendu
entendis	entendîtes	eus entendu	eûtes entendu
entendit	entendirent	eut entendu	eurent entendu
4 futur		**11 futur antérieur**	
entendrai	entendrons	aurai entendu	aurons entendu
entendras	entendrez	auras entendu	aurez entendu
entendra	entendront	aura entendu	auront entendu
5 conditionnel		**12 conditionnel passé**	
entendrais	entendrions	aurais entendu	aurions entendu
entendrais	entendriez	aurais entendu	auriez entendu
entendrait	entendraient	aurait entendu	auraient entendu
6 présent du subjonctif		**13 passé du subjonctif**	
entende	entendions	aie entendu	ayons entendu
entendes	entendiez	aies entendu	ayez entendu
entende	entendent	ait entendu	aient entendu
7 imparfait du subjonctif		**14 plus-que-parfait du subjonctif**	
entendisse	entendissions	eusse entendu	eussions entendu
entendisses	entendissiez	eusses entendu	eussiez entendu
entendît	entendissent	eût entendu	eussent entendu

Impératif
entends
entendons
entendez

J'ai entendu dire qu'on mange bien dans ce restaurant.   I've heard that a person can have a good meal in this restaurant.

Qu'entendez-vous par là?   What do you mean by that?

un entendement understanding	bien entendu of course
sous-entendre to imply	C'est entendu! It's understood! Agreed!
un sous-entendu innuendo	s'entendre avec qqn to get along with
une sous-entente implication	someone, to understand each other
Je m'entends bien avec ma sœur.	
I get along very well with my sister.	

109

entrer	Part. pr. **entrant**	Part. passé **entré(e)(s)**

to enter, to come in, to go in

Regular -er verb

The Seven Simple Tenses		The Seven Compound Tenses	
Singular	Plural	Singular	Plural
1 présent de l'indicatif		8 passé composé	
entre	**entrons**	**suis entré(e)**	**sommes entré(e)s**
entres	**entrez**	**es entré(e)**	**êtes entré(e)(s)**
entre	**entrent**	**est entré(e)**	**sont entré(e)s**
2 imparfait de l'indicatif		9 plus-que-parfait de l'indicatif	
entrais	**entrions**	**étais entré(e)**	**étions entré(e)s**
entrais	**entriez**	**étais entré(e)**	**étiez entré(e)(s)**
entrait	**entraient**	**était entré(e)**	**étaient entré(e)s**
3 passé simple		10 passé antérieur	
entrai	**entrâmes**	**fus entré(e)**	**fûmes entré(e)s**
entras	**entrâtes**	**fus entré(e)**	**fûtes entré(e)(s)**
entra	**entrèrent**	**fut entré(e)**	**furent entré(e)s**
4 futur		11 futur antérieur	
entrerai	**entrerons**	**serai entré(e)**	**serons entré(e)s**
entreras	**entrerez**	**seras entré(e)**	**serez entré(e)(s)**
entrera	**entreront**	**sera entré(e)**	**seront entré(e)s**
5 conditionnel		12 conditionnel passé	
entrerais	**entrerions**	**serais entré(e)**	**serions entré(e)s**
entrerais	**entreriez**	**serais entré(e)**	**seriez entré(e)(s)**
entrerait	**entreraient**	**serait entré(e)**	**seraient entré(e)s**
6 présent du subjonctif		13 passé du subjonctif	
entre	**entrions**	**sois entré(e)**	**soyons entré(e)s**
entres	**entriez**	**sois entré(e)**	**soyez entré(e)(s)**
entre	**entrent**	**soit entré(e)**	**soient entré(e)s**
7 imparfait du subjonctif		14 plus-que-parfait du subjonctif	
entrasse	**entrassions**	**fusse entré(e)**	**fussions entré(e)s**
entrasses	**entrassiez**	**fusses entré(e)**	**fussiez entré(e)(s)**
entrât	**entrassent**	**fût entré(e)**	**fussent entré(e)s**

Impératif
entre
entrons
entrez

entrée interdite no entry	**entrer dans les détails** to go into the details
l'entrée *f.* **des données** data input, data entry	**l'entrée** *f.* entrance
entrer des données to enter/input data (computer)	**entrer par la fenêtre** to enter through the window
	entrer dans + noun to enter (into) + noun

See also **rentrer**.

This verb is conjugated with **avoir** when it has a direct object. **Ma mère a entré la clé dans la serrure pour ouvrir la porte.** My mother put the key in the lock to open the door. But: **Ma mère est entrée dans la maison.** My mother went in the house.

Regular -er verb endings; spelling change: -oyer verbs must change   to send
y to i in front of a mute e; future and conditional stem is enverr-.

The Seven Simple Tenses		The Seven Compound Tenses	
Singular	Plural	Singular	Plural
1 présent de l'indicatif		8 passé composé	
envoie	**envoyons**	**ai envoyé**	**avons envoyé**
envoies	**envoyez**	**as envoyé**	**avez envoyé**
envoie	**envoient**	**a envoyé**	**ont envoyé**
2 imparfait de l'indicatif		9 plus-que-parfait de l'indicatif	
envoyais	**envoyions**	**avais envoyé**	**avions envoyé**
envoyais	**envoyiez**	**avais envoyé**	**aviez envoyé**
envoyait	**envoyaient**	**avait envoyé**	**avaient envoyé**
3 passé simple		10 passé antérieur	
envoyai	**envoyâmes**	**eus envoyé**	**eûmes envoyé**
envoyas	**envoyâtes**	**eus envoyé**	**eûtes envoyé**
envoya	**envoyèrent**	**eut envoyé**	**eurent envoyé**
4 futur		11 futur antérieur	
enverrai	**enverrons**	**aurai envoyé**	**aurons envoyé**
enverras	**enverrez**	**auras envoyé**	**aurez envoyé**
enverra	**enverront**	**aura envoyé**	**auront envoyé**
5 conditionnel		12 conditionnel passé	
enverrais	**enverrions**	**aurais envoyé**	**aurions envoyé**
enverrais	**enverriez**	**aurais envoyé**	**auriez envoyé**
enverrait	**enverraient**	**aurait envoyé**	**auraient envoyé**
6 présent du subjonctif		13 passé du subjonctif	
envoie	**envoyions**	**aie envoyé**	**ayons envoyé**
envoies	**envoyiez**	**aies envoyé**	**ayez envoyé**
envoie	**envoient**	**ait envoyé**	**aient envoyé**
7 imparfait du subjonctif		14 plus-que-parfait du subjonctif	
envoyasse	**envoyassions**	**eusse envoyé**	**eussions envoyé**
envoyasses	**envoyassiez**	**eusses envoyé**	**eussiez envoyé**
envoyât	**envoyassent**	**eût envoyé**	**eussent envoyé**
		Impératif	
		envoie	
		envoyons	
		envoyez	

Hier j'ai envoyé une lettre à des amis en France.   Yesterday I sent a letter to some friends in France.

Où est-ce que je peux envoyer un courriel/un courrier électronique?   Where can I send an e-mail?

envoyer chercher   to send for
un envoi   envoy
envoyeur, envoyeuse   sender
renvoyer   to send away (back), to discharge someone

to marry, to wed   Regular -er verb

The Seven Simple Tenses		The Seven Compound Tenses	
Singular	Plural	Singular	Plural
1 présent de l'indicatif		8 passé composé	
épouse	**épousons**	**ai épousé**	**avons épousé**
épouses	**épousez**	**as épousé**	**avez épousé**
épouse	**épousent**	**a épousé**	**ont épousé**
2 imparfait de l'indicatif		9 plus-que-parfait de l'indicatif	
épousais	**épousions**	**avais épousé**	**avions épousé**
épousais	**épousiez**	**avais épousé**	**aviez épousé**
épousait	**épousaient**	**avait épousé**	**avaient épousé**
3 passé simple		10 passé antérieur	
épousai	**épousâmes**	**eus épousé**	**eûmes épousé**
épousas	**épousâtes**	**eus épousé**	**eûtes épousé**
épousa	**épousèrent**	**eut épousé**	**eurent épousé**
4 futur		11 futur antérieur	
épouserai	**épouserons**	**aurai épousé**	**aurons épousé**
épouseras	**épouserez**	**auras épousé**	**aurez épousé**
épousera	**épouseront**	**aura épousé**	**auront épousé**
5 conditionnel		12 conditionnel passé	
épouserais	**épouserions**	**aurais épousé**	**aurions épousé**
épouserais	**épouseriez**	**aurais épousé**	**auriez épousé**
épouserait	**épouseraient**	**aurait épousé**	**auraient épousé**
6 présent du subjonctif		13 passé du subjonctif	
épouse	**épousions**	**aie épousé**	**ayons épousé**
épouses	**épousiez**	**aies épousé**	**ayez épousé**
épouse	**épousent**	**ait épousé**	**aient épousé**
7 imparfait du subjonctif		14 plus-que-parfait du subjonctif	
épousasse	**épousassions**	**eusse épousé**	**eussions épousé**
épousasses	**épousassiez**	**eusses épousé**	**eussiez épousé**
épousât	**épousassent**	**eût épousé**	**eussent épousé**
		Impératif	
		épouse	
		épousons	
		épousez	

Mon frère a épousé une Française.   My brother married a French woman.

un époux husband, spouse
une épouse wife, spouse
les nouveaux mariés the newlyweds
se marier avec quelqu'un to get married to someone
épouser une grosse fortune to marry into money

Regular **-er** verb endings: spelling change: to hope
é changes to è before syllable with mute e.

The Seven Simple Tenses		The Seven Compound Tenses	
Singular	Plural	Singular	Plural
1 présent de l'indicatif		8 passé composé	
espère	**espérons**	**ai espéré**	**avons espéré**
espères	**espérez**	**as espéré**	**avez espéré**
espère	**espèrent**	**a espéré**	**ont espéré**
2 imparfait de l'indicatif		9 plus-que-parfait de l'indicatif	
espérais	**espérions**	**avais espéré**	**avions espéré**
espérais	**espériez**	**avais espéré**	**aviez espéré**
espérait	**espéraient**	**avait espéré**	**avaient espéré**
3 passé simple		10 passé antérieur	
espérai	**espérâmes**	**eus espéré**	**eûmes espéré**
espéras	**espérâtes**	**eus espéré**	**eûtes espéré**
espéra	**espérèrent**	**eut espéré**	**eurent espéré**
4 futur		11 futur antérieur	
espérerai	**espérerons**	**aurai espéré**	**aurons espéré**
espéreras	**espérerez**	**auras espéré**	**aurez espéré**
espérera	**espéreront**	**aura espéré**	**auront espéré**
5 conditionnel		12 conditionnel passé	
espérerais	**espérerions**	**aurais espéré**	**aurions espéré**
espérerais	**espéreriez**	**aurais espéré**	**auriez espéré**
espérerait	**espéreraient**	**aurait espéré**	**auraient espéré**
6 présent du subjonctif		13 passé du subjonctif	
espère	**espérions**	**aie espéré**	**ayons espéré**
espères	**espériez**	**aies espéré**	**ayez espéré**
espère	**espèrent**	**ait espéré**	**aient espéré**
7 imparfait du subjonctif		14 plus-que-parfait du subjonctif	
espérasse	**espérassions**	**eusse espéré**	**eussions espéré**
espérasses	**espérassiez**	**eusses espéré**	**eussiez espéré**
espérât	**espérassent**	**eût espéré**	**eussent espéré**
		Impératif	
		espère	
		espérons	
		espérez	

J'espère que Paul viendra mais je n'espère pas que son frère vienne.   I hope that Paul will come, but I don't hope that his brother will come.

l'espérance *f.*   hope, expectation
plein d'espérance   hopeful, full of hope
l'espoir *m.*   hope
avoir bon espoir de réussir   to have good hopes of succeeding
désespérer de   to despair of; **se désespérer**   to be in despair
le désespoir   despair; **un désespoir d'amour**   disappointed love

Note: The Académie française now allows the accent grave (`` ` ``) in the future (e.g., **j'espèrerai**) and conditional (e.g., **j'espèrerais**) of this verb.   **113**

to try, to try on	Regular -er verb endings: spelling change: -ayer verbs may change y to i in front of a mute e or may keep y.

The Seven Simple Tenses		The Seven Compound Tenses	
Singular	Plural	Singular	Plural

1 présent de l'indicatif

essaie or essaye	essayons		
essaies or essayes	essayez		
essaie or essaye	essaient or essayent		

8 passé composé

ai essayé	avons essayé
as essayé	avez essayé
a essayé	ont essayé

2 imparfait de l'indicatif

essayais	essayions
essayais	essayiez
essayait	essayaient

9 plus-que-parfait de l'indicatif

avais essayé	avions essayé
avais essayé	aviez essayé
avait essayé	avaient essayé

3 passé simple

essayai	essayâmes
essayas	essayâtes
essaya	essayèrent

10 passé antérieur

eus essayé	eûmes essayé
eus essayé	eûtes essayé
eut essayé	eurent essayé

4 futur

essaierai or essayerai	essaierons or essayerons
essaieras or essayeras	essaierez or essayerez
essaiera or essayera	essaieront or essayeront

11 futur antérieur

aurai essayé	aurons essayé
auras essayé	aurez essayé
aura essayé	auront essayé

5 conditionnel

essaierais or essayerais	essaierions or essayerions
essaierais or essayerais	essaieriez or essayeriez
essaierait or essayerait	essaieraient or essayeraient

12 conditionnel passé

aurais essayé	aurions essayé
aurais essayé	auriez essayé
aurait essayé	auraient essayé

6 présent du subjonctif

essaie or essaye	essayions
essaies or essayes	essayiez
essaie or essaye	essaient or essayent

13 passé du subjonctif

aie essayé	ayons essayé
aies essayé	ayez essayé
ait essayé	aient essayé

7 imparfait du subjonctif

essayasse	essayassions
essayasses	essayassiez
essayât	essayassent

14 plus-que-parfait du subjonctif

eusse essayé	eussions essayé
eusses essayé	eussiez essayé
eût essayé	eussent essayé

Impératif

essaie or essaye
essayons
essayez

---

un essai essay	essayeur, essayeuse fitter (clothing)
essayiste essayist	essayage *m.* fitting (clothing)
essayer de faire qqch to try	une salle/un salon d'essayage
to do something	fitting room

Regular -er verb endings: spelling change: -uyer   to wipe
verbs must change y to i in front of a mute e.

The Seven Simple Tenses		The Seven Compound Tenses	
Singular	Plural	Singular	Plural
1 présent de l'indicatif		8 passé composé	
essuie	**essuyons**	**ai essuyé**	**avons essuyé**
essuies	**essuyez**	**as essuyé**	**avez essuyé**
essuie	**essuient**	**a essuyé**	**ont essuyé**
2 imparfait de l'indicatif		9 plus-que-parfait de l'indicatif	
essuyais	**essuyions**	**avais essuyé**	**avions essuyé**
essuyais	**essuyiez**	**avais essuyé**	**aviez essuyé**
essuyait	**essuyaient**	**avait essuyé**	**avaient essuyé**
3 passé simple		10 passé antérieur	
essuyai	**essuyâmes**	**eus essuyé**	**eûmes essuyé**
essuyas	**essuyâtes**	**eus essuyé**	**eûtes essuyé**
essuya	**essuyèrent**	**eut essuyé**	**eurent essuyé**
4 futur		11 futur antérieur	
essuierai	**essuierons**	**aurai essuyé**	**aurons essuyé**
essuieras	**essuierez**	**auras essuyé**	**aurez essuyé**
essuiera	**essuieront**	**aura essuyé**	**auront essuyé**
5 conditionnel		12 conditionnel passé	
essuierais	**essuierions**	**aurais essuyé**	**aurions essuyé**
essuierais	**essuieriez**	**aurais essuyé**	**auriez essuyé**
essuierait	**essuieraient**	**aurait essuyé**	**auraient essuyé**
6 présent du subjonctif		13 passé du subjonctif	
essuie	**essuyions**	**aie essuyé**	**ayons essuyé**
essuies	**essuyiez**	**aies essuyé**	**ayez essuyé**
essuie	**essuient**	**ait essuyé**	**aient essuyé**
7 imparfait du subjonctif		14 plus-que-parfait du subjonctif	
essuyasse	**essuyassions**	**eusse essuyé**	**eussions essuyé**
essuyasses	**essuyassiez**	**eusses essuyé**	**eussiez essuyé**
essuyât	**essuyassent**	**eût essuyé**	**eussent essuyé**
		Impératif	
		essuie	
		essuyons	
		essuyez	

un essuie-mains hand towel	**un essuie-verres** glass cloth
un essuie-glace windshield wiper	**s'essuyer** to wipe oneself
l'essuyage *m.* wiping	**s'essuyer le front** to wipe one's brow

S'il vous plaît, essuyez vos pieds avant d'entrer.   Please wipe your feet before entering.

Notre équipe a essuyé une défaite dans le championnat.   Our team suffered a defeat in the championship. (Note: This does not mean "wiped defeat.")

éteindre	Part. pr. **éteignant**	Part. passé **éteint**

to extinguish, to shut down (computer), to turn off — Irregular verb

The Seven Simple Tenses		The Seven Compound Tenses	
Singular	Plural	Singular	Plural
1 présent de l'indicatif		**8 passé composé**	
éteins	éteignons	ai éteint	avons éteint
éteins	éteignez	as éteint	avez éteint
éteint	éteignent	a éteint	ont éteint
2 imparfait de l'indicatif		**9 plus-que-parfait de l'indicatif**	
éteignais	éteignions	avais éteint	avions éteint
éteignais	éteigniez	avais éteint	aviez éteint
éteignait	éteignaient	avait éteint	avaient éteint
3 passé simple		**10 passé antérieur**	
éteignis	éteignîmes	eus éteint	eûmes éteint
éteignis	éteignîtes	eus éteint	eûtes éteint
éteignit	éteignirent	eut éteint	eurent éteint
4 futur		**11 futur antérieur**	
éteindrai	éteindrons	aurai éteint	aurons éteint
éteindras	éteindrez	auras éteint	aurez éteint
éteindra	éteindront	aura éteint	auront éteint
5 conditionnel		**12 conditionnel passé**	
éteindrais	éteindrions	aurais éteint	aurions éteint
éteindrais	éteindriez	aurais éteint	auriez éteint
éteindrait	éteindraient	aurait éteint	auraient éteint
6 présent du subjonctif		**13 passé du subjonctif**	
éteigne	éteignions	aie éteint	ayons éteint
éteignes	éteigniez	aies éteint	ayez éteint
éteigne	éteignent	ait éteint	aient éteint
7 imparfait du subjonctif		**14 plus-que-parfait du subjonctif**	
éteignisse	éteignissions	eusse éteint	eussions éteint
éteignisses	éteignissiez	eusses éteint	eussiez éteint
éteignît	éteignissent	eût éteint	eussent éteint

Impératif
éteins
éteignons
éteignez

J'éteins la lumière. Bonne nuit!   I'm turning out the light. Good night!
Les pompiers ont éteint l'incendie après une lutte de trois heures.   The firemen put out the fire after a three-hour struggle.

éteint, éteinte   extinct
un éteignoir   extinguisher, snuffer
s'éteindre   to flicker out, to die out, to die
éteindre le feu   to put out the fire
éteindre la lumière   to turn off the light

Reflexive regular -re verb

to stretch oneself, to stretch out,
to lie down

The Seven Simple Tenses		The Seven Compound Tenses	
Singular	Plural	Singular	Plural
1 présent de l'indicatif		**8 passé composé**	
m'étends	nous étendons	me suis étendu(e)	nous sommes étendu(e)s
t'étends	vous étendez	t'es étendu(e)	vous êtes étendu(e)(s)
s'étend	s'étendent	s'est étendu(e)	se sont étendu(e)s
2 imparfait de l'indicatif		**9 plus-que-parfait de l'indicatif**	
m'étendais	nous étendions	m'étais étendu(e)	nous étions étendu(e)s
t'étendais	vous étendiez	t'étais étendu(e)	vous étiez étendu(e)(s)
s'étendait	s'étendaient	s'était étendu(e)	s'étaient étendu(e)s
3 passé simple		**10 passé antérieur**	
m'étendis	nous étendîmes	me fus étendu(e)	nous fûmes étendu(e)s
t'étendis	vous étendîtes	te fus étendu(e)	vous fûtes étendu(e)(s)
s'étendit	s'étendirent	se fut étendu(e)	se furent étendu(e)s
4 futur		**11 futur antérieur**	
m'étendrai	nous étendrons	me serai étendu(e)	nous serons étendu(e)s
t'étendras	vous étendrez	te seras étendu(e)	vous serez étendu(e)(s)
s'étendra	s'étendront	se sera étendu(e)	se seront étendu(e)s
5 conditionnel		**12 conditionnel passé**	
m'étendrais	nous étendrions	me serais étendu(e)	nous serions étendu(e)s
t'étendrais	vous étendriez	te serais étendu(e)	vous seriez étendu(e)(s)
s'étendrait	s'étendraient	se serait étendu(e)	se seraient étendu(e)s
6 présent du subjonctif		**13 passé du subjonctif**	
m'étende	nous étendions	me sois étendu(e)	nous soyons étendu(e)s
t'étendes	vous étendiez	te sois étendu(e)	vous soyez étendu(e)(s)
s'étende	s'étendent	se soit étendu(e)	se soient étendu(e)s
7 imparfait du subjonctif		**14 plus-que-parfait du subjonctif**	
m'étendisse	nous étendissions	me fusse étendu(e)	nous fussions étendu(e)s
t'étendisses	vous étendissiez	te fusses étendu(e)	vous fussiez étendu(e)(s)
s'étendît	s'étendissent	se fût étendu(e)	se fussent étendu(e)s

Impératif
étends-toi; ne t'étends pas
étendons-nous; ne nous étendons pas
étendez-vous; ne vous étendez pas

Ma mère était si fatiguée qu'elle est allée directement au lit et elle s'est étendue.
My mother was so tired that she went straight to bed and lay down.

étendre le linge to hang out the wash	**l'étendue** *f.* area, extent
étendre la main to hold out your hand	
étendre le bras to extend your arm	
étendre d'eau to water down	
s'étendre sur qqch to dwell on something	

étonner	Part. pr. étonnant	Part. passé étonné

to amaze, to astonish, to stun, to surprise

Regular -er verb

The Seven Simple Tenses		The Seven Compound Tenses	
Singular	Plural	Singular	Plural
1 présent de l'indicatif		**8 passé composé**	
étonne	étonnons	ai étonné	avons étonné
étonnes	étonnez	as étonné	avez étonné
étonne	étonnent	a étonné	ont étonné
2 imparfait de l'indicatif		**9 plus-que-parfait de l'indicatif**	
étonnais	étonnions	avais étonné	avions étonné
étonnais	étonniez	avais étonné	aviez étonné
étonnait	étonnaient	avait étonné	avaient étonné
3 passé simple		**10 passé antérieur**	
étonnai	étonnâmes	eus étonné	eûmes étonné
étonnas	étonnâtes	eus étonné	eûtes étonné
étonna	étonnèrent	eut étonné	eurent étonné
4 futur		**11 futur antérieur**	
étonnerai	étonnerons	aurai étonné	aurons étonné
étonneras	étonnerez	auras étonné	aurez étonné
étonnera	étonneront	aura étonné	auront étonné
5 conditionnel		**12 conditionnel passé**	
étonnerais	étonnerions	aurais étonné	aurions étonné
étonnerais	étonneriez	aurais étonné	auriez étonné
étonnerait	étonneraient	aurait étonné	auraient étonné
6 présent du subjonctif		**13 passé du subjonctif**	
étonne	étonnions	aie étonné	ayons étonné
étonnes	étonniez	aies étonné	ayez étonné
étonne	étonnent	ait étonné	aient étonné
7 imparfait du subjonctif		**14 plus-que-parfait du subjonctif**	
étonnasse	étonnassions	eusse étonné	eussions étonné
étonnasses	étonnassiez	eusses étonné	eussiez étonné
étonnât	étonnassent	eût étonné	eussent étonné

Impératif
étonne
étonnons
étonnez

étonnant, étonnante   astonishing
C'est bien étonnant!   It's quite astonishing!
l'étonnement *m.*   astonishment, amazement
s'étonner de   to be astonished at
Cela m'étonne!   That astonishes me!
Cela ne m'étonne pas!   That does not surprise me!

Irregular verb   to be

The Seven Simple Tenses		The Seven Compound Tenses	
Singular	Plural	Singular	Plural
1 présent de l'indicatif		**8 passé composé**	
suis	sommes	ai été	avons été
es	êtes	as été	avez été
est	sont	a été	ont été
2 imparfait de l'indicatif		**9 plus-que-parfait de l'indicatif**	
étais	étions	avais été	avions été
étais	étiez	avais été	aviez été
était	étaient	avait été	avaient été
3 passé simple		**10 passé antérieur**	
fus	fûmes	eus été	eûmes été
fus	fûtes	eus été	eûtes été
fut	furent	eut été	eurent été
4 futur		**11 futur antérieur**	
serai	serons	aurai été	aurons été
seras	serez	auras été	aurez été
sera	seront	aura été	auront été
5 conditionnel		**12 conditionnel passé**	
serais	serions	aurais été	aurions été
serais	seriez	aurais été	auriez été
serait	seraient	aurait été	auraient été
6 présent du subjonctif		**13 passé du subjonctif**	
sois	soyons	aie été	ayons été
sois	soyez	aies été	ayez été
soit	soient	ait été	aient été
7 imparfait du subjonctif		**14 plus-que-parfait du subjonctif**	
fusse	fussions	eusse été	eussions été
fusses	fussiez	eusses été	eussiez été
fût	fussent	eût été	eussent été
		Impératif	
		sois	
		soyons	
		soyez	

être en train de + inf.   to be in the act of + pres. part., to be in the process of, to be busy + pres. part.; **Mon père est en train d'écrire une lettre à mes grands-parents.**   My father is busy writing a letter to my grandparents.

être à l'heure   to be on time
être à temps   to be in time
être pressé(e)   to be in a hurry
être à qqn   to belong to someone;
    Ce stylo est à moi. This pen is mine.
être en retard   to be late

Je suis à vous.   I am at your service.
Je suis d'avis que. . .   I am of the opinion that. . .
être ou ne pas être   to be or not to be

étudier Part. pr. **étudiant** Part. passé **étudié**

to study

Regular -er verb

The Seven Simple Tenses		The Seven Compound Tenses	
Singular	Plural	Singular	Plural
1 présent de l'indicatif		**8 passé composé**	
étudie	étudions	ai étudié	avons étudié
étudies	étudiez	as étudié	avez étudié
étudie	étudient	a étudié	ont étudié
2 imparfait de l'indicatif		**9 plus-que-parfait de l'indicatif**	
étudiais	étudiions	avais étudié	avions étudié
étudiais	étudiiez	avais étudié	aviez étudié
étudiait	étudiaient	avait étudié	avaient étudié
3 passé simple		**10 passé antérieur**	
étudiai	étudiâmes	eus étudié	eûmes étudié
étudias	étudiâtes	eus étudié	eûtes étudié
étudia	étudièrent	eut étudié	eurent étudié
4 futur		**11 futur antérieur**	
étudierai	étudierons	aurai étudié	aurons étudié
étudieras	étudierez	auras étudié	aurez étudié
étudiera	étudieront	aura étudié	auront étudié
5 conditionnel		**12 conditionnel passé**	
étudierais	étudierions	aurais étudié	aurions étudié
étudierais	étudieriez	aurais étudié	auriez étudié
étudierait	étudieraient	aurait étudié	auraient étudié
6 présent du subjonctif		**13 passé du subjonctif**	
étudie	étudiions	aie étudié	ayons étudié
étudies	étudiiez	aies étudié	ayez étudié
étudie	étudient	ait étudié	aient étudié
7 imparfait du subjonctif		**14 plus-que-parfait du subjonctif**	
étudiasse	étudiassions	eusse étudié	eussions étudié
étudiasses	étudiassiez	eusses étudié	eussiez étudié
étudiât	étudiassent	eût étudié	eussent étudié

Impératif
étudie
étudions
étudiez

Depuis combien de temps étudiez-vous le français? How long have you been studying French?

J'étudie le français depuis deux ans. I have been studying French for two years.

étudier à fond to study thoroughly	**s'amuser au lieu d'étudier** to have
un étudiant, une étudiante student	a good time instead of studying
l'étude f. study; **les études** studies	**étudier qqch de près** to study
faire ses études to study, to go to school	something closely
à l'étude under consideration, under study	**s'étudier** to analyze oneself
une salle d'études study hall	

Reflexive regular -er verb   to excuse oneself, to apologize

The Seven Simple Tenses		The Seven Compound Tenses	
Singular	Plural	Singular	Plural
1 présent de l'indicatif		**8 passé composé**	
m'excuse	nous excusons	me suis excusé(e)	nous sommes excusé(e)s
t'excuses	vous excusez	t'es excusé(e)	vous êtes excusé(e)(s)
s'excuse	s'excusent	s'est excusé(e)	se sont excusé(e)s
2 imparfait de l'indicatif		**9 plus-que-parfait de l'indicatif**	
m'excusais	nous excusions	m'étais excusé(e)	nous étions excusé(e)s
t'excusais	vous excusiez	t'étais excusé(e)	vous étiez excusé(e)(s)
s'excusait	s'excusaient	s'était excusé(e)	s'étaient excusé(e)s
3 passé simple		**10 passé antérieur**	
m'excusai	nous excusâmes	me fus excusé(e)	nous fûmes excusé(e)s
t'excusas	vous excusâtes	te fus excusé(e)	vous fûtes excusé(e)(s)
s'excusa	s'excusèrent	se fut excusé(e)	se furent excusé(e)s
4 futur		**11 futur antérieur**	
m'excuserai	nous excuserons	me serai excusé(e)	nous serons excusé(e)s
t'excuseras	vous excuserez	te seras excusé(e)	vous serez excusé(e)(s)
s'excusera	s'excuseront	se sera excusé(e)	se seront excusé(e)s
5 conditionnel		**12 conditionnel passé**	
m'excuserais	nous excuserions	me serais excusé(e)	nous serions excusé(e)s
t'excuserais	vous excuseriez	te serais excusé(e)	vous seriez excusé(e)(s)
s'excuserait	s'excuseraient	se serait excusé(e)	se seraient excusé(e)s
6 présent du subjonctif		**13 passé du subjonctif**	
m'excuse	nous excusions	me sois excusé(e)	nous soyons excusé(e)s
t'excuses	vous excusiez	te sois excusé(e)	vous soyez excusé(e)(s)
s'excuse	s'excusent	se soit excusé(e)	se soient excusé(e)s
7 imparfait du subjonctif		**14 plus-que-parfait du subjonctif**	
m'excusasse	nous excusassions	me fusse excusé(e)	nous fussions excusé(e)s
t'excusasses	vous excusassiez	te fusses excusé(e)	vous fussiez excusé(e)(s)
s'excusât	s'excusassent	se fût excusé(e)	se fussent excusé(e)s

Impératif
excuse-toi; ne t'excuse pas
excusons-nous; ne nous excusons pas
excusez-vous; ne vous excusez pas

L'élève:	**Je m'excuse, madame. Excusez-moi. Je m'excuse de vous déranger. Est-ce que vous m'excusez? Est-ce que je vous dérange?**
La maîtresse:	**Oui, je t'excuse. Non, tu ne me déranges pas. Que veux-tu?**
L'élève:	**Est-ce que je peux quitter la salle de classe pour aller aux toilettes?**
La maîtresse:	**Oui, vas-y.**

s'excuser de   to apologize for
Veuillez m'excuser.   Please (Be good enough to) excuse me.
Qui s'excuse s'accuse.   A guilty conscience needs no accuser.

| to demand, to require | Regular -er verb endings: spelling change: retain the ge before a or o to keep the soft g sound of the verb. |

The Seven Simple Tenses		The Seven Compound Tenses	
Singular	Plural	Singular	Plural
1 présent de l'indicatif		8 passé composé	
exige	**exigeons**	**ai exigé**	**avons exigé**
exiges	**exigez**	**as exigé**	**avez exigé**
exige	**exigent**	**a exigé**	**ont exigé**
2 imparfait de l'indicatif		9 plus-que-parfait de l'indicatif	
exigeais	**exigions**	**avais exigé**	**avions exigé**
exigeais	**exigiez**	**avais exigé**	**aviez exigé**
exigeait	**exigeaient**	**avait exigé**	**avaient exigé**
3 passé simple		10 passé antérieur	
exigeai	**exigeâmes**	**eus exigé**	**eûmes exigé**
exigeas	**exigeâtes**	**eus exigé**	**eûtes exigé**
exigea	**exigèrent**	**eut exigé**	**eurent exigé**
4 futur		11 futur antérieur	
exigerai	**exigerons**	**aurai exigé**	**aurons exigé**
exigeras	**exigerez**	**auras exigé**	**aurez exigé**
exigera	**exigeront**	**aura exigé**	**auront exigé**
5 conditionnel		12 conditionnel passé	
exigerais	**exigerions**	**aurais exigé**	**aurions exigé**
exigerais	**exigeriez**	**aurais exigé**	**auriez exigé**
exigerait	**exigeraient**	**aurait exigé**	**auraient exigé**
6 présent du subjonctif		13 passé du subjonctif	
exige	**exigions**	**aie exigé**	**ayons exigé**
exiges	**exigiez**	**aies exigé**	**ayez exigé**
exige	**exigent**	**ait exigé**	**aient exigé**
7 imparfait du subjonctif		14 plus-que-parfait du subjonctif	
exigeasse	**exigeassions**	**eusse exigé**	**eussions exigé**
exigeasses	**exigeassiez**	**eusses exigé**	**eussiez exigé**
exigeât	**exigeassent**	**eût exigé**	**eussent exigé**

	Impératif
	exige
	exigeons
	exigez

| *La maîtresse de français:* | Paul, viens ici. Ta composition est pleine de fautes. J'exige que tu la refasses. Rends-la-moi dans dix minutes. |
| *L'élève:* | Ce n'est pas de ma faute, madame. C'est mon père qui l'a écrite. Dois-je la refaire? |

exigeant, exigeante exacting
l'exigence f. exigency, requirement
exiger des soins attentifs to demand great care
les exigences requirements

Regular -er verb

The Seven Simple Tenses		The Seven Compound Tenses	
Singular	Plural	Singular	Plural
1 présent de l'indicatif		**8 passé composé**	
explique	expliquons	ai expliqué	avons expliqué
expliques	expliquez	as expliqué	avez expliqué
explique	expliquent	a expliqué	ont expliqué
2 imparfait de l'indicatif		**9 plus-que-parfait de l'indicatif**	
expliquais	expliquions	avais expliqué	avions expliqué
expliquais	expliquiez	avais expliqué	aviez expliqué
expliquait	expliquaient	avait expliqué	avaient expliqué
3 passé simple		**10 passé antérieur**	
expliquai	expliquâmes	eus expliqué	eûmes expliqué
expliquas	expliquâtes	eus expliqué	eûtes expliqué
expliqua	expliquèrent	eut expliqué	eurent expliqué
4 futur		**11 futur antérieur**	
expliquerai	expliquerons	aurai expliqué	aurons expliqué
expliqueras	expliquerez	auras expliqué	aurez expliqué
expliquera	expliqueront	aura expliqué	auront expliqué
5 conditionnel		**12 conditionnel passé**	
expliquerais	expliquerions	aurais expliqué	aurions expliqué
expliquerais	expliqueriez	aurais expliqué	auriez expliqué
expliquerait	expliqueraient	aurait expliqué	auraient expliqué
6 présent du subjonctif		**13 passé du subjonctif**	
explique	expliquions	aie expliqué	ayons expliqué
expliques	expliquiez	aies expliqué	ayez expliqué
explique	expliquent	ait expliqué	aient expliqué
7 imparfait du subjonctif		**14 plus-que-parfait du subjonctif**	
expliquasse	expliquassions	eusse expliqué	eussions expliqué
expliquasses	expliquassiez	eusses expliqué	eussiez expliqué
expliquât	expliquassent	eût expliqué	eussent expliqué

Impératif
explique
expliquons
expliquez

---

explicite explicit	**explicatif, explicative** explanatory
explicitement explicitly	**s'expliciter** to be explicit
l'explication f. explanation	**une explication de texte**
explicable explainable	interpretation, critical analysis of a text

Note the difference in meaning in the following two sentences. See p. xxix (b).

J'ai étudié la leçon que le professeur avait expliquée.   I studied the lesson that the teacher had explained.

J'avais étudié la leçon que le professeur a expliquée.   I had studied the lesson that the teacher explained.

se fâcher   Part. pr. se fâchant   Part. passé fâché(e)(s)

to become angry, to get angry   Reflexive regular -er verb

The Seven Simple Tenses		The Seven Compound Tenses	
Singular	Plural	Singular	Plural
1 présent de l'indicatif		**8 passé composé**	
me fâche	nous fâchons	me suis fâché(e)	nous sommes fâché(e)s
te fâches	vous fâchez	t'es fâché(e)	vous êtes fâché(e)(s)
se fâche	se fâchent	s'est fâché(e)	se sont fâché(e)s
2 imparfait de l'indicatif		**9 plus-que-parfait de l'indicatif**	
me fâchais	nous fâchions	m'étais fâché(e)	nous étions fâché(e)s
te fâchais	vous fâchiez	t'étais fâché(e)	vous étiez fâché(e)(s)
se fâchait	se fâchaient	s'était fâché(e)	s'étaient fâché(e)s
3 passé simple		**10 passé antérieur**	
me fâchai	nous fâchâmes	me fus fâché(e)	nous fûmes fâché(e)s
te fâchas	vous fâchâtes	te fus fâché(e)	vous fûtes fâché(e)(s)
se fâcha	se fâchèrent	se fut fâché(e)	se furent fâché(e)s
4 futur		**11 futur antérieur**	
me fâcherai	nous fâcherons	me serai fâché(e)	nous serons fâché(e)s
te fâcheras	vous fâcherez	te seras fâché(e)	vous serez fâché(e)(s)
se fâchera	se fâcheront	se sera fâché(e)	se seront fâché(e)s
5 conditionnel		**12 conditionnel passé**	
me fâcherais	nous fâcherions	me serais fâché(e)	nous serions fâché(e)s
te fâcherais	vous fâcheriez	te serais fâché(e)	vous seriez fâché(e)(s)
se fâcherait	se fâcheraient	se serait fâché(e)	se seraient fâché(e)s
6 présent du subjonctif		**13 passé du subjonctif**	
me fâche	nous fâchions	me sois fâché(e)	nous soyons fâché(e)s
te fâches	vous fâchiez	te sois fâché(e)	vous soyez fâché(e)(s)
se fâche	se fâchent	se soit fâché(e)	se soient fâché(e)s
7 imparfait du subjonctif		**14 plus-que-parfait du subjonctif**	
me fâchasse	nous fâchassions	me fusse fâché(e)	nous fussions fâché(e)s
te fâchasses	vous fâchassiez	te fusses fâché(e)	vous fussiez fâché(e)(s)
se fâchât	se fâchassent	se fût fâché(e)	se fussent fâché(e)s

Impératif
fâche-toi; ne te fâche pas
fâchons-nous; ne nous fâchons pas
fâchez-vous; ne vous fâchez pas

---

fâcher qqn to anger someone, to offend someone
se fâcher contre qqn to become angry at someone
une fâcherie tiff, quarrel
C'est fâcheux! It's a nuisance! It's annoying!
fâcheusement unfortunately
se fâcher tout rouge to turn red with anger
Ce que vous dites me fâche beaucoup. What you are saying distresses me very much.

124

Irregular verb   to fail

The Seven Simple Tenses		The Seven Compound Tenses	
Singular	Plural	Singular	Plural
1 présent de l'indicatif		**8 passé composé**	
faux	faillons	ai failli	avons failli
faux	faillez	as failli	avez failli
faut	faillent	a failli	ont failli
2 imparfait de l'indicatif		**9 plus-que-parfait de l'indicatif**	
faillais	faillions	avais failli	avions failli
faillais	failliez	avais failli	aviez failli
faillait	faillaient	avait failli	avaient failli
3 passé simple		**10 passé antérieur**	
faillis	faillîmes	eus failli	eûmes failli
faillis	faillîtes	eus failli	eûtes failli
faillit	faillirent	eut failli	eurent failli
4 futur		**11 futur antérieur**	
faillirai *or* faudrai	faillirons *or* faudrons	aurai failli	aurons failli
failliras *or* faudras	faillirez *or* faudrez	auras failli	aurez failli
faillira *or* faudra	failliront *or* faudront	aura failli	auront failli
5 conditionnel		**12 conditionnel passé**	
faillirais *or* faudrais	faillirions *or* faudrions	aurais failli	aurions failli
faillirais *or* faudrais	failliriez *or* faudriez	aurais failli	auriez failli
faillirait *or* faudrait	failliraient *or* faudraient	aurait failli	auraient failli
6 présent du subjonctif		**13 passé du subjonctif**	
faille	faillions	aie failli	ayons failli
failles	failliez	aies failli	ayez failli
faille	faillent	ait failli	aient failli
7 imparfait du subjonctif		**14 plus-que-parfait du subjonctif**	
faillisse	faillissions	eusse failli	eussions failli
faillisses	faillissiez	eusses failli	eussiez failli
faillît	faillissent	eût failli	eussent failli

Impératif
—

la faillite bankruptcy, failure	**défaillir** to weaken, to faint
failli, faillie bankrupt	**défaillant, défaillante** feeble
J'ai failli tomber. I almost fell.	**une défaillance** faint (swoon)
faire faillite to go bankrupt	**être en faillite** to be bankrupt

Note: The conjugated forms of this verb are used most of the time in the **passé simple** and compound tenses. The other tenses are rarely used.

faire	Part. pr. **faisant**	Part. passé **fait**

to do, to make

Irregular verb

The Seven Simple Tenses		The Seven Compound Tenses	
Singular	Plural	Singular	Plural
1 présent de l'indicatif		8 passé composé	
fais	faisons	ai fait	avons fait
fais	faites	as fait	avez fait
fait	font	a fait	ont fait
2 imparfait de l'indicatif		9 plus-que-parfait de l'indicatif	
faisais	faisions	avais fait	avions fait
faisais	faisiez	avais fait	aviez fait
faisait	faisaient	avait fait	avaient fait
3 passé simple		10 passé antérieur	
fis	fîmes	eus fait	eûmes fait
fis	fîtes	eus fait	eûtes fait
fit	firent	eut fait	eurent fait
4 futur		11 futur antérieur	
ferai	ferons	aurai fait	aurons fait
feras	ferez	auras fait	aurez fait
fera	feront	aura fait	auront fait
5 conditionnel		12 conditionnel passé	
ferais	ferions	aurais fait	aurions fait
ferais	feriez	aurais fait	auriez fait
ferait	feraient	aurait fait	auraient fait
6 présent du subjonctif		13 passé du subjonctif	
fasse	fassions	aie fait	ayons fait
fasses	fassiez	aies fait	ayez fait
fasse	fassent	ait fait	aient fait
7 imparfait du subjonctif		14 plus-que-parfait du subjonctif	
fisse	fissions	eusse fait	eussions fait
fisses	fissiez	eusses fait	eussiez fait
fît	fissent	eût fait	eussent fait

	Impératif	
	fais	
	faisons	
	faites	

---

faire beau   to be beautiful weather
faire chaud   to be warm weather
faire froid   to be cold weather
faire de l'autostop   to hitchhike
faire attention à qqn ou à qqch   to pay
   attention to someone or to something

faire une promenade   to take a walk
faire le ménage   to do the housework
faire un voyage   to take a trip
faire du vélo   to ride a bike
faire un appel (téléphonique)   to
   make a (telephone) call

Il fait beau aujourd'hui.   The weather's nice today.
Cela ne fait rien.   That doesn't matter. That makes no difference.
Faites comme chez vous! (formal, plural)   Make yourself/yourselves at home!
Fais comme chez toi! (informal)   Make yourself at home!

126

Impersonal verb	to be necessary, must, to be lacking to (à), to need

The Seven Simple Tenses	The Seven Compound Tenses
Singular	Singular
1 présent de l'indicatif **il faut**	8 passé composé **il a fallu**
2 imparfait de l'indicatif **il fallait**	9 plus-que-parfait de l'indicatif **il avait fallu**
3 passé simple **il fallut**	10 passé antérieur **il eut fallu**
4 futur **il faudra**	11 futur antérieur **il aura fallu**
5 conditionnel **il faudrait**	12 conditionnel passé **il aurait fallu**
6 présent du subjonctif **qu'il faille**	13 passé du subjonctif **qu'il ait fallu**
7 imparfait du subjonctif **qu'il fallût**	14 plus-que-parfait du subjonctif **qu'il eût fallu**

Impératif
—

comme il faut   as is proper
agir comme il faut   to behave properly
Il me faut de l'argent.   I need some
  money.
Il faut manger pour vivre.   It is
  necessary to eat in order to live.
	Il ne faut pas parler sans politesse.
	  One must not talk impolitely.
	Il faut . . . It is necessary; one must . . .
	Il ne faut pas . . . One must not . . .
	Peu s'en faut . . . It takes only a little . . .
	Il s'en faut de beaucoup . . . It takes
	  a lot . . .

This is an impersonal verb and it is used in the tenses given above with the subject **il**.

fermer	Part. pr. **fermant**	Part. passé **fermé**

to close

Regular -er verb

The Seven Simple Tenses		The Seven Compound Tenses	
Singular	Plural	Singular	Plural

1 présent de l'indicatif		8 passé composé	
ferme	fermons	ai fermé	avons fermé
fermes	fermez	as fermé	avez fermé
ferme	ferment	a fermé	ont fermé

2 imparfait de l'indicatif		9 plus-que-parfait de l'indicatif	
fermais	fermions	avais fermé	avions fermé
fermais	fermiez	avais fermé	aviez fermé
fermait	fermaient	avait fermé	avaient fermé

3 passé simple		10 passé antérieur	
fermai	fermâmes	eus fermé	eûmes fermé
fermas	fermâtes	eus fermé	eûtes fermé
ferma	fermèrent	eut fermé	eurent fermé

4 futur		11 futur antérieur	
fermerai	fermerons	aurai fermé	aurons fermé
fermeras	fermerez	auras fermé	aurez fermé
fermera	fermeront	aura fermé	auront fermé

5 conditionnel		12 conditionnel passé	
fermerais	fermerions	aurais fermé	aurions fermé
fermerais	fermeriez	aurais fermé	auriez fermé
fermerait	fermeraient	aurait fermé	auraient fermé

6 présent du subjonctif		13 passé du subjonctif	
ferme	fermions	aie fermé	ayons fermé
fermes	fermiez	aies fermé	ayez fermé
ferme	ferment	ait fermé	aient fermé

7 imparfait du subjonctif		14 plus-que-parfait du subjonctif	
fermasse	fermassions	eusse fermé	eussions fermé
fermasses	fermassiez	eusses fermé	eussiez fermé
fermât	fermassent	eût fermé	eussent fermé

Impératif
ferme
fermons
fermez

Fermez la porte, s'il vous plaît.   Please close the door.
Je fermais la porte quand j'ai entendu le téléphone sonner.   I was closing the door when I heard the phone ring.

enfermer to shut in	**renfermer** to enclose
fermer à clef to lock	**une fermeture** closing, shutting
fermer au verrou to bolt	**une fermeture éclair, une**
Ferme-la! Shut up! Zip it!	**fermeture à glissière** zipper
fermer le robinet to turn off the tap	**l'heure de fermer** closing time
	fermer un programme to close a program (computer)

128

Reflexive regular -er verb   to depend on, to rely on, to trust in

The Seven Simple Tenses		The Seven Compound Tenses	
Singular	Plural	Singular	Plural
1 présent de l'indicatif		**8 passé composé**	
me fie	nous fions	me suis fié(e)	nous sommes fié(e)s
te fies	vous fiez	t'es fié(e)	vous êtes fié(e)(s)
se fie	se fient	s'est fié(e)	se sont fié(e)s
2 imparfait de l'indicatif		**9 plus-que-parfait de l'indicatif**	
me fiais	nous fiions	m'étais fié(e)	nous étions fié(e)s
te fiais	vous fiiez	t'étais fié(e)	vous étiez fié(e)(s)
se fiait	se fiaient	s'était fié(e)	s'étaient fié(e)s
3 passé simple		**10 passé antérieur**	
me fiai	nous fiâmes	me fus fié(e)	nous fûmes fié(e)s
te fias	vous fiâtes	te fus fié(e)	vous fûtes fié(e)(s)
se fia	se fièrent	se fut fié(e)	se furent fié(e)s
4 futur		**11 futur antérieur**	
me fierai	nous fierons	me serai fié(e)	nous serons fié(e)s
te fieras	vous fierez	te seras fié(e)	vous serez fié(e)(s)
se fiera	se fieront	se sera fié(e)	se seront fié(e)s
5 conditionnel		**12 conditionnel passé**	
me fierais	nous fierions	me serais fié(e)	nous serions fié(e)s
te fierais	vous fieriez	te serais fié(e)	vous seriez fié(e)(s)
se fierait	se fieraient	se serait fié(e)	se seraient fié(e)s
6 présent du subjonctif		**13 passé du subjonctif**	
me fie	nous fiions	me sois fié(e)	nous soyons fié(e)s
te fies	vous fiiez	te sois fié(e)	vous soyez fié(e)(s)
se fie	se fient	se soit fié(e)	se soient fié(e)s
7 imparfait du subjonctif		**14 plus-que-parfait du subjonctif**	
me fiasse	nous fiassions	me fusse fié(e)	nous fussions fié(e)s
te fiasses	vous fiassiez	te fusses fié(e)	vous fussiez fié(e)(s)
se fiât	se fiassent	se fût fié(e)	se fussent fié(e)s

Impératif
fie-toi; ne te fie pas
fions-nous; ne nous fions pas
fiez-vous; ne vous fiez pas

---

la confiance confidence, trust
avoir confiance en soi to be self-confident
confier à to confide to
se méfier de to mistrust, to distrust, to beware of
la méfiance mistrust, distrust
fiable reliable, trustworthy
Ne vous fiez pas aux apparences.
    Don't trust appearances.

se fier à to depend on, to trust in, to rely on
se confier à to trust to, to confide in

129

finir	Part. pr. **finissant**	Part. passé **fini**

to finish, to end, to terminate, to complete Regular **-ir** verb

The Seven Simple Tenses		The Seven Compound Tenses	
Singular	Plural	Singular	Plural
1 présent de l'indicatif		8 passé composé	
finis	**finissons**	**ai fini**	**avons fini**
finis	**finissez**	**as fini**	**avez fini**
finit	**finissent**	**a fini**	**ont fini**
2 imparfait de l'indicatif		9 plus-que-parfait de l'indicatif	
finissais	**finissions**	**avais fini**	**avions fini**
finissais	**finissiez**	**avais fini**	**aviez fini**
finissait	**finissaient**	**avait fini**	**avaient fini**
3 passé simple		10 passé antérieur	
finis	**finîmes**	**eus fini**	**eûmes fini**
finis	**finîtes**	**eus fini**	**eûtes fini**
finit	**finirent**	**eut fini**	**eurent fini**
4 futur		11 futur antérieur	
finirai	**finirons**	**aurai fini**	**aurons fini**
finiras	**finirez**	**auras fini**	**aurez fini**
finira	**finiront**	**aura fini**	**auront fini**
5 conditionnel		12 conditionnel passé	
finirais	**finirions**	**aurais fini**	**aurions fini**
finirais	**finiriez**	**aurais fini**	**auriez fini**
finirait	**finiraient**	**aurait fini**	**auraient fini**
6 présent du subjonctif		13 passé du subjonctif	
finisse	**finissions**	**aie fini**	**ayons fini**
finisses	**finissiez**	**aies fini**	**ayez fini**
finisse	**finissent**	**ait fini**	**aient fini**
7 imparfait du subjonctif		14 plus-que-parfait du subjonctif	
finisse	**finissions**	**eusse fini**	**eussions fini**
finisses	**finissiez**	**eusses fini**	**eussiez fini**
finît	**finissent**	**eût fini**	**eussent fini**
		Impératif	
		finis	
		finissons	
		finissez	

finir de + inf.   to finish + pr. part.
J'ai fini de travailler pour aujourd'hui.   I have finished working for today.

finir par + inf.   to end up by + pr. part.
Louis a fini par quitter son emploi pour reprendre ses études à l'université.
Louis ended up quitting his job to resume his studies at the university.

la fin   the end; **la fin de semaine**   weekend; **C'est fini!**   It's all over!
afin de   in order to; **enfin**   finally; **finalement**   finally
mettre fin à   to put an end to; **final, finale**   final; **définir**   to define
Tout est bien qui finit bien.   All's well that ends well.

130

Regular -er verb endings: spelling change: c changes   to force
to ç before a or o to keep s sound.

The Seven Simple Tenses		The Seven Compound Tenses	
Singular	Plural	Singular	Plural

1 présent de l'indicatif		8 passé composé	
force	**forçons**	**ai forcé**	**avons forcé**
forces	**forcez**	**as forcé**	**avez forcé**
force	**forcent**	**a forcé**	**ont forcé**
2 imparfait de l'indicatif		9 plus-que-parfait de l'indicatif	
forçais	**forcions**	**avais forcé**	**avions forcé**
forçais	**forciez**	**avais forcé**	**aviez forcé**
forçait	**forçaient**	**avait forcé**	**avaient forcé**
3 passé simple		10 passé antérieur	
forçai	**forçâmes**	**eus forcé**	**eûmes forcé**
forças	**forçâtes**	**eus forcé**	**eûtes forcé**
força	**forcèrent**	**eut forcé**	**eurent forcé**
4 futur		11 futur antérieur	
forcerai	**forcerons**	**aurai forcé**	**aurons forcé**
forceras	**forcerez**	**auras forcé**	**aurez forcé**
forcera	**forceront**	**aura forcé**	**auront forcé**
5 conditionnel		12 conditionnel passé	
forcerais	**forcerions**	**aurais forcé**	**aurions forcé**
forcerais	**forceriez**	**aurais forcé**	**auriez forcé**
forcerait	**forceraient**	**aurait forcé**	**auraient forcé**
6 présent du subjonctif		13 passé du subjonctif	
force	**forcions**	**aie forcé**	**ayons forcé**
forces	**forciez**	**aies forcé**	**ayez forcé**
force	**forcent**	**ait forcé**	**aient forcé**
7 imparfait du subjonctif		14 plus-que-parfait du subjonctif	
forçasse	**forçassions**	**eusse forcé**	**eussions forcé**
forçasses	**forçassiez**	**eusses forcé**	**eussiez forcé**
forçât	**forçassent**	**eût forcé**	**eussent forcé**

Impératif
force
forçons
forcez

---

forcer la porte de qqn   to force one's way into someone's house
être forcé de faire qqch   to be obliged to do something
se forcer la voix   to strain one's voice
un forçat   a convict
à force de   by dint of, by means of
la force   strength, force; **avec force**   forcefully, with force
forcément   necessarily, inevitably
forcer qqn à faire qqch   to force someone to do something

frapper Part. pr. **frappant** Part. passé **frappé**

to knock, to hit, to frap, to rap, to strike (hit) Regular -er verb

The Seven Simple Tenses		The Seven Compound Tenses	
Singular	Plural	Singular	Plural
1 présent de l'indicatif		8 passé composé	
frappe	frappons	ai frappé	avons frappé
frappes	frappez	as frappé	avez frappé
frappe	frappent	a frappé	ont frappé
2 imparfait de l'indicatif		9 plus-que-parfait de l'indicatif	
frappais	frappions	avais frappé	avions frappé
frappais	frappiez	avais frappé	aviez frappé
frappait	frappaient	avait frappé	avaient frappé
3 passé simple		10 passé antérieur	
frappai	frappâmes	eus frappé	eûmes frappé
frappas	frappâtes	eus frappé	eûtes frappé
frappa	frappèrent	eut frappé	eurent frappé
4 futur		11 futur antérieur	
frapperai	frapperons	aurai frappé	aurons frappé
frapperas	frapperez	auras frappé	aurez frappé
frappera	frapperont	aura frappé	auront frappé
5 conditionnel		12 conditionnel passé	
frapperais	frapperions	aurais frappé	aurions frappé
frapperais	frapperiez	aurais frappé	auriez frappé
frapperait	frapperaient	aurait frappé	auraient frappé
6 présent du subjonctif		13 passé du subjonctif	
frappe	frappions	aie frappé	ayons frappé
frappes	frappiez	aies frappé	ayez frappé
frappe	frappent	ait frappé	aient frappé
7 imparfait du subjonctif		14 plus-que-parfait du subjonctif	
frappasse	frappassions	eusse frappé	eussions frappé
frappasses	frappassiez	eusses frappé	eussiez frappé
frappât	frappassent	eût frappé	eussent frappé

Impératif
frappe
frappons
frappez

---

se frapper la poitrine to beat one's chest
le frappage striking (medals, coins)
une faute de frappe a typing mistake
frapper à la porte to knock on the door
frapper du pied to stamp one's foot
entrer sans frapper enter without knocking
C'est frappant! It's striking!

frappé (frappée) de stricken with
le frappement beating, striking
frappé à mort mortally wounded
un lait frappé a milkshake

Part. pr. —	Part. passé **frit**		**frire**

Defective verb   to fry

The Seven Simple Tenses		The Seven Compound Tenses	
Singular	Plural	Singular	Plural
1 présent de l'indicatif		**8 passé composé**	
fris		**ai frit**	**avons frit**
fris		**as frit**	**avez frit**
frit		**a frit**	**ont frit**
		9 plus-que-parfait de l'indicatif	
		avais frit	**avions frit**
		avais frit	**aviez frit**
		avait frit	**avaient frit**
		10 passé antérieur	
		eus frit	**eûmes frit**
		eus frit	**eûtes frit**
		eut frit	**eurent frit**
4 futur		**11 futur antérieur**	
frirai	**frirons**	**aurai frit**	**aurons frit**
friras	**frirez**	**auras frit**	**aurez frit**
frira	**friront**	**aura frit**	**auront frit**
5 conditionnel		**12 conditionnel passé**	
frirais	**fririons**	**aurais frit**	**aurions frit**
frirais	**fririez**	**aurais frit**	**auriez frit**
frirait	**friraient**	**aurait frit**	**auraient frit**
		13 passé du subjonctif	
		aie frit	**ayons frit**
		aies frit	**ayez frit**
		ait frit	**aient frit**
		14 plus-que-parfait du subjonctif	
		eusse frit	**eussions frit**
		eusses frit	**eussiez frit**
		eût frit	**eussent frit**

Impératif
fris
faisons frire
faites frire

---

faire frire to fry (see note below)   **des pommes de terre frites** fried potatoes
pommes frites French fries   (French style)
une friteuse frying basket   **un bifteck frites, un steak-frites** steak
la friture frying   with French fries

Note: This verb is generally used only in the persons and tenses given above. To supply the forms that are lacking, use the appropriate form of **faire** plus the infinitive **frire**, e.g., the plural of the present indicative is: **nous faisons frire, vous faites frire, ils font frire**.

to flee, to fly off, to shun, to leak   Irregular verb

The Seven Simple Tenses		The Seven Compound Tenses	
Singular	Plural	Singular	Plural
1 présent de l'indicatif		8 passé composé	
fuis	fuyons	ai fui	avons fui
fuis	fuyez	as fui	avez fui
fuit	fuient	a fui	ont fui
2 imparfait de l'indicatif		9 plus-que-parfait de l'indicatif	
fuyais	fuyions	avais fui	avions fui
fuyais	fuyiez	avais fui	aviez fui
fuyait	fuyaient	avait fui	avaient fui
3 passé simple		10 passé antérieur	
fuis	fuîmes	eus fui	eûmes fui
fuis	fuîtes	eus fui	eûtes fui
fuit	fuirent	eut fui	eurent fui
4 futur		11 futur antérieur	
fuirai	fuirons	aurai fui	aurons fui
fuiras	fuirez	auras fui	aurez fui
fuira	fuiront	aura fui	auront fui
5 conditionnel		12 conditionnel passé	
fuirais	fuirions	aurais fui	aurions fui
fuirais	fuiriez	aurais fui	auriez fui
fuirait	fuiraient	aurait fui	auraient fui
6 présent du subjonctif		13 passé du subjonctif	
fuie	fuyions	aie fui	ayons fui
fuies	fuyiez	aies fui	ayez fui
fuie	fuient	ait fui	aient fui
7 imparfait du subjonctif		14 plus-que-parfait du subjonctif	
fuisse	fuissions	eusse fui	eussions fui
fuisses	fuissiez	eusses fui	eussiez fui
fuît	fuissent	eût fui	eussent fui
		Impératif	
		fuis	
		fuyons	
		fuyez	

faire fuir to put to flight		**s'enfuir de** to flee from, to run away from
la fuite flight		**fugitif, fugitive** fugitive, fleeting, runaway
prendre la fuite to take to flight		**fugitivement** fugitively
une fuite de gaz gas leak		
faire une fugue to run away, to elope		

Regular -er verb   to smoke, to steam

The Seven Simple Tenses		The Seven Compound Tenses	
Singular	Plural	Singular	Plural

1 présent de l'indicatif		8 passé composé	
fume	fumons	ai fumé	avons fumé
fumes	fumez	as fumé	avez fumé
fume	fument	a fumé	ont fumé

2 imparfait de l'indicatif		9 plus-que-parfait de l'indicatif	
fumais	fumions	avais fumé	avions fumé
fumais	fumiez	avais fumé	aviez fumé
fumait	fumaient	avait fumé	avaient fumé

3 passé simple		10 passé antérieur	
fumai	fumâmes	eus fumé	eûmes fumé
fumas	fumâtes	eus fumé	eûtes fumé
fuma	fumèrent	eut fumé	eurent fumé

4 futur		11 futur antérieur	
fumerai	fumerons	aurai fumé	aurons fumé
fumeras	fumerez	auras fumé	aurez fumé
fumera	fumeront	aura fumé	auront fumé

5 conditionnel		12 conditionnel passé	
fumerais	fumerions	aurais fumé	aurions fumé
fumerais	fumeriez	aurais fumé	auriez fumé
fumerait	fumeraient	aurait fumé	auraient fumé

6 présent du subjonctif		13 passé du subjonctif	
fume	fumions	aie fumé	ayons fumé
fumes	fumiez	aies fumé	ayez fumé
fume	fument	ait fumé	aient fumé

7 imparfait du subjonctif		14 plus-que-parfait du subjonctif	
fumasse	fumassions	eusse fumé	eussions fumé
fumasses	fumassiez	eusses fumé	eussiez fumé
fumât	fumassent	eût fumé	eussent fumé

	Impératif
	fume
	fumons
	fumez

Le père: **Je te défends de fumer. C'est une mauvaise habitude.**   I forbid you to smoke. It's a bad habit.

Le fils: **Alors, pourquoi fumes-tu, papa?**   Then why do you smoke, Dad?

Défense de fumer No smoking allowed
la fumée smoke
un rideau de fumée smoke screen
parfumer to perfume
compartiment (pour) fumeurs
  smoking car (on a train)

fumeux, fumeuse smoky
un fume-cigare cigar holder
un fume-cigarette cigarette holder
un fumeur, une fumeuse smoker
  (person who smokes)
non-fumeur non-smoking

to win, to earn, to gain   Regular **-er** verb

The Seven Simple Tenses		The Seven Compound Tenses	
Singular	Plural	Singular	Plural
1 présent de l'indicatif		**8 passé composé**	
gagne	gagnons	ai gagné	avons gagné
gagnes	gagnez	as gagné	avez gagné
gagne	gagnent	a gagné	ont gagné
2 imparfait de l'indicatif		**9 plus-que-parfait de l'indicatif**	
gagnais	gagnions	avais gagné	avions gagné
gagnais	gagniez	avais gagné	aviez gagné
gagnait	gagnaient	avait gagné	avaient gagné
3 passé simple		**10 passé antérieur**	
gagnai	gagnâmes	eus gagné	eûmes gagné
gagnas	gagnâtes	eus gagné	eûtes gagné
gagna	gagnèrent	eut gagné	eurent gagné
4 futur		**11 futur antérieur**	
gagnerai	gagnerons	aurai gagné	aurons gagné
gagneras	gagnerez	auras gagné	aurez gagné
gagnera	gagneront	aura gagné	auront gagné
5 conditionnel		**12 conditionnel passé**	
gagnerais	gagnerions	aurais gagné	aurions gagné
gagnerais	gagneriez	aurais gagné	auriez gagné
gagnerait	gagneraient	aurait gagné	auraient gagné
6 présent du subjonctif		**13 passé du subjonctif**	
gagne	gagnions	aie gagné	ayons gagné
gagnes	gagniez	aies gagné	ayez gagné
gagne	gagnent	ait gagné	aient gagné
7 imparfait du subjonctif		**14 plus-que-parfait du subjonctif**	
gagnasse	gagnassions	eusse gagné	eussions gagné
gagnasses	gagnassiez	eusses gagné	eussiez gagné
gagnât	gagnassent	eût gagné	eussent gagné

Impératif
gagne
gagnons
gagnez

---

gagner sa vie to earn one's living
gagner du poids to gain weight
gagner de l'argent to earn money
gagnable obtainable
gagner du temps to save time
un gagne-pain job
un gagnant, une gagnante a winner

regagner to regain, to recover, to win back
regagner le temps perdu to make up (to recover) time lost
gagner le gros lot to win the jackpot
Vous n'y gagnerez rien de bon. You will get nothing good out of it.

Regular **-er** verb   to guard, to keep, to retain

The Seven Simple Tenses		The Seven Compound Tenses	
Singular	Plural	Singular	Plural
1 présent de l'indicatif		8 passé composé	
garde	gardons	ai gardé	avons gardé
gardes	gardez	as gardé	avez gardé
garde	gardent	a gardé	ont gardé
2 imparfait de l'indicatif		9 plus-que-parfait de l'indicatif	
gardais	gardions	avais gardé	avions gardé
gardais	gardiez	avais gardé	aviez gardé
gardait	gardaient	avait gardé	avaient gardé
3 passé simple		10 passé antérieur	
gardai	gardâmes	eus gardé	eûmes gardé
gardas	gardâtes	eus gardé	eûtes gardé
garda	gardèrent	eut gardé	eurent gardé
4 futur		11 futur antérieur	
garderai	garderons	aurai gardé	aurons gardé
garderas	garderez	auras gardé	aurez gardé
gardera	garderont	aura gardé	auront gardé
5 conditionnel		12 conditionnel passé	
garderais	garderions	aurais gardé	aurions gardé
garderais	garderiez	aurais gardé	auriez gardé
garderait	garderaient	aurait gardé	auraient gardé
6 présent du subjonctif		13 passé du subjonctif	
garde	gardions	aie gardé	ayons gardé
gardes	gardiez	aies gardé	ayez gardé
garde	gardent	ait gardé	aient gardé
7 imparfait du subjonctif		14 plus-que-parfait du subjonctif	
gardasse	gardassions	eusse gardé	eussions gardé
gardasses	gardassiez	eusses gardé	eussiez gardé
gardât	gardassent	eût gardé	eussent gardé

Impératif
garde
gardons
gardez

Raoul garde tout son argent dans son matelas.   Ralph keeps all his money in his mattress.

se garder   to protect oneself
se garder de tomber   to take care not to fall
un gardien, une gardienne   guardian
prendre garde de   to take care not to
une gardienne d'enfants   babysitter
une garde-robe   wardrobe (closet)
un gardien de but   goalie
regarder   to look at, to watch, to consider, to regard

un garde-manger   pantry
un garde-vue   eyeshade (visor)
En garde!   On guard!
Dieu m'en garde!   God forbid!
un garde-fou   guard rail
un chien de garde, une chienne de garde   guard dog

gâter	Part. pr. gâtant	Part. passé gâté

to spoil, to damage

Regular -er verb

The Seven Simple Tenses		The Seven Compound Tenses	
Singular	Plural	Singular	Plural
1 présent de l'indicatif		8 passé composé	
gâte	gâtons	ai gâté	avons gâté
gâtes	gâtez	as gâté	avez gâté
gâte	gâtent	a gâté	ont gâté
2 imparfait de l'indicatif		9 plus-que-parfait de l'indicatif	
gâtais	gâtions	avais gâté	avions gâté
gâtais	gâtiez	avais gâté	aviez gâté
gâtait	gâtaient	avait gâté	avaient gâté
3 passé simple		10 passé antérieur	
gâtai	gâtâmes	eus gâté	eûmes gâté
gâtas	gâtâtes	eus gâté	eûtes gâté
gâta	gâtèrent	eut gâté	eurent gâté
4 futur		11 futur antérieur	
gâterai	gâterons	aurai gâté	aurons gâté
gâteras	gâterez	auras gâté	aurez gâté
gâtera	gâteront	aura gâté	auront gâté
5 conditionnel		12 conditionnel passé	
gâterais	gâterions	aurais gâté	aurions gâté
gâterais	gâteriez	aurais gâté	auriez gâté
gâterait	gâteraient	aurait gâté	auraient gâté
6 présent du subjonctif		13 passé du subjonctif	
gâte	gâtions	aie gâté	ayons gâté
gâtes	gâtiez	aies gâté	ayez gâté
gâte	gâtent	ait gâté	aient gâté
7 imparfait du subjonctif		14 plus-que-parfait du subjonctif	
gâtasse	gâtassions	eusse gâté	eussions gâté
gâtasses	gâtassiez	eusses gâté	eussiez gâté
gâtât	gâtassent	eût gâté	eussent gâté

Impératif
gâte
gâtons
gâtez

Marcel est un enfant gâté. Je n'aime pas jouer avec lui. Il gâte tout. Il demande toujours des gâteries.   Marcel is a spoiled child. I don't like to play with him. He spoils everything. He always asks for treats.

gâter un enfant   to spoil a child
se gâter   to pamper oneself
faire des dégâts   to cause damage

un enfant gâté   a spoiled child
une gâterie   a treat

Regular -er verb endings: spelling change: **to freeze**
e changes to è before syllable with mute e.

The Seven Simple Tenses		The Seven Compound Tenses	
Singular	Plural	Singular	Plural
1 présent de l'indicatif		8 passé composé	
gèle	gelons	ai gelé	avons gelé
gèles	gelez	as gelé	avez gelé
gèle	gèlent	a gelé	ont gelé
2 imparfait de l'indicatif		9 plus-que-parfait de l'indicatif	
gelais	gelions	avais gelé	avions gelé
gelais	geliez	avais gelé	aviez gelé
gelait	gelaient	avait gelé	avaient gelé
3 passé simple		10 passé antérieur	
gelai	gelâmes	eus gelé	eûmes gelé
gelas	gelâtes	eus gelé	eûtes gelé
gela	gelèrent	eut gelé	eurent gelé
4 futur		11 futur antérieur	
gèlerai	gèlerons	aurai gelé	aurons gelé
gèleras	gèlerez	auras gelé	aurez gelé
gèlera	gèleront	aura gelé	auront gelé
5 conditionnel		12 conditionnel passé	
gèlerais	gèlerions	aurais gelé	aurions gelé
gèlerais	gèleriez	aurais gelé	auriez gelé
gèlerait	gèleraient	aurait gelé	auraient gelé
6 présent du subjonctif		13 passé du subjonctif	
gèle	gelions	aie gelé	ayons gelé
gèles	geliez	aies gelé	ayez gelé
gèle	gèlent	ait gelé	aient gelé
7 imparfait du subjonctif		14 plus-que-parfait du subjonctif	
gelasse	gelassions	eusse gelé	eussions gelé
gelasses	gelassiez	eusses gelé	eussiez gelé
gelât	gelassent	eût gelé	eussent gelé
		Impératif	
		gèle	
		gelons	
		gelez	

Je ne veux pas sortir aujourd'hui parce qu'il gèle. Quand je me suis levé ce matin, j'ai regardé par la fenêtre et j'ai vu de la gelée partout.

Il gèle! It's freezing!	congeler to congeal, to freeze
Qu'il gèle! Let it freeze!	la congélation congelation, freezing, icing
le gel frost, freezing	le point de congélation freezing point
la gelée frost	à la gelée jellied
le congélateur freezer	

139

goûter   Part. pr. goûtant   Part. passé goûté

to taste, to have a snack, to enjoy   Regular -er verb

The Seven Simple Tenses		The Seven Compound Tenses	
Singular	Plural	Singular	Plural
1 présent de l'indicatif		8 passé composé	
goûte	goûtons	ai goûté	avons goûté
goûtes	goûtez	as goûté	avez goûté
goûte	goûtent	a goûté	ont goûté
2 imparfait de l'indicatif		9 plus-que-parfait de l'indicatif	
goûtais	goûtions	avais goûté	avions goûté
goûtais	goûtiez	avais goûté	aviez goûté
goûtait	goûtaient	avait goûté	avaient goûté
3 passé simple		10 passé antérieur	
goûtai	goûtâmes	eus goûté	eûmes goûté
goûtas	goûtâtes	eus goûté	eûtes goûté
goûta	goûtèrent	eut goûté	eurent goûté
4 futur		11 futur antérieur	
goûterai	goûterons	aurai goûté	aurons goûté
goûteras	goûterez	auras goûté	aurez goûté
goûtera	goûteront	aura goûté	auront goûté
5 conditionnel		12 conditionnel passé	
goûterais	goûterions	aurais goûté	aurions goûté
goûterais	goûteriez	aurais goûté	auriez goûté
goûterait	goûteraient	aurait goûté	auraient goûté
6 présent du subjonctif		13 passé du subjonctif	
goûte	goûtions	aie goûté	ayons goûté
goûtes	goûtiez	aies goûté	ayez goûté
goûte	goûtent	ait goûté	aient goûté
7 imparfait du subjonctif		14 plus-que-parfait du subjonctif	
goûtasse	goûtassions	eusse goûté	eussions goûté
goûtasses	goûtassiez	eusses goûté	eussiez goûté
goûtât	goûtassent	eût goûté	eussent goûté

Impératif
goûte
goûtons
goûtez

Quand j'arrive chez moi de l'école l'après-midi, j'ai l'habitude de prendre le goûter à quatre heures.

le goûter snack, bite to eat	de mauvais goût in bad taste
goûter sur l'herbe to have a picnic	avoir un goût de to taste like
à chacun son goût to each his own	goûter de to eat or drink something for
goûter à to drink or eat only a small	the first time
quantity	dégoûter to disgust
le goût taste	C'est dégoûtant! It's disgusting!

Note: The Académie française now allows **goûter** and related words to be
spelled without the circumflex accent (^): **gouter**.

Regular **-ir** verb   to grow (up, taller), to increase

The Seven Simple Tenses		The Seven Compound Tenses	
Singular	Plural	Singular	Plural
1 présent de l'indicatif		**8 passé composé**	
grandis	**grandissons**	**ai grandi**	**avons grandi**
grandis	**grandissez**	**as grandi**	**avez grandi**
grandit	**grandissent**	**a grandi**	**ont grandi**
2 imparfait de l'indicatif		**9 plus-que-parfait de l'indicatif**	
grandissais	**grandissions**	**avais grandi**	**avions grandi**
grandissais	**grandissiez**	**avais grandi**	**aviez grandi**
grandissait	**grandissaient**	**avait grandi**	**avaient grandi**
3 passé simple		**10 passé antérieur**	
grandis	**grandîmes**	**eus grandi**	**eûmes grandi**
grandis	**grandîtes**	**eus grandi**	**eûtes grandi**
grandit	**grandirent**	**eut grandi**	**eurent grandi**
4 futur		**11 futur antérieur**	
grandirai	**grandirons**	**aurai grandi**	**aurons grandi**
grandiras	**grandirez**	**auras grandi**	**aurez grandi**
grandira	**grandiront**	**aura grandi**	**auront grandi**
5 conditionnel		**12 conditionnel passé**	
grandirais	**grandirions**	**aurais grandi**	**aurions grandi**
grandirais	**grandiriez**	**aurais grandi**	**auriez grandi**
grandirait	**grandiraient**	**aurait grandi**	**auraient grandi**
6 présent du subjonctif		**13 passé du subjonctif**	
grandisse	**grandissions**	**aie grandi**	**ayons grandi**
grandisses	**grandissiez**	**aies grandi**	**ayez grandi**
grandisse	**grandissent**	**ait grandi**	**aient grandi**
7 imparfait du subjonctif		**14 plus-que-parfait du subjonctif**	
grandisse	**grandissions**	**eusse grandi**	**eussions grandi**
grandisses	**grandissiez**	**eusses grandi**	**eussiez grandi**
grandît	**grandissent**	**eût grandi**	**eussent grandi**

	Impératif
	grandis
	grandissons
	grandissez

Voyez-vous comme Joseph et Joséphine ont grandi? C'est incroyable! Quel âge ont-ils maintenant?

le grandissement growth	**agrandir** to expand, to enlarge
grandiose grandiose, grand	**un agrandissement** enlargement,
grand, grande tall	extension, aggrandizement
la grandeur size, greatness, grandeur	**un enfant grandi trop vite**
grandiosement grandiosely	a lanky child (grew tall too fast)

141

gronder	Part. pr. **grondant**	Part. passé **grondé**

to chide, to reprimand, to scold   Regular -er verb

The Seven Simple Tenses		The Seven Compound Tenses	
Singular	Plural	Singular	Plural
1 présent de l'indicatif		8 passé composé	
gronde	grondons	ai grondé	avons grondé
grondes	grondez	as grondé	avez grondé
gronde	grondent	a grondé	ont grondé
2 imparfait de l'indicatif		9 plus-que-parfait de l'indicatif	
grondais	grondions	avais grondé	avions grondé
grondais	grondiez	avais grondé	aviez grondé
grondait	grondaient	avait grondé	avaient grondé
3 passé simple		10 passé antérieur	
grondai	grondâmes	eus grondé	eûmes grondé
grondas	grondâtes	eus grondé	eûtes grondé
gronda	grondèrent	eut grondé	eurent grondé
4 futur		11 futur antérieur	
gronderai	gronderons	aurai grondé	aurons grondé
gronderas	gronderez	auras grondé	aurez grondé
grondera	gronderont	aura grondé	auront grondé
5 conditionnel		12 conditionnel passé	
gronderais	gronderions	aurais grondé	aurions grondé
gronderais	gronderiez	aurais grondé	auriez grondé
gronderait	gronderaient	aurait grondé	auraient grondé
6 présent du subjonctif		13 passé du subjonctif	
gronde	grondions	aie grondé	ayons grondé
grondes	grondiez	aies grondé	ayez grondé
gronde	grondent	ait grondé	aient grondé
7 imparfait du subjonctif		14 plus-que-parfait du subjonctif	
grondasse	grondassions	eusse grondé	eussions grondé
grondasses	grondassiez	eusses grondé	eussiez grondé
grondât	grondassent	eût grondé	eussent grondé

	Impératif
	gronde
	grondons
	grondez

—Victor, pourquoi pleures-tu?

—La maitresse de mathématiques m'a grondé.

—Pourquoi est-ce qu'elle t'a grondé? Qu'est-ce que tu as fait?

—Ce n'est pas parce que j'ai fait quelque chose. C'est parce que je n'ai rien fait. Je n'ai pas préparé la leçon.

—Alors, tu mérites une gronderie et une réprimande.

—Elle gronde à chaque instant.

grondeur, grondeuse *adj.* scolding
une gronderie a scolding

à chaque instant constantly
Il nous a parlé d'un ton grondeur.
     He spoke to us in a scolding tone.

Regular -ir verb   to cure, to heal, to remedy, to recover

The Seven Simple Tenses		The Seven Compound Tenses	
Singular	Plural	Singular	Plural
1 présent de l'indicatif		**8 passé composé**	
guéris	guérissons	ai guéri	avons guéri
guéris	guérissez	as guéri	avez guéri
guérit	guérissent	a guéri	ont guéri
2 imparfait de l'indicatif		**9 plus-que-parfait de l'indicatif**	
guérissais	guérissions	avais guéri	avions guéri
guérissais	guérissiez	avais guéri	aviez guéri
guérissait	guérissaient	avait guéri	avaient guéri
3 passé simple		**10 passé antérieur**	
guéris	guérîmes	eus guéri	eûmes guéri
guéris	guérîtes	eus guéri	eûtes guéri
guérit	guérirent	eut guéri	eurent guéri
4 futur		**11 futur antérieur**	
guérirai	guérirons	aurai guéri	aurons guéri
guériras	guérirez	auras guéri	aurez guéri
guérira	guériront	aura guéri	auront guéri
5 conditionnel		**12 conditionnel passé**	
guérirais	guéririons	aurais guéri	aurions guéri
guérirais	guéririez	aurais guéri	auriez guéri
guérirait	guériraient	aurait guéri	auraient guéri
6 présent du subjonctif		**13 passé du subjonctif**	
guérisse	guérissions	aie guéri	ayons guéri
guérisses	guérissiez	aies guéri	ayez guéri
guérisse	guérissent	ait guéri	aient guéri
7 imparfait du subjonctif		**14 plus-que-parfait du subjonctif**	
guérisse	guérissions	eusse guéri	eussions guéri
guérisses	guérissiez	eusses guéri	eussiez guéri
guérît	guérissent	eût guéri	eussent guéri
		Impératif	
		guéris	
		guérissons	
		guérissez	

Madame Gérard est tombée dans l'escalier la semaine dernière et elle s'est blessée au genou. Elle est allée chez le médecin et maintenant elle est guérie. Mrs. Gérard fell down the stairs last week and hurt her knee. She went to the doctor and now she is healed.

une guérison   healing, cure
guérisseur, guérisseuse   healer, faith healer
guérissable   curable

guérir de   to recover from, to cure of
la guérison par la foi   faith healing

s'habiller

Part. pr. **s'habillant** Part. passé **habillé(e)(s)**

to get dressed, to dress (oneself)

Reflexive regular -er verb

The Seven Simple Tenses		The Seven Compound Tenses	
Singular	Plural	Singular	Plural
1 présent de l'indicatif		**8 passé composé**	
m'habille	nous habillons	me suis habillé(e)	nous sommes habillé(e)s
t'habilles	vous habillez	t'es habillé(e)	vous êtes habillé(e)(s)
s'habille	s'habillent	s'est habillé(e)	se sont habillé(e)s
2 imparfait de l'indicatif		**9 plus-que-parfait de l'indicatif**	
m'habillais	nous habillions	m'étais habillé(e)	nous étions habillé(e)s
t'habillais	vous habilliez	t'étais habillé(e)	vous étiez habillé(e)(s)
s'habillait	s'habillaient	s'était habillé(e)	s'étaient habillé(e)s
3 passé simple		**10 passé antérieur**	
m'habillai	nous habillâmes	me fus habillé(e)	nous fûmes habillé(e)s
t'habillas	vous habillâtes	te fus habillé(e)	vous fûtes habillé(e)(s)
s'habilla	s'habillèrent	se fut habillé(e)	se furent habillé(e)s
4 futur		**11 futur antérieur**	
m'habillerai	nous habillerons	me serai habillé(e)	nous serons habillé(e)s
t'habilleras	vous habillerez	te seras habillé(e)	vous serez habillé(e)(s)
s'habillera	s'habilleront	se sera habillé(e)	se seront habillé(e)s
5 conditionnel		**12 conditionnel passé**	
m'habillerais	nous habillerions	me serais habillé(e)	nous serions habillé(e)s
t'habillerais	vous habilleriez	te serais habillé(e)	vous seriez habillé(e)(s)
s'habillerait	s'habilleraient	se serait habillé(e)	se seraient habillé(e)s
6 présent du subjonctif		**13 passé du subjonctif**	
m'habille	nous habillions	me sois habillé(e)	nous soyons habillé(e)s
t'habilles	vous habilliez	te sois habillé(e)	vous soyez habillé(e)(s)
s'habille	s'habillent	se soit habillé(e)	se soient habillé(e)s
7 imparfait du subjonctif		**14 plus-que-parfait du subjonctif**	
m'habillasse	nous habillassions	me fusse habillé(e)	nous fussions habillé(e)s
t'habillasses	vous habillassiez	te fusses habillé(e)	vous fussiez habillé(e)(s)
s'habillât	s'habillassent	se fût habillé(e)	se fussent habillé(e)s

Impératif
habille-toi; ne t'habille pas
habillons-nous; ne nous habillons pas
habillez-vous; ne vous habillez pas

---

un **habit** costume, outfit
les **habits** clothes
habiller qqn to dress someone
habillement *m.* garment, wearing apparel
L'habit ne fait pas le moine. Clothes don't make the person (the monk).

déshabiller to undress
se déshabiller to undress oneself, to get undressed
habiller de to clothe with
l'habit de gala formal wear
l'habit militaire military dress

Regular -er verb to live (in), to dwell (in), to inhabit

The Seven Simple Tenses		The Seven Compound Tenses	
Singular	Plural	Singular	Plural
1 présent de l'indicatif		8 passé composé	
habite	**habitons**	**ai habité**	**avons habité**
habites	**habitez**	**as habité**	**avez habité**
habite	**habitent**	**a habité**	**ont habité**
2 imparfait de l'indicatif		9 plus-que-parfait de l'indicatif	
habitais	**habitions**	**avais habité**	**avions habité**
habitais	**habitiez**	**avais habité**	**aviez habité**
habitait	**habitaient**	**avait habité**	**avaient habité**
3 passé simple		10 passé antérieur	
habitai	**habitâmes**	**eus habité**	**eûmes habité**
habitas	**habitâtes**	**eus habité**	**eûtes habité**
habita	**habitèrent**	**eut habité**	**eurent habité**
4 futur		11 futur antérieur	
habiterai	**habiterons**	**aurai habité**	**aurons habité**
habiteras	**habiterez**	**auras habité**	**aurez habité**
habitera	**habiteront**	**aura habité**	**auront habité**
5 conditionnel		12 conditionnel passé	
habiterais	**habiterions**	**aurais habité**	**aurions habité**
habiterais	**habiteriez**	**aurais habité**	**auriez habité**
habiterait	**habiteraient**	**aurait habité**	**auraient habité**
6 présent du subjonctif		13 passé du subjonctif	
habite	**habitions**	**aie habité**	**ayons habité**
habites	**habitiez**	**aies habité**	**ayez habité**
habite	**habitent**	**ait habité**	**aient habité**
7 imparfait du subjonctif		14 plus-que-parfait du subjonctif	
habitasse	**habitassions**	**eusse habité**	**eussions habité**
habitasses	**habitassiez**	**eusses habité**	**eussiez habité**
habitât	**habitassent**	**eût habité**	**eussent habité**

Impératif
habite
habitons
habitez

—Où habitez-vous?
—J'habite 27 rue Duparc dans une petite maison blanche.
—Avec qui habitez-vous?
—J'habite avec mes parents, mes frères, mes soeurs, et mon chien.

une habitation dwelling, residence, abode
un habitat habitat
un habitant inhabitant
H.L.M. (habitation à loyer modéré)
 lodging at a moderate rental

l'amélioration de l'habitat
 improvement of living conditions
habiter à la campagne to live in
 the country
habiter la banlieue to live in the
 suburbs

Note: Be careful! **Habitable** means *habitable* or *inhabitable*.
But **inhabitable** means *uninhabitable*.

haïr

Part. pr. **haïssant**   Part. passé **haï**

to hate   Irregular verb

The Seven Simple Tenses		The Seven Compound Tenses	
Singular	Plural	Singular	Plural
1 présent de l'indicatif		8 passé composé	
hais	haïssons	ai haï	avons haï
hais	haïssez	as haï	avez haï
hait	haïssent	a haï	ont haï
2 imparfait de l'indicatif		9 plus-que-parfait de l'indicatif	
haïssais	haïssions	avais haï	avions haï
haïssais	haïssiez	avais haï	aviez haï
haïssait	haïssaient	avait haï	avaient haï
3 passé simple		10 passé antérieur	
haïs	haïmes	eus haï	eûmes haï
haïs	haïtes	eus haï	eûtes haï
haït	haïrent	eut haï	eurent haï
4 futur		11 futur antérieur	
haïrai	haïrons	aurai haï	aurons haï
haïras	haïrez	auras haï	aurez haï
haïra	haïront	aura haï	auront haï
5 conditionnel		12 conditionnel passé	
haïrais	haïrions	aurais haï	aurions haï
haïrais	haïriez	aurais haï	auriez haï
haïrait	haïraient	aurait haï	auraient haï
6 présent du subjonctif		13 passé du subjonctif	
haïsse	haïssions	aie haï	ayons haï
haïsses	haïssiez	aies haï	ayez haï
haïsse	haïssent	ait haï	aient haï
7 imparfait du subjonctif		14 plus-que-parfait du subjonctif	
haïsse	haïssions	eusse haï	eussions haï
haïsses	haïssiez	eusses haï	eussiez haï
haït	haïssent	eût haï	eussent haï
		Impératif	
		hais	
		haïssons	
		haïssez	

Je hais le mensonge, je hais la médiocrité, et je hais la calomnie. Ces choses sont haïssables.   I hate lying, I hate mediocrity, and I hate slander. These things are detestable.

haïssable   detestable, hateful
la haine   hatred, hate
haineux, haineuse   hateful, heinous

haïr qqn comme la peste
to hate somebody like poison

This verb begins with an aspirate h; make no liaison and use je instead of j'.

146

Regular -er verb   to insist

The Seven Simple Tenses		The Seven Compound Tenses	
Singular	Plural	Singular	Plural
1 présent de l'indicatif		8 passé composé	
insiste	**insistons**	**ai insisté**	**avons insisté**
insistes	**insistez**	**as insisté**	**avez insisté**
insiste	**insistent**	**a insisté**	**ont insisté**
2 imparfait de l'indicatif		9 plus-que-parfait de l'indicatif	
insistais	**insistions**	**avais insisté**	**avions insisté**
insistais	**insistiez**	**avais insisté**	**aviez insisté**
insistait	**insistaient**	**avait insisté**	**avaient insisté**
3 passé simple		10 passé antérieur	
insistai	**insistâmes**	**eus insisté**	**eûmes insisté**
insistas	**insistâtes**	**eus insisté**	**eûtes insisté**
insista	**insistèrent**	**eut insisté**	**eurent insisté**
4 futur		11 futur antérieur	
insisterai	**insisterons**	**aurai insisté**	**aurons insisté**
insisteras	**insisterez**	**auras insisté**	**aurez insisté**
insistera	**insisteront**	**aura insisté**	**auront insisté**
5 conditionnel		12 conditionnel passé	
insisterais	**insisterions**	**aurais insisté**	**aurions insisté**
insisterais	**insisteriez**	**aurais insisté**	**auriez insisté**
insisterait	**insisteraient**	**aurait insisté**	**auraient insisté**
6 présent du subjonctif		13 passé du subjonctif	
insiste	**insistions**	**aie insisté**	**ayons insisté**
insistes	**insistiez**	**aies insisté**	**ayez insisté**
insiste	**insistent**	**ait insisté**	**aient insisté**
7 imparfait du subjonctif		14 plus-que-parfait du subjonctif	
insistasse	**insistassions**	**eusse insisté**	**eussions insisté**
insistasses	**insistassiez**	**eusses insisté**	**eussiez insisté**
insistât	**insistassent**	**eût insisté**	**eussent insisté**
		Impératif	
		insiste	
		insistons	
		insistez	

Madame Albertine insiste beaucoup sur la discipline dans cette école.
Mrs. Albertine insists a great deal on discipline in this school.

insistant, insistante insistent, persistent	**insister sur** to insist upon
l'insistance f. insistence	**inutile d'insister (sur cela)** useless to insist (on that)

to instruct   Irregular verb

The Seven Simple Tenses		The Seven Compound Tenses	
Singular	Plural	Singular	Plural
1 présent de l'indicatif		8 passé composé	
instruis	**instruisons**	**ai instruit**	**avons instruit**
instruis	**instruisez**	**as instruit**	**avez instruit**
instruit	**instruisent**	**a instruit**	**ont instruit**
2 imparfait de l'indicatif		9 plus-que-parfait de l'indicatif	
instruisais	**instruisions**	**avais instruit**	**avions instruit**
instruisais	**instruisiez**	**avais instruit**	**aviez instruit**
instruisait	**instruisaient**	**avait instruit**	**avaient instruit**
3 passé simple		10 passé antérieur	
instruisis	**instruisîmes**	**eus instruit**	**eûmes instruit**
instruisis	**instruisîtes**	**eus instruit**	**eûtes instruit**
instruisit	**instruisirent**	**eut instruit**	**eurent instruit**
4 futur		11 futur antérieur	
instruirai	**instruirons**	**aurai instruit**	**aurons instruit**
instruiras	**instruirez**	**auras instruit**	**aurez instruit**
instruira	**instruiront**	**aura instruit**	**auront instruit**
5 conditionnel		12 conditionnel passé	
instruirais	**instruirions**	**aurais instruit**	**aurions instruit**
instruirais	**instruiriez**	**aurais instruit**	**auriez instruit**
instruirait	**instruiraient**	**aurait instruit**	**auraient instruit**
6 présent du subjonctif		13 passé du subjonctif	
instruise	**instruisions**	**aie instruit**	**ayons instruit**
instruises	**instruisiez**	**aies instruit**	**ayez instruit**
instruise	**instruisent**	**ait instruit**	**aient instruit**
7 imparfait du subjonctif		14 plus-que-parfait du subjonctif	
instruisisse	**instruisissions**	**eusse instruit**	**eussions instruit**
instruisisses	**instruisissiez**	**eusses instruit**	**eussiez instruit**
instruisît	**instruisissent**	**eût instruit**	**eussent instruit**
		Impératif	
		instruis	
		instruisons	
		instruisez	

instruit, instruite educated
instruction *f.* instruction, teaching
sans instruction uneducated
instructeur, instructrice instructor
instructif, instructive instructive
les instructions instructions

s'instruire to teach oneself, to educate oneself
l'instruction publique public education
bien instruit (instruite), fort instruit (instruite) well educated

Part. pr. **interdisant**   Part. passé **interdit**   **interdire**

Irregular verb   to forbid, to prohibit

The Seven Simple Tenses		The Seven Compound Tenses	
Singular	Plural	Singular	Plural

1 présent de l'indicatif		8 passé composé	
interdis	interdisons	ai interdit	avons interdit
interdis	interdisez	as interdit	avez interdit
interdit	interdisent	a interdit	ont interdit

2 imparfait de l'indicatif		9 plus-que-parfait de l'indicatif	
interdisais	interdisions	avais interdit	avions interdit
interdisais	interdisiez	avais interdit	aviez interdit
interdisait	interdisaient	avait interdit	avaient interdit

3 passé simple		10 passé antérieur	
interdis	interdîmes	eus interdit	eûmes interdit
interdis	interdîtes	eus interdit	eûtes interdit
interdit	interdirent	eut interdit	eurent interdit

4 futur		11 futur antérieur	
interdirai	interdirons	aurai interdit	aurons interdit
interdiras	interdirez	auras interdit	aurez interdit
interdira	interdiront	aura interdit	auront interdit

5 conditionnel		12 conditionnel passé	
interdirais	interdirions	aurais interdit	aurions interdit
inerdirais	interdiriez	aurais interdit	auriez interdit
interdirait	interdiraient	aurait interdit	auraient interdit

6 présent du subjonctif		13 passé du subjonctif	
interdise	interdisions	aie interdit	ayons interdit
interdises	interdisiez	aies interdit	ayez interdit
interdise	interdisent	ait interdit	aient interdit

7 imparfait du subjonctif		14 plus-que-parfait du subjonctif	
interdisse	interdissions	eusse interdit	eussions interdit
interdisses	interdissiez	eusses interdit	eussiez interdit
interdît	interdissent	eût interdit	eussent interdit

Impératif
interdis
interdisons
interdisez

Je vous interdis de m'interrompre constamment.   I forbid you to interrupt me constantly.

interdire qqch à qqn   to forbid someone something
l'interdit *m.*   interdict; *adj.* **les jeux interdits**   forbidden games
l'interdiction *f.*   interdiction, prohibition
Il est interdit de marcher sur l'herbe.   Do not walk on the grass.
interdire à qqn de faire qqch   to forbid someone from doing something
STATIONNEMENT INTERDIT   NO PARKING

interrompre Part. pr. **interrompant** Part. passé **interrompu**

to interrupt

Regular -re verb endings: spelling change:
3rd person sing. of Tense No. 1 adds t.

The Seven Simple Tenses | The Seven Compound Tenses

Singular	Plural	Singular	Plural
1 présent de l'indicatif		8 passé composé	
interromps	**interrompons**	**ai interrompu**	**avons interrompu**
interromps	**interrompez**	**as interrompu**	**avez interrompu**
interrompt	**interrompent**	**a interrompu**	**ont interrompu**
2 imparfait de l'indicatif		9 plus-que-parfait de l'indicatif	
interrompais	**interrompions**	**avais interrompu**	**avions interrompu**
interrompais	**interrompiez**	**avais interrompu**	**aviez interrompu**
interrompait	**interrompaient**	**avait interrompu**	**avaient interrompu**
3 passé simple		10 passé antérieur	
interrompis	**interrompîmes**	**eus interrompu**	**eûmes interrompu**
interrompis	**interrompîtes**	**eus interrompu**	**eûtes interrompu**
interrompit	**interrompirent**	**eut interrompu**	**eurent interrompu**
4 futur		11 futur antérieur	
interromprai	**interromprons**	**aurai interrompu**	**aurons interrompu**
interrompras	**interromprez**	**auras interrompu**	**aurez interrompu**
interrompra	**interrompront**	**aura interrompu**	**auront interrompu**
5 conditionnel		12 conditionnel passé	
interromprais	**interromprions**	**aurais interrompu**	**aurions interrompu**
interromprais	**interrompriez**	**aurais interrompu**	**auriez interrompu**
interromprait	**interrompraient**	**aurait interrompu**	**auraient interrompu**
6 présent du subjonctif		13 passé du subjonctif	
interrompe	**interrompions**	**aie interrompu**	**ayons interrompu**
interrompes	**interrompiez**	**aies interrompu**	**ayez interrompu**
interrompe	**interrompent**	**ait interrompu**	**aient interrompu**
7 imparfait du subjonctif		14 plus-que-parfait du subjonctif	
interrompisse	**interrompissions**	**eusse interrompu**	**eussions interrompu**
interrompisses	**interrompissiez**	**eusses interrompu**	**eussiez interrompu**
interrompît	**interrompissent**	**eût interrompu**	**eussent interrompu**

Impératif
interromps
interrompons
interrompez

—Maurice, tu m'interromps à chaque instant. Cesse de m'interrompre, s'il te plaît!   Maurice, you interrupt me at every moment. Stop interrupting me, please!

une **interruption** interruption
interrompu, interrompue interrupted
un **interrupteur** light switch

un **interrupteur**, une **interruptrice**
interrupter

Irregular verb   to introduce, to show in

The Seven Simple Tenses		The Seven Compound Tenses	
Singular	Plural	Singular	Plural
1 présent de l'indicatif		8 passé composé	
introduis	**introduisons**	**ai introduit**	**avons introduit**
introduis	**introduisez**	**as introduit**	**avez introduit**
introduit	**introduisent**	**a introduit**	**ont introduit**
2 imparfait de l'indicatif		9 plus-que-parfait de l'indicatif	
introduisais	**introduisions**	**avais introduit**	**avions introduit**
introduisais	**introduisiez**	**avais introduit**	**aviez introduit**
introduisait	**introduisaient**	**avait introduit**	**avaient introduit**
3 passé simple		10 passé antérieur	
introduisis	**introduisîmes**	**eus introduit**	**eûmes introduit**
introduisis	**introduisîtes**	**eus introduit**	**eûtes introduit**
introduisit	**introduisirent**	**eut introduit**	**eurent introduit**
4 futur		11 futur antérieur	
introduirai	**introduirons**	**aurai introduit**	**aurons introduit**
introduiras	**introduirez**	**auras introduit**	**aurez introduit**
introduira	**introduiront**	**aura introduit**	**auront introduit**
5 conditionnel		12 conditionnel passé	
introduirais	**introduirions**	**aurais introduit**	**aurions introduit**
introduirais	**introduiriez**	**aurais introduit**	**auriez introduit**
introduirait	**introduiraient**	**aurait introduit**	**auraient introduit**
6 présent du subjonctif		13 passé du subjonctif	
introduise	**introduisions**	**aie introduit**	**ayons introduit**
introduises	**introduisiez**	**aies introduit**	**ayez introduit**
introduise	**introduisent**	**ait introduit**	**aient introduit**
7 imparfait du subjonctif		14 plus-que-parfait du subjonctif	
introduisisse	**introduisissions**	**eusse introduit**	**eussions introduit**
introduisisses	**introduisissiez**	**eusses introduit**	**eussiez introduit**
introduisît	**introduisissent**	**eût introduit**	**eussent introduit**

Impératif
introduis
introduisons
introduisez

---

introductoire   introductory
introducteur, introductrice   introducer
introductif, introductive   introductory
introduction *f.*   introduction

See also **conduire**, **produire**, and **traduire**.

J'ai introduit la clef dans la serrure.
  I inserted the key into the lock.

inviter	Part. pr. **invitant**	Part. passé **invité**

to invite

Regular -er verb

The Seven Simple Tenses		The Seven Compound Tenses	
Singular	Plural	Singular	Plural
1 présent de l'indicatif		8 passé composé	
invite	**invitons**	**ai invité**	**avons invité**
invites	**invitez**	**as invité**	**avez invité**
invite	**invitent**	**a invité**	**ont invité**
2 imparfait de l'indicatif		9 plus-que-parfait de l'indicatif	
invitais	**invitions**	**avais invité**	**avions invité**
invitais	**invitiez**	**avais invité**	**aviez invité**
invitait	**invitaient**	**avait invité**	**avaient invité**
3 passé simple		10 passé antérieur	
invitai	**invitâmes**	**eus invité**	**eûmes invité**
invitas	**invitâtes**	**eus invité**	**eûtes invité**
invita	**invitèrent**	**eut invité**	**eurent invité**
4 futur		11 futur antérieur	
inviterai	**inviterons**	**aurai invité**	**aurons invité**
inviteras	**inviterez**	**auras invité**	**aurez invité**
invitera	**inviteront**	**aura invité**	**auront invité**
5 conditionnel		12 conditionnel passé	
inviterais	**inviterions**	**aurais invité**	**aurions invité**
inviterais	**inviteriez**	**aurais invité**	**auriez invité**
inviterait	**inviteraient**	**aurait invité**	**auraient invité**
6 présent du subjonctif		13 passé du subjonctif	
invite	**invitions**	**aie invité**	**ayons invité**
invites	**invitiez**	**aies invité**	**ayez invité**
invite	**invitent**	**ait invité**	**aient invité**
7 imparfait du subjonctif		14 plus-que-parfait du subjonctif	
invitasse	**invitassions**	**eusse invité**	**eussions invité**
invitasses	**invitassiez**	**eusses invité**	**eussiez invité**
invitât	**invitassent**	**eût invité**	**eussent invité**

Impératif
invite
invitons
invitez

C'est moi qui invite! My treat!

Elle s'est invitée. She invited herself.

J'ai invité mes meilleurs amis à dîner chez moi. I invited my best friends to have dinner at my place.

l'invitation f. invitation

les invités the guests

sur l'invitation de at the invitation of

sans invitation without invitation, uninvited

inviter qqn à faire qqch
to invite someone to do something

152

Regular -er verb endings: spelling change: to throw, to cast
t becomes tt before syllable with mute e.

The Seven Simple Tenses		The Seven Compound Tenses	
Singular	Plural	Singular	Plural
1 présent de l'indicatif		**8 passé composé**	
jette	**jetons**	**ai jeté**	**avons jeté**
jettes	**jetez**	**as jeté**	**avez jeté**
jette	**jettent**	**a jeté**	**ont jeté**
2 imparfait de l'indicatif		**9 plus-que-parfait de l'indicatif**	
jetais	**jetions**	**avais jeté**	**avions jeté**
jetais	**jetiez**	**avais jeté**	**aviez jeté**
jetait	**jetaient**	**avait jeté**	**avaient jeté**
3 passé simple		**10 passé antérieur**	
jetai	**jetâmes**	**eus jeté**	**eûmes jeté**
jetas	**jetâtes**	**eus jeté**	**eûtes jeté**
jeta	**jetèrent**	**eut jeté**	**eurent jeté**
4 futur		**11 futur antérieur**	
jetterai	**jetterons**	**aurai jeté**	**aurons jeté**
jetteras	**jetterez**	**auras jeté**	**aurez jeté**
jettera	**jetteront**	**aura jeté**	**auront jeté**
5 conditionnel		**12 conditionnel passé**	
jetterais	**jetterions**	**aurais jeté**	**aurions jeté**
jetterais	**jetteriez**	**aurais jeté**	**auriez jeté**
jetterait	**jetteraient**	**aurait jeté**	**auraient jeté**
6 présent du subjonctif		**13 passé du subjonctif**	
jette	**jetions**	**aie jeté**	**ayons jeté**
jettes	**jetiez**	**aies jeté**	**ayez jeté**
jette	**jettent**	**ait jeté**	**aient jeté**
7 imparfait du subjonctif		**14 plus-que-parfait du subjonctif**	
jetasse	**jetassions**	**eusse jeté**	**eussions jeté**
jetasses	**jetassiez**	**eusses jeté**	**eussiez jeté**
jetât	**jetassent**	**eût jeté**	**eussent jeté**

Impératif
jette
jetons
jetez

jeter un cri   to utter a cry
jeter son argent par la fenêtre   to throw one's money out the window
se jeter sur (contre)   to throw oneself at (against)
un jeton de téléphone   telephone slug
une jetée   jetty
un jet d'eau   fountain
jeter un coup d'oeil à   to glance at; **se jeter au cou de qqn**
    to throw oneself at somebody
rejeter   to reject, to throw back; **projeter**   to plan, to project

joindre	Part. pr. joignant	Part. passé joint

to join, to contact — Irregular verb

The Seven Simple Tenses		The Seven Compound Tenses	

Singular	Plural	Singular	Plural
1 présent de l'indicatif		**8 passé composé**	
joins	joignons	ai joint	avons joint
joins	joignez	as joint	avez joint
joint	joignent	a joint	ont joint
2 imparfait de l'indicatif		**9 plus-que-parfait de l'indicatif**	
joignais	joignions	avais joint	avions joint
joignais	joigniez	avais joint	aviez joint
joignait	joignaient	avait joint	avaient joint
3 passé simple		**10 passé antérieur**	
joignis	joignîmes	eus joint	eûmes joint
joignis	joignîtes	eus joint	eûtes joint
joignit	joignirent	eut joint	eurent joint
4 futur		**11 futur antérieur**	
joindrai	joindrons	aurai joint	aurons joint
joindras	joindrez	auras joint	aurez joint
joindra	joindront	aura joint	auront joint
5 conditionnel		**12 conditionnel passé**	
joindrais	joindrions	aurais joint	aurions joint
joindrais	joindriez	aurais joint	auriez joint
joindrait	joindraient	aurait joint	auraient joint
6 présent du subjonctif		**13 passé du subjonctif**	
joigne	joignions	aie joint	ayons joint
joignes	joigniez	aies joint	ayez joint
joigne	joignent	ait joint	aient joint
7 imparfait du subjonctif		**14 plus-que-parfait du subjonctif**	
joignisse	joignissions	eusse joint	eussions joint
joignisses	joignissiez	eusses joint	eussiez joint
joignît	joignissent	eût joint	eussent joint

Impératif
joins
joignons
joignez

---

joindre les deux bouts   to make ends meet
les jointures des doigts   knuckles
joint, jointe   joined
joignant, joignante   adjoining
ci-joint   herewith, attached
joindre à   to join to, to add to

les talons joints   heels together
se joindre à la discussion   to join in the discussion
joindre par téléphone   to reach by telephone
rejoindre   to rejoin, to join together
se rejoindre   to meet, to come together

154

Regular -er verb   to play, to act (in a play), to gamble

The Seven Simple Tenses		The Seven Compound Tenses	
Singular	Plural	Singular	Plural
1 présent de l'indicatif		**8 passé composé**	
joue	**jouons**	**ai joué**	**avons joué**
joues	**jouez**	**as joué**	**avez joué**
joue	**jouent**	**a joué**	**ont joué**
2 imparfait de l'indicatif		**9 plus-que-parfait de l'indicatif**	
jouais	**jouions**	**avais joué**	**avions joué**
jouais	**jouiez**	**avais joué**	**aviez joué**
jouait	**jouaient**	**avait joué**	**avaient joué**
3 passé simple		**10 passé antérieur**	
jouai	**jouâmes**	**eus joué**	**eûmes joué**
jouas	**jouâtes**	**eus joué**	**eûtes joué**
joua	**jouèrent**	**eut joué**	**eurent joué**
4 futur		**11 futur antérieur**	
jouerai	**jouerons**	**aurai joué**	**aurons joué**
joueras	**jouerez**	**auras joué**	**aurez joué**
jouera	**joueront**	**aura joué**	**auront joué**
5 conditionnel		**12 conditionnel passé**	
jouerais	**jouerions**	**aurais joué**	**aurions joué**
jouerais	**joueriez**	**aurais joué**	**auriez joué**
jouerait	**joueraient**	**aurait joué**	**auraient joué**
6 présent du subjonctif		**13 passé du subjonctif**	
joue	**jouions**	**aie joué**	**ayons joué**
joues	**jouiez**	**aies joué**	**ayez joué**
joue	**jouent**	**ait joué**	**aient joué**
7 imparfait du subjonctif		**14 plus-que-parfait du subjonctif**	
jouasse	**jouassions**	**eusse joué**	**eussions joué**
jouasses	**jouassiez**	**eusses joué**	**eussiez joué**
jouât	**jouassent**	**eût joué**	**eussent joué**
		Impératif	
		joue	
		jouons	
		jouez	

jouer au tennis   to play tennis
jouer aux cartes   to play cards
jouer du piano   to play the piano
jouer un tour à qqn   to play a trick
on someone
un jouet   toy, plaything
joueur, joueuse   player, gambler
jouer sur les mots   to play with words
déjouer   to baffle, to thwart

jouer un rôle   to play a part
jouer une partie de qqch   to play a game
of something
jouer de la flûte   to play the flute
se jouer de   to make fun of, to deride
un joujou, des joujoux   toy, toys
(child's language)

to let, to allow, to leave   Regular -er verb

The Seven Simple Tenses		The Seven Compound Tenses	
Singular	Plural	Singular	Plural
1 présent de l'indicatif		8 passé composé	
laisse	laissons	ai laissé	avons laissé
laisses	laissez	as laissé	avez laissé
laisse	laissent	a laissé	ont laissé
2 imparfait de l'indicatif		9 plus-que-parfait de l'indicatif	
laissais	laissions	avais laissé	avions laissé
laissais	laissiez	avais laissé	aviez laissé
laissait	laissaient	avait laissé	avaient laissé
3 passé simple		10 passé antérieur	
laissai	laissâmes	eus laissé	eûmes laissé
laissas	laissâtes	eus laissé	eûtes laissé
laissa	laissèrent	eut laissé	eurent laissé
4 futur		11 futur antérieur	
laisserai	laisserons	aurai laissé	aurons laissé
laisseras	laisserez	auras laissé	aurez laissé
laissera	laisseront	aura laissé	auront laissé
5 conditionnel		12 conditionnel passé	
laisserais	laisserions	aurais laissé	aurions laissé
laisserais	laisseriez	aurais laissé	auriez laissé
laisserait	laisseraient	aurait laissé	auraient laissé
6 présent du subjonctif		13 passé du subjonctif	
laisse	laissions	aie laissé	ayons laissé
laisses	laissiez	aies laissé	ayez laissé
laisse	laissent	ait laissé	aient laissé
7 imparfait du subjonctif		14 plus-que-parfait du subjonctif	
laissasse	laissassions	eusse laissé	eussions laissé
laissasses	laissassiez	eusses laissé	eussiez laissé
laissât	laissassent	eût laissé	eussent laissé

Impératif
laisse
laissons
laissez

J'ai laissé mes devoirs chez moi.   I left my homework at home.
Laissez-moi tranquille!   Leave me alone!
Laissez-moi passer, s'il vous plaît.   Please let me get by.

laissez-faire   do not interfere;   Laissez-moi faire.   Let me do as I please.
une laisse   a leash;   délaisser   to abandon, to forsake
laisser entrer   to let in, to allow to enter;   laisser tomber   to drop
laisser aller   to let go;   se laisser aller   to let oneself go
C'était fâcheux! (See se fâcher)

Regular -er verb endings: spelling change: to hurl, to launch, to throw
c changes to ç before a or o to keep s sound.

The Seven Simple Tenses		The Seven Compound Tenses	
Singular	Plural	Singular	Plural
1 présent de l'indicatif		8 passé composé	
lance	lançons	ai lancé	avons lancé
lances	lancez	as lancé	avez lancé
lance	lancent	a lancé	ont lancé
2 imparfait de l'indicatif		9 plus-que-parfait de l'indicatif	
lançais	lancions	avais lancé	avions lancé
lançais	lanciez	avais lancé	aviez lancé
lançait	lançaient	avait lancé	avaient lancé
3 passé simple		10 passé antérieur	
lançai	lançâmes	eus lancé	eûmes lancé
lanças	lançâtes	eus lancé	eûtes lancé
lança	lancèrent	eut lancé	eurent lancé
4 futur		11 futur antérieur	
lancerai	lancerons	aurai lancé	aurons lancé
lanceras	lancerez	auras lancé	aurez lancé
lancera	lanceront	aura lancé	auront lancé
5 conditionnel		12 conditionnel passé	
lancerais	lancerions	aurais lancé	aurions lancé
lancerais	lanceriez	aurais lancé	auriez lancé
lancerait	lanceraient	aurait lancé	auraient lancé
6 présent du subjonctif		13 passé du subjonctif	
lance	lancions	aie lancé	ayons lancé
lances	lanciez	aies lancé	ayez lancé
lance	lancent	ait lancé	aient lancé
7 imparfait du subjonctif		14 plus-que-parfait du subjonctif	
lançasse	lançassions	eusse lancé	eussions lancé
lançasses	lançassiez	eusses lancé	eussiez lancé
lançât	lançassent	eût lancé	eussent lancé
		Impératif	
		lance	
		lançons	
		lancez	

---

se lancer contre   to throw oneself at, against
un départ lancé   a flying start (sports)
une lance   a spear
lancer une balle en l'air
   to throw a ball in the air
lancer une plaisanterie   to crack a joke
un lancement   hurling, casting

le lancement d'un disque, d'un
   livre, etc.   ceremony to launch a
   new record, book, etc.
un lanceur   thrower, pitcher (sports)
lancer un cri   to cry out
lancer une idée en l'air
   to toss out an idea

laver	Part. pr. **lavant**	Part. passé **lavé**
to wash		Regular -er verb

The Seven Simple Tenses		The Seven Compound Tenses	
Singular	Plural	Singular	Plural
1 présent de l'indicatif		8 passé composé	
lave	lavons	ai lavé	avons lavé
laves	lavez	as lavé	avez lavé
lave	lavent	a lavé	ont lavé
2 imparfait de l'indicatif		9 plus-que-parfait de l'indicatif	
lavais	lavions	avais lavé	avions lavé
lavais	laviez	avais lavé	aviez lavé
lavait	lavaient	avait lavé	avaient lavé
3 passé simple		10 passé antérieur	
lavai	lavâmes	eus lavé	eûmes lavé
lavas	lavâtes	eus lavé	eûtes lavé
lava	lavèrent	eut lavé	eurent lavé
4 futur		11 futur antérieur	
laverai	laverons	aurai lavé	aurons lavé
laveras	laverez	auras lavé	aurez lavé
lavera	laveront	aura lavé	auront lavé
5 conditionnel		12 conditionnel passé	
laverais	laverions	aurais lavé	aurions lavé
laverais	laveriez	aurais lavé	auriez lavé
laverait	laveraient	aurait lavé	auraient lavé
6 présent du subjonctif		13 passé du subjonctif	
lave	lavions	aie lavé	ayons lavé
laves	laviez	aies lavé	ayez lavé
lave	lavent	ait lavé	aient lavé
7 imparfait du subjonctif		14 plus-que-parfait du subjonctif	
lavasse	lavassions	eusse lavé	eussions lavé
lavasses	lavassiez	eusses lavé	eussiez lavé
lavât	lavassent	eût lavé	eussent lavé
		Impératif	
		lave	
		lavons	
		lavez	

Note: In the following examples, la voiture is the direct object:
Marie lave la voiture.   Marie is washing the car.
Marie a lavé la voiture.   Marie washed the car.
Marie l'a lavée.   Marie washed it.

le lavage washing	**un laveur, une laveuse** washer
le lavement enema	**une machine à laver** washing machine
la lavette dish mop	**un lave-vaisselle** dishwasher
la lavure dishwater	**un lavabo** washbasin, sink

See also se laver.

158

Reflexive regular -er verb   to wash oneself

The Seven Simple Tenses		The Seven Compound Tenses	
Singular	Plural	Singular	Plural
1 présent de l'indicatif		**8 passé composé**	
me lave	nous lavons	me suis lavé(e)	nous sommes lavé(e)s
te laves	vous lavez	t'es lavé(e)	vous êtes lavé(e)(s)
se lave	se lavent	s'est lavé(e)	se sont lavé(e)s
2 imparfait de l'indicatif		**9 plus-que-parfait de l'indicatif**	
me lavais	nous lavions	m'étais lavé(e)	nous étions lavé(e)s
te lavais	vous laviez	t'étais lavé(e)	vous étiez lavé(e)(s)
se lavait	se lavaient	s'était lavé(e)	s'étaient lavé(e)s
3 passé simple		**10 passé antérieur**	
me lavai	nous lavâmes	me fus lavé(e)	nous fûmes lavé(e)s
te lavas	vous lavâtes	te fus lavé(e)	vous fûtes lavé(e)(s)
se lava	se lavèrent	se fut lavé(e)	se furent lavé(e)s
4 futur		**11 futur antérieur**	
me laverai	nous laverons	me serai lavé(e)	nous serons lavé(e)s
te laveras	vous laverez	te seras lavé(e)	vous serez lavé(e)(s)
se lavera	se laveront	se sera lavé(e)	se seront lavé(e)s
5 conditionnel		**12 conditionnel passé**	
me laverais	nous laverions	me serais lavé(e)	nous serions lavé(e)s
te laverais	vous laveriez	te serais lavé(e)	vous seriez lavé(e)(s)
se laverait	se laveraient	se serait lavé(e)	se seraient lavé(e)s
6 présent du subjonctif		**13 passé du subjonctif**	
me lave	nous lavions	me sois lavé(e)	nous soyons lavé(e)s
te laves	vous laviez	te sois lavé(e)	vous soyez lavé(e)(s)
se lave	se lavent	se soit lavé(e)	se soient lavé(e)s
7 imparfait du subjonctif		**14 plus-que-parfait du subjonctif**	
me lavasse	nous lavassions	me fusse lavé(e)	nous fussions lavé(e)s
te lavasses	vous lavassiez	te fusses lavé(e)	vous fussiez lavé(e)(s)
se lavât	se lavassent	se fût lavé(e)	se fussent lavé(e)s

Impératif
lave-toi; ne te lave pas
lavons-nous; ne nous lavons pas
lavez-vous; ne vous lavez pas

Note: In the following example, **se/s'** is the direct object pronoun:
Marie se lave.   Marie is washing herself.
Marie s'est lavée.   Marie washed herself.

Note: In the following, **les mains** is the direct object and **se/s'** is the indirect object:
Marie se lave les mains.   Marie is washing her hands.
Marie s'est lavé les mains.   Marie washed her hands. (No agreement because there is no *preceding* direct object pronoun.)

se laver les mains de qqch   to wash one's hands of something

For words related to se laver, see the verb laver.

lever	Part. pr. levant	Part. passé levé

to lift, to raise

Regular -er verb: spelling change: e changes to è before syllable with mute e.

The Seven Simple Tenses		The Seven Compound Tenses	
Singular	Plural	Singular	Plural

1 présent de l'indicatif		8 passé composé	
lève	levons	ai levé	avons levé
lèves	levez	as levé	avez levé
lève	lèvent	a levé	ont levé

2 imparfait de l'indicatif		9 plus-que-parfait de l'indicatif	
levais	levions	avais levé	avions levé
levais	leviez	avais levé	aviez levé
levait	levaient	avait levé	avaient levé

3 passé simple		10 passé antérieur	
levai	levâmes	eus levé	eûmes levé
levas	levâtes	eus levé	eûtes levé
leva	levèrent	eut levé	eurent levé

4 futur		11 futur antérieur	
lèverai	lèverons	aurai levé	aurons levé
lèveras	lèverez	auras levé	aurez levé
lèvera	lèveront	aura levé	auront levé

5 conditionnel		12 conditionnel passé	
lèverais	lèverions	aurais levé	aurions levé
lèverais	lèveriez	aurais levé	auriez levé
lèverait	lèveraient	aurait levé	auraient levé

6 présent du subjonctif		13 passé du subjonctif	
lève	levions	aie levé	ayons levé
lèves	leviez	aies levé	ayez levé
lève	lèvent	ait levé	aient levé

7 imparfait du subjonctif		14 plus-que-parfait du subjonctif	
levasse	levassions	eusse levé	eussions levé
levasses	levassiez	eusses levé	eussiez levé
levât	levassent	eût levé	eussent levé

Impératif
lève
levons
levez

---

voter à main levée   to vote by a show of hands
le levage   raising, lifting
faire lever qqn   to get someone out of bed
le levant   the East
le levain   leaven
du pain sans levain   unleavened bread
le lever du soleil   sunrise

se relever   to get up on one's feet
lever la main   to raise one's hand
élever   to raise, to rear, to bring up
enlever   to remove
relever   to raise again, to pick up

Part. pr. **se levant**   Part. passé **levé(e)(s)**   **se lever**

Regular -er verb: spelling change: e changes   to get up
to è before syllable with mute e.

The Seven Simple Tenses		The Seven Compound Tenses	
Singular	Plural	Singular	Plural
1 présent de l'indicatif		8 passé composé	
me lève	**nous levons**	**me suis levé(e)**	**nous sommes levé(e)s**
te lèves	**vous levez**	**t'es levé(e)**	**vous êtes levé(e)(s)**
se lève	**se lèvent**	**s'est levé(e)**	**se sont levé(e)s**
2 imparfait de l'indicatif		9 plus-que-parfait de l'indicatif	
me levais	**nous levions**	**m'étais levé(e)**	**nous étions levé(e)s**
te levais	**vous leviez**	**t'étais levé(e)**	**vous étiez levé(e)(s)**
se levait	**se levaient**	**s'était levé(e)**	**s'étaient levé(e)s**
3 passé simple		10 passé antérieur	
me levai	**nous levâmes**	**me fus levé(e)**	**nous fûmes levé(e)s**
te levas	**vous levâtes**	**te fus levé(e)**	**vous fûtes levé(e)(s)**
se leva	**se levèrent**	**se fut levé(e)**	**se furent levé(e)s**
4 futur		11 futur antérieur	
me lèverai	**nous lèverons**	**me serai levé(e)**	**nous serons levé(e)s**
te lèveras	**vous lèverez**	**te seras levé(e)**	**vous serez levé(e)(s)**
se lèvera	**se lèveront**	**se sera levé(e)**	**se seront levé(e)s**
5 conditionnel		12 conditionnel passé	
me lèverais	**nous lèverions**	**me serais levé(e)**	**nous serions levé(e)s**
te lèverais	**vous lèveriez**	**te serais levé(e)**	**vous seriez levé(e)(s)**
se lèverait	**se lèveraient**	**se serait levé(e)**	**se seraient levé(e)s**
6 présent du subjonctif		13 passé du subjonctif	
me lève	**nous levions**	**me sois levé(e)**	**nous soyons levé(e)s**
te lèves	**vous leviez**	**te sois levé(e)**	**vous soyez levé(e)(s)**
se lève	**se lèvent**	**se soit levé(e)**	**se soient levé(e)s**
7 imparfait du subjonctif		14 plus-que-parfait du subjonctif	
me levasse	**nous levassions**	**me fusse levé(e)**	**nous fussions levé(e)s**
te levasses	**vous levassiez**	**te fusses levé(e)**	**vous fussiez levé(e)(s)**
se levât	**se levassent**	**se fût levé(e)**	**se fussent levé(e)s**

Impératif
lève-toi; ne te lève pas
levons-nous; ne nous levons pas
levez-vous; ne vous levez pas

Caroline s'est levée après le petit déjeuner.   Caroline got up after breakfast.
Après s'être levée, elle a quitté la maison.   After getting up, she left the house.
Lève-toi! Il est temps de partir.   Get up! It's time to leave!

For words related to se lever, see the verb lever.

161

lire	Part. pr. lisant	Part. passé lu

to read

Irregular verb

The Seven Simple Tenses		The Seven Compound Tenses	
Singular	Plural	Singular	Plural
1 présent de l'indicatif		8 passé composé	
lis	lisons	ai lu	avons lu
lis	lisez	as lu	avez lu
lit	lisent	a lu	ont lu
2 imparfait de l'indicatif		9 plus-que-parfait de l'indicatif	
lisais	lisions	avais lu	avions lu
lisais	lisiez	avais lu	aviez lu
lisait	lisaient	avait lu	avaient lu
3 passé simple		10 passé antérieur	
lus	lûmes	eus lu	eûmes lu
lus	lûtes	eus lu	eûtes lu
lut	lurent	eut lu	eurent lu
4 futur		11 futur antérieur	
lirai	lirons	aurai lu	aurons lu
liras	lirez	auras lu	aurez lu
lira	liront	aura lu	auront lu
5 conditionnel		12 conditionnel passé	
lirais	lirions	aurais lu	aurions lu
lirais	liriez	aurais lu	auriez lu
lirait	liraient	aurait lu	auraient lu
6 présent du subjonctif		13 passé du subjonctif	
lise	lisions	aie lu	ayons lu
lises	lisiez	aies lu	ayez lu
lise	lisent	ait lu	aient lu
7 imparfait du subjonctif		14 plus-que-parfait du subjonctif	
lusse	lussions	eusse lu	eussions lu
lusses	lussiez	eusses lu	eussiez lu
lût	lussent	eût lu	eussent lu

Impératif
lis
lisons
lisez

C'est un livre à lire.   It's a book worth reading.
lisible   legible, readable
lisiblement   legibly
lecteur, lectrice   reader (a person who reads)
un lecteur d'épreuves, une lectrice d'épreuves   proofreader
la lecture   reading
lectures pour la jeunesse   juvenile reading

lire à haute voix   to read aloud
lire à voix basse   to read in a low voice
lire tout bas   to read to oneself
relire   to reread
Dans l'espoir de vous lire . . .   Hoping to receive a letter from you soon . . .

Defective and impersonal verb   to shine

The Seven Simple Tenses   The Seven Compound Tenses

Singular	Plural	Singular	Plural

1   présent de l'indicatif
il luit

   8   passé composé
il a lui

2   imparfait de l'indicatif
il luisait

   9   plus-que-parfait de l'indicatif
il avait lui

3   passé simple
—

  10   passé antérieur
il eut lui

4   futur
il luira

  11   futur antérieur
il aura lui

5   conditionnel
il luirait

  12   conditionnel passé
il aurait lui

6   présent du subjonctif
qu'il luise

  13   passé du subjonctif
qu'il ait lui

7   imparfait du subjonctif
—

  14   plus-que-parfait du subjonctif
qu'il eût lui

Impératif
Qu'il luise!   Let it shine!

---

la lueur   glimmer, gleam, glow   Le soleil luit.   The sun is shining.
luisant, luisante   shining   J'ai le nez qui luit.   My nose is shiny.
une lueur d'espoir   a glimmer of hope

Note: This verb is used ordinarily when referring to the sun.

to reduce (one's weight), to grow thin, to lose weight   Regular -ir verb

The Seven Simple Tenses		The Seven Compound Tenses	
Singular	Plural	Singular	Plural
1 présent de l'indicatif		8 passé composé	
maigris	maigrissons	ai maigri	avons maigri
maigris	maigrissez	as maigri	avez maigri
maigrit	maigrissent	a maigri	ont maigri
2 imparfait de l'indicatif		9 plus-que-parfait de l'indicatif	
maigrissais	maigrissions	avais maigri	avions maigri
maigrissais	maigrissiez	avais maigri	aviez maigri
maigrissait	maigrissaient	avait maigri	avaient maigri
3 passé simple		10 passé antérieur	
maigris	maigrîmes	eus maigri	eûmes maigri
maigris	maigrîtes	eus maigri	eûtes maigri
maigrit	maigrirent	eut maigri	eurent maigri
4 futur		11 futur antérieur	
maigrirai	maigrirons	aurai maigri	aurons maigri
maigriras	maigrirez	auras maigri	aurez maigri
maigrira	maigriront	aura maigri	auront maigri
5 conditionnel		12 conditionnel passé	
maigrirais	maigririons	aurais maigri	aurions maigri
maigrirais	maigririez	aurais maigri	auriez maigri
maigrirait	maigriraient	aurait maigri	auraient maigri
6 présent du subjonctif		13 passé du subjonctif	
maigrisse	maigrissions	aie maigri	ayons maigri
maigrisses	maigrissiez	aies maigri	ayez maigri
maigrisse	maigrissent	ait maigri	aient maigri
7 imparfait du subjonctif		14 plus-que-parfait du subjonctif	
maigrisse	maigrissions	eusse maigri	eussions maigri
maigrisses	maigrissiez	eusses maigri	eussiez maigri
maigrît	maigrissent	eût maigri	eussent maigri
		Impératif	
		maigris	
		maigrissons	
		maigrissez	

---

maigre thin
la maigreur thinness
maigrement meagerly
se faire maigrir to slim down one's
   weight
être au régime pour maigrir to be on
   a diet to lose weight

s'amaigrir to lose weight
faire maigre to abstain from meat
maigre comme un clou as thin as a nail
   (rail)

Regular -er verb endings: spelling change: retain the   to eat
ge before a or o to keep the soft g sound of the verb.

The Seven Simple Tenses		The Seven Compound Tenses	
Singular	Plural	Singular	Plural
1 présent de l'indicatif		8 passé composé	
mange	**mangeons**	**ai mangé**	**avons mangé**
manges	**mangez**	**as mangé**	**avez mangé**
mange	**mangent**	**a mangé**	**ont mangé**
2 imparfait de l'indicatif		9 plus-que-parfait de l'indicatif	
mangeais	**mangions**	**avais mangé**	**avions mangé**
mangeais	**mangiez**	**avais mangé**	**aviez mangé**
mangeait	**mangeaient**	**avait mangé**	**avaient mangé**
3 passé simple		10 passé antérieur	
mangeai	**mangeâmes**	**eus mangé**	**eûmes mangé**
mangeas	**mangeâtes**	**eus mangé**	**eûtes mangé**
mangea	**mangèrent**	**eut mangé**	**eurent mangé**
4 futur		11 futur antérieur	
mangerai	**mangerons**	**aurai mangé**	**aurons mangé**
mangeras	**mangerez**	**auras mangé**	**aurez mangé**
mangera	**mangeront**	**aura mangé**	**auront mangé**
5 conditionnel		12 conditionnel passé	
mangerais	**mangerions**	**aurais mangé**	**aurions mangé**
mangerais	**mangeriez**	**aurais mangé**	**auriez mangé**
mangerait	**mangeraient**	**aurait mangé**	**auraient mangé**
6 présent du subjonctif		13 passé du subjonctif	
mange	**mangions**	**aie mangé**	**ayons mangé**
manges	**mangiez**	**aies mangé**	**ayez mangé**
mange	**mangent**	**ait mangé**	**aient mangé**
7 imparfait du subjonctif		14 plus-que-parfait du subjonctif	
mangeasse	**mangeassions**	**eusse mangé**	**eussions mangé**
mangeasses	**mangeassiez**	**eusses mangé**	**eussiez mangé**
mangeât	**mangeassent**	**eût mangé**	**eussent mangé**

Impératif
mange
mangeons
mangez

---

le manger   food
gros mangeur   big eater
manger de l'argent   to spend money foolishly
ne pas manger à sa faim   not to have much to eat
manger à sa faim   to eat until filled
manger comme quatre   to eat like a horse

une mangeoire   manger
manger comme un oiseau   to eat like a bird
L'appétit vient en mangeant.   The more you have, the more you want. (Literally: Appetite comes while eating.)

manquer	Part. pr. manquant	Part. passé manqué

to miss, to lack

Regular -er verb

The Seven Simple Tenses		The Seven Compound Tenses	
Singular	Plural	Singular	Plural

1 présent de l'indicatif		8 passé composé	
manque	manquons	ai manqué	avons manqué
manques	manquez	as manqué	avez manqué
manque	manquent	a manqué	ont manqué

2 imparfait de l'indicatif		9 plus-que-parfait de l'indicatif	
manquais	manquions	avais manqué	avions manqué
manquais	manquiez	avais manqué	aviez manqué
manquait	manquaient	avait manqué	avaient manqué

3 passé simple		10 passé antérieur	
manquai	manquâmes	eus manqué	eûmes manqué
manquas	manquâtes	eus manqué	eûtes manqué
manqua	manquèrent	eut manqué	eurent manqué

4 futur		11 futur antérieur	
manquerai	manquerons	aurai manqué	aurons manqué
manqueras	manquerez	auras manqué	aurez manqué
manquera	manqueront	aura manqué	auront manqué

5 conditionnel		12 conditionnel passé	
manquerais	manquerions	aurais manqué	aurions manqué
manquerais	manqueriez	aurais manqué	auriez manqué
manquerait	manqueraient	aurait manqué	auraient manqué

6 présent du subjonctif		13 passé du subjonctif	
manque	manquions	aie manqué	ayons manqué
manques	manquiez	aies manqué	ayez manqué
manque	manquent	ait manqué	aient manqué

7 imparfait du subjonctif		14 plus-que-parfait du subjonctif	
manquasse	manquassions	eusse manqué	eussions manqué
manquasses	manquassiez	eusses manqué	eussiez manqué
manquât	manquassent	eût manqué	eussent manqué

Impératif
manque
manquons
manquez

---

manquer à to lack; Le courage lui manque. He lacks courage.
Elle me manque. I miss her.
Est-ce que je te manque? Do you miss me?
manquer de qqch to be lacking something; manquer de sucre to be out of sugar
Ne manquez pas de venir. Don't fail to come.

un mariage manqué a broken engagement
un héros manqué a would-be hero
Il me manque un euro. I am lacking (I need) one euro.
manquer de + inf. to fail to, to almost do something
Paul a manqué de venir. Paul failed to come.
manquer à sa parole to go back on one's word

Regular -er verb   to walk, to march, to run (machine), to function

The Seven Simple Tenses		The Seven Compound Tenses	
Singular	Plural	Singular	Plural

1 présent de l'indicatif		8 passé composé	
marche	marchons	ai marché	avons marché
marches	marchez	as marché	avez marché
marche	marchent	a marché	ont marché

2 imparfait de l'indicatif		9 plus-que-parfait de l'indicatif	
marchais	marchions	avais marché	avions marché
marchais	marchiez	avais marché	aviez marché
marchait	marchaient	avait marché	avaient marché

3 passé simple		10 passé antérieur	
marchai	marchâmes	eus marché	eûmes marché
marchas	marchâtes	eus marché	eûtes marché
marcha	marchèrent	eut marché	eurent marché

4 futur		11 futur antérieur	
marcherai	marcherons	aurai marché	aurons marché
marcheras	marcherez	auras marché	aurez marché
marchera	marcheront	aura marché	auront marché

5 conditionnel		12 conditionnel passé	
marcherais	marcherions	aurais marché	aurions marché
marcherais	marcheriez	aurais marché	auriez marché
marcherait	marcheraient	aurait marché	auraient marché

6 présent du subjonctif		13 passé du subjonctif	
marche	marchions	aie marché	ayons marché
marches	marchiez	aies marché	ayez marché
marche	marchent	ait marché	aient marché

7 imparfait du subjonctif		14 plus-que-parfait du subjonctif	
marchasse	marchassions	eusse marché	eussions marché
marchasses	marchassiez	eusses marché	eussiez marché
marchât	marchassent	eût marché	eussent marché

Impératif
marche
marchons
marchez

---

la marche   march, walking
ralentir sa marche   to slow down one's pace
le marché   market
le marché aux fleurs   flower market
le marché aux puces   flea market
à bon marché   cheap
faire marcher qqn   to put someone on
une démarche   gait, walk
faire une démarche   to take a step

marcher bien   to function (go, run, work) well
marcher sur les pas de qqn   to follow in someone's footsteps
faire marcher qqch   to make something go (run, function)
Ça ne marche plus.   It's out of order.

se méfier   Part. pr. se méfiant   Part. passé méfié(e)(s)

to beware, to distrust, to mistrust   Reflexive regular -er verb

The Seven Simple Tenses		The Seven Compound Tenses	
Singular	Plural	Singular	Plural
1 présent de l'indicatif		8 passé composé	
me méfie	nous méfions	me suis méfié(e)	nous sommes méfié(e)s
te méfies	vous méfiez	t'es méfié(e)	vous êtes méfié(e)(s)
se méfie	se méfient	s'est méfié(e)	se sont méfié(e)s
2 imparfait de l'indicatif		9 plus-que-parfait de l'indicatif	
me méfiais	nous méfiions	m'étais méfié(e)	nous étions méfié(e)s
te méfiais	vous méfiiez	t'étais méfié(e)	vous étiez méfié(e)(s)
se méfiait	se méfiaient	s'était méfié(e)	s'étaient méfié(e)s
3 passé simple		10 passé antérieur	
me méfiai	nous méfiâmes	me fus méfié(e)	nous fûmes méfié(e)s
te méfias	vous méfiâtes	te fus méfié(e)	vous fûtes méfié(e)(s)
se méfia	se méfièrent	se fut méfié(e)	se furent méfié(e)s
4 futur		11 futur antérieur	
me méfierai	nous méfierons	me serai méfié(e)	nous serons méfié(e)s
te méfieras	vous méfierez	te seras méfié(e)	vous serez méfié(e)(s)
se méfiera	se méfieront	se sera méfié(e)	se seront méfié(e)s
5 conditionnel		12 conditionnel passé	
me méfierais	nous méfierions	me serais méfié(e)	nous serions méfié(e)s
te méfierais	vous méfieriez	te serais méfié(e)	vous seriez méfié(e)(s)
se méfierait	se méfieraient	se serait méfié(e)	se seraient méfié(e)s
6 présent du subjonctif		13 passé du subjonctif	
me méfie	nous méfiions	me sois méfié(e)	nous soyons méfié(e)s
te méfies	vous méfiiez	te sois méfié(e)	vous soyez méfié(e)(s)
se méfie	se méfient	se soit méfié(e)	se soient méfié(e)s
7 imparfait du subjonctif		14 plus-que-parfait du subjonctif	
me méfiasse	nous méfiassions	me fusse méfié(e)	nous fussions méfié(e)s
te méfiasses	vous méfiassiez	te fusses méfié(e)	vous fussiez méfié(e)(s)
se méfiât	se méfiassent	se fût méfié(e)	se fussent méfié(e)s

Impératif
méfie-toi; ne te méfie pas
méfions-nous; ne nous méfions pas
méfiez-vous; ne vous méfiez pas

se méfier de   to distrust, to mistrust
Méfiez-vous!   Watch out!
méfiant, méfiante   distrustful
la méfiance   distrust, mistrust
un méfait   misdeed, wrongdoing
Il faut vous méfier.   You must be
    careful.

Méfiez-vous de lui (d'elle).   Do not
    trust him (her).
être sans méfiance   to be completely
    trusting
avoir de la méfiance envers quelqu'un
    to mistrust someone

Regular -er verb: spelling change: e changes   to lead, to control
to è before syllable with mute e.

The Seven Simple Tenses		The Seven Compound Tenses	
Singular	Plural	Singular	Plural
1 présent de l'indicatif		8 passé composé	
mène	**menons**	**ai mené**	**avons mené**
mènes	**menez**	**as mené**	**avez mené**
mène	**mènent**	**a mené**	**ont mené**
2 imparfait de l'indicatif		9 plus-que-parfait de l'indicatif	
menais	**menions**	**avais mené**	**avions mené**
menais	**meniez**	**avais mené**	**aviez mené**
menait	**menaient**	**avait mené**	**avaient mené**
3 passé simple		10 passé antérieur	
menai	**menâmes**	**eus mené**	**eûmes mené**
menas	**menâtes**	**eus mené**	**eûtes mené**
mena	**menèrent**	**eut mené**	**eurent mené**
4 futur		11 futur antérieur	
mènerai	**mènerons**	**aurai mené**	**aurons mené**
mèneras	**mènerez**	**auras mené**	**aurez mené**
mènera	**mèneront**	**aura mené**	**auront mené**
5 conditionnel		12 conditionnel passé	
mènerais	**mènerions**	**aurais mené**	**aurions mené**
mènerais	**mèneriez**	**aurais mené**	**auriez mené**
mènerait	**mèneraient**	**aurait mené**	**auraient mené**
6 présent du subjonctif		13 passé du subjonctif	
mène	**menions**	**aie mené**	**ayons mené**
mènes	**meniez**	**aies mené**	**ayez mené**
mène	**mènent**	**ait mené**	**aient mené**
7 imparfait du subjonctif		14 plus-que-parfait du subjonctif	
menasse	**menassions**	**eusse mené**	**eussions mené**
menasses	**menassiez**	**eusses mené**	**eussiez mené**
menât	**menassent**	**eût mené**	**eussent mené**
		Impératif	
		mène	
		menons	
		menez	

---

un meneur, une meneuse   leader
Cela ne mène à rien.   That leads to nothing.
mener qqn par le bout du nez   to lead someone around by the nose
mener une vie vagabonde   to lead a vagabond life
mener tout le monde   to be bossy with everyone
mener la bande   to lead the group
Cela vous mènera loin.   That will take you a long way.

See also emmener.

mentir	Part. pr. **mentant**	Part. passé **menti**

to lie, to tell a lie

Irregular verb

The Seven Simple Tenses		The Seven Compound Tenses	
Singular	Plural	Singular	Plural
1 présent de l'indicatif		8 passé composé	
mens	**mentons**	**ai menti**	**avons menti**
mens	**mentez**	**as menti**	**avez menti**
ment	**mentent**	**a menti**	**ont menti**
2 imparfait de l'indicatif		9 plus-que-parfait de l'indicatif	
mentais	**mentions**	**avais menti**	**avions menti**
mentais	**mentiez**	**avais menti**	**aviez menti**
mentait	**mentaient**	**avait menti**	**avaient menti**
3 passé simple		10 passé antérieur	
mentis	**mentîmes**	**eus menti**	**eûmes menti**
mentis	**mentîtes**	**eus menti**	**eûtes menti**
mentit	**mentirent**	**eut menti**	**eurent menti**
4 futur		11 futur antérieur	
mentirai	**mentirons**	**aurai menti**	**aurons menti**
mentiras	**mentirez**	**auras menti**	**aurez menti**
mentira	**mentiront**	**aura menti**	**auront menti**
5 conditionnel		12 conditionnel passé	
mentirais	**mentirions**	**aurais menti**	**aurions menti**
mentirais	**mentiriez**	**aurais menti**	**auriez menti**
mentirait	**mentiraient**	**aurait menti**	**auraient menti**
6 présent du subjonctif		13 passé du subjonctif	
mente	**mentions**	**aie menti**	**ayons menti**
mentes	**mentiez**	**aies menti**	**ayez menti**
mente	**mentent**	**ait menti**	**aient menti**
7 imparfait du subjonctif		14 plus-que-parfait du subjonctif	
mentisse	**mentissions**	**eusse menti**	**eussions menti**
mentisses	**mentissiez**	**eusses menti**	**eussiez menti**
mentît	**mentissent**	**eût menti**	**eussent menti**
		Impératif	
		mens	
		mentons	
		mentez	

---

un mensonge a lie
dire des mensonges to tell lies
un menteur, une menteuse a liar
démentir to belie, to deny, to falsify, to refute
une menterie fib

Ce sont des mensonges. It's all a pack of lies.
Tu mens! You're a liar!
sans mentir quite honestly

Irregular verb   to put, to place, to put on (clothing)

The Seven Simple Tenses		The Seven Compound Tenses	
Singular	Plural	Singular	Plural
1 présent de l'indicatif		**8 passé composé**	
mets	mettons	ai mis	avons mis
mets	mettez	as mis	avez mis
met	mettent	a mis	ont mis
2 imparfait de l'indicatif		**9 plus-que-parfait de l'indicatif**	
mettais	mettions	avais mis	avions mis
mettais	mettiez	avais mis	aviez mis
mettait	mettaient	avait mis	avaient mis
3 passé simple		**10 passé antérieur**	
mis	mîmes	eus mis	eûmes mis
mis	mîtes	eus mis	eûtes mis
mit	mirent	eut mis	eurent mis
4 futur		**11 futur antérieur**	
mettrai	mettrons	aurai mis	aurons mis
mettras	mettrez	auras mis	aurez mis
mettra	mettront	aura mis	auront mis
5 conditionnel		**12 conditionnel passé**	
mettrais	mettrions	aurais mis	aurions mis
mettrais	mettriez	aurais mis	auriez mis
mettrait	mettraient	aurait mis	auraient mis
6 présent du subjonctif		**13 passé du subjonctif**	
mette	mettions	aie mis	ayons mis
mettes	mettiez	aies mis	ayez mis
mette	mettent	ait mis	aient mis
7 imparfait du subjonctif		**14 plus-que-parfait du subjonctif**	
misse	missions	eusse mis	eussions mis
misses	missiez	eusses mis	eussiez mis
mît	missent	eût mis	eussent mis
		Impératif	
		mets	
		mettons	
		mettez	

mettre la table to set the table	mettre au courant to inform
mettre de côté to lay aside, to save	mettre le couvert to set the table
mettre en cause to question	mettre au point to make clear
mettre qqn à la porte to kick somebody	mettre la télé to turn on the TV
out the door	mettre la radio to turn on the radio

Try reading aloud as fast as you can this play on the sound mi: Mimi a mis ses amis
à Miami.   Mimi dropped off her friends in Miami.

This play on the sound **mi** was used at the Institut de Phonétique, Université de
Paris (en Sorbonne), where the first author of this book studied French phonetics.
(See "About the Authors," page iv.) In common usage, it is more common to say,
"Mimi a déposé (or transporté) ses amis à Miami," but that's not as amusing!   **171**
See also **admettre, permettre, promettre, remettre,** and **soumettre.**

se mettre   Part. pr. **se mettant**   Part. passé **mis(e)(es)**

to begin, to start, to place oneself   Reflexive irregular verb

The Seven Simple Tenses		The Seven Compound Tenses	
Singular	Plural	Singular	Plural
1 présent de l'indicatif		8 passé composé	
me mets	nous mettons	me suis mis(e)	nous sommes mis(es)
te mets	vous mettez	t'es mis(e)	vous êtes mis(e)(es)
se met	se mettent	s'est mis(e)	se sont mis(es)
2 imparfait de l'indicatif		9 plus-que-parfait de l'indicatif	
me mettais	nous mettions	m'étais mis(e)	nous étions mis(es)
te mettais	vous mettiez	t'étais mis(e)	vous étiez mis(e)(es)
se mettait	se mettaient	s'était mis(e)	s'étaient mis(es)
3 passé simple		10 passé antérieur	
me mis	nous mîmes	me fus mis(e)	nous fûmes mis(es)
te mis	vous mîtes	te fus mis(e)	vous fûtes mis(e)(es)
se mit	se mirent	se fut mis(e)	se furent mis(es)
4 futur		11 futur antérieur	
me mettrai	nous mettrons	me serai mis(e)	nous serons mis(es)
te mettras	vous mettrez	te seras mis(e)	vous serez mis(e)(es)
se mettra	se mettront	se sera mis(e)	se seront mis(es)
5 conditionnel		12 conditionnel passé	
me mettrais	nous mettrions	me serais mis(e)	nous serions mis(es)
te mettrais	vous mettriez	te serais mis(e)	vous seriez mis(e)(es)
se mettrait	se mettraient	se serait mis(e)	se seraient mis(es)
6 présent du subjonctif		13 passé du subjonctif	
me mette	nous mettions	me sois mis(e)	nous soyons mis(es)
te mettes	vous mettiez	te sois mis(e)	vous soyez mis(e)(es)
se mette	se mettent	se soit mis(e)	se soient mis(es)
7 imparfait du subjonctif		14 plus-que-parfait du subjonctif	
me misse	nous missions	me fusse mis(e)	nous fussions mis(es)
te misses	vous missiez	te fusses mis(e)	vous fussiez mis(e)(es)
se mît	se missent	se fût mis(e)	se fussent mis(es)

Impératif
mets-toi; ne te mets pas
mettons-nous; ne nous mettons pas
mettez-vous; ne vous mettez pas

---

se mettre à + inf.   to begin, to start + inf.
se mettre à table   to go sit at the table
se mettre en colère   to get angry
mettable   wearable; se mettre en grande toilette   to dress for an occasion;
    se mettre en smoking   to put on a dinner jacket
mettre en scène   to stage; un metteur en scène   director of a play, film
Il ne faut pas se mettre à l'eau de peur de la pluie.   One shouldn't jump in the
    water out of fear of the rain.

See also mettre.

Regular -er verb   to go up, to ascend, to take up, to bring up, to mount

The Seven Simple Tenses		The Seven Compound Tenses	
Singular	Plural	Singular	Plural
1 présent de l'indicatif		8 passé composé	
monte	montons	**suis monté(e)**	**sommes monté(e)s**
montes	montez	**es monté(e)**	**êtes monté(e)(s)**
monte	montent	**est monté(e)**	**sont monté(e)s**
2 imparfait de l'indicatif		9 plus-que-parfait de l'indicatif	
montais	montions	**étais monté(e)**	**étions monté(e)s**
montais	montiez	**étais monté(e)**	**étiez monté(e)(s)**
montait	montaient	**était monté(e)**	**étaient monté(e)s**
3 passé simple		10 passé antérieur	
montai	montâmes	**fus monté(e)**	**fûmes monté(e)s**
montas	montâtes	**fus monté(e)**	**fûtes monté(e)(s)**
monta	montèrent	**fut monté(e)**	**furent monté(e)s**
4 futur		11 futur antérieur	
monterai	monterons	**serai monté(e)**	**serons monté(e)s**
monteras	monterez	**seras monté(e)**	**serez monté(e)(s)**
montera	monteront	**sera monté(e)**	**seront monté(e)s**
5 conditionnel		12 conditionnel passé	
monterais	monterions	**serais monté(e)**	**serions monté(e)s**
monterais	monteriez	**serais monté(e)**	**seriez monté(e)(s)**
monterait	monteraient	**serait monté(e)**	**seraient monté(e)s**
6 présent du subjonctif		13 passé du subjonctif	
monte	montions	**sois monté(e)**	**soyons monté(e)s**
montes	montiez	**sois monté(e)**	**soyez monté(e)(s)**
monte	montent	**soit monté(e)**	**soient monté(e)s**
7 imparfait du subjonctif		14 plus-que-parfait du subjonctif	
montasse	montassions	**fusse monté(e)**	**fussions monté(e)s**
montasses	montassiez	**fusses monté(e)**	**fussiez monté(e)(s)**
montât	montassent	**fût monté(e)**	**fussent monté(e)s**

Impératif
monte
montons
montez

This verb is conjugated with avoir when it has a direct object.

Examples: **J'ai monté l'escalier.**   I went up the stairs.
            J'ai monté les valises.   I brought up the suitcases.

BUT: **Elle est montée vite.**   She went up quickly.

See also descendre.

monter à bicyclette   to ride a bicycle
monter dans un train   to get on a train
monter une pièce de théâtre   to stage a play

to show, to display, to exhibit, to point out   Regular -er verb

The Seven Simple Tenses		The Seven Compound Tenses	
Singular	Plural	Singular	Plural
1 présent de l'indicatif		8 passé composé	
montre	montrons	ai montré	avons montré
montres	montrez	as montré	avez montré
montre	montrent	a montré	ont montré
2 imparfait de l'indicatif		9 plus-que-parfait de l'indicatif	
montrais	montrions	avais montré	avions montré
montrais	montriez	avais montré	aviez montré
montrait	montraient	avait montré	avaient montré
3 passé simple		10 passé antérieur	
montrai	montrâmes	eus montré	eûmes montré
montras	montrâtes	eus montré	eûtes montré
montra	montrèrent	eut montré	eurent montré
4 futur		11 futur antérieur	
montrerai	montrerons	aurai montré	aurons montré
montreras	montrerez	auras montré	aurez montré
montrera	montreront	aura montré	auront montré
5 conditionnel		12 conditionnel passé	
montrerais	montrerions	aurais montré	aurions montré
montrerais	montreriez	aurais montré	auriez montré
montrerait	montreraient	aurait montré	auraient montré
6 présent du subjonctif		13 passé du subjonctif	
montre	montrions	aie montré	ayons montré
montres	montriez	aies montré	ayez montré
montre	montrent	ait montré	aient montré
7 imparfait du subjonctif		14 plus-que-parfait du subjonctif	
montrasse	montrassions	eusse montré	eussions montré
montrasses	montrassiez	eusses montré	eussiez montré
montrât	montrassent	eût montré	eussent montré
		Impératif	
		montre	
		montrons	
		montrez	

une montre   a watch, display
une montre-bracelet   wristwatch
faire montre de sa richesse   to display, to show off one's wealth
Quelle heure est-il à votre montre?   What time is it on your watch?
se faire montrer la porte   to be put out the door, to be shown out the door
démontrer   to demonstrate
se démontrer   to be proved
se montrer   to show oneself, to appear
montrer du doigt   to point out, to show, to indicate by pointing

Regular -re verb   to bite

The Seven Simple Tenses		The Seven Compound Tenses	
Singular	Plural	Singular	Plural
1 présent de l'indicatif		8 passé composé	
mords	**mordons**	**ai mordu**	**avons mordu**
mords	**mordez**	**as mordu**	**avez mordu**
mord	**mordent**	**a mordu**	**ont mordu**
2 imparfait de l'indicatif		9 plus-que-parfait de l'indicatif	
mordais	**mordions**	**avais mordu**	**avions mordu**
mordais	**mordiez**	**avais mordu**	**aviez mordu**
mordait	**mordaient**	**avait mordu**	**avaient mordu**
3 passé simple		10 passé antérieur	
mordis	**mordîmes**	**eus mordu**	**eûmes mordu**
mordis	**mordîtes**	**eus mordu**	**eûtes mordu**
mordit	**mordirent**	**eut mordu**	**eurent mordu**
4 futur		11 futur antérieur	
mordrai	**mordrons**	**aurai mordu**	**aurons mordu**
mordras	**mordrez**	**auras mordu**	**aurez mordu**
mordra	**mordront**	**aura mordu**	**auront mordu**
5 conditionnel		12 conditionnel passé	
mordrais	**mordrions**	**aurais mordu**	**aurions mordu**
mordrais	**mordriez**	**aurais mordu**	**auriez mordu**
mordrait	**mordraient**	**aurait mordu**	**auraient mordu**
6 présent du subjonctif		13 passé du subjonctif	
morde	**mordions**	**aie mordu**	**ayons mordu**
mordes	**mordiez**	**aies mordu**	**ayez mordu**
morde	**mordent**	**ait mordu**	**aient mordu**
7 imparfait du subjonctif		14 plus-que-parfait du subjonctif	
mordisse	**mordissions**	**eusse mordu**	**eussions mordu**
mordisses	**mordissiez**	**eusses mordu**	**eussiez mordu**
mordît	**mordissent**	**eût mordu**	**eussent mordu**
		Impératif	
		mords	
		mordons	
		mordez	

Chien qui aboie ne mord pas.   A barking dog does not bite. (**aboyer,** to bark)
Tous les chiens qui aboient ne mordent pas.   All dogs that bark do not bite.
mordre la poussière   to bite the dust
se mordre les lèvres   to bite one's lips
mordeur, mordeuse   biter (one who bites)
mordiller   to bite playfully, to nibble
mordant, mordante   biting, trenchant
une morsure   bite
un mordu de l'ordinateur   a computer fanatic, buff
C'est un mordu du jazz.   He's a fan of jazz.

mourir	Part. pr. **mourant**	Part. passé **mort(e)(s)**

to die

Irregular verb

The Seven Simple Tenses		The Seven Compound Tenses	
Singular	Plural	Singular	Plural
1 présent de l'indicatif		**8 passé composé**	
meurs	**mourons**	**suis mort(e)**	**sommes mort(e)s**
meurs	**mourez**	**es mort(e)**	**êtes mort(e)(s)**
meurt	**meurent**	**est mort(e)**	**sont mort(e)s**
2 imparfait de l'indicatif		**9 plus-que-parfait de l'indicatif**	
mourais	**mourions**	**étais mort(e)**	**étions mort(e)s**
mourais	**mouriez**	**étais mort(e)**	**étiez mort(e)(s)**
mourait	**mouraient**	**était mort(e)**	**étaient mort(e)s**
3 passé simple		**10 passé antérieur**	
mourus	**mourûmes**	**fus mort(e)**	**fûmes mort(e)s**
mourus	**mourûtes**	**fus mort(e)**	**fûtes mort(e)(s)**
mourut	**moururent**	**fut mort(e)**	**furent mort(e)s**
4 futur		**11 futur antérieur**	
mourrai	**mourrons**	**serai mort(e)**	**serons mort(e)s**
mourras	**mourrez**	**seras mort(e)**	**serez mort(e)(s)**
mourra	**mourront**	**sera mort(e)**	**seront mort(e)s**
5 conditionnel		**12 conditionnel passé**	
mourrais	**mourrions**	**serais mort(e)**	**serions mort(e)s**
mourrais	**mourriez**	**serais mort(e)**	**seriez mort(e)(s)**
mourrait	**mourraient**	**serait mort(e)**	**seraient mort(e)s**
6 présent du subjonctif		**13 passé du subjonctif**	
meure	**mourions**	**sois mort(e)**	**soyons mort(e)s**
meures	**mouriez**	**sois mort(e)**	**soyez mort(e)(s)**
meure	**meurent**	**soit mort(e)**	**soient mort(e)s**
7 imparfait du subjonctif		**14 plus-que-parfait du subjonctif**	
mourusse	**mourussions**	**fusse mort(e)**	**fussions mort(e)s**
mourusses	**mourussiez**	**fusses mort(e)**	**fussiez mort(e)(s)**
mourût	**mourussent**	**fût mort(e)**	**fussent mort(e)s**

Impératif
meurs
mourons
mourez

---

mourir de faim   to starve to death
la mort   death
Elle est mourante.   She is dying. Elle se meurt.   She is dying.
mourir d'ennui   to be bored to death
mourir de chagrin   to die of a broken heart
mourir de soif   to die of thirst
mourir de rire   to die laughing
mourir d'envie de faire qqch   to be very eager to do something
C'est triste à mourir.   It's horribly sad.

176

Part. pr. **mouvant**   Part. passé **mû, mue**   **mouvoir**

Irregular verb   to move

The Seven Simple Tenses | The Seven Compound Tenses

Singular	Plural		Singular	Plural

1 présent de l'indicatif

meus	mouvons		ai mû	avons mû
meus	mouvez		as mû	avez mû
meut	meuvent		a mû	ont mû

2 imparfait de l'indicatif

mouvais	mouvions		avais mû	avions mû
mouvais	mouviez		avais mû	aviez mû
mouvait	mouvaient		avait mû	avaient mû

3 passé simple

mus	mûmes		eus mû	eûmes mû
mus	mûtes		eus mû	eûtes mû
mut	murent		eut mû	eurent mû

4 futur

mouvrai	mouvrons		aurai mû	aurons mû
mouvras	mouvrez		auras mû	aurez mû
mouvra	mouvront		aura mû	auront mû

5 conditionnel

mouvrais	mouvrions		aurais mû	aurions mû
mouvrais	mouvriez		aurais mû	auriez mû
mouvrait	mouvraient		aurait mû	auraient mû

6 présent du subjonctif

meuve	mouvions		aie mû	ayons mû
meuves	mouviez		aies mû	ayez mû
meuve	meuvent		ait mû	aient mû

7 imparfait du subjonctif

musse	mussions		eusse mû	eussions mû
musses	mussiez		eusses mû	eussiez mû
mût	mussent		eût mû	eussent mû

2 imparfait de l'indicatif — *8 passé composé*

9 plus-que-parfait de l'indicatif

10 passé antérieur

11 futur antérieur

12 conditionnel passé

13 passé du subjonctif

14 plus-que-parfait du subjonctif

Impératif
meus
mouvons
mouvez

émouvoir to move, to affect (emotionally)
s'émouvoir to be moved, to be touched, to be affected (emotionally)
faire mouvoir to move, to set in motion
promouvoir to promote

Do not confuse this verb with **déménager**, which means to move from one dwelling to another or from one city to another.

nager	Part. pr. **nageant**	Part. passé **nagé**

to swim

Regular -er verb endings: spelling change: retain the ge before a or o to keep the soft g sound of the verb.

The Seven Simple Tenses		The Seven Compound Tenses	
Singular	Plural	Singular	Plural

1 présent de l'indicatif		8 passé composé	
nage	**nageons**	**ai nagé**	**avons nagé**
nages	**nagez**	**as nagé**	**avez nagé**
nage	**nagent**	**a nagé**	**ont nagé**

2 imparfait de l'indicatif		9 plus-que-parfait de l'indicatif	
nageais	**nagions**	**avais nagé**	**avions nagé**
nageais	**nagiez**	**avais nagé**	**aviez nagé**
nageait	**nageaient**	**avait nagé**	**avaient nagé**

3 passé simple		10 passé antérieur	
nageai	**nageâmes**	**eus nagé**	**eûmes nagé**
nageas	**nageâtes**	**eus nagé**	**eûtes nagé**
nagea	**nagèrent**	**eut nagé**	**eurent nagé**

4 futur		11 futur antérieur	
nagerai	**nagerons**	**aurai nagé**	**aurons nagé**
nageras	**nagerez**	**auras nagé**	**aurez nagé**
nagera	**nageront**	**aura nagé**	**auront nagé**

5 conditionnel		12 conditionnel passé	
nagerais	**nagerions**	**aurais nagé**	**aurions nagé**
nagerais	**nageriez**	**aurais nagé**	**auriez nagé**
nagerait	**nageraient**	**aurait nagé**	**auraient nagé**

6 présent du subjonctif		13 passé du subjonctif	
nage	**nagions**	**aie nagé**	**ayons nagé**
nages	**nagiez**	**aies nagé**	**ayez nagé**
nage	**nagent**	**ait nagé**	**aient nagé**

7 imparfait du subjonctif		14 plus-que-parfait du subjonctif	
nageasse	**nageassions**	**eusse nagé**	**eussions nagé**
nageasses	**nageassiez**	**eusses nagé**	**eussiez nagé**
nageât	**nageassent**	**eût nagé**	**eussent nagé**

Impératif
nage
nageons
nagez

---

un nageur, une nageuse   swimmer
la piscine   swimming pool
savoir nager   to know how to swim
la natation   swimming
nager entre deux eaux   to sit on the
  fence; to avoid a commitment
la nage   swimming; la nage libre
  freestyle swimming

se sauver à la nage   to swim to safety
faire de la natation   to swim
nager comme un poisson   to swim like
  a fish
aller nager   to go swimming

Irregular verb   to be born

The Seven Simple Tenses		The Seven Compound Tenses	
Singular	Plural	Singular	Plural
1 présent de l'indicatif		8 passé composé	
nais	naissons	suis né(e)	sommes né(e)s
nais	naissez	es né(e)	êtes né(e)(s)
naît	naissent	est né(e)	sont né(e)s
2 imparfait de l'indicatif		9 plus-que-parfait de l'indicatif	
naissais	naissions	étais né(e)	étions né(e)s
naissais	naissiez	étais né(e)	étiez né(e)(s)
naissait	naissaient	était né(e)	étaient né(e)s
3 passé simple		10 passé antérieur	
naquis	naquîmes	fus né(e)	fûmes né(e)s
naquis	naquîtes	fus né(e)	fûtes né(e)(s)
naquit	naquirent	fut né(e)	furent né(e)s
4 futur		11 futur antérieur	
naîtrai	naîtrons	serai né(e)	serons né(e)s
naîtras	naîtrez	seras né(e)	serez né(e)(s)
naîtra	naîtront	sera né(e)	seront né(e)s
5 conditionnel		12 conditionnel passé	
naîtrais	naîtrions	serais né(e)	serions né(e)s
naîtrais	naîtriez	serais né(e)	seriez né(e)(s)
naîtrait	naîtraient	serait né(e)	seraient né(e)s
6 présent du subjonctif		13 passé du subjonctif	
naisse	naissions	sois né(e)	soyons né(e)s
naisses	naissiez	sois né(e)	soyez né(e)(s)
naisse	naissent	soit né(e)	soient né(e)s
7 imparfait du subjonctif		14 plus-que-parfait du subjonctif	
naquisse	naquissions	fusse né(e)	fussions né(e)s
naquisses	naquissiez	fusses né(e)	fussiez né(e)(s)
naquît	naquissent	fût né(e)	fussent né(e)s

Impératif
nais
naissons
naissez

---

la naissance   birth
un anniversaire de naissance   a birthday anniversary
donner naissance à   to give birth to; la naissance du monde   beginning of the
   world
Anne est Française de naissance.   Anne was born French.
renaître   to be born again
faire naître   to cause, to give rise to
Je ne suis pas né(e) d'hier!   I wasn't born yesterday!
la Nativité   Nativity

neiger	Part. pr. neigeant	Part. passé neigé
to snow		Impersonal verb

The Seven Simple Tenses	The Seven Compound Tenses
Singular	Singular
1 présent de l'indicatif **il neige**	8 passé composé **il a neigé**
2 imparfait de l'indicatif **il neigeait**	9 plus-que-parfait de l'indicatif **il avait neigé**
3 passé simple **il neigea**	10 passé antérieur **il eut neigé**
4 futur **il neigera**	11 futur antérieur **il aura neigé**
5 conditionnel **il neigerait**	12 conditionnel passé **il aurait neigé**
6 présent du subjonctif **qu'il neige**	13 passé du subjonctif **qu'il ait neigé**
7 imparfait du subjonctif **qu'il neigeât**	14 plus-que-parfait du subjonctif **qu'il eût neigé**

Impératif
Qu'il neige! (Let it snow!)

la neige   snow
un bonhomme de neige   a snowman
neige fondue   slush
neigeux, neigeuse   snowy
Blanche-Neige   Snow-White
une boule de neige   snowball
lancer des boules de neige   to throw snowballs
une chute de neige   snowfall
déneiger   to clear the snow
un chasse-neige   snow plow

Regular -er verb endings: spelling change: -oyer   to clean
verbs must change y to i in front of a mute e.

The Seven Simple Tenses		The Seven Compound Tenses	
Singular	Plural	Singular	Plural
1 présent de l'indicatif		8 passé composé	
nettoie	**nettoyons**	**ai nettoyé**	**avons nettoyé**
nettoies	**nettoyez**	**as nettoyé**	**avez nettoyé**
nettoie	**nettoient**	**a nettoyé**	**ont nettoyé**
2 imparfait de l'indicatif		9 plus-que-parfait de l'indicatif	
nettoyais	**nettoyions**	**avais nettoyé**	**avions nettoyé**
nettoyais	**nettoyiez**	**avais nettoyé**	**aviez nettoyé**
nettoyait	**nettoyaient**	**avait nettoyé**	**avaient nettoyé**
3 passé simple		10 passé antérieur	
nettoyai	**nettoyâmes**	**eus nettoyé**	**eûmes nettoyé**
nettoyas	**nettoyâtes**	**eus nettoyé**	**eûtes nettoyé**
nettoya	**nettoyèrent**	**eut nettoyé**	**eurent nettoyé**
4 futur		11 futur antérieur	
nettoierai	**nettoierons**	**aurai nettoyé**	**aurons nettoyé**
nettoieras	**nettoierez**	**auras nettoyé**	**aurez nettoyé**
nettoiera	**nettoieront**	**aura nettoyé**	**auront nettoyé**
5 conditionnel		12 conditionnel passé	
nettoierais	**nettoierions**	**aurais nettoyé**	**aurions nettoyé**
nettoierais	**nettoieriez**	**aurais nettoyé**	**auriez nettoyé**
nettoierait	**nettoieraient**	**aurait nettoyé**	**auraient nettoyé**
6 présent du subjonctif		13 passé du subjonctif	
nettoie	**nettoyions**	**aie nettoyé**	**ayons nettoyé**
nettoies	**nettoyiez**	**aies nettoyé**	**ayez nettoyé**
nettoie	**nettoient**	**ait nettoyé**	**aient nettoyé**
7 imparfait du subjonctif		14 plus-que-parfait du subjonctif	
nettoyasse	**nettoyassions**	**eusse nettoyé**	**eussions nettoyé**
nettoyasses	**nettoyassiez**	**eusses nettoyé**	**eussiez nettoyé**
nettoyât	**nettoyassent**	**eût nettoyé**	**eussent nettoyé**
		Impératif	
		nettoie	
		nettoyons	
		nettoyez	

---

le nettoyage   cleaning; le nettoyage à sec   dry cleaning
nettoyer à sec   to dry clean
une nettoyeuse   cleaning machine
un nettoyeur de fenêtres   window cleaner
un nettoyant   cleanser
Elle refuse nettement.   She flatly refuses.
se faire nettoyer au jeu   to be cleaned out at gambling

to feed, to nourish   Regular -ir verb

The Seven Simple Tenses		The Seven Compound Tenses	
Singular	Plural	Singular	Plural
1 présent de l'indicatif		8 passé composé	
nourris	nourrissons	ai nourri	avons nourri
nourris	nourrissez	as nourri	avez nourri
nourrit	nourrissent	a nourri	ont nourri
2 imparfait de l'indicatif		9 plus-que-parfait de l'indicatif	
nourrissais	nourrissions	avais nourri	avions nourri
nourrissais	nourrissiez	avais nourri	aviez nourri
nourrissait	nourrissaient	avait nourri	avaient nourri
3 passé simple		10 passé antérieur	
nourris	nourrîmes	eus nourri	eûmes nourri
nourris	nourrîtes	eus nourri	eûtes nourri
nourrit	nourrirent	eut nourri	eurent nourri
4 futur		11 futur antérieur	
nourrirai	nourrirons	aurai nourri	aurons nourri
nourriras	nourrirez	auras nourri	aurez nourri
nourrira	nourriront	aura nourri	auront nourri
5 conditionnel		12 conditionnel passé	
nourrirais	nourririons	aurais nourri	aurions nourri
nourrirais	nourririez	aurais nourri	auriez nourri
nourrirait	nourriraient	aurait nourri	auraient nourri
6 présent du subjonctif		13 passé du subjonctif	
nourrisse	nourrissions	aie nourri	ayons nourri
nourrisses	nourrissiez	aies nourri	ayez nourri
nourrisse	nourrissent	ait nourri	aient nourri
7 imparfait du subjonctif		14 plus-que-parfait du subjonctif	
nourrisse	nourrissions	eusse nourri	eussions nourri
nourrisses	nourrissiez	eusses nourri	eussiez nourri
nourrît	nourrissent	eût nourri	eussent nourri
		Impératif	
		nourris	
		nourrissons	
		nourrissez	

---

la nourriture   nourishment, food
une nourrice   wet nurse
bien nourri   well fed; mal nourri
   poorly fed
nourrissant, nourrissante   nourishing

un nourrisson   infant
nourricier, nourricière   nutritious
une mère nourricière   foster mother
un père nourricier   foster father
se nourrir   to feed oneself

Irregular verb   to harm, to hinder

The Seven Simple Tenses		The Seven Compound Tenses	
Singular	Plural	Singular	Plural

1 présent de l'indicatif		8 passé composé	
nuis	nuisons	ai nui	avons nui
nuis	nuisez	as nui	avez nui
nuit	nuisent	a nui	ont nui

2 imparfait de l'indicatif		9 plus-que-parfait de l'indicatif	
nuisais	nuisions	avais nui	avions nui
nuisais	nuisiez	avais nui	aviez nui
nuisait	nuisaient	avait nui	avaient nui

3 passé simple		10 passé antérieur	
nuisis	nuisîmes	eus nui	eûmes nui
nuisis	nuisîtes	eus nui	eûtes nui
nuisit	nuisirent	eut nui	eurent nui

4 futur		11 futur antérieur	
nuirai	nuirons	aurai nui	aurons nui
nuiras	nuirez	auras nui	aurez nui
nuira	nuiront	aura nui	auront nui

5 conditionnel		12 conditionnel passé	
nuirais	nuirions	aurais nui	aurions nui
nuirais	nuiriez	aurais nui	auriez nui
nuirait	nuiraient	aurait nui	auraient nui

6 présent du subjonctif		13 passé du subjonctif	
nuise	nuisions	aie nui	ayons nui
nuises	nuisiez	aies nui	ayez nui
nuise	nuisent	ait nui	aient nui

7 imparfait du subjonctif		14 plus-que-parfait du subjonctif	
nuisisse	nuisissions	eusse nui	eussions nui
nuisisses	nuisissiez	eusses nui	eussiez nui
nuisît	nuisissent	eût nui	eussent nui

Impératif
nuis
nuisons
nuisez

---

la nuisance nuisance
la nuisibilité harmfulness
nuisible harmful
les nuisances sonores noise
pollution

nuire à to do harm to, to be injurious to,
to be harmful to
Cela peut nuire à la réputation de votre famille.
That may harm the reputation of your family.

obéir	Part. pr. obéissant	Part. passé obéi

to obey — Regular -ir verb

The Seven Simple Tenses		The Seven Compound Tenses	

Singular	Plural	Singular	Plural
1 présent de l'indicatif		**8 passé composé**	
obéis	obéissons	ai obéi	avons obéi
obéis	obéissez	as obéi	avez obéi
obéit	obéissent	a obéi	ont obéi
2 imparfait de l'indicatif		**9 plus-que-parfait de l'indicatif**	
obéissais	obéissions	avais obéi	avions obéi
obéissais	obéissiez	avais obéi	aviez obéi
obéissait	obéissaient	avait obéi	avaient obéi
3 passé simple		**10 passé antérieur**	
obéis	obéîmes	eus obéi	eûmes obéi
obéis	obéîtes	eus obéi	eûtes obéi
obéit	obéirent	eut obéi	eurent obéi
4 futur		**11 futur antérieur**	
obéirai	obéirons	aurai obéi	aurons obéi
obéiras	obéirez	auras obéi	aurez obéi
obéira	obéiront	aura obéi	auront obéi
5 conditionnel		**12 conditionnel passé**	
obéirais	obéirions	aurais obéi	aurions obéi
obéirais	obéiriez	aurais obéi	auriez obéi
obéirait	obéiraient	aurait obéi	auraient obéi
6 présent du subjonctif		**13 passé du subjonctif**	
obéisse	obéissions	aie obéi	ayons obéi
obéisses	obéissiez	aies obéi	ayez obéi
obéisse	obéissent	ait obéi	aient obéi
7 imparfait du subjonctif		**14 plus-que-parfait du subjonctif**	
obéisse	obéissions	eusse obéi	eussions obéi
obéisses	obéissiez	eusses obéi	eussiez obéi
obéît	obéissent	eût obéi	eussent obéi

Impératif
obéis
obéissons
obéissez

---

obéir à qqn   to obey someone
désobéir à qqn   to disobey someone
l'obéissance *f.*   obedience
obéissant, obéissante   obedient

désobéissant, désobéissante   disobedient
obéir à ses **instincts**   to obey one's
   instincts

Regular -er verb endings: spelling change: retain the   to oblige
ge before a or o to keep the soft g sound of the verb.

The Seven Simple Tenses		The Seven Compound Tenses	
Singular	Plural	Singular	Plural
1 présent de l'indicatif		**8 passé composé**	
oblige	**obligeons**	**ai obligé**	**avons obligé**
obliges	**obligez**	**as obligé**	**avez obligé**
oblige	**obligent**	**a obligé**	**ont obligé**
2 imparfait de l'indicatif		**9 plus-que-parfait de l'indicatif**	
obligeais	**obligions**	**avais obligé**	**avions obligé**
obligeais	**obligiez**	**avais obligé**	**aviez obligé**
obligeait	**obligeaient**	**avait obligé**	**avaient obligé**
3 passé simple		**10 passé antérieur**	
obligeai	**obligeâmes**	**eus obligé**	**eûmes obligé**
obligeas	**obligeâtes**	**eus obligé**	**eûtes obligé**
obligea	**obligèrent**	**eut obligé**	**eurent obligé**
4 futur		**11 futur antérieur**	
obligerai	**obligerons**	**aurai obligé**	**aurons obligé**
obligeras	**obligerez**	**auras obligé**	**aurez obligé**
obligera	**obligeront**	**aura obligé**	**auront obligé**
5 conditionnel		**12 conditionnel passé**	
obligerais	**obligerions**	**aurais obligé**	**aurions obligé**
obligerais	**obligeriez**	**aurais obligé**	**auriez obligé**
obligerait	**obligeraient**	**aurait obligé**	**auraient obligé**
6 présent du subjonctif		**13 passé du subjonctif**	
oblige	**obligions**	**aie obligé**	**ayons obligé**
obliges	**obligiez**	**aies obligé**	**ayez obligé**
oblige	**obligent**	**ait obligé**	**aient obligé**
7 imparfait du subjonctif		**14 plus-que-parfait du subjonctif**	
obligeasse	**obligeassions**	**eusse obligé**	**eussions obligé**
obligeasses	**obligeassiez**	**eusses obligé**	**eussiez obligé**
obligeât	**obligeassent**	**eût obligé**	**eussent obligé**
		Impératif	
		oblige	
		obligeons	
		obligez	

obligatoire   obligatory
obligation *f.*   obligation
avoir beaucoup d'obligation à qqn   to be much obliged to someone
obligeant, obligeante   obliging
se montrer obligeant envers qqn   to show kindness to someone
obligé, obligée   obliged
Noblesse oblige.   Nobility obliges. (i.e., the moral obligation of a highborn person
  is to show honorable conduct)

to obtain, to get   Irregular verb

The Seven Simple Tenses		The Seven Compound Tenses	
Singular	Plural	Singular	Plural
1 présent de l'indicatif		8 passé composé	
obtiens	obtenons	ai obtenu	avons obtenu
obtiens	obtenez	as obtenu	avez obtenu
obtient	obtiennent	a obtenu	ont obtenu
2 imparfait de l'indicatif		9 plus-que-parfait de l'indicatif	
obtenais	obtenions	avais obtenu	avions obtenu
obtenais	obteniez	avais obtenu	aviez obtenu
obtenait	obtenaient	avait obtenu	avaient obtenu
3 passé simple		10 passé antérieur	
obtins	obtînmes	eus obtenu	eûmes obtenu
obtins	obtîntes	eus obtenu	eûtes obtenu
obtint	obtinrent	eut obtenu	eurent obtenu
4 futur		11 futur antérieur	
obtiendrai	obtiendrons	aurai obtenu	aurons obtenu
obtiendras	obtiendrez	auras obtenu	aurez obtenu
obtiendra	obtiendront	aura obtenu	auront obtenu
5 conditionnel		12 conditionnel passé	
obtiendrais	obtiendrions	aurais obtenu	aurions obtenu
obtiendrais	obtiendriez	aurais obtenu	auriez obtenu
obtiendrait	obtiendraient	aurait obtenu	auraient obtenu
6 présent du subjonctif		13 passé du subjonctif	
obtienne	obtenions	aie obtenu	ayons obtenu
obtiennes	obteniez	aies obtenu	ayez obtenu
obtienne	obtiennent	ait obtenu	aient obtenu
7 imparfait du subjonctif		14 plus-que-parfait du subjonctif	
obtinsse	obtinssions	eusse obtenu	eussions obtenu
obtinsses	obtinssiez	eusses obtenu	eussiez obtenu
obtînt	obtinssent	eût obtenu	eussent obtenu
		Impératif	
		obtiens	
		obtenons	
		obtenez	

l'obtention   obtainment
obtenir de qqn qqch de force   to get something out of someone by force
s'obtenir de   to be obtained from

See also **tenir**.

Regular **-er** verb

to occupy

The Seven Simple Tenses		The Seven Compound Tenses	
Singular	Plural	Singular	Plural
1 présent de l'indicatif		**8 passé composé**	
occupe	occupons	ai occupé	avons occupé
occupes	occupez	as occupé	avez occupé
occupe	occupent	a occupé	ont occupé
2 imparfait de l'indicatif		**9 plus-que-parfait de l'indicatif**	
occupais	occupions	avais occupé	avions occupé
occupais	occupiez	avais occupé	aviez occupé
occupait	occupaient	avait occupé	avaient occupé
3 passé simple		**10 passé antérieur**	
occupai	occupâmes	eus occupé	eûmes occupé
occupas	occupâtes	eus occupé	eûtes occupé
occupa	occupèrent	eut occupé	eurent occupé
4 futur		**11 futur antérieur**	
occuperai	occuperons	aurai occupé	aurons occupé
occuperas	occuperez	auras occupé	aurez occupé
occupera	occuperont	aura occupé	auront occupé
5 conditionnel		**12 conditionnel passé**	
occuperais	occuperions	aurais occupé	aurions occupé
occuperais	occuperiez	aurais occupé	auriez occupé
occuperait	occuperaient	aurait occupé	auraient occupé
6 présent du subjonctif		**13 passé du subjonctif**	
occupe	occupions	aie occupé	ayons occupé
occupes	occupiez	aies occupé	ayez occupé
occupe	occupent	ait occupé	aient occupé
7 imparfait du subjonctif		**14 plus-que-parfait du subjonctif**	
occupasse	occupassions	eusse occupé	eussions occupé
occupasses	occupassiez	eusses occupé	eussiez occupé
occupât	occupassent	eût occupé	eussent occupé
		Impératif	
		occupe	
		occupons	
		occupez	

occupation *f.* occupation
être occupé(e)   to be busy
occuper qqn   to keep someone busy
occuper trop de place   to take up too much room
occupant, occupante   occupying; **du travail occupant**   engrossing work
occuper l'attention de qqn   to hold someone's attention
préoccuper   to preoccupy; **une préoccupation**   preoccupation
La ligne est occupée.   The line is busy.

s'occuper   Part. pr. s'occupant   Part. passé occupé(e)(s)

to be busy, to keep oneself busy   Reflexive regular -er verb

The Seven Simple Tenses		The Seven Compound Tenses	
Singular	Plural	Singular	Plural
1 présent de l'indicatif		8 passé composé	
m'occupe	nous occupons	me suis occupé(e)	nous sommes occupé(e)s
t'occupes	vous occupez	t'es occupé(e)	vous êtes occupé(e)(s)
s'occupe	s'occupent	s'est occupé(e)	se sont occupé(e)s
2 imparfait de l'indicatif		9 plus-que-parfait de l'indicatif	
m'occupais	nous occupions	m'étais occupé(e)	nous étions occupé(e)s
t'occupais	vous occupiez	t'étais occupé(e)	vous étiez occupé(e)(s)
s'occupait	s'occupaient	s'était occupé(e)	s'étaient occupé(e)s
3 passé simple		10 passé antérieur	
m'occupai	nous occupâmes	me fus occupé(e)	nous fûmes occupé(e)s
t'occupas	vous occupâtes	te fus occupé(e)	vous fûtes occupé(e)(s)
s'occupa	s'occupèrent	se fut occupé(e)	se furent occupé(e)s
4 futur		11 futur antérieur	
m'occuperai	nous occuperons	me serai occupé(e)	nous serons occupé(e)s
t'occuperas	vous occuperez	te seras occupé(e)	vous serez occupé(e)(s)
s'occupera	s'occuperont	se sera occupé(e)	se seront occupé(e)s
5 conditionnel		12 conditionnel passé	
m'occuperais	nous occuperions	me serais occupé(e)	nous serions occupé(e)s
t'occuperais	vous occuperiez	te serais occupé(e)	vous seriez occupé(e)(s)
s'occuperait	s'occuperaient	se serait occupé(e)	se seraient occupé(e)s
6 présent du subjonctif		13 passé du subjonctif	
m'occupe	nous occupions	me sois occupé(e)	nous soyons occupé(e)s
t'occupes	vous occupiez	te sois occupé(e)	vous soyez occupé(e)(s)
s'occupe	s'occupent	se soit occupé(e)	se soient occupé(e)s
7 imparfait du subjonctif		14 plus-que-parfait du subjonctif	
m'occupasse	nous occupassions	me fusse occupé(e)	nous fussions occupé(e)s
t'occupasses	vous occupassiez	te fusses occupé(e)	vous fussiez occupé(e)(s)
s'occupât	s'occupassent	se fût occupé(e)	se fussent occupé(e)s

Impératif
occupe-toi; ne t'occupe pas
occupons-nous; ne nous occupons pas
occupez-vous; ne vous occupez pas

s'occuper de ses affaires   to mind one's own business
Je m'occupe de mes affaires.   I mind my own business.
s'occuper des enfants   to look after children
s'occuper de   to look after, to tend to
s'occuper à   to be engaged in

Occupez-vous de vos affaires!   Mind your own business!
Ne vous occupez pas de mes affaires!   Don't mind my business!
Est-ce qu'on s'occupe de vous?   Is someone helping you?

See also occuper.

188

Irregular verb   to offer

The Seven Simple Tenses		The Seven Compound Tenses	
Singular	Plural	Singular	Plural
1 présent de l'indicatif		8 passé composé	
offre	offrons	ai offert	avons offert
offres	offrez	as offert	avez offert
offre	offrent	a offert	ont offert
2 imparfait de l'indicatif		9 plus-que-parfait de l'indicatif	
offrais	offrions	avais offert	avions offert
offrais	offriez	avais offert	aviez offert
offrait	offraient	avait offert	avaient offert
3 passé simple		10 passé antérieur	
offris	offrîmes	eus offert	eûmes offert
offris	offrîtes	eus offert	eûtes offert
offrit	offrirent	eut offert	eurent offert
4 futur		11 futur antérieur	
offrirai	offrirons	aurai offert	aurons offert
offriras	offrirez	auras offert	aurez offert
offrira	offriront	aura offert	auront offert
5 conditionnel		12 conditionnel passé	
offrirais	offririons	aurais offert	aurions offert
offrirais	offririez	aurais offert	auriez offert
offrirait	offriraient	aurait offert	auraient offert
6 présent du subjonctif		13 passé du subjonctif	
offre	offrions	aie offert	ayons offert
offres	offriez	aies offert	ayez offert
offre	offrent	ait offert	aient offert
7 imparfait du subjonctif		14 plus-que-parfait du subjonctif	
offrisse	offrissions	eusse offert	eussions offert
offrisses	offrissiez	eusses offert	eussiez offert
offrît	offrissent	eût offert	eussent offert

Impératif
offre
offrons
offrez

---

offrir qqch à qqn   to offer (to present)   **C'est pour offrir?** Is it to give as a gift?
  something to someone   **une offre d'emploi** a job offer
une offre an offer, a proposal
une offrande gift, offering
l'offre et la demande supply and demand

to omit   Irregular verb

The Seven Simple Tenses		The Seven Compound Tenses	
Singular	Plural	Singular	Plural
1 présent de l'indicatif		**8 passé composé**	
omets	omettons	ai omis	avons omis
omets	omettez	as omis	avez omis
omet	omettent	a omis	ont omis
2 imparfait de l'indicatif		**9 plus-que-parfait de l'indicatif**	
omettais	omettions	avais omis	avions omis
omettais	omettiez	avais omis	aviez omis
omettait	omettaient	avait omis	avaient omis
3 passé simple		**10 passé antérieur**	
omis	omîmes	eus omis	eûmes omis
omis	omîtes	eus omis	eûtes omis
omit	omirent	eut omis	eurent omis
4 futur		**11 futur antérieur**	
omettrai	omettrons	aurai omis	aurons omis
omettras	omettrez	auras omis	aurez omis
omettra	omettront	aura omis	auront omis
5 conditionnel		**12 conditionnel passé**	
omettrais	omettrions	aurais omis	aurions omis
omettrais	omettriez	aurais omis	auriez omis
omettrait	omettraient	aurait omis	auraient omis
6 présent du subjonctif		**13 passé du subjonctif**	
omette	omettions	aie omis	ayons omis
omettes	omettiez	aies omis	ayez omis
omette	omettent	ait omis	aient omis
7 imparfait du subjonctif		**14 plus-que-parfait du subjonctif**	
omisse	omissions	eusse omis	eussions omis
omisses	omissiez	eusses omis	eussiez omis
omît	omissent	eût omis	eussent omis
		Impératif	
		omets	
		omettons	
		omettez	

omettre de faire qqch   to neglect to do something
une omission   an omission
omis, omise   omitted
commettre   to commit

See also **admettre**, **mettre**, **permettre**, **promettre**, **remettre**, and **soumettre**.

Regular -er verb   to forget

The Seven Simple Tenses		The Seven Compound Tenses	
Singular	Plural	Singular	Plural
1 présent de l'indicatif		8 passé composé	
oublie	**oublions**	**ai oublié**	**avons oublié**
oublies	**oubliez**	**as oublié**	**avez oublié**
oublie	**oublient**	**a oublié**	**ont oublié**
2 imparfait de l'indicatif		9 plus-que-parfait de l'indicatif	
oubliais	**oubliions**	**avais oublié**	**avions oublié**
oubliais	**oubliiez**	**avais oublié**	**aviez oublié**
oubliait	**oubliaient**	**avait oublié**	**avaient oublié**
3 passé simple		10 passé antérieur	
oubliai	**oubliâmes**	**eus oublié**	**eûmes oublié**
oublias	**oubliâtes**	**eus oublié**	**eûtes oublié**
oublia	**oublièrent**	**eut oublié**	**eurent oublié**
4 futur		11 futur antérieur	
oublierai	**oublierons**	**aurai oublié**	**aurons oublié**
oublieras	**oublierez**	**auras oublié**	**aurez oublié**
oubliera	**oublieront**	**aura oublié**	**auront oublié**
5 conditionnel		12 conditionnel passé	
oublierais	**oublierions**	**aurais oublié**	**aurions oublié**
oublierais	**oublieriez**	**aurais oublié**	**auriez oublié**
oublierait	**oublieraient**	**aurait oublié**	**auraient oublié**
6 présent du subjonctif		13 passé du subjonctif	
oublie	**oubliions**	**aie oublié**	**ayons oublié**
oublies	**oubliiez**	**aies oublié**	**ayez oublié**
oublie	**oublient**	**ait oublié**	**aient oublié**
7 imparfait du subjonctif		14 plus-que-parfait du subjonctif	
oubliasse	**oubliassions**	**eusse oublié**	**eussions oublié**
oubliasses	**oubliassiez**	**eusses oublié**	**eussiez oublié**
oubliât	**oubliassent**	**eût oublié**	**eussent oublié**

Impératif
oublie
oublions
oubliez

---

un oubli oversight; oblivion
oubliable forgettable
inoubliable unforgettable
s'oublier to forget oneself, to be
  unmindful of oneself
tomber dans l'oubli to be forgotten
  (over time)
Nous n'oublierons jamais.
  We will never forget.

oublier de faire qqch to forget
  to do something
oublieux, oublieuse oblivious; **oublieux de**
  unmindful of

ouvrir		Part. pr. **ouvrant**	Part. passé **ouvert**

to open

Irregular verb

The Seven Simple Tenses		The Seven Compound Tenses	
Singular	Plural	Singular	Plural
1 présent de l'indicatif		8 passé composé	
ouvre	**ouvrons**	**ai ouvert**	**avons ouvert**
ouvres	**ouvrez**	**as ouvert**	**avez ouvert**
ouvre	**ouvrent**	**a ouvert**	**ont ouvert**
2 imparfait de l'indicatif		9 plus-que-parfait de l'indicatif	
ouvrais	**ouvrions**	**avais ouvert**	**avions ouvert**
ouvrais	**ouvriez**	**avais ouvert**	**aviez ouvert**
ouvrait	**ouvraient**	**avait ouvert**	**avaient ouvert**
3 passé simple		10 passé antérieur	
ouvris	**ouvrîmes**	**eus ouvert**	**eûmes ouvert**
ouvris	**ouvrîtes**	**eus ouvert**	**eûtes ouvert**
ouvrit	**ouvrirent**	**eut ouvert**	**eurent ouvert**
4 futur		11 futur antérieur	
ouvrirai	**ouvrirons**	**aurai ouvert**	**aurons ouvert**
ouvriras	**ouvrirez**	**auras ouvert**	**aurez ouvert**
ouvrira	**ouvriront**	**aura ouvert**	**auront ouvert**
5 conditionnel		12 conditionnel passé	
ouvrirais	**ouvririons**	**aurais ouvert**	**aurions ouvert**
ouvrirais	**ouvririez**	**aurais ouvert**	**auriez ouvert**
ouvrirait	**ouvriraient**	**aurait ouvert**	**auraient ouvert**
6 présent du subjonctif		13 passé du subjonctif	
ouvre	**ouvrions**	**aie ouvert**	**ayons ouvert**
ouvres	**ouvriez**	**aies ouvert**	**ayez ouvert**
ouvre	**ouvrent**	**ait ouvert**	**aient ouvert**
7 imparfait du subjonctif		14 plus-que-parfait du subjonctif	
ouvrisse	**ouvrissions**	**eusse ouvert**	**eussions ouvert**
ouvrisses	**ouvrissiez**	**eusses ouvert**	**eussiez ouvert**
ouvrît	**ouvrissent**	**eût ouvert**	**eussent ouvert**

Impératif
ouvre
ouvrons
ouvrez

---

ouvert, ouverte   open
ouverture *f.* opening
ouvrir le gaz   to turn on the gas
ouvrir de force   to force open
un ouvre-boîte (des ouvre-boîtes)   can
  opener
un ouvre-bouteille (des ouvre-
  bouteilles)   bottle opener

les heures ouvrables   business hours
ouvrir une session   to log in, log on
  (computer)
rouvrir   to reopen, to open again
entrouvrir   to open just a bit
entrouvert, entrouverte   ajar
s'ouvrir à   to confide in

Irregular verb   to appear, to seem

The Seven Simple Tenses		The Seven Compound Tenses	
Singular	Plural	Singular	Plural
1 présent de l'indicatif		8 passé composé	
parais	paraissons	ai paru	avons paru
parais	paraissez	as paru	avez paru
paraît	paraissent	a paru	ont paru
2 imparfait de l'indicatif		9 plus-que-parfait de l'indicatif	
paraissais	paraissions	avais paru	avions paru
paraissais	paraissiez	avais paru	aviez paru
paraissait	paraissaient	avait paru	avaient paru
3 passé simple		10 passé antérieur	
parus	parûmes	eus paru	eûmes paru
parus	parûtes	eus paru	eûtes paru
parut	parurent	eut paru	eurent paru
4 futur		11 futur antérieur	
paraîtrai	paraîtrons	aurai paru	aurons paru
paraîtras	paraîtrez	auras paru	aurez paru
paraîtra	paraîtront	aura paru	auront paru
5 conditionnel		12 conditionnel passé	
paraîtrais	paraîtrions	aurais paru	aurions paru
paraîtrais	paraîtriez	aurais paru	auriez paru
paraîtrait	paraîtraient	aurait paru	auraient paru
6 présent du subjonctif		13 passé du subjonctif	
paraisse	paraissions	aie paru	ayons paru
paraisses	paraissiez	aies paru	ayez paru
paraisse	paraissent	ait paru	aient paru
7 imparfait du subjonctif		14 plus-que-parfait du subjonctif	
parusse	parussions	eusse paru	eussions paru
parusses	parussiez	eusses paru	eussiez paru
parût	parussent	eût paru	eussent paru

	Impératif
	parais
	paraissons
	paraissez

---

apparition f.   apparition, appearance
Cela me paraît incroyable.   That seems unbelievable to me.
Le jour paraît.   Day is breaking.
apparaître to appear, to come into view
disparaître to disappear
réapparaître to reappear
Ce livre vient de paraître.   This book has just been published.
la parution (act of) publication

Note: The Académie française now allows **paraître** and related words to be spelled without the circumflex accent: **disparaitre, paraitre, il parait,** etc.

pardonner Part. pr. **pardonnant** Part. passé **pardonné**

to pardon, to forgive

Regular -er verb

The Seven Simple Tenses		The Seven Compound Tenses	
Singular	Plural	Singular	Plural

1 présent de l'indicatif

pardonne	pardonnons		
pardonnes	pardonnez		
pardonne	pardonnent		

8 passé composé

ai pardonné		avons pardonné	
as pardonné		avez pardonné	
a pardonné		ont pardonné	

2 imparfait de l'indicatif

pardonnais	pardonnions
pardonnais	pardonniez
pardonnait	pardonnaient

9 plus-que-parfait de l'indicatif

avais pardonné	avions pardonné
avais pardonné	aviez pardonné
avait pardonné	avaient pardonné

3 passé simple

pardonnai	pardonnâmes
pardonnas	pardonnâtes
pardonna	pardonnèrent

10 passé antérieur

eus pardonné	eûmes pardonné
eus pardonné	eûtes pardonné
eut pardonné	eurent pardonné

4 futur

pardonnerai	pardonnerons
pardonneras	pardonnerez
pardonnera	pardonneront

11 futur antérieur

aurai pardonné	aurons pardonné
auras pardonné	aurez pardonné
aura pardonné	auront pardonné

5 conditionnel

pardonnerais	pardonnerions
pardonnerais	pardonneriez
pardonnerait	pardonneraient

12 conditionnel passé

aurais pardonné	aurions pardonné
aurais pardonné	auriez pardonné
aurait pardonné	auraient pardonné

6 présent du subjonctif

pardonne	pardonnions
pardonnes	pardonniez
pardonne	pardonnent

13 passé du subjonctif

aie pardonné	ayons pardonné
aies pardonné	ayez pardonné
ait pardonné	aient pardonné

7 imparfait du subjonctif

pardonnasse	pardonnassions
pardonnasses	pardonnassiez
pardonnât	pardonnassent

14 plus-que-parfait du subjonctif

eusse pardonné	eussions pardonné
eusses pardonné	eussiez pardonné
eût pardonné	eussent pardonné

Impératif
pardonne
pardonnons
pardonnez

---

pardonner à qqn de qqch   to forgive someone for something
  J'ai pardonné à mon ami d'être arrivé en retard.   I forgave my friend for
  having arrived late.
un pardon   forgiveness, pardon
un don   gift
pardonnable   forgivable, pardonable
impardonnable   unforgivable
Pardonnez-moi.   Pardon me.

Regular -er verb　　　　　　　　　　　　　　　　to talk, to speak

The Seven Simple Tenses		The Seven Compound Tenses	
Singular	Plural	Singular	Plural
1　présent de l'indicatif		8　passé composé	
parle	**parlons**	**ai parlé**	**avons parlé**
parles	**parlez**	**as parlé**	**avez parlé**
parle	**parlent**	**a parlé**	**ont parlé**
2　imparfait de l'indicatif		9　plus-que-parfait de l'indicatif	
parlais	**parlions**	**avais parlé**	**avions parlé**
parlais	**parliez**	**avais parlé**	**aviez parlé**
parlait	**parlaient**	**avait parlé**	**avaient parlé**
3　passé simple		10　passé antérieur	
parlai	**parlâmes**	**eus parlé**	**eûmes parlé**
parlas	**parlâtes**	**eus parlé**	**eûtes parlé**
parla	**parlèrent**	**eut parlé**	**eurent parlé**
4　futur		11　futur antérieur	
parlerai	**parlerons**	**aurai parlé**	**aurons parlé**
parleras	**parlerez**	**auras parlé**	**aurez parlé**
parlera	**parleront**	**aura parlé**	**auront parlé**
5　conditionnel		12　conditionnel passé	
parlerais	**parlerions**	**aurais parlé**	**aurions parlé**
parlerais	**parleriez**	**aurais parlé**	**auriez parlé**
parlerait	**parleraient**	**aurait parlé**	**auraient parlé**
6　présent du subjonctif		13　passé du subjonctif	
parle	**parlions**	**aie parlé**	**ayons parlé**
parles	**parliez**	**aies parlé**	**ayez parlé**
parle	**parlent**	**ait parlé**	**aient parlé**
7　imparfait du subjonctif		14　plus-que-parfait du subjonctif	
parlasse	**parlassions**	**eusse parlé**	**eussions parlé**
parlasses	**parlassiez**	**eusses parlé**	**eussiez parlé**
parlât	**parlassent**	**eût parlé**	**eussent parlé**

Impératif
parle
parlons
parlez

---

parler à haute voix　to speak in a loud voice; **parler haut**　to speak loudly
parler à voix basse　to speak in a soft voice; **parler bas**　to speak softly
la parole　spoken word; **parler à**　to talk to; **parler de**　to talk about (of)
selon la parole du Christ　according to Christ's words
le don de la parole　the gift of gab
parler affaires　to talk business, to talk shop
sans parler de . . .　not to mention . . .
parler pour qqn　to speak for someone; **parler contre qqn**　to speak against
　someone
un parloir　parlor (room where people talk)

partir	Part. pr. **partant**	Part. passé **parti(e)(s)**

to leave, to depart   Irregular verb

The Seven Simple Tenses		The Seven Compound Tenses	
Singular	Plural	Singular	Plural
1 présent de l'indicatif		8 passé composé	
pars	**partons**	**suis parti(e)**	**sommes parti(e)s**
pars	**partez**	**es parti(e)**	**êtes parti(e)(s)**
part	**partent**	**est parti(e)**	**sont parti(e)s**
2 imparfait de l'indicatif		9 plus-que-parfait de l'indicatif	
partais	**partions**	**étais parti(e)**	**étions parti(e)s**
partais	**partiez**	**étais parti(e)**	**étiez parti(e)(s)**
partait	**partaient**	**était parti(e)**	**étaient parti(e)s**
3 passé simple		10 passé antérieur	
partis	**partîmes**	**fus parti(e)**	**fûmes parti(e)s**
partis	**partîtes**	**fus parti(e)**	**fûtes parti(e)(s)**
partit	**partirent**	**fut parti(e)**	**furent parti(e)s**
4 futur		11 futur antérieur	
partirai	**partirons**	**serai parti(e)**	**serons parti(e)s**
partiras	**partirez**	**seras parti(e)**	**serez parti(e)(s)**
partira	**partiront**	**sera parti(e)**	**seront parti(e)s**
5 conditionnel		12 conditionnel passé	
partirais	**partirions**	**serais parti(e)**	**serions parti(e)s**
partirais	**partiriez**	**serais parti(e)**	**seriez parti(e)(s)**
partirait	**partiraient**	**serait parti(e)**	**seraient parti(e)s**
6 présent du subjonctif		13 passé du subjonctif	
parte	**partions**	**sois parti(e)**	**soyons parti(e)s**
partes	**partiez**	**sois parti(e)**	**soyez parti(e)(s)**
parte	**partent**	**soit parti(e)**	**soient parti(e)s**
7 imparfait du subjonctif		14 plus-que-parfait du subjonctif	
partisse	**partissions**	**fusse parti(e)**	**fussions parti(e)s**
partisses	**partissiez**	**fusses parti(e)**	**fussiez parti(e)(s)**
partît	**partissent**	**fût parti(e)**	**fussent parti(e)s**

	Impératif
	pars
	partons
	partez

A quelle heure part le train pour Paris? At what time does the train for Paris leave?
à partir de maintenant from now on; à partir d'aujourd'hui from today on
le départ departure
partir en voyage to go on a trip
partir en vacances to leave for a vacation
repartir to leave again, to set out again (use être as auxiliary); to reply (use avoir as auxiliary)
Note: Be careful! répartir (to divide up, share) is a regular -ir verb.
Le chat parti, les souris dansent. When the cat is away, the mice will play.

Part. pr. passant Part. passé passé **passer**

Regular -er verb to pass, to spend (time)

The Seven Simple Tenses		The Seven Compound Tenses	
Singular	Plural	Singular	Plural
1 présent de l'indicatif		8 passé composé	
passe	passons	ai passé	avons passé
passes	passez	as passé	avez passé
passe	passent	a passé	ont passé
2 imparfait de l'indicatif		9 plus-que-parfait de l'indicatif	
passais	passions	avais passé	avions passé
passais	passiez	avais passé	aviez passé
passait	passaient	avait passé	avaient passé
3 passé simple		10 passé antérieur	
passai	passâmes	eus passé	eûmes passé
passas	passâtes	eus passé	eûtes passé
passa	passèrent	eut passé	eurent passé
4 futur		11 futur antérieur	
passerai	passerons	aurai passé	aurons passé
passeras	passerez	auras passé	aurez passé
passera	passeront	aura passé	auront passé
5 conditionnel		12 conditionnel passé	
passerais	passerions	aurais passé	aurions passé
passerais	passeriez	aurais passé	auriez passé
passerait	passeraient	aurait passé	auraient passé
6 présent du subjonctif		13 passé du subjonctif	
passe	passions	aie passé	ayons passé
passes	passiez	aies passé	ayez passé
passe	passent	ait passé	aient passé
7 imparfait du subjonctif		14 plus-que-parfait du subjonctif	
passasse	passassions	eusse passé	eussions passé
passasses	passassiez	eusses passé	eussiez passé
passât	passassent	eût passé	eussent passé
		Impératif	
		passe	
		passons	
		passez	

This verb is conjugated with être to indicate a state.

Example: Ses soupçons sont passés en certitudes.

This verb is conjugated with être when it means *to pass by, go by:*
Example: **Elle est passée chez moi.** She came by my house.

BUT: This verb is conjugated with avoir when it has a direct object:
Examples: **Elle m'a passé le sel.** She passed me the salt.
  Elle a passé un examen. She took an exam.

repasser to pass again; to iron
dépasser to protrude, to exceed, to surpass, to pass (a vehicle)

See also se passer. **197**

se passer	Part. pr. se passant	Part. passé **passé**
to happen, to take place		Impersonal verb

The Seven Simple Tenses	The Seven Compound Tenses
Singular	Singular
1 présent de l'indicatif **il se passe**	8 passé composé **il s'est passé**
2 imparfait de l'indicatif **il se passait**	9 plus-que-parfait de l'indicatif **il s'était passé**
3 passé simple **il se passa**	10 passé antérieur **il se fut passé**
4 futur **il se passera**	11 futur antérieur **il se sera passé**
5 conditionnel **il se passerait**	12 conditionnel passé **il se serait passé**
6 présent du subjonctif **qu'il se passe**	13 passé du subjonctif **qu'il se soit passé**
7 imparfait du subjonctif **qu'il se passât**	14 plus-que-parfait du subjonctif **qu'il se fût passé**

Impératif
Qu'il se passe! (Let it happen!)

Que se passe-t-il? What's going on? What's happening?
Qu'est-ce qui se passe? What's going on? What's happening?
Qu'est-ce qui s'est passé? What happened?
se passer de qqch to do without something
Je peux me passer de fumer. I can do without smoking.

This verb is impersonal and is generally used in the 3rd person sing. only.

See also **passer**.

198

Regular -er verb

to skate

The Seven Simple Tenses		The Seven Compound Tenses	
Singular	Plural	Singular	Plural

1 présent de l'indicatif		8 passé composé	
patine	**patinons**	**ai patiné**	**avons patiné**
patines	**patinez**	**as patiné**	**avez patiné**
patine	**patinent**	**a patiné**	**ont patiné**

2 imparfait de l'indicatif		9 plus-que-parfait de l'indicatif	
patinais	**patinions**	**avais patiné**	**avions patiné**
patinais	**patiniez**	**avais patiné**	**aviez patiné**
patinait	**patinaient**	**avait patiné**	**avaient patiné**

3 passé simple		10 passé antérieur	
patinai	**patinâmes**	**eus patiné**	**eûmes patiné**
patinas	**patinâtes**	**eus patiné**	**eûtes patiné**
patina	**patinèrent**	**eut patiné**	**eurent patiné**

4 futur		11 futur antérieur	
patinerai	**patinerons**	**aurai patiné**	**aurons patiné**
patineras	**patinerez**	**auras patiné**	**aurez patiné**
patinera	**patineront**	**aura patiné**	**auront patiné**

5 conditionnel		12 conditionnel passé	
patinerais	**patinerions**	**aurais patiné**	**aurions patiné**
patinerais	**patineriez**	**aurais patiné**	**auriez patiné**
patinerait	**patineraient**	**aurait patiné**	**auraient patiné**

6 présent du subjonctif		13 passé du subjonctif	
patine	**patinions**	**aie patiné**	**ayons patiné**
patines	**patiniez**	**aies patiné**	**ayez patiné**
patine	**patinent**	**ait patiné**	**aient patiné**

7 imparfait du subjonctif		14 plus-que-parfait du subjonctif	
patinasse	**patinassions**	**eusse patiné**	**eussions patiné**
patinasses	**patinassiez**	**eusses patiné**	**eussiez patiné**
patinât	**patinassent**	**eût patiné**	**eussent patiné**

	Impératif
	patine
	patinons
	patinez

patiner sur glace to skate on ice	**les patins à roues alignées** inline skates
une patinette scooter	**une patinoire** skating rink
un patineur, une patineuse skater	**patiner sur roulettes, patiner à roulettes** to roller skate
le patinage skating	
le patinage artistique figure skating	**le patinage à roulettes** roller skating
le patinage de vitesse speed skating	

payer	Part. pr. **payant**	Part. passé **payé**

to pay (for) — Regular -er verb endings: spelling change: -ayer verbs may change y to i before a mute e or may keep y.

The Seven Simple Tenses		The Seven Compound Tenses	
Singular	Plural	Singular	Plural
1 présent de l'indicatif		**8 passé composé**	
paie or **paye**	**payons**	**ai payé**	**avons payé**
paies or **payes**	**payez**	**as payé**	**avez payé**
paie or **paye**	**paient** or **payent**	**a payé**	**ont payé**
2 imparfait de l'indicatif		**9 plus-que-parfait de l'indicatif**	
payais	**payions**	**avais payé**	**avions payé**
payais	**payiez**	**avais payé**	**aviez payé**
payait	**payaient**	**avait payé**	**avaient payé**
3 passé simple		**10 passé antérieur**	
payai	**payâmes**	**eus payé**	**eûmes payé**
payas	**payâtes**	**eus payé**	**eûtes payé**
paya	**payèrent**	**eut payé**	**eurent payé**
4 futur		**11 futur antérieur**	
paierai or **payerai**	**paierons** or **payerons**	**aurai payé**	**aurons payé**
paieras or **payeras**	**paierez** or **payerez**	**auras payé**	**aurez payé**
paiera or **payera**	**paieront** or **payeront**	**aura payé**	**auront payé**
5 conditionnel		**12 conditionnel passé**	
paierais or **payerais**	**paierions** or **payerions**	**aurais payé**	**aurions payé**
paierais or **payerais**	**paieriez** or **payeriez**	**aurais payé**	**auriez payé**
paierait or **payerait**	**paieraient** or **payeraient**	**aurait payé**	**auraient payé**
6 présent du subjonctif		**13 passé du subjonctif**	
paie or **paye**	**payions**	**aie payé**	**ayons payé**
paies or **payes**	**payiez**	**aies payé**	**ayez payé**
paie or **paye**	**paient** or **payent**	**ait payé**	**aient payé**
7 imparfait du subjonctif		**14 plus-que-parfait du subjonctif**	
payasse	**payassions**	**eusse payé**	**eussions payé**
payasses	**payassiez**	**eusses payé**	**eussiez payé**
payât	**payassent**	**eût payé**	**eussent payé**

Impératif
paie or **paye**
payons
payez

Payez à la caisse, s'il vous plaît. Pay at the cashier, please.	**payer cher/peu** to pay a lot/little
avoir de quoi payer to have the means to pay	**payer comptant, payer en espèces** to pay in cash
	un paiement (or **payement**) payment

200

Regular -er verb endings: spelling change: to sin, to commit a sin
é changes to è before syllable with mute e.

The Seven Simple Tenses		The Seven Compound Tenses	
Singular	Plural	Singular	Plural

1 présent de l'indicatif

pèche	péchons		
pèches	péchez		
pèche	pèchent		

8 passé composé

ai péché	avons péché		
as péché	avez péché		
a péché	ont péché		

2 imparfait de l'indicatif

péchais	péchions
péchais	péchiez
péchait	péchaient

9 plus-que-parfait de l'indicatif

avais péché	avions péché
avais péché	aviez péché
avait péché	avaient péché

3 passé simple

péchai	péchâmes
péchas	péchâtes
pécha	péchèrent

10 passé antérieur

eus péché	eûmes péché
eus péché	eûtes péché
eut péché	eurent péché

4 futur

pécherai	pécherons
pécheras	pécherez
péchera	pécheront

11 futur antérieur

aurai péché	aurons péché
auras péché	aurez péché
aura péché	auront péché

5 conditionnel

pécherais	pécherions
pécherais	pécheriez
pécherait	pécheraient

12 conditionnel passé

aurais péché	aurions péché
aurais péché	auriez péché
aurait péché	auraient péché

6 présent du subjonctif

pèche	péchions
pèches	péchiez
pèche	pèchent

13 passé du subjonctif

aie péché	ayons péché
aies péché	ayez péché
ait péché	aient péché

7 imparfait du subjonctif

péchasse	péchassions
péchasses	péchassiez
péchât	péchassent

14 plus-que-parfait du subjonctif

eusse péché	eussions péché
eusses péché	eussiez péché
eût péché	eussent péché

Impératif
—

---

le péché   sin
un pécheur, une pécheresse   sinner
à tout péché miséricorde   forgiveness for every sin
commettre, faire un péché   to commit sin
vivre dans le péché   to lead a sinful life
les sept péchés capitaux   the seven deadly sins

Do not confuse this verb with **pêcher**, *to fish*.
Note: The Académie française now allows the accent grave (`) in the future
(je pècherai, tu pècheras, etc.) and conditional (je pècherais, tu pècherais,
etc.) of this verb.

pêcher	Part. pr. pêchant	Part. passé pêché
to fish		Regular -er verb

The Seven Simple Tenses		The Seven Compound Tenses	
Singular	Plural	Singular	Plural

1 présent de l'indicatif		8 passé composé	
pêche	pêchons	ai pêché	avons pêché
pêches	pêchez	as pêché	avez pêché
pêche	pêchent	a pêché	ont pêché

2 imparfait de l'indicatif		9 plus-que-parfait de l'indicatif	
pêchais	pêchions	avais pêché	avions pêché
pêchais	pêchiez	avais pêché	aviez pêché
pêchait	pêchaient	avait pêché	avaient pêché

3 passé simple		10 passé antérieur	
pêchai	pêchâmes	eus pêché	eûmes pêché
pêchas	pêchâtes	eus pêché	eûtes pêché
pêcha	pêchèrent	eut pêché	eurent pêché

4 futur		11 futur antérieur	
pêcherai	pêcherons	aurai pêché	aurons pêché
pêcheras	pêcherez	auras pêché	aurez pêché
pêchera	pêcheront	aura pêché	auront pêché

5 conditionnel		12 conditionnel passé	
pêcherais	pêcherions	aurais pêché	aurions pêché
pêcherais	pêcheriez	aurais pêché	auriez pêché
pêcherait	pêcheraient	aurait pêché	auraient pêché

6 présent du subjonctif		13 passé du subjonctif	
pêche	pêchions	aie pêché	ayons pêché
pêches	pêchiez	aies pêché	ayez pêché
pêche	pêchent	ait pêché	aient pêché

7 imparfait du subjonctif		14 plus-que-parfait du subjonctif	
pêchasse	pêchassions	eusse pêché	eussions pêché
pêchasses	pêchassiez	eusses pêché	eussiez pêché
pêchât	pêchassent	eût pêché	eussent pêché

	Impératif
	pêche
	pêchons
	pêchez

Samedi nous irons à la pêche. Je connais un lac à la campagne où il y a beaucoup de poissons.

aller à la pêche   to go fishing
un pêcheur   fisherman; une pêcheuse
   fisherwoman
un bateau pêcheur   fishing boat
la pêche au filet   net fishing

un pêcheur de perles   pearl diver
repêcher   to fish out
le repêchage   recovery, (act of)
   fishing out

Do not confuse this verb with pécher, *to sin*. And do not confuse une pêche (peach), which is a fruit, with a verb form of pêcher and with the noun la pêche, which means *fishing*, the sport.

202

Reflexive regular -er verb   to comb one's hair

The Seven Simple Tenses		The Seven Compound Tenses	
Singular	Plural	Singular	Plural
1 présent de l'indicatif		8 passé composé	
me peigne	nous peignons	me suis peigné(e)	nous sommes peigné(e)s
te peignes	vous peignez	t'es peigné(e)	vous êtes peigné(e)(s)
se peigne	se peignent	s'est peigné(e)	se sont peigné(e)s
2 imparfait de l'indicatif		9 plus-que-parfait de l'indicatif	
me peignais	nous peignions	m'étais peigné(e)	nous étions peigné(e)s
te peignais	vous peigniez	t'étais peigné(e)	vous étiez peigné(e)(s)
se peignait	se peignaient	s'était peigné(e)	s'étaient peigné(e)s
3 passé simple		10 passé antérieur	
me peignai	nous peignâmes	me fus peigné(e)	nous fûmes peigné(e)s
te peignas	vous peignâtes	te fus peigné(e)	vous fûtes peigné(e)(s)
se peigna	se peignèrent	se fut peigné(e)	se furent peigné(e)s
4 futur		11 futur antérieur	
me peignerai	nous peignerons	me serai peigné(e)	nous serons peigné(e)s
te peigneras	vous peignerez	te seras peigné(e)	vous serez peigné(e)(s)
se peignera	se peigneront	se sera peigné(e)	se seront peigné(e)s
5 conditionnel		12 conditionnel passé	
me peignerais	nous peignerions	me serais peigné(e)	nous serions peigné(e)s
te peignerais	vous peigneriez	te serais peigné(e)	vous seriez peigné(e)(s)
se peignerait	se peigneraient	se serait peigné(e)	se seraient peigné(e)s
6 présent du subjonctif		13 passé du subjonctif	
me peigne	nous peignions	me sois peigné(e)	nous soyons peigné(e)s
te peignes	vous peigniez	te sois peigné(e)	vous soyez peigné(e)(s)
se peigne	se peignent	se soit peigné(e)	se soient peigné(e)s
7 imparfait du subjonctif		14 plus-que-parfait du subjonctif	
me peignasse	nous peignassions	me fusse peigné(e)	nous fussions peigné(e)s
te peignasses	vous peignassiez	te fusses peigné(e)	vous fussiez peigné(e)(s)
se peignât	se peignassent	se fût peigné(e)	se fussent peigné(e)s

Impératif
peigne-toi; ne te peigne pas
peignons-nous; ne nous peignons pas
peignez-vous; ne vous peignez pas

Mon frère a peigné notre petit chien. Ma mère a lavé les cheveux de ma petite soeur et elle l'a peignée. Après cela, elle s'est lavé les cheveux et elle s'est peignée.

peigner qqn to comb someone	**mal peigné(e)(s)** untidy hair, disheveled
un peigne a comb	**bien peigné(e)(s)** well combed
un peignoir dressing gown	**un peignoir de bain** bathrobe

peindre	Part. pr. **peignant**	Part. passé **peint**

to paint, to portray   Irregular verb

The Seven Simple Tenses		The Seven Compound Tenses	
Singular	Plural	Singular	Plural
1 présent de l'indicatif		8 passé composé	
peins	**peignons**	**ai peint**	**avons peint**
peins	**peignez**	**as peint**	**avez peint**
peint	**peignent**	**a peint**	**ont peint**
2 imparfait de l'indicatif		9 plus-que-parfait de l'indicatif	
peignais	**peignions**	**avais peint**	**avions peint**
peignais	**peigniez**	**avais peint**	**aviez peint**
peignait	**peignaient**	**avait peint**	**avaient peint**
3 passé simple		10 passé antérieur	
peignis	**peignîmes**	**eus peint**	**eûmes peint**
peignis	**peignîtes**	**eus peint**	**eûtes peint**
peignit	**peignirent**	**eut peint**	**eurent peint**
4 futur		11 futur antérieur	
peindrai	**peindrons**	**aurai peint**	**aurons peint**
peindras	**peindrez**	**auras peint**	**aurez peint**
peindra	**peindront**	**aura peint**	**auront peint**
5 conditionnel		12 conditionnel passé	
peindrais	**peindrions**	**aurais peint**	**aurions peint**
peindrais	**peindriez**	**aurais peint**	**auriez peint**
peindrait	**peindraient**	**aurait peint**	**auraient peint**
6 présent du subjonctif		13 passé du subjonctif	
peigne	**peignions**	**aie peint**	**ayons peint**
peignes	**peigniez**	**aies peint**	**ayez peint**
peigne	**peignent**	**ait peint**	**aient peint**
7 imparfait du subjonctif		14 plus-que-parfait du subjonctif	
peignisse	**peignissions**	**eusse peint**	**eussions peint**
peignisses	**peignissiez**	**eusses peint**	**eussiez peint**
peignît	**peignissent**	**eût peint**	**eussent peint**

	Impératif
	peins
	peignons
	peignez

—Qui a **peint** ce tableau?   Who painted this picture?
—Mon fils l'a **peint.**   My son painted it.

une peinture painting, picture	un peintre painter
un tableau painting, picture	un artiste peintre artist
une peinture à l'huile oil painting	une femme peintre woman artist
peintre en bâtiments house painter	une palette de peintre artist's palette
dépeindre to depict, to describe	se faire peindre to have one's portrait
PEINTURE FRAÎCHE WET PAINT	painted

Part. pr. pensant		Part. passé pensé		**penser**
Regular -er verb				to think

The Seven Simple Tenses		The Seven Compound Tenses	
Singular	Plural	Singular	Plural

1 présent de l'indicatif		8 passé composé	
pense	pensons	ai pensé	avons pensé
penses	pensez	as pensé	avez pensé
pense	pensent	a pensé	ont pensé

2 imparfait de l'indicatif		9 plus-que-parfait de l'indicatif	
pensais	pensions	avais pensé	avions pensé
pensais	pensiez	avais pensé	aviez pensé
pensait	pensaient	avait pensé	avaient pensé

3 passé simple		10 passé antérieur	
pensai	pensâmes	eus pensé	eûmes pensé
pensas	pensâtes	eus pensé	eûtes pensé
pensa	pensèrent	eut pensé	eurent pensé

4 futur		11 futur antérieur	
penserai	penserons	aurai pensé	aurons pensé
penseras	penserez	auras pensé	aurez pensé
pensera	penseront	aura pensé	auront pensé

5 conditionnel		12 conditionnel passé	
penserais	penserions	aurais pensé	aurions pensé
penserais	penseriez	aurais pensé	auriez pensé
penserait	penseraient	aurait pensé	auraient pensé

6 présent du subjonctif		13 passé du subjonctif	
pense	pensions	aie pensé	ayons pensé
penses	pensiez	aies pensé	ayez pensé
pense	pensent	ait pensé	aient pensé

7 imparfait du subjonctif		14 plus-que-parfait du subjonctif	
pensasse	pensassions	eusse pensé	eussions pensé
pensasses	pensassiez	eusses pensé	eussiez pensé
pensât	pensassent	eût pensé	eussent pensé

Impératif
pense
pensons
pensez

—Je pense à mon examen de français. À quoi penses-tu?   I'm thinking about
  my French test. What are you thinking about?
—Moi? Je pense à nos vacances.   Me? I'm thinking about our vacation.

penser à   to think of, to think about; penser de   to think about (i.e., to have an
  opinion about)
un pense-bête   reminder (e.g., string around one's finger)
repenser   to rethink

Note: If you want to say that you're making up your mind (reflecting on something),
use réfléchir.

perdre	Part. pr. **perdant**	Part. passé **perdu**

to lose

Regular -re verb

The Seven Simple Tenses		The Seven Compound Tenses	
Singular	Plural	Singular	Plural
1 présent de l'indicatif		**8 passé composé**	
perds	perdons	ai perdu	avons perdu
perds	perdez	as perdu	avez perdu
perd	perdent	a perdu	ont perdu
2 imparfait de l'indicatif		**9 plus-que-parfait de l'indicatif**	
perdais	perdions	avais perdu	avions perdu
perdais	perdiez	avais perdu	aviez perdu
perdait	perdaient	avait perdu	avaient perdu
3 passé simple		**10 passé antérieur**	
perdis	perdîmes	eus perdu	eûmes perdu
perdis	perdîtes	eus perdu	eûtes perdu
perdit	perdirent	eut perdu	eurent perdu
4 futur		**11 futur antérieur**	
perdrai	perdrons	aurai perdu	aurons perdu
perdras	perdrez	auras perdu	aurez perdu
perdra	perdront	aura perdu	auront perdu
5 conditionnel		**12 conditionnel passé**	
perdrais	perdrions	aurais perdu	aurions perdu
perdrais	perdriez	aurais perdu	auriez perdu
perdrait	perdraient	aurait perdu	auraient perdu
6 présent du subjonctif		**13 passé du subjonctif**	
perde	perdions	aie perdu	ayons perdu
perdes	perdiez	aies perdu	ayez perdu
perde	perdent	ait perdu	aient perdu
7 imparfait du subjonctif		**14 plus-que-parfait du subjonctif**	
perdisse	perdissions	eusse perdu	eussions perdu
perdisses	perdissiez	eusses perdu	eussiez perdu
perdît	perdissent	eût perdu	eussent perdu

Impératif
perds
perdons
perdez

À cause du verglas, le chauffeur a perdu la maîtrise de sa voiture.   Because of the black ice, the driver lost control of his car.

se perdre to lose oneself, to lose one's way, to be ruined
perdre son temps to waste one's time
perdre son chemin to lose one's way
perdre pied to lose one's footing
perdre l'esprit to go out of one's mind
perdre le nord, perdre la boule to go crazy

Vous n'avez rien à perdre.   You have nothing to lose.
une perte a loss
perdre de vue to lose sight of
perdre la raison to take leave of one's senses

206

Regular -ir verb   to perish, to die

The Seven Simple Tenses		The Seven Compound Tenses	
Singular	Plural	Singular	Plural
1 présent de l'indicatif		8 passé composé	
péris	périssons	ai péri	avons péri
péris	périssez	as péri	avez péri
périt	périssent	a péri	ont péri
2 imparfait de l'indicatif		9 plus-que-parfait de l'indicatif	
périssais	périssions	avais péri	avions péri
périssais	périssiez	avais péri	aviez péri
périssait	périssaient	avait péri	avaient péri
3 passé simple		10 passé antérieur	
péris	pérîmes	eus péri	eûmes péri
péris	pérîtes	eus péri	eûtes péri
périt	périrent	eut péri	eurent péri
4 futur		11 futur antérieur	
périrai	périrons	aurai péri	aurons péri
périras	périrez	auras péri	aurez péri
périra	périront	aura péri	auront péri
5 conditionnel		12 conditionnel passé	
périrais	péririons	aurais péri	aurions péri
périrais	péririez	aurais péri	auriez péri
périrait	périraient	aurait péri	auraient péri
6 présent du subjonctif		13 passé du subjonctif	
périsse	périssions	aie péri	ayons péri
périsses	périssiez	aies péri	ayez péri
périsse	périssent	ait péri	aient péri
7 imparfait du subjonctif		14 plus-que-parfait du subjonctif	
périsse	périssions	eusse péri	eussions péri
périsses	périssiez	eusses péri	eussiez péri
pérît	périssent	eût péri	eussent péri
		Impératif	
		péris	
		périssons	
		périssez	

---

faire périr   to kill
s'ennuyer à périr   to be bored to death
périssable   perishable
périr d'ennui   to be bored to death
péri en mer   lost at sea

périr de froid   to freeze to death
les denrées périssables
   perishable foods
impérissable   imperishable,
   eternal

permettre	Part. pr. permettant	Part. passé **permis**

to permit, to allow, to let   Irregular verb

The Seven Simple Tenses		The Seven Compound Tenses	
Singular	Plural	Singular	Plural
1 présent de l'indicatif		8 passé composé	
permets	permettons	ai permis	avons permis
permets	permettez	as permis	avez permis
permet	permettent	a permis	ont permis
2 imparfait de l'indicatif		9 plus-que-parfait de l'indicatif	
permettais	permettions	avais permis	avions permis
permettais	permettiez	avais permis	aviez permis
permettait	permettaient	avait permis	avaient permis
3 passé simple		10 passé antérieur	
permis	permîmes	eus permis	eûmes permis
permis	permîtes	eus permis	eûtes permis
permit	permirent	eut permis	eurent permis
4 futur		11 futur antérieur	
permettrai	permettrons	aurai permis	aurons permis
permettras	permettrez	auras permis	aurez permis
permettra	permettront	aura permis	auront permis
5 conditionnel		12 conditionnel passé	
permettrais	permettrions	aurais permis	aurions permis
permettrais	permettriez	aurais permis	auriez permis
permettrait	permettraient	aurait permis	auraient permis
6 présent du subjonctif		13 passé du subjonctif	
permette	permettions	aie permis	ayons permis
permettes	permettiez	aies permis	ayez permis
permette	permettent	ait permis	aient permis
7 imparfait du subjonctif		14 plus-que-parfait du subjonctif	
permisse	permissions	eusse permis	eussions permis
permisses	permissiez	eusses permis	eussiez permis
permît	permissent	eût permis	eussent permis

Impératif
permets
permettons
permettez

La maîtresse de français a permis à l'élève de quitter la salle de classe quelques minutes avant la fin de la leçon.   The French teacher allowed the student to leave the classroom a few minutes before the end of the lesson.

permettre à qqn de faire qqch   to permit (to allow) someone to do something
Vous permettez?   May I? Do you mind?   la permission   permission
s'il est permis   if it is allowed, permitted   se permettre de faire qqch   to take
un permis   permit   the liberty of doing something;
un permis de conduire   driving license   to venture to do something

See also admettre, mettre, promettre, remettre, and soumettre.

208

Regular -er verb endings: spelling change: to place, to put
c changes to ç before a or o to keep s sound.

The Seven Simple Tenses		The Seven Compound Tenses	
Singular	Plural	Singular	Plural
1 présent de l'indicatif		**8 passé composé**	
place	plaçons	ai placé	avons placé
places	placez	as placé	avez placé
place	placent	a placé	ont placé
2 imparfait de l'indicatif		**9 plus-que-parfait de l'indicatif**	
plaçais	placions	avais placé	avions placé
plaçais	placiez	avais placé	aviez placé
plaçait	plaçaient	avait placé	avaient placé
3 passé simple		**10 passé antérieur**	
plaçai	plaçâmes	eus placé	eûmes placé
plaças	plaçâtes	eus placé	eûtes placé
plaça	placèrent	eut placé	eurent placé
4 futur		**11 futur antérieur**	
placerai	placerons	aurai placé	aurons placé
placeras	placerez	auras placé	aurez placé
placera	placeront	aura placé	auront placé
5 conditionnel		**12 conditionnel passé**	
placerais	placerions	aurais placé	aurions placé
placerais	placeriez	aurais placé	auriez placé
placerait	placeraient	aurait placé	auraient placé
6 présent du subjonctif		**13 passé du subjonctif**	
place	placions	aie placé	ayons placé
places	placiez	aies placé	ayez placé
place	placent	ait placé	aient placé
7 imparfait du subjonctif		**14 plus-que-parfait du subjonctif**	
plaçasse	plaçassions	eusse placé	eussions placé
plaçasses	plaçassiez	eusses placé	eussiez placé
plaçât	plaçassent	eût placé	eussent placé
		Impératif	
		place	
		plaçons	
		placez	

Nous pouvons déjeuner maintenant. Ma place est ici près de la fenêtre, ta place est là-bas près de la porte. Marie, place-toi à côté de Pierre. Combien de places y a-t-il? Y a-t-il assez de places pour tout le monde?

une place   a seat, a place
chaque chose à sa place   everything in its place
un placement   placing
un bureau de placement   employment agency
se placer   to place oneself, to take a seat, to find employment
remplacer   to replace

to pity   Irregular verb

The Seven Simple Tenses		The Seven Compound Tenses	
Singular	Plural	Singular	Plural
1 présent de l'indicatif		8 passé composé	
plains	plaignons	ai plaint	avons plaint
plains	plaignez	as plaint	avez plaint
plaint	plaignent	a plaint	ont plaint
2 imparfait de l'indicatif		9 plus-que-parfait de l'indicatif	
plaignais	plaignions	avais plaint	avions plaint
plaignais	plaigniez	avais plaint	aviez plaint
plaignait	plaignaient	avait plaint	avaient plaint
3 passé simple		10 passé antérieur	
plaignis	plaignîmes	eus plaint	eûmes plaint
plaignis	plaignîtes	eus plaint	eûtes plaint
plaignit	plaignirent	eut plaint	eurent plaint
4 futur		11 futur antérieur	
plaindrai	plaindrons	aurai plaint	aurons plaint
plaindras	plaindrez	auras plaint	aurez plaint
plaindra	plaindront	aura plaint	auront plaint
5 conditionnel		12 conditionnel passé	
plaindrais	plaindrions	aurais plaint	aurions plaint
plaindrais	plaindriez	aurais plaint	auriez plaint
plaindrait	plaindraient	aurait plaint	auraient plaint
6 présent du subjonctif		13 passé du subjonctif	
plaigne	plaignions	aie plaint	ayons plaint
plaignes	plaigniez	aies plaint	ayez plaint
plaigne	plaignent	ait plaint	aient plaint
7 imparfait du subjonctif		14 plus-que-parfait du subjonctif	
plaignisse	plaignissions	eusse plaint	eussions plaint
plaignisses	plaignissiez	eusses plaint	eussiez plaint
plaignît	plaignissent	eût plaint	eussent plaint
		Impératif	
		plains	
		plaignons	
		plaignez	

Pauvre Madame Bayou! Elle a des ennuis et je la plains.

une plainte   groan, moan, protest, complaint
porter plainte contre   to bring charges against
déposer/faire une plainte   to file a complaint
plaintif, plaintive   plaintive
plaintivement   plaintively, mournfully

Je te plains.   I feel for you; I feel sorry for you; I pity you.
être à plaindre   to be pitied
Elle est à plaindre.   She is to be pitied.

For additional related words, see se plaindre.

Reflexive irregular verb   to complain, to lament, to moan

The Seven Simple Tenses		The Seven Compound Tenses	
Singular	Plural	Singular	Plural
1 présent de l'indicatif		8 passé composé	
me plains	nous plaignons	me suis plaint(e)	nous sommes plaint(e)s
te plains	vous plaignez	t'es plaint(e)	vous êtes plaint(e)(s)
se plaint	se plaignent	s'est plaint(e)	se sont plaint(e)s
2 imparfait de l'indicatif		9 plus-que-parfait de l'indicatif	
me plaignais	nous plaignions	m'étais plaint(e)	nous étions plaint(e)s
te plaignais	vous plaigniez	t'étais plaint(e)	vous étiez plaint(e)(s)
se plaignait	se plaignaient	s'était plaint(e)	s'étaient plaint(e)s
3 passé simple		10 passé antérieur	
me plaignis	nous plaignîmes	me fus plaint(e)	nous fûmes plaint(e)s
te plaignis	vous plaignîtes	te fus plaint(e)	vous fûtes plaint(e)(s)
se plaignit	se plaignirent	se fut plaint(e)	se furent plaint(e)s
4 futur		11 futur antérieur	
me plaindrai	nous plaindrons	me serai plaint(e)	nous serons plaint(e)s
te plaindras	vous plaindrez	te seras plaint(e)	vous serez plaint(e)(s)
se plaindra	se plaindront	se sera plaint(e)	se seront plaint(e)s
5 conditionnel		12 conditionnel passé	
me plaindrais	nous plaindrions	me serais plaint(e)	nous serions plaint(e)s
te plaindrais	vous plaindriez	te serais plaint(e)	vous seriez plaint(e)(s)
se plaindrait	se plaindraient	se serait plaint(e)	se seraient plaint(e)s
6 présent du subjonctif		13 passé du subjonctif	
me plaigne	nous plaignions	me sois plaint(e)	nous soyons plaint(e)s
te plaignes	vous plaigniez	te sois plaint(e)	vous soyez plaint(e)(s)
se plaigne	se plaignent	se soit plaint(e)	se soient plaint(e)s
7 imparfait du subjonctif		14 plus-que-parfait du subjonctif	
me plaignisse	nous plaignissions	me fusse plaint(e)	nous fussions plaint(e)s
te plaignisses	vous plaignissiez	te fusses plaint(e)	vous fussiez plaint(e)(s)
se plaignît	se plaignissent	se fût plaint(e)	se fussent plaint(e)s

	Impératif
	plains-toi; ne te plains pas
	plaignons-nous; ne nous plaignons pas
	plaignez-vous; ne vous plaignez pas

Quelle jeune fille! Elle se plaint toujours de tout! Hier elle s'est plainte de son professeur de français, aujourd'hui elle se plaint de ses devoirs, et je suis certain que demain elle se plaindra du temps.

se plaindre du temps   to complain about the weather
se plaindre de qqn ou de qqch   to complain of, to find fault with someone or something
avoir bonne raison de se plaindre   to have good reason to complain

For other words related to this verb, see **plaindre**.

plaire	Part. pr. plaisant	Part. passé plu
to please		Irregular verb

The Seven Simple Tenses		The Seven Compound Tenses	
Singular	Plural	Singular	Plural
1 présent de l'indicatif		**8 passé composé**	
plais	plaisons	ai plu	avons plu
plais	plaisez	as plu	avez plu
plaît	plaisent	a plu	ont plu
2 imparfait de l'indicatif		**9 plus-que-parfait de l'indicatif**	
plaisais	plaisions	avais plu	avions plu
plaisais	plaisiez	avais plu	aviez plu
plaisait	plaisaient	avait plu	avaient plu
3 passé simple		**10 passé antérieur**	
plus	plûmes	eus plu	eûmes plu
plus	plûtes	eus plu	eûtes plu
plut	plurent	eut plu	eurent plu
4 futur		**11 futur antérieur**	
plairai	plairons	aurai plu	aurons plu
plairas	plairez	auras plu	aurez plu
plaira	plairont	aura plu	auront plu
5 conditionnel		**12 conditionnel passé**	
plairais	plairions	aurais plu	aurions plu
plairais	plairiez	aurais plu	auriez plu
plairait	plairaient	aurait plu	auraient plu
6 présent du subjonctif		**13 passé du subjonctif**	
plaise	plaisions	aie plu	ayons plu
plaises	plaisiez	aies plu	ayez plu
plaise	plaisent	ait plu	aient plu
7 imparfait du subjonctif		**14 plus-que-parfait du subjonctif**	
plusse	plussions	eusse plu	eussions plu
plusses	plussiez	eusses plu	eussiez plu
plût	plussent	eût plu	eussent plu
		Impératif	
		plais	
		plaisons	
		plaisez	

plaire à qqn to please, to be pleasing to someone; **Son mariage a plu à sa famille.**
Her (his) marriage pleased her (his) family. **Est-ce que ce cadeau lui plaira?**
Will this present please her (him)? Will this gift be pleasing to her (to him)?
se plaire à to take pleasure in; **Robert se plaît à ennuyer son petit frère.** Robert
takes pleasure in bothering his little brother.
le plaisir delight, pleasure; **complaire à** to please; **déplaire à** to displease
s'il vous plaît; s'il te plaît please (if it is pleasing to you)
Il a beaucoup plu hier et cela m'a beaucoup plu. It rained a lot yesterday and that
pleased me a great deal. (See **pleuvoir.**)

212

Regular -er verb   to cry, to weep, to mourn

The Seven Simple Tenses		The Seven Compound Tenses	
Singular	Plural	Singular	Plural

1 présent de l'indicatif

		8 passé composé	
pleure	**pleurons**	**ai pleuré**	**avons pleuré**
pleures	**pleurez**	**as pleuré**	**avez pleuré**
pleure	**pleurent**	**a pleuré**	**ont pleuré**

2 imparfait de l'indicatif

		9 plus-que-parfait de l'indicatif	
pleurais	**pleurions**	**avais pleuré**	**avions pleuré**
pleurais	**pleuriez**	**avais pleuré**	**aviez pleuré**
pleurait	**pleuraient**	**avait pleuré**	**avaient pleuré**

3 passé simple

		10 passé antérieur	
pleurai	**pleurâmes**	**eus pleuré**	**eûmes pleuré**
pleuras	**pleurâtes**	**eus pleuré**	**eûtes pleuré**
pleura	**pleurèrent**	**eut pleuré**	**eurent pleuré**

4 futur

		11 futur antérieur	
pleurerai	**pleurerons**	**aurai pleuré**	**aurons pleuré**
pleureras	**pleurerez**	**auras pleuré**	**aurez pleuré**
pleurera	**pleureront**	**aura pleuré**	**auront pleuré**

5 conditionnel

		12 conditionnel passé	
pleurerais	**pleurerions**	**aurais pleuré**	**aurions pleuré**
pleurerais	**pleureriez**	**aurais pleuré**	**auriez pleuré**
pleurerait	**pleureraient**	**aurait pleuré**	**auraient pleuré**

6 présent du subjonctif

		13 passé du subjonctif	
pleure	**pleurions**	**aie pleuré**	**ayons pleuré**
pleures	**pleuriez**	**aies pleuré**	**ayez pleuré**
pleure	**pleurent**	**ait pleuré**	**aient pleuré**

7 imparfait du subjonctif

		14 plus-que-parfait du subjonctif	
pleurasse	**pleurassions**	**eusse pleuré**	**eussions pleuré**
pleurasses	**pleurassiez**	**eusses pleuré**	**eussiez pleuré**
pleurât	**pleurassent**	**eût pleuré**	**eussent pleuré**

Impératif
pleure
pleurons
pleurez

---

pleurer toutes les larmes de son corps to cry one's eyes out
une larme a tear
un pleur a tear
pleurard, pleurarde whimpering person
une pièce pleurnicharde soap opera
larmoyant, larmoyante tearful, lachrymose
pleurnicher to snivel, to whine
un pleurnicheur, une pleurnicheuse crybaby

pleuvoir	Part. pr. pleuvant	Part. passé **plu**
to rain		Impersonal verb

The Seven Simple Tenses	The Seven Compound Tenses
Singular	Singular
1 présent de l'indicatif **il pleut**	8 passé composé **il a plu**
2 imparfait de l'indicatif **il pleuvait**	9 plus-que-parfait de l'indicatif **il avait plu**
3 passé simple **il plut**	10 passé antérieur **il eut plu**
4 futur **il pleuvra**	11 futur antérieur **il aura plu**
5 conditionnel **il pleuvrait**	12 conditionnel passé **il aurait plu**
6 présent du subjonctif **qu'il pleuve**	13 passé du subjonctif **qu'il ait plu**
7 imparfait du subjonctif **qu'il plût**	14 plus-que-parfait du subjonctif **qu'il eût plu**

Impératif
Qu'il pleuve! (Let it rain!)

Hier il a plu, il pleut maintenant, et je suis certain qu'il pleuvra demain.

la pluie the rain	**bruiner** to drizzle
pluvieux, pluvieuse rainy	**Il pleut à seaux.** It's raining buckets.
pleuvoter to drizzle	**Il pleut à verse.** It's raining hard.
un parapluie umbrella	

Il a beaucoup plu hier et cela m'a beaucoup plu.   It rained a lot yesterday and that pleased me a great deal. (See **plaire**.)

Do not confuse the past part. of this verb with the past part. of **plaire**, which is identical.

Regular -er verb to wear, to carry

The Seven Simple Tenses		The Seven Compound Tenses	
Singular	Plural	Singular	Plural

1 présent de l'indicatif		8 passé composé	
porte	portons	ai porté	avons porté
portes	portez	as porté	avez porté
porte	portent	a porté	ont porté

2 imparfait de l'indicatif		9 plus-que-parfait de l'indicatif	
portais	portions	avais porté	avions porté
portais	portiez	avais porté	aviez porté
portait	portaient	avait porté	avaient porté

3 passé simple		10 passé antérieur	
portai	portâmes	eus porté	eûmes porté
portas	portâtes	eus porté	eûtes porté
porta	portèrent	eut porté	eurent porté

4 futur		11 futur antérieur	
porterai	porterons	aurai porté	aurons porté
porteras	porterez	auras porté	aurez porté
portera	porteront	aura porté	auront porté

5 conditionnel		12 conditionnel passé	
porterais	porterions	aurais porté	aurions porté
porterais	porteriez	aurais porté	auriez porté
porterait	porteraient	aurait porté	auraient porté

6 présent du subjonctif		13 passé du subjonctif	
porte	portions	aie porté	ayons porté
portes	portiez	aies porté	ayez porté
porte	portent	ait porté	aient porté

7 imparfait du subjonctif		14 plus-que-parfait du subjonctif	
portasse	portassions	eusse porté	eussions porté
portasses	portassiez	eusses porté	eussiez porté
portât	portassent	eût porté	eussent porté

Impératif
porte
portons
portez

porter la main sur qqn to raise one's hand against someone
porter son âge to look one's age
se porter to feel (health); **Comment vous portez-vous aujourd'hui?** How do
  you feel today?

apporter to bring things	comporter to comprise
exporter to export	déporter to deport
importer to import; to matter, to be	se comporter to behave
of importance	emporter to carry away; **Autant**
un porte-monnaie change purse	**en emporte le vent** (*Gone with the Wind*)
(des porte-monnaie)	un portable cell phone, laptop computer

pousser	Part. pr. **poussant**	Part. passé **poussé**
to push, to grow		Regular -er verb

The Seven Simple Tenses		The Seven Compound Tenses	
Singular	Plural	Singular	Plural

1 présent de l'indicatif		8 passé composé	
pousse	**poussons**	**ai poussé**	**avons poussé**
pousses	**poussez**	**as poussé**	**avez poussé**
pousse	**poussent**	**a poussé**	**ont poussé**

2 imparfait de l'indicatif		9 plus-que-parfait de l'indicatif	
poussais	**poussions**	**avais poussé**	**avions poussé**
poussais	**poussiez**	**avais poussé**	**aviez poussé**
poussait	**poussaient**	**avait poussé**	**avaient poussé**

3 passé simple		10 passé antérieur	
poussai	**poussâmes**	**eus poussé**	**eûmes poussé**
poussas	**poussâtes**	**eus poussé**	**eûtes poussé**
poussa	**poussèrent**	**eut poussé**	**eurent poussé**

4 futur		11 futur antérieur	
pousserai	**pousserons**	**aurai poussé**	**aurons poussé**
pousseras	**pousserez**	**auras poussé**	**aurez poussé**
poussera	**pousseront**	**aura poussé**	**auront poussé**

5 conditionnel		12 conditionnel passé	
pousserais	**pousserions**	**aurais poussé**	**aurions poussé**
pousserais	**pousseriez**	**aurais poussé**	**auriez poussé**
pousserait	**pousseraient**	**aurait poussé**	**auraient poussé**

6 présent du subjonctif		13 passé du subjonctif	
pousse	**poussions**	**aie poussé**	**ayons poussé**
pousses	**poussiez**	**aies poussé**	**ayez poussé**
pousse	**poussent**	**ait poussé**	**aient poussé**

7 imparfait du subjonctif		14 plus-que-parfait du subjonctif	
poussasse	**poussassions**	**eusse poussé**	**eussions poussé**
poussasses	**poussassiez**	**eusses poussé**	**eussiez poussé**
poussât	**poussassent**	**eût poussé**	**eussent poussé**

	Impératif
	pousse
	poussons
	poussez

une poussée a push, a thrust
pousser qqn à faire qqch to egg someone on to do something
Robert pousse une barbe. Robert is growing a beard.
pousser un cri to utter a cry; pousser un soupir to heave a sigh
une poussette a stroller
repousser to repulse, to drive back; to grow in again, to grow back in
se pousser to push oneself; to push each other
un pousse-pousse rickshaw
pousser qqn à bout to corner someone

Irregular verb   to be able, can

| The Seven Simple Tenses | | The Seven Compound Tenses | |

Singular	Plural	Singular	Plural
1 présent de l'indicatif		**8 passé composé**	
peux* *or* **puis**	**pouvons**	ai pu	avons pu
peux	**pouvez**	as pu	avez pu
peut	**peuvent**	a pu	ont pu
2 imparfait de l'indicatif		**9 plus-que-parfait de l'indicatif**	
pouvais	**pouvions**	avais pu	avions pu
pouvais	**pouviez**	avais pu	aviez pu
pouvait	**pouvaient**	avait pu	avaient pu
3 passé simple		**10 passé antérieur**	
pus	**pûmes**	eus pu	eûmes pu
pus	**pûtes**	eus pu	eûtes pu
put	**purent**	eut pu	eurent pu
4 futur		**11 futur antérieur**	
pourrai	**pourrons**	aurai pu	aurons pu
pourras	**pourrez**	auras pu	aurez pu
pourra	**pourront**	aura pu	auront pu
5 conditionnel		**12 conditionnel passé**	
pourrais	**pourrions**	aurais pu	aurions pu
pourrais	**pourriez**	aurais pu	auriez pu
pourrait	**pourraient**	aurait pu	auraient pu
6 présent du subjonctif		**13 passé du subjonctif**	
puisse	**puissions**	aie pu	ayons pu
puisses	**puissiez**	aies pu	ayez pu
puisse	**puissent**	ait pu	aient pu
7 imparfait du subjonctif		**14 plus-que-parfait du subjonctif**	
pusse	**pussions**	eusse pu	eussions pu
pusses	**pussiez**	eusses pu	eussiez pu
pût	**pussent**	eût pu	eussent pu

Impératif
—

---

si l'on peut dire   if one may say so
se pouvoir: Cela se peut.   That may be. (That's possible.)
le pouvoir   power
avoir du pouvoir sur soi-même   to have self-control
n'y pouvoir rien   not to be able to do anything about it; **Que me voulez-vous?**
   What do you want from me? **Je n'y peux rien.**   I can't help it; I can't do anything
   about it.
Puis-je entrer? Est-ce que je peux entrer?   May I come in?

*In the affirmative, it is correct to say "**Je peux.**" In the inverted interrogative, you
should say "**Puis-je?**"

préférer	Part. pr. **préférant**	Part. passé **préféré**

to prefer	Regular -er verb endings: spelling change: é changes to è before syllable with mute e.

The Seven Simple Tenses	The Seven Compound Tenses

Singular	Plural	Singular	Plural

1 présent de l'indicatif

préfère	préférons
préfères	préférez
préfère	préfèrent

8 passé composé

ai préféré	avons préféré
as préféré	avez préféré
a préféré	ont préféré

2 imparfait de l'indicatif

préférais	préférions
préférais	préfériez
préférait	préféraient

9 plus-que-parfait de l'indicatif

avais préféré	avions préféré
avais préféré	aviez préféré
avait préféré	avaient préféré

3 passé simple

préférai	préférâmes
préféras	préférâtes
préféra	préférèrent

10 passé antérieur

eus préféré	eûmes préféré
eus préféré	eûtes préféré
eut préféré	eurent préféré

4 futur

préférerai	préférerons
préféreras	préférerez
préférera	préféreront

11 futur antérieur

aurai préféré	aurons préféré
auras préféré	aurez préféré
aura préféré	auront préféré

5 conditionnel

préférerais	préférerions
préférerais	préféreriez
préférerait	préféreraient

12 conditionnel passé

aurais préféré	aurions préféré
aurais préféré	auriez préféré
aurait préféré	auraient préféré

6 présent du subjonctif

préfère	préférions
préfères	préfériez
préfère	préfèrent

13 passé du subjonctif

aie préféré	ayons préféré
aies préféré	ayez préféré
ait préféré	aient préféré

7 imparfait du subjonctif

préférasse	préférassions
préférasses	préférassiez
préférât	préférassent

14 plus-que-parfait de subjonctif

eusse préféré	eussions préféré
eusses préféré	eussiez préféré
eût préféré	eussent préféré

Impératif
préfère
préférons
préférez

—Qu'est-ce que vous préférez faire ce soir?
—Je préfère aller voir un bon film. Et vous?
—Je préfère rester à la maison. Ne préféreriez-vous pas rester ici avec moi?

une préférence a preference	**préférablement** preferably
préférentiel, préférentielle preferential	**de préférence à** in preference to
préférable preferable	

Note: The Académie française now allows the accent grave (`) in the future
(je préfèrerai, tu préfèreras, etc.) and conditional (je préfèrerais, tu préfèrerais,
etc.) of this verb.

Irregular verb   to take

The Seven Simple Tenses		The Seven Compound Tenses	
Singular	Plural	Singular	Plural
1 présent de l'indicatif		**8 passé composé**	
prends	prenons	ai pris	avons pris
prends	prenez	as pris	avez pris
prend	prennent	a pris	ont pris
2 imparfait de l'indicatif		**9 plus-que-parfait de l'indicatif**	
prenais	prenions	avais pris	avions pris
prenais	preniez	avais pris	aviez pris
prenait	prenaient	avait pris	avaient pris
3 passé simple		**10 passé antérieur**	
pris	prîmes	eus pris	eûmes pris
pris	prîtes	eus pris	eûtes pris
prit	prirent	eut pris	eurent pris
4 futur		**11 futur antérieur**	
prendrai	prendrons	aurai pris	aurons pris
prendras	prendrez	auras pris	aurez pris
prendra	prendront	aura pris	auront pris
5 conditionnel		**12 conditionnel passé**	
prendrais	prendrions	aurais pris	aurions pris
prendrais	prendriez	aurais pris	auriez pris
prendrait	prendraient	aurait pris	auraient pris
6 présent du subjonctif		**13 passé du subjonctif**	
prenne	prenions	aie pris	ayons pris
prennes	preniez	aies pris	ayez pris
prenne	prennent	ait pris	aient pris
7 imparfait du subjonctif		**14 plus-que-parfait du subjonctif**	
prisse	prissions	eusse pris	eussions pris
prisses	prissiez	eusses pris	eussiez pris
prît	prissent	eût pris	eussent pris

Impératif
prends
prenons
prenez

—Qui a pris les fleurs qui étaient sur la table?   Who took the flowers that were on the table?
—C'est moi qui les ai prises.   I took them. (It is I who took them.)

à tout prendre on the whole, all in all
un preneur, une preneuse taker, purchaser
s'y prendre to go about it, to handle it, to set about it
Je ne sais comment m'y prendre. I don't know how to go about it.
C'est à prendre ou à laisser. Take it or leave it.
prendre à témoin to call to witness

See also **apprendre**, **comprendre**, and **reprendre**.

préparer	Part. pr. **préparant**	Part. passé **préparé**

to prepare

Regular -er verb

The Seven Simple Tenses		The Seven Compound Tenses	
Singular	Plural	Singular	Plural

1 présent de l'indicatif		8 passé composé	
prépare	**préparons**	**ai préparé**	**avons préparé**
prépares	**préparez**	**as préparé**	**avez préparé**
prépare	**préparent**	**a préparé**	**ont préparé**

2 imparfait de l'indicatif		9 plus-que-parfait de l'indicatif	
préparais	**préparions**	**avais préparé**	**avions préparé**
préparais	**prépariez**	**avais préparé**	**aviez préparé**
préparait	**préparaient**	**avait préparé**	**avaient préparé**

3 passé simple		10 passé antérieur	
préparai	**préparâmes**	**eus préparé**	**eûmes préparé**
préparas	**préparâtes**	**eus préparé**	**eûtes préparé**
prépara	**préparèrent**	**eut préparé**	**eurent préparé**

4 futur		11 futur antérieur	
préparerai	**préparerons**	**aurai préparé**	**aurons préparé**
prépareras	**préparerez**	**auras préparé**	**aurez préparé**
préparera	**prépareront**	**aura préparé**	**auront préparé**

5 conditionnel		12 conditionnel passé	
préparerais	**préparerions**	**aurais préparé**	**aurions préparé**
préparerais	**prépareriez**	**aurais préparé**	**auriez préparé**
préparerait	**prépareraient**	**aurait préparé**	**auraient préparé**

6 présent du subjonctif		13 passé du subjonctif	
prépare	**préparions**	**aie préparé**	**ayons préparé**
prépares	**prépariez**	**aies préparé**	**ayez préparé**
prépare	**préparent**	**ait préparé**	**aient préparé**

7 imparfait du subjonctif		14 plus-que-parfait du subjonctif	
préparasse	**préparassions**	**eusse préparé**	**eussions préparé**
préparasses	**préparassiez**	**eusses préparé**	**eussiez préparé**
préparât	**préparassent**	**eût préparé**	**eussent préparé**

Impératif
prépare
préparons
préparez

Si Albert avait préparé sa leçon, il aurait reçu une bonne note. Il prépare toujours ses leçons mais cette fois il ne les a pas préparées.

la préparation preparation
les préparatifs *m.* preparations
préparatoire preparatory
se préparer to prepare oneself
préparer un examen to study for an exam

Regular -er verb   to lend

The Seven Simple Tenses | The Seven Compound Tenses

Singular	Plural	Singular	Plural
1 présent de l'indicatif		8 passé composé	
prête	**prêtons**	**ai prêté**	**avons prêté**
prêtes	**prêtez**	**as prêté**	**avez prêté**
prête	**prêtent**	**a prêté**	**ont prêté**
2 imparfait de l'indicatif		9 plus-que-parfait de l'indicatif	
prêtais	**prêtions**	**avais prêté**	**avions prêté**
prêtais	**prêtiez**	**avais prêté**	**aviez prêté**
prêtait	**prêtaient**	**avait prêté**	**avaient prêté**
3 passé simple		10 passé antérieur	
prêtai	**prêtâmes**	**eus prêté**	**eûmes prêté**
prêtas	**prêtâtes**	**eus prêté**	**eûtes prêté**
prêta	**prêtèrent**	**eut prêté**	**eurent prêté**
4 futur		11 futur antérieur	
prêterai	**prêterons**	**aurai prêté**	**aurons prêté**
prêteras	**prêterez**	**auras prêté**	**aurez prêté**
prêtera	**prêteront**	**aura prêté**	**auront prêté**
5 conditionnel		12 conditionnel passé	
prêterais	**prêterions**	**aurais prêté**	**aurions prêté**
prêterais	**prêteriez**	**aurais prêté**	**auriez prêté**
prêterait	**prêteraient**	**aurait prêté**	**auraient prêté**
6 présent du subjonctif		13 passé du subjonctif	
prête	**prêtions**	**aie prêté**	**ayons prêté**
prêtes	**prêtiez**	**aies prêté**	**ayez prêté**
prête	**prêtent**	**ait prêté**	**aient prêté**
7 imparfait du subjonctif		14 plus-que-parfait du subjonctif	
prêtasse	**prêtassions**	**eusse prêté**	**eussions prêté**
prêtasses	**prêtassiez**	**eusses prêté**	**eussiez prêté**
prêtât	**prêtassent**	**eût prêté**	**eussent prêté**

Impératif
prête
prêtons
prêtez

---

prêter à intérêt   to lend at interest
prêter attention à qqn ou à qqch   to pay attention to someone or something
un prêteur sur gages   pawnbroker
prêter la main à qqn   to give a helping hand to someone
prêter secours à qqn   to go to someone's rescue (help)
apprêter   to prepare, to get (something) ready
s'apprêter   to get oneself ready
prêter l'oreille   to listen, to lend an ear

Note: Don't confuse **prêter** with **emprunter** (to borrow).

produire	Part. pr. **produisant**	Part. passé **produit**

to produce   Irregular verb

The Seven Simple Tenses	The Seven Compound Tenses

Singular	Plural	Singular	Plural
1 présent de l'indicatif		**8 passé composé**	
produis	**produisons**	**ai produit**	**avons produit**
produis	**produisez**	**as produit**	**avez produit**
produit	**produisent**	**a produit**	**ont produit**
2 imparfait de l'indicatif		**9 plus-que-parfait de l'indicatif**	
produisais	**produisions**	**avais produit**	**avions produit**
produisais	**produisiez**	**avais produit**	**aviez produit**
produisait	**produisaient**	**avait produit**	**avaient produit**
3 passé simple		**10 passé antérieur**	
produisis	**produisîmes**	**eus produit**	**eûmes produit**
produisis	**produisîtes**	**eus produit**	**eûtes produit**
produisit	**produisirent**	**eut produit**	**eurent produit**
4 futur		**11 futur antérieur**	
produirai	**produirons**	**aurai produit**	**aurons produit**
produiras	**produirez**	**auras produit**	**aurez produit**
produira	**produiront**	**aura produit**	**auront produit**
5 conditionnel		**12 conditionnel passé**	
produirais	**produirions**	**aurais produit**	**aurions produit**
produirais	**produiriez**	**aurais produit**	**auriez produit**
produirait	**produiraient**	**aurait produit**	**auraient produit**
6 présent du subjonctif		**13 passé du subjonctif**	
produise	**produisions**	**aie produit**	**ayons produit**
produises	**produisiez**	**aies produit**	**ayez produit**
produise	**produisent**	**ait produit**	**aient produit**
7 imparfait du subjonctif		**14 plus-que-parfait du subjonctif**	
produisisse	**produisissions**	**eusse produit**	**eussions produit**
produisisses	**produisissiez**	**eusses produit**	**eussiez produit**
produisît	**produisissent**	**eût produit**	**eussent produit**

	Impératif
	produis
	produisons
	produisez

---

un produit product
la production production
productible producible
productif, productive productive
la productivité productivity
se produire to happen, to occur, to be
  brought about

le produit national brut the gross
  national product
les produits alimentaires food
  products
se produire en public to appear in
  public

See also **conduire**, **introduire**, and **traduire**.

Part. pr. **se promenant**   Part. passé **promené(e)(s)**   **se promener**

Regular -er verb endings: spelling change: to take a walk
e changes to è before syllable with mute e.

The Seven Simple Tenses		The Seven Compound Tenses	

Singular   Plural

Singular   Plural

1 présent de l'indicatif

me promène	nous promenons
te promènes	vous promenez
se promène	se promènent

8 passé composé

me suis	nous sommes	
t'es	vous êtes	+ promené(e)(s)
s'est	se sont	

2 imparfait de l'indicatif

me promenais	nous promenions
te promenais	vous promeniez
se promenait	se promenaient

9 plus-que-parfait de l'indicatif

m'étais	nous étions	
t'étais	vous étiez	+ promené(e)(s)
s'était	s'étaient	

3 passé simple

me promenai	nous promenâmes
te promenas	vous promenâtes
se promena	se promenèrent

10 passé antérieur

me fus	nous fûmes	
te fus	vous fûtes	+ promené(e)(s)
se fut	se furent	

4 futur

me promènerai	nous promènerons
te promèneras	vous promènerez
se promènera	se promèneront

11 futur antérieur

me serai	nous serons	
te seras	vous serez	+ promené(e)(s)
se sera	se seront	

5 conditionnel

me promènerais	nous promènerions
te promènerais	vous promèneriez
se promènerait	se promèneraient

12 conditionnel passé

me serais	nous serions	
te serais	vous seriez	+ promené(e)(s)
se serait	se seraient	

6 présent du subjonctif

me promène	nous promenions
te promènes	vous promeniez
se promène	se promènent

13 passé du subjonctif

me sois	nous soyons	
te sois	vous soyez	+ promené(e)(s)
se soit	se soient	

7 imparfait du subjonctif

me promenasse	nous promenassions
te promenasses	vous promenassiez
se promenât	se promenassent

14 plus-que-parfait du subjonctif

me fusse	nous fussions	
te fusses	vous fussiez	+ promené(e)(s)
se fût	se fussent	

Impératif
promène-toi; ne te promène pas
promenons-nous; ne nous promenons pas
promenez-vous; ne vous promenez pas

Je me promène tous les matins.   I take a walk every morning.
Cette promenade est merveilleuse.   This walk is marvelous.
Janine et Robert se sont promenés dans le parc.   Janine and Robert took a walk
    in the park.
faire une promenade   to take a walk
faire une promenade en voiture   to go for a drive
promener son chien   to take one's dog out for a walk
promener ses regards sur   to cast one's eyes on, to look over
un promenoir   indoor mall for walking, strolling

promettre	Part. pr. **promettant**	Part. passé **promis**

to promise

Irregular verb

The Seven Simple Tenses		The Seven Compound Tenses	
Singular	Plural	Singular	Plural
1 présent de l'indicatif		8 passé composé	
promets	**promettons**	**ai promis**	**avons promis**
promets	**promettez**	**as promis**	**avez promis**
promet	**promettent**	**a promis**	**ont promis**
2 imparfait de l'indicatif		9 plus-que-parfait de l'indicatif	
promettais	**promettions**	**avais promis**	**avions promis**
promettais	**promettiez**	**avais promis**	**aviez promis**
promettait	**promettaient**	**avait promis**	**avaient promis**
3 passé simple		10 passé antérieur	
promis	**promîmes**	**eus promis**	**eûmes promis**
promis	**promîtes**	**eus promis**	**eûtes promis**
promit	**promirent**	**eut promis**	**eurent promis**
4 futur		11 futur antérieur	
promettrai	**promettrons**	**aurai promis**	**aurons promis**
promettras	**promettrez**	**auras promis**	**aurez promis**
promettra	**promettront**	**aura promis**	**auront promis**
5 conditionnel		12 conditionnel passé	
promettrais	**promettrions**	**aurais promis**	**aurions promis**
promettrais	**promettriez**	**aurais promis**	**auriez promis**
promettrait	**promettraient**	**aurait promis**	**auraient promis**
6 présent du subjonctif		13 passé du subjonctif	
promette	**promettions**	**aie promis**	**ayons promis**
promettes	**promettiez**	**aies promis**	**ayez promis**
promette	**promettent**	**ait promis**	**aient promis**
7 imparfait du subjonctif		14 plus-que-parfait du subjonctif	
promisse	**promissions**	**eusse promis**	**eussions promis**
promisses	**promissiez**	**eusses promis**	**eussiez promis**
promît	**promissent**	**eût promis**	**eussent promis**

Impératif
promets
promettons
promettez

promettre de faire qqch   to promise to do something
une promesse   promise
tenir sa promesse   to keep one's promise
promettre à qqn de faire qqch   to promise someone to do something
Ça promet!   It looks promising!
se promettre   to promise oneself

See also **admettre, mettre, permettre, remettre,** and **soumettre.**

Part. pr. **prononçant** Part. passé **prononcé** **prononcer**

Regular -er verb endings: spelling change: **to pronounce, to declare**
c changes to ç before a or o to keep s sound.

The Seven Simple Tenses		The Seven Compound Tenses	
Singular	Plural	Singular	Plural
1 présent de l'indicatif		8 passé composé	
prononce	prononçons	ai prononcé	avons prononcé
prononces	prononcez	as prononcé	avez prononcé
prononce	prononcent	a prononcé	ont prononcé
2 imparfait de l'indicatif		9 plus-que-parfait de l'indicatif	
prononçais	prononcions	avais prononcé	avions prononcé
prononçais	prononciez	avais prononcé	aviez prononcé
prononçait	prononçaient	avait prononcé	avaient prononcé
3 passé simple		10 passé antérieur	
prononçai	prononçâmes	eus prononcé	eûmes prononcé
prononças	prononçâtes	eus prononcé	eûtes prononcé
prononça	prononcèrent	eut prononcé	eurent prononcé
4 futur		11 futur antérieur	
prononcerai	prononcerons	aurai prononcé	aurons prononcé
prononceras	prononcerez	auras prononcé	aurez prononcé
prononcera	prononceront	aura prononcé	auront prononcé
5 conditionnel		12 conditionnel passé	
prononcerais	prononcerions	aurais prononcé	aurions prononcé
prononcerais	prononceriez	aurais prononcé	auriez prononcé
prononcerait	prononceraient	aurait prononcé	auraient prononcé
6 présent du subjonctif		13 passé du subjonctif	
prononce	prononcions	aie prononcé	ayons prononcé
prononces	prononciez	aies prononcé	ayez prononcé
prononce	prononcent	ait prononcé	aient prononcé
7 imparfait du subjonctif		14 plus-que-parfait du subjonctif	
prononçasse	prononçassions	eusse prononcé	eussions prononcé
prononçasses	prononçassiez	eusses prononcé	eussiez prononcé
prononçât	prononçassent	eût prononcé	eussent prononcé

Impératif
prononce
prononçons
prononcez

prononcer un discours   to deliver a speech
la prononciation   pronunciation
prononçable   pronounceable
se prononcer pour   to decide in favor of
énoncer   to enunciate

annoncer   to announce
dénoncer   to denounce
se prononcer   to declare, to be pronounced (as a word)
se prononcer contre   to decide against

225

prouver   Part. pr. **prouvant**   Part. passé **prouvé**

to prove

Regular -er verb

The Seven Simple Tenses		The Seven Compound Tenses	
Singular	Plural	Singular	Plural
1 présent de l'indicatif		8 passé composé	
prouve	**prouvons**	**ai prouvé**	**avons prouvé**
prouves	**prouvez**	**as prouvé**	**avez prouvé**
prouve	**prouvent**	**a prouvé**	**ont prouvé**
2 imparfait de l'indicatif		9 plus-que-parfait de l'indicatif	
prouvais	**prouvions**	**avais prouvé**	**avions prouvé**
prouvais	**prouviez**	**avais prouvé**	**aviez prouvé**
prouvait	**prouvaient**	**avait prouvé**	**avaient prouvé**
3 passé simple		10 passé antérieur	
prouvai	**prouvâmes**	**eus prouvé**	**eûmes prouvé**
prouvas	**prouvâtes**	**eus prouvé**	**eûtes prouvé**
prouva	**prouvèrent**	**eut prouvé**	**eurent prouvé**
4 futur		11 futur antérieur	
prouverai	**prouverons**	**aurai prouvé**	**aurons prouvé**
prouveras	**prouverez**	**auras prouvé**	**aurez prouvé**
prouvera	**prouveront**	**aura prouvé**	**auront prouvé**
5 conditionnel		12 conditionnel passé	
prouverais	**prouverions**	**aurais prouvé**	**aurions prouvé**
prouverais	**prouveriez**	**aurais prouvé**	**auriez prouvé**
prouverait	**prouveraient**	**aurait prouvé**	**auraient prouvé**
6 présent du subjonctif		13 passé du subjonctif	
prouve	**prouvions**	**aie prouvé**	**ayons prouvé**
prouves	**prouviez**	**aies prouvé**	**ayez prouvé**
prouve	**prouvent**	**ait prouvé**	**aient prouvé**
7 imparfait du subjonctif		14 plus-que-parfait du subjonctif	
prouvasse	**prouvassions**	**eusse prouvé**	**eussions prouvé**
prouvasses	**prouvassiez**	**eusses prouvé**	**eussiez prouvé**
prouvât	**prouvassent**	**eût prouvé**	**eussent prouvé**
		Impératif	
		prouve	
		prouvons	
		prouvez	

une preuve   proof
comme preuve   by way of proof
prouvable   provable
une épreuve   test, proof
approuver   to approve of
désapprouver   to disapprove of
éprouver   to test, to try, to experience

éprouver de la sympathie pour   to feel
  sympathy for
mettre à l'épreuve   to put to the test
avoir la preuve de   to have proof of
faire la preuve de qqch   to prove
  something

Defective verb

The Seven Simple Tenses

Singular	Plural
1 présent de l'indicatif	
pue	**puons**
pues	**puez**
pue	**puent**

Singular	Plural
2 imparfait de l'indicatif	
puais	**puions**
puais	**puiez**
puait	**puaient**

Singular	Plural
4 futur	
puerai	**puerons**
pueras	**puerez**
puera	**pueront**

Singular	Plural
5 conditionnel	
puerais	**puerions**
puerais	**pueriez**
puerait	**pueraient**

---

puant, puante stinking; conceited
la puanteur stink, foul smell
Robert est un type puant. Robert is a stinker.
Cet ivrogne pue l'alcool; je me bouche le nez. This drunkard stinks of alcohol;
I'm blocking my nose.
Joseph, ta chambre pue la porcherie. Joseph, your room smells like a pigsty.

Note: This verb is used mainly in the above tenses. If you need to use this verb in
all 14 tenses and the imperative, use the endings for a regular -er verb such as
aimer (p. 10) or **manquer** (p. 166).

punir	Part. pr. **punissant**	Part. passé **puni**
to punish		Regular -**ir** verb

The Seven Simple Tenses	The Seven Compound Tenses

Singular	Plural	Singular	Plural
1 présent de l'indicatif		8 passé composé	
punis	**punissons**	**ai puni**	**avons puni**
punis	**punissez**	**as puni**	**avez puni**
punit	**punissent**	**a puni**	**ont puni**
2 imparfait de l'indicatif		9 plus-que-parfait de l'indicatif	
punissais	**punissions**	**avais puni**	**avions puni**
punissais	**punissiez**	**avais puni**	**aviez puni**
punissait	**punissaient**	**avait puni**	**avaient puni**
3 passé simple		10 passé antérieur	
punis	**punîmes**	**eus puni**	**eûmes puni**
punis	**punîtes**	**eus puni**	**eûtes puni**
punit	**punirent**	**eut puni**	**eurent puni**
4 futur		11 futur antérieur	
punirai	**punirons**	**aurai puni**	**aurons puni**
puniras	**punirez**	**auras puni**	**aurez puni**
punira	**puniront**	**aura puni**	**auront puni**
5 conditionnel		12 conditionnel passé	
punirais	**punirions**	**aurais puni**	**aurions puni**
punirais	**puniriez**	**aurais puni**	**auriez puni**
punirait	**puniraient**	**aurait puni**	**auraient puni**
6 présent du subjonctif		13 passé du subjonctif	
punisse	**punissions**	**aie puni**	**ayons puni**
punisses	**punissiez**	**aies puni**	**ayez puni**
punisse	**punissent**	**ait puni**	**aient puni**
7 imparfait du subjonctif		14 plus-que-parfait du subjonctif	
punisse	**punissions**	**eusse puni**	**eussions puni**
punisses	**punissiez**	**eusses puni**	**eussiez puni**
punît	**punissent**	**eût puni**	**eussent puni**

	Impératif
	punis
	punissons
	punissez

---

punisseur, punisseuse punisher	**échapper à la punition** to escape
punissable punishable	punishment
punition *f.* punishment	**la peine capitale** capital punishment
punitif, punitive punitive	**en punition** as a punishment

Proverb: **La punition boite, mais elle arrive.** Punishment is lame, but it comes.
(Justice may be slow.)

Regular **-er** verb to leave

The Seven Simple Tenses The Seven Compound Tenses

Singular	Plural	Singular	Plural
1 présent de l'indicatif		8 passé composé	
quitte	quittons	ai quitté	avons quitté
quittes	quittez	as quitté	avez quitté
quitte	quittent	a quitté	ont quitté
2 imparfait de l'indicatif		9 plus-que-parfait de l'indicatif	
quittais	quittions	avais quitté	avions quitté
quittais	quittiez	avais quitté	aviez quitté
quittait	quittaient	avait quitté	avaient quitté
3 passé simple		10 passé antérieur	
quittai	quittâmes	eus quitté	eûmes quitté
quittas	quittâtes	eus quitté	eûtes quitté
quitta	quittèrent	eut quitté	eurent quitté
4 futur		11 futur antérieur	
quitterai	quitterons	aurai quitté	aurons quitté
quitteras	quitterez	auras quitté	aurez quitté
quittera	quitteront	aura quitté	auront quitté
5 conditionnel		12 conditionnel passé	
quitterais	quitterions	aurais quitté	aurions quitté
quitterais	quitteriez	aurais quitté	auriez quitté
quitterait	quitteraient	aurait quitté	auraient quitté
6 présent du subjonctif		13 passé du subjonctif	
quitte	quittions	aie quitté	ayons quitté
quittes	quittiez	aies quitté	ayez quitté
quitte	quittent	ait quitté	aient quitté
7 imparfait du subjonctif		14 plus-que-parfait du subjonctif	
quittasse	quittassions	eusse quitté	eussions quitté
quittasses	quittassiez	eusses quitté	eussiez quitté
quittât	quittassent	eût quitté	eussent quitté

Impératif
quitte
quittons
quittez

---

une quittance acquittance, discharge
quitter son chapeau to take off one's hat
se quitter to separate, to leave each other
Ne quittez pas, s'il vous plaît. Hold the
line, please! (on the phone)
être quitte to be free of an obligation
quitte ou double double or nothing
Avant quelle heure dois-je quitter la chambre?
Before what time must I leave (check out of) the room?

acquitter to acquit
s'acquitter de to fulfill
un acquittement acquittal
Je vous ai payé la dette; maintenant
nous sommes quittes! I paid
you the debt; now we're even!

raconter	Part. pr. **racontant**	Part. passé **raconté**

to relate, to tell about, to narrate — Regular -er verb

The Seven Simple Tenses		The Seven Compound Tenses	
Singular	Plural	Singular	Plural
1 présent de l'indicatif		8 passé composé	
raconte	racontons	ai raconté	avons raconté
racontes	racontez	as raconté	avez raconté
raconte	racontent	a raconté	ont raconté
2 imparfait de l'indicatif		9 plus-que-parfait de l'indicatif	
racontais	racontions	avais raconté	avions raconté
racontais	racontiez	avais raconté	aviez raconté
racontait	racontaient	avait raconté	avaient raconté
3 passé simple		10 passé antérieur	
racontai	racontâmes	eus raconté	eûmes raconté
racontas	racontâtes	eus raconté	eûtes raconté
raconta	racontèrent	eut raconté	eurent raconté
4 futur		11 futur antérieur	
raconterai	raconterons	aurai raconté	aurons raconté
raconteras	raconterez	auras raconté	aurez raconté
racontera	raconteront	aura raconté	auront raconté
5 conditionnel		12 conditionnel passé	
raconterais	raconterions	aurais raconté	aurions raconté
raconterais	raconteriez	aurais raconté	auriez raconté
raconterait	raconteraient	aurait raconté	auraient raconté
6 présent du subjonctif		13 passé du subjonctif	
raconte	racontions	aie raconté	ayons raconté
racontes	racontiez	aies raconté	ayez raconté
raconte	racontent	ait raconté	aient raconté
7 imparfait du subjonctif		14 plus-que-parfait du subjonctif	
racontasse	racontassions	eusse raconté	eussions raconté
racontasses	racontassiez	eusses raconté	eussiez raconté
racontât	racontassent	eût raconté	eussent raconté

	Impératif
	raconte
	racontons
	racontez

Mon professeur de français aime nous raconter des anecdotes en français dans la classe de français. C'est un bon raconteur.   My French teacher likes to tell us anecdotes in French during French class. He's a good storyteller.

un raconteur   storyteller
Qu'est-ce que vous racontez?   What are you talking about?
le racontar   gossip

See also conter.

Regular -er verb endings: spelling change: to call again, to call back,
l becomes ll before syllable with a mute e.   to recall, to remind

The Seven Simple Tenses		The Seven Compound Tenses	
Singular	Plural	Singular	Plural
1 présent de l'indicatif		8 passé composé	
rappelle	**rappelons**	**ai rappelé**	**avons rappelé**
rappelles	**rappelez**	**as rappelé**	**avez rappelé**
rappelle	**rappellent**	**a rappelé**	**ont rappelé**
2 imparfait de l'indicatif		9 plus-que-parfait de l'indicatif	
rappelais	**rappelions**	**avais rappelé**	**avions rappelé**
rappelais	**rappeliez**	**avais rappelé**	**aviez rappelé**
rappelait	**rappelaient**	**avait rappelé**	**avaient rappelé**
3 passé simple		10 passé antérieur	
rappelai	**rappelâmes**	**eus rappelé**	**eûmes rappelé**
rappelas	**rappelâtes**	**eus rappelé**	**eûtes rappelé**
rappela	**rappelèrent**	**eut rappelé**	**eurent rappelé**
4 futur		11 futur antérieur	
rappellerai	**rappellerons**	**aurai rappelé**	**aurons rappelé**
rappelleras	**rappellerez**	**auras rappelé**	**aurez rappelé**
rappellera	**rappelleront**	**aura rappelé**	**auront rappelé**
5 conditionnel		12 conditionnel passé	
rappellerais	**rappellerions**	**aurais rappelé**	**aurions rappelé**
rappellerais	**rappelleriez**	**aurais rappelé**	**auriez rappelé**
rappellerait	**rappelleraient**	**aurait rappelé**	**auraient rappelé**
6 présent du subjonctif		13 passé du subjonctif	
rappelle	**rappelions**	**aie rappelé**	**ayons rappelé**
rappelles	**rappeliez**	**aies rappelé**	**ayez rappelé**
rappelle	**rappellent**	**ait rappelé**	**aient rappelé**
7 imparfait du subjonctif		14 plus-que-parfait du subjonctif	
rappelasse	**rappelassions**	**eusse rappelé**	**eussions rappelé**
rappelasses	**rappelassiez**	**eusses rappelé**	**eussiez rappelé**
rappelât	**rappelassent**	**eût rappelé**	**eussent rappelé**
		Impératif	
		rappelle	
		rappelons	
		rappelez	

—Je ne peux pas vous parler maintenant. Rappelez-moi demain.
—D'accord. Je vous rappellerai demain.

un rappel   recall, callback, recalling
rappeler à la vie   to restore to life
Rappelez-moi votre nom.   Remind me of your name.
rappeler qqn à l'ordre   to call someone to order

See also **appeler**, **s'appeler**, and **se rappeler**.

se rappeler   Part. pr. **se rappelant**   Part. passé **rappelé(e)(s)**

to remember, to recall, to recollect	Regular -er verb endings: reflexive verb: spelling change: **l** becomes **ll** before syllable with a mute e

The Seven Simple Tenses		The Seven Compound Tenses	
Singular	Plural	Singular	Plural

1 présent de l'indicatif		8 passé composé	
me rappelle	nous rappelons	me suis	nous sommes
te rappelles	vous rappelez	t'es	vous êtes + rappelé(e)(s)
se rappelle	se rappellent	s'est	se sont

2 imparfait de l'indicatif		9 plus-que-parfait de l'indicatif	
me rappelais	nous rappelions	m'étais	nous étions
te rappelais	vous rappeliez	t'étais	vous étiez + rappelé(e)(s)
se rappelait	se rappelaient	s'était	s'étaient

3 passé simple		10 passé antérieur	
me rappelai	nous rappelâmes	me fus	nous fûmes
te rappelas	vous rappelâtes	te fus	vous fûtes + rappelé(e)(s)
se rappela	se rappelèrent	se fut	se furent

4 futur		11 futur antérieur	
me rappellerai	nous rappellerons	me serai	nous serons
te rappelleras	vous rappellerez	te seras	vous serez + rappelé(e)(s)
se rappellera	se rappelleront	se sera	se seront

5 conditionnel		12 conditionnel passé	
me rappellerais	nous rappellerions	me serais	nous serions
te rappellerais	vous rappelleriez	te serais	vous seriez + rappelé(e)(s)
se rappellerait	se rappelleraient	se serait	se seraient

6 présent du subjonctif		13 passé du subjonctif	
me rappelle	nous rappelions	me sois	nous soyons
te rappelles	vous rappeliez	te sois	vous soyez + rappelé(e)(s)
se rappelle	se rappellent	se soit	se soient

7 imparfait du subjonctif		14 plus-que-parfait du subjonctif	
me rappelasse	nous rappelassions	me fusse	nous fussions
te rappelasses	vous rappelassiez	te fusses	vous fussiez + rappelé(e)(s)
se rappelât	se rappelassent	se fût	se fussent

Impératif
rappelle-toi; ne te rappelle pas
rappelons-nous; ne nous rappelons pas
rappelez-vous; ne vous rappelez pas

Je me rappelle bien le jour où j'ai connu ma femme.   I remember well the day I met my wife.

Rappelez-vous que nous avons un examen lundi prochain!   Remember that we have a test next Monday!

See also **appeler**, **s'appeler**, and **rappeler**.

Irregular verb with spelling change: **c** changes   to receive, to get
to **ç** before **a** or **u** to keep **s** sound.

The Seven Simple Tenses		The Seven Compound Tenses	
Singular	Plural	Singular	Plural
1 présent de l'indicatif		8 passé composé	
reçois	**recevons**	**ai reçu**	**avons reçu**
reçois	**recevez**	**as reçu**	**avez reçu**
reçoit	**reçoivent**	**a reçu**	**ont reçu**
2 imparfait de l'indicatif		9 plus-que-parfait de l'indicatif	
recevais	**recevions**	**avais reçu**	**avions reçu**
recevais	**receviez**	**avais reçu**	**aviez reçu**
recevait	**recevaient**	**avait reçu**	**avaient reçu**
3 passé simple		10 passé antérieur	
reçus	**reçûmes**	**eus reçu**	**eûmes reçu**
reçus	**reçûtes**	**eus reçu**	**eûtes reçu**
reçut	**reçurent**	**eut reçu**	**eurent reçu**
4 futur		11 futur antérieur	
recevrai	**recevrons**	**aurai reçu**	**aurons reçu**
recevras	**recevrez**	**auras reçu**	**aurez reçu**
recevra	**recevront**	**aura reçu**	**auront reçu**
5 conditionnel		12 conditionnel passé	
recevrais	**recevrions**	**aurais reçu**	**aurions reçu**
recevrais	**recevriez**	**aurais reçu**	**auriez reçu**
recevrait	**recevraient**	**aurait reçu**	**auraient reçu**
6 présent du subjonctif		13 passé du subjonctif	
reçoive	**recevions**	**aie reçu**	**ayons reçu**
reçoives	**receviez**	**aies reçu**	**ayez reçu**
reçoive	**reçoivent**	**ait reçu**	**aient reçu**
7 imparfait du subjonctif		14 plus-que-parfait du subjonctif	
reçusse	**reçussions**	**eusse reçu**	**eussions reçu**
reçusses	**reçussiez**	**eusses reçu**	**eussiez reçu**
reçût	**reçussent**	**eût reçu**	**eussent reçu**

Impératif
reçois
recevons
recevez

---

réceptif, réceptive   receptive
une réception   reception, welcome
un, une réceptionniste   receptionist
un reçu   a receipt
au reçu de   on receipt of

recevable   receivable
un receveur, une receveuse   receiver
être reçu à un examen   to pass an exam
Est-ce que tu as reçu mon courriel?
    Did you receive my e-mail?

Proverb: **Il y a plus de bonheur à donner qu'à recevoir.**   It is better to give than
  to receive.

réfléchir
Part. pr. **réfléchissant**   Part. passé **réfléchi**

to think, to meditate, to reflect, to ponder   Regular -ir verb

The Seven Simple Tenses		The Seven Compound Tenses	
Singular	Plural	Singular	Plural
1 présent de l'indicatif		8 passé composé	
réfléchis	**réfléchissons**	**ai réfléchi**	**avons réfléchi**
réfléchis	**réfléchissez**	**as réfléchi**	**avez réfléchi**
réfléchit	**réfléchissent**	**a réfléchi**	**ont réfléchi**
2 imparfait de l'indicatif		9 plus-que-parfait de l'indicatif	
réfléchissais	**réfléchissions**	**avais réfléchi**	**avions réfléchi**
réfléchissais	**réfléchissiez**	**avais réfléchi**	**aviez réfléchi**
réfléchissait	**réfléchissaient**	**avait réfléchi**	**avaient réfléchi**
3 passé simple		10 passé antérieur	
réfléchis	**réfléchîmes**	**eus réfléchi**	**eûmes réfléchi**
réfléchis	**réfléchîtes**	**eus réfléchi**	**eûtes réfléchi**
réfléchit	**réfléchirent**	**eut réfléchi**	**eurent réfléchi**
4 futur		11 futur antérieur	
réfléchirai	**réfléchirons**	**aurai réfléchi**	**aurons réfléchi**
réfléchiras	**réfléchirez**	**auras réfléchi**	**aurez réfléchi**
réfléchira	**réfléchiront**	**aura réfléchi**	**auront réfléchi**
5 conditionnel		12 conditionnel passé	
réfléchirais	**réfléchirions**	**aurais réfléchi**	**aurions réfléchi**
réfléchirais	**réfléchiriez**	**aurais réfléchi**	**auriez réfléchi**
réfléchirait	**réfléchiraient**	**aurait réfléchi**	**auraient réfléchi**
6 présent du subjonctif		13 passé du subjonctif	
réfléchisse	**réfléchissions**	**aie réfléchi**	**ayons réfléchi**
réfléchisses	**réfléchissiez**	**aies réfléchi**	**ayez réfléchi**
réfléchisse	**réfléchissent**	**ait réfléchi**	**aient réfléchi**
7 imparfait du subjonctif		14 plus-que-parfait du subjonctif	
réfléchisse	**réfléchissions**	**eusse réfléchi**	**eussions réfléchi**
réfléchisses	**réfléchissiez**	**eusses réfléchi**	**eussiez réfléchi**
réfléchît	**réfléchissent**	**eût réfléchi**	**eussent réfléchi**

	Impératif
	réfléchis
	réfléchissons
	réfléchissez

Mathilde: **Yvette, vas-tu au bal samedi soir?**
Yvette: **Je ne sais pas si j'y vais. Je demande à réfléchir.**
Mathilde: **Bon, alors, réfléchis avant de me donner ta réponse.**

réfléchir à qqch   to think over (ponder) something
réfléchir avant de parler   to think before speaking
La mer réfléchit le ciel.   The sea reflects the sky.
Il faut que j'y réfléchisse.   I must think it over.
un reflet   reflection
tout bien réfléchi   after careful thought

234

Regular -er verb   to refuse, to withhold

The Seven Simple Tenses | The Seven Compound Tenses

Singular	Plural	Singular	Plural
1 présent de l'indicatif		8 passé composé	
refuse	refusons	ai refusé	avons refusé
refuses	refusez	as refusé	avez refusé
refuse	refusent	a refusé	ont refusé
2 imparfait de l'indicatif		9 plus-que-parfait de l'indicatif	
refusais	refusions	avais refusé	avions refusé
refusais	refusiez	avais refusé	aviez refusé
refusait	refusaient	avait refusé	avaient refusé
3 passé simple		10 passé antérieur	
refusai	refusâmes	eus refusé	eûmes refusé
refusas	refusâtes	eus refusé	eûtes refusé
refusa	refusèrent	eut refusé	eurent refusé
4 futur		11 futur antérieur	
refuserai	refuserons	aurai refusé	aurons refusé
refuseras	refuserez	auras refusé	aurez refusé
refusera	refuseront	aura refusé	auront refusé
5 conditionnel		12 conditionnel passé	
refuserais	refuserions	aurais refusé	aurions refusé
refuserais	refuseriez	aurais refusé	auriez refusé
refuserait	refuseraient	aurait refusé	auraient refusé
6 présent du subjonctif		13 passé du subjonctif	
refuse	refusions	aie refusé	ayons refusé
refuses	refusiez	aies refusé	ayez refusé
refuse	refusent	ait refusé	aient refusé
7 imparfait du subjonctif		14 plus-que-parfait du subjonctif	
refusasse	refusassions	eusse refusé	eussions refusé
refusasses	refusassiez	eusses refusé	eussiez refusé
refusât	refusassent	eût refusé	eussent refusé
		Impératif	
		refuse	
		refusons	
		refusez	

Je refuse absolument de vous écouter. Sortez, s'il vous plaît! Si vous refusez, vous le regretterez.

refuser de faire qqch   to refuse to do something
se refuser qqch   to deny oneself something
refusable   refusable
un refus   refusal
refuser l'entrée à qqn   to turn someone away
Elle a été refusée.   She was refused.

regarder	Part. pr. **regardant**	Part. passé **regardé**

to look (at), to watch | Regular **-er** verb

The Seven Simple Tenses		The Seven Compound Tenses	
Singular	Plural	Singular	Plural
1 présent de l'indicatif		8 passé composé	
regarde	regardons	ai regardé	avons regardé
regardes	regardez	as regardé	avez regardé
regarde	regardent	a regardé	ont regardé
2 imparfait de l'indicatif		9 plus-que-parfait de l'indicatif	
regardais	regardions	avais regardé	avions regardé
regardais	regardiez	avais regardé	aviez regardé
regardait	regardaient	avait regardé	avaient regardé
3 passé simple		10 passé antérieur	
regardai	regardâmes	eus regardé	eûmes regardé
regardas	regardâtes	eus regardé	eûtes regardé
regarda	regardèrent	eut regardé	eurent regardé
4 futur		11 futur antérieur	
regarderai	regarderons	aurai regardé	aurons regardé
regarderas	regarderez	auras regardé	aurez regardé
regardera	regarderont	aura regardé	auront regardé
5 conditionnel		12 conditionnel passé	
regarderais	regarderions	aurais regardé	aurions regardé
regarderais	regarderiez	aurais regardé	auriez regardé
regarderait	regarderaient	aurait regardé	auraient regardé
6 présent du subjonctif		13 passé du subjonctif	
regarde	regardions	aie regardé	ayons regardé
regardes	regardiez	aies regardé	ayez regardé
regarde	regardent	ait regardé	aient regardé
7 imparfait du subjonctif		14 plus-que-parfait du subjonctif	
regardasse	regardassions	eusse regardé	eussions regardé
regardasses	regardassiez	eusses regardé	eussiez regardé
regardât	regardassent	eût regardé	eussent regardé

	Impératif
	regarde
	regardons
	regardez

—Qu'est-ce que tu regardes, Bernard?
—Je regarde le ciel. Il est beau et clair.
—Pourquoi ne me regardes-tu pas?

regarder qqch   to look at (to watch) something
un regard   glance, look; au regard de   compared to, with regard to
regarder la télé   to watch TV
Cela ne vous regarde pas.   That's none of your business.

Part. pr. **remarquant**   Part. passé **remarqué**   **remarquer**

Regular -er verb   to remark, to notice, to observe, to distinguish

The Seven Simple Tenses   The Seven Compound Tenses

Singular	Plural	Singular	Plural
1 présent de l'indicatif		8 passé composé	
remarque	**remarquons**	**ai remarqué**	**avons remarqué**
remarques	**remarquez**	**as remarqué**	**avez remarqué**
remarque	**remarquent**	**a remarqué**	**ont remarqué**
2 imparfait de l'indicatif		9 plus-que-parfait de l'indicatif	
remarquais	**remarquions**	**avais remarqué**	**avions remarqué**
remarquais	**remarquiez**	**avais remarqué**	**aviez remarqué**
remarquait	**remarquaient**	**avait remarqué**	**avaient remarqué**
3 passé simple		10 passé antérieur	
remarquai	**remarquâmes**	**eus remarqué**	**eûmes remarqué**
remarquas	**remarquâtes**	**eus remarqué**	**eûtes remarqué**
remarqua	**remarquèrent**	**eut remarqué**	**eurent remarqué**
4 futur		11 futur antérieur	
remarquerai	**remarquerons**	**aurai remarqué**	**aurons remarqué**
remarqueras	**remarquerez**	**auras remarqué**	**aurez remarqué**
remarquera	**remarqueront**	**aura remarqué**	**auront remarqué**
5 conditionnel		12 conditionnel passé	
remarquerais	**remarquerions**	**aurais remarqué**	**aurions remarqué**
remarquerais	**remarqueriez**	**aurais remarqué**	**auriez remarqué**
remarquerait	**remarqueraient**	**aurait remarqué**	**auraient remarqué**
6 présent du subjonctif		13 passé du subjonctif	
remarque	**remarquions**	**aie remarqué**	**ayons remarqué**
remarques	**remarquiez**	**aies remarqué**	**ayez remarqué**
remarque	**remarquent**	**ait remarqué**	**aient remarqué**
7 imparfait du subjonctif		14 plus-que-parfait du subjonctif	
remarquasse	**remarquassions**	**eusse remarqué**	**eussions remarqué**
remarquasses	**remarquassiez**	**eusses remarqué**	**eussiez remarqué**
remarquât	**remarquassent**	**eût remarqué**	**eussent remarqué**

Impératif
remarque
remarquons
remarquez

---

une remarque   remark, observation, comment; **marquer**   to mark
faire remarquer qqch à qqn   to bring something to someone's attention, to point
   out something to someone
se faire remarquer   to make oneself noticed, draw attention
remarquable   remarkable

Erich Maria Remarque, romancier, est l'auteur du roman *All Quiet on the Western
   Front.* **Son nom de famille est d'origine française.**

remettre	Part. pr. remettant	Part. passé remis

to give back, to postpone, to put (on) again,   Irregular verb
to replace, to put back

The Seven Simple Tenses		The Seven Compound Tenses	
Singular	Plural	Singular	Plural
1 présent de l'indicatif		8 passé composé	
remets	**remettons**	**ai remis**	**avons remis**
remets	**remettez**	**as remis**	**avez remis**
remet	**remettent**	**a remis**	**ont remis**
2 imparfait de l'indicatif		9 plus-que-parfait de l'indicatif	
remettais	**remettions**	**avais remis**	**avions remis**
remettais	**remettiez**	**avais remis**	**aviez remis**
remettait	**remettaient**	**avait remis**	**avaient remis**
3 passé simple		10 passé antérieur	
remis	**remîmes**	**eus remis**	**eûmes remis**
remis	**remîtes**	**eus remis**	**eûtes remis**
remit	**remirent**	**eut remis**	**eurent remis**
4 futur		11 futur antérieur	
remettrai	**remettrons**	**aurai remis**	**aurons remis**
remettras	**remettrez**	**auras remis**	**aurez remis**
remettra	**remettront**	**aura remis**	**auront remis**
5 conditionnel		12 conditionnel passé	
remettrais	**remettrions**	**aurais remis**	**aurions remis**
remettrais	**remettriez**	**aurais remis**	**auriez remis**
remettrait	**remettraient**	**aurait remis**	**auraient remis**
6 présent du subjonctif		13 passé du subjonctif	
remette	**remettions**	**aie remis**	**ayons remis**
remettes	**remettiez**	**aies remis**	**ayez remis**
remette	**remettent**	**ait remis**	**aient remis**
7 imparfait du subjonctif		14 plus-que-parfait du subjonctif	
remisse	**remissions**	**eusse remis**	**eussions remis**
remisses	**remissiez**	**eusses remis**	**eussiez remis**
remît	**remissent**	**eût remis**	**eussent remis**
		Impératif	
		remets	
		remettons	
		remettez	

—Où avez-vous remis les fleurs que je vous ai données?
—Je les ai remises là-bas. Ne les voyez-vous pas?

se remettre de   to recover from
se remettre à faire qqch   to start to do something again
s'en remettre à   to depend on, to rely on
Remettez-vous!   Pull yourself together!
une remise   remittance, postponement, discount

See also **admettre**, **mettre**, **permettre**, **promettre**, and **soumettre**.

Part. pr. **remplaçant**	Part. passé **remplacé**		**remplacer**

Regular -er verb endings: spelling change: c changes **to replace**
to ç before a or o to keep s sound.

The Seven Simple Tenses		The Seven Compound Tenses	
Singular	Plural	Singular	Plural

1 présent de l'indicatif		8 passé composé	
remplace	**remplaçons**	**ai remplacé**	**avons remplacé**
remplaces	**remplacez**	**as remplacé**	**avez remplacé**
remplace	**remplacent**	**a remplacé**	**ont remplacé**

2 imparfait de l'indicatif		9 plus-que-parfait de l'indicatif	
remplaçais	**remplacions**	**avais remplacé**	**avions remplacé**
remplaçais	**remplaciez**	**avais remplacé**	**aviez remplacé**
remplaçait	**remplaçaient**	**avait remplacé**	**avaient remplacé**

3 passé simple		10 passé antérieur	
remplaçai	**remplaçâmes**	**eus remplacé**	**eûmes remplacé**
remplaças	**remplaçâtes**	**eus remplacé**	**eûtes remplacé**
remplaça	**remplacèrent**	**eut remplacé**	**eurent remplacé**

4 futur		11 futur antérieur	
remplacerai	**remplacerons**	**aurai remplacé**	**aurons remplacé**
remplaceras	**remplacerez**	**auras remplacé**	**aurez remplacé**
remplacera	**remplaceront**	**aura remplacé**	**auront remplacé**

5 conditionnel		12 conditionnel passé	
remplacerais	**remplacerions**	**aurais remplacé**	**aurions remplacé**
remplacerais	**remplaceriez**	**aurais remplacé**	**auriez remplacé**
remplacerait	**remplaceraient**	**aurait remplacé**	**auraient remplacé**

6 présent du subjonctif		13 passé du subjonctif	
remplace	**remplacions**	**aie remplacé**	**ayons remplacé**
remplaces	**remplaciez**	**aies remplacé**	**ayez remplacé**
remplace	**remplacent**	**ait remplacé**	**aient remplacé**

7 imparfait du subjonctif		14 plus-que-parfait du subjonctif	
remplaçasse	**remplaçassions**	**eusse remplacé**	**eussions remplacé**
remplaçasses	**remplaçassiez**	**eusses remplacé**	**eussiez remplacé**
remplaçât	**remplaçassent**	**eût remplacé**	**eussent remplacé**

		Impératif	
		remplace	
		remplaçons	
		remplacez	

remplacer par to replace with
un remplacement replacement (thing)
un remplaçant, une remplaçante replacement (person), substitute
remplaçable replaceable
irremplaçable irreplaceable
en remplacement de in place of

See also **placer**.

remplir	Part. pr. **remplissant**	Part. passé **rempli**

to fill, to fulfill, to fill in, to fill out

Regular **-ir** verb

The Seven Simple Tenses		The Seven Compound Tenses	
Singular	Plural	Singular	Plural
1 présent de l'indicatif		8 passé composé	
remplis	**remplissons**	**ai rempli**	**avons rempli**
remplis	**remplissez**	**as rempli**	**avez rempli**
remplit	**remplissent**	**a rempli**	**ont rempli**
2 imparfait de l'indicatif		9 plus-que-parfait de l'indicatif	
remplissais	**remplissions**	**avais rempli**	**avions rempli**
remplissais	**remplissiez**	**avais rempli**	**aviez rempli**
remplissait	**remplissaient**	**avait rempli**	**avaient rempli**
3 passé simple		10 passé antérieur	
remplis	**remplîmes**	**eus rempli**	**eûmes rempli**
remplis	**remplîtes**	**eus rempli**	**eûtes rempli**
remplit	**remplirent**	**eut rempli**	**eurent rempli**
4 futur		11 futur antérieur	
remplirai	**remplirons**	**aurai rempli**	**aurons rempli**
rempliras	**remplirez**	**auras rempli**	**aurez rempli**
remplira	**rempliront**	**aura rempli**	**auront rempli**
5 conditionnel		12 conditionnel passé	
remplirais	**remplirions**	**aurais rempli**	**aurions rempli**
remplirais	**rempliriez**	**aurais rempli**	**auriez rempli**
remplirait	**rempliraient**	**aurait rempli**	**auraient rempli**
6 présent du subjonctif		13 passé du subjonctif	
remplisse	**remplissions**	**aie rempli**	**ayons rempli**
remplisses	**remplissiez**	**aies rempli**	**ayez rempli**
remplisse	**remplissent**	**ait rempli**	**aient rempli**
7 imparfait du subjonctif		14 plus-que-parfait du subjonctif	
remplisse	**remplissions**	**eusse rempli**	**eussions rempli**
remplisses	**remplissiez**	**eusses rempli**	**eussiez rempli**
remplît	**remplissent**	**eût rempli**	**eussent rempli**

Impératif
remplis
remplissons
remplissez

---

remplir de to fill with
remplir qqch de qqch to fill something
 with something
se remplir to fill up
un remplissage filling up
emplir to fill
remplir quelqu'un d'admiration
 to fill someone with admiration

remplir des conditions to fulfill
 requirements, conditions
remplir une tâche to carry out
 (perform) a task

240

Regular -er verb   to meet, to encounter

The Seven Simple Tenses		The Seven Compound Tenses	
Singular	Plural	Singular	Plural
1 présent de l'indicatif		8 passé composé	
rencontre	**rencontrons**	**ai rencontré**	**avons rencontré**
rencontres	**rencontrez**	**as rencontré**	**avez rencontré**
rencontre	**rencontrent**	**a rencontré**	**ont rencontré**
2 imparfait de l'indicatif		9 plus-que-parfait de l'indicatif	
rencontrais	**rencontrions**	**avais rencontré**	**avions rencontré**
rencontrais	**rencontriez**	**avais rencontré**	**aviez rencontré**
rencontrait	**rencontraient**	**avait rencontré**	**avaient rencontré**
3 passé simple		10 passé antérieur	
rencontrai	**rencontrâmes**	**eus rencontré**	**eûmes rencontré**
rencontras	**rencontrâtes**	**eus rencontré**	**eûtes rencontré**
rencontra	**rencontrèrent**	**eut rencontré**	**eurent rencontré**
4 futur		11 futur antérieur	
rencontrerai	**rencontrerons**	**aurai rencontré**	**aurons rencontré**
rencontreras	**rencontrerez**	**auras rencontré**	**aurez rencontré**
rencontrera	**rencontreront**	**aura rencontré**	**auront rencontré**
5 conditionnel		12 conditionnel passé	
rencontrerais	**rencontrerions**	**aurais rencontré**	**aurions rencontré**
rencontrerais	**rencontreriez**	**aurais rencontré**	**auriez rencontré**
rencontrerait	**rencontreraient**	**aurait rencontré**	**auraient rencontré**
6 présent du subjonctif		13 passé du subjonctif	
rencontre	**rencontrions**	**aie rencontré**	**ayons rencontré**
rencontres	**rencontriez**	**aies rencontré**	**ayez rencontré**
rencontre	**rencontrent**	**ait rencontré**	**aient rencontré**
7 imparfait du subjonctif		14 plus-que-parfait du subjonctif	
recontrasse	**rencontrassions**	**eusse rencontré**	**eussions rencontré**
rencontrasses	**rencontrassiez**	**eusses rencontré**	**eussiez rencontré**
rencontrât	**rencontrassent**	**eût rencontré**	**eussent rencontré**
		Impératif	
		rencontre	
		rencontrons	
		rencontrez	

se rencontrer   to meet each other
une rencontre   encounter, meeting
aller à la rencontre de qqn   to go to meet someone
rencontrer par hasard   to meet someone by chance (bump into)
une rencontre au sommet   summit meeting
faire une rencontre inattendue   to have an unexpected encounter

rendre	Part. pr. **rendant**	Part. passé **rendu**

to give back, to return (something), to render; to vomit   Regular -re verb

The Seven Simple Tenses		The Seven Compound Tenses	
Singular	Plural	Singular	Plural
1 présent de l'indicatif		8 passé composé	
rends	rendons	ai rendu	avons rendu
rends	rendez	as rendu	avez rendu
rend	rendent	a rendu	ont rendu
2 imparfait de l'indicatif		9 plus-que-parfait de l'indicatif	
rendais	rendions	avais rendu	avions rendu
rendais	rendiez	avais rendu	aviez rendu
rendait	rendaient	avait rendu	avaient rendu
3 passé simple		10 passé antérieur	
rendis	rendîmes	eus rendu	eûmes rendu
rendis	rendîtes	eus rendu	eûtes rendu
rendit	rendirent	eut rendu	eurent rendu
4 futur		11 futur antérieur	
rendrai	rendrons	aurai rendu	aurons rendu
rendras	rendrez	auras rendu	aurez rendu
rendra	rendront	aura rendu	auront rendu
5 conditionnel		12 conditionnel passé	
rendrais	rendrions	aurais rendu	aurions rendu
rendrais	rendriez	aurais rendu	auriez rendu
rendrait	rendraient	aurait rendu	auraient rendu
6 présent du subjonctif		13 passé du subjonctif	
rende	rendions	aie rendu	ayons rendu
rendes	rendiez	aies rendu	ayez rendu
rende	rendent	ait rendu	aient rendu
7 imparfait du subjonctif		14 plus-que-parfait du subjonctif	
rendisse	rendissions	eusse rendu	eussions rendu
rendisses	rendissiez	eusses rendu	eussiez rendu
rendît	rendissent	eût rendu	eussent rendu

	Impératif
	rends
	rendons
	rendez

---

un rendez-vous appointment, date
un compte rendu report, account
se rendre à to surrender to
se rendre compte de to realize
rendre un service à qqn to do someone a favor
rendre qqn + adj. to make someone + adj.
rendre grâce à qqn to give thanks to someone

rendre service à qqn to be of service to someone
rendre compte de qqch to give an account of something
rendre qqch to return something
se rendre aux urnes to vote
rendre visite à to pay a visit to
Pendant les vacances nous rendrons visite à notre grand-père. During vacation we will pay a visit to our grandfather.

242

Regular -er verb   to return

The Seven Simple Tenses		The Seven Compound Tenses	
Singular	Plural	Singular	Plural
1 présent de l'indicatif		8 passé composé	
rentre	rentrons	suis rentré(e)	sommes rentré(e)s
rentres	rentrez	es rentré(e)	êtes rentré(e)(s)
rentre	rentrent	est rentré(e)	sont rentré(e)s
2 imparfait de l'indicatif		9 plus-que-parfait de l'indicatif	
rentrais	rentrions	étais rentré(e)	étions rentré(e)s
rentrais	rentriez	étais rentré(e)	étiez rentré(e)(s)
rentrait	rentraient	était rentré(e)	étaient rentré(e)s
3 passé simple		10 passé antérieur	
rentrai	rentrâmes	fus rentré(e)	fûmes rentré(e)s
rentras	rentrâtes	fus rentré(e)	fûtes rentré(e)(s)
rentra	rentrèrent	fut rentré(e)	furent rentré(e)s
4 futur		11 futur antérieur	
rentrerai	rentrerons	serai rentré(e)	serons rentré(e)s
rentreras	rentrerez	seras rentré(e)	serez rentré(e)(s)
rentrera	rentreront	sera rentré(e)	seront rentré(e)s
5 conditionnel		12 conditionnel passé	
rentrerais	rentrerions	serais rentré(e)	serions rentré(e)s
rentrerais	rentreriez	serais rentré(e)	seriez rentré(e)(s)
rentrerait	rentreraient	serait rentré(e)	seraient rentré(e)s
6 présent du subjonctif		13 passé du subjonctif	
rentre	rentrions	sois rentré(e)	soyons rentré(e)s
rentres	rentriez	sois rentré(e)	soyez rentré(e)(s)
rentre	rentrent	soit rentré(e)	soient rentré(e)s
7 imparfait du subjonctif		14 plus-que-parfait du subjonctif	
rentrasse	rentrassions	fusse rentré(e)	fussions rentré(e)s
rentrasses	rentrassiez	fusses rentré(e)	fussiez rentré(e)(s)
rentrât	rentrassent	fût rentré(e)	fussent rentré(e)s

Impératif
rentre
rentrons
rentrez

This verb is conjugated with **avoir** when it has a direct object.

Example: **Elle a rentré le chat dans la maison.**   She brought (took) the cat into the house.
BUT: **Elle est rentrée tôt.**   She returned home early.

rentrer chez soi   to go back home
rentrer les enfants   to take the children home
rentrer ses larmes   to hold back one's tears
la rentrée   return, homecoming
la rentrée des classes   back to school

répéter	Part. pr. **répétant**	Part. passé **répété**

to repeat, to rehearse

Regular -er verb: spelling change: é changes to è before syllable with mute e.

The Seven Simple Tenses		The Seven Compound Tenses	
Singular	Plural	Singular	Plural
1 présent de l'indicatif		8 passé composé	
répète	**répétons**	**ai répété**	**avons répété**
répètes	**répétez**	**as répété**	**avez répété**
répète	**répètent**	**a répété**	**ont répété**
2 imparfait de l'indicatif		9 plus-que-parfait de l'indicatif	
répétais	**répétions**	**avais répété**	**avions répété**
répétais	**répétiez**	**avais répété**	**aviez répété**
répétait	**répétaient**	**avait répété**	**avaient répété**
3 passé simple		10 passé antérieur	
répétai	**répétâmes**	**eus répété**	**eûmes répété**
répétas	**répétâtes**	**eus répété**	**eûtes répété**
répéta	**répétèrent**	**eut répété**	**eurent répété**
4 futur		11 futur antérieur	
répéterai	**répéterons**	**aurai répété**	**aurons répété**
répéteras	**répéterez**	**auras répété**	**aurez répété**
répétera	**répéteront**	**aura répété**	**auront répété**
5 conditionnel		12 conditionnel passé	
répéterais	**répéterions**	**aurais répété**	**aurions répété**
répéterais	**répéteriez**	**aurais répété**	**auriez répété**
répéterait	**répéteraient**	**aurait répété**	**auraient répété**
6 présent du subjonctif		13 passé du subjonctif	
répète	**répétions**	**aie répété**	**ayons répété**
répètes	**répétiez**	**aies répété**	**ayez répété**
répète	**répètent**	**ait répété**	**aient répété**
7 imparfait du subjonctif		14 plus-que-parfait du subjonctif	
répétasse	**répétassions**	**eusse répété**	**eussions répété**
répétasses	**répétassiez**	**eusses répété**	**eussiez répété**
répétât	**répétassent**	**eût répété**	**eussent répété**

Impératif
répète
répétons
répétez

répéter une pièce de théâtre   to rehearse a play
une répétition   repetition
La pièce est en répétition.   The play is in rehearsal.
se répéter   to repeat oneself; to recur
répétailler   to keep on repeating

Note: The Académie française now allows the accent grave (`) in the future (**je répèterai, tu répèteras,** etc.) and conditional (**je répèterais, tu répèterais,** etc.) of this verb.

244

Regular -re verb   to respond, to reply, to answer

The Seven Simple Tenses		The Seven Compound Tenses	
Singular	Plural	Singular	Plural
1 présent de l'indicatif		8 passé composé	
réponds	**répondons**	**ai répondu**	**avons répondu**
réponds	**répondez**	**as répondu**	**avez répondu**
répond	**répondent**	**a répondu**	**ont répondu**
2 imparfait de l'indicatif		9 plus-que-parfait de l'indicatif	
répondais	**répondions**	**avais répondu**	**avions répondu**
répondais	**répondiez**	**avais répondu**	**aviez répondu**
répondait	**répondaient**	**avait répondu**	**avaient répondu**
3 passé simple		10 passé antérieur	
répondis	**répondîmes**	**eus répondu**	**eûmes répondu**
répondis	**répondîtes**	**eus répondu**	**eûtes répondu**
répondit	**répondirent**	**eut répondu**	**eurent répondu**
4 futur		11 futur antérieur	
répondrai	**répondrons**	**aurai répondu**	**aurons répondu**
répondras	**répondrez**	**auras répondu**	**aurez répondu**
répondra	**répondront**	**aura répondu**	**auront répondu**
5 conditionnel		12 conditionnel passé	
répondrais	**répondrions**	**aurais répondu**	**aurions répondu**
répondrais	**répondriez**	**aurais répondu**	**auriez répondu**
répondrait	**répondraient**	**aurait répondu**	**auraient répondu**
6 présent du subjonctif		13 passé du subjonctif	
réponde	**répondions**	**aie répondu**	**ayons répondu**
répondes	**répondiez**	**aies répondu**	**ayez répondu**
réponde	**répondent**	**ait répondu**	**aient répondu**
7 imparfait du subjonctif		14 plus-que-parfait du subjonctif	
répondisse	**répondissions**	**eusse répondu**	**eussions répondu**
répondisses	**répondissiez**	**eusses répondu**	**eussiez répondu**
répondît	**répondissent**	**eût répondu**	**eussent répondu**

	Impératif
	réponds
	répondons
	répondez

répondre à qqn   to answer someone; to reply to someone
répondre de qqn   to be responsible for, to vouch for someone
répondre de qqch   to vouch for something, to guarantee something
une réponse   answer, reply; **en réponse à votre lettre ...**   in reply to your letter ...
pour répondre à la question de ...   in answer to the question of ...
un répondeur téléphonique   telephone answering machine
un coupon-réponse   reply coupon or reply card
Elle m'a répondu en claquant la porte.   She answered me by slamming the door.

se reposer
Part. pr. se reposant   Part. passé reposé(e)(s)

to rest

Reflexive regular -er verb

The Seven Simple Tenses		The Seven Compound Tenses	
Singular	Plural	Singular	Plural
1 présent de l'indicatif		8 passé composé	
me repose	nous reposons	me suis reposé(e)	nous sommes reposé(e)s
te reposes	vous reposez	t'es reposé(e)	vous êtes reposé(e)(s)
se repose	se reposent	s'est reposé(e)	se sont reposé(e)s
2 imparfait de l'indicatif		9 plus-que-parfait de l'indicatif	
me reposais	nous reposions	m'étais reposé(e)	nous étions reposé(e)s
te reposais	vous reposiez	t'étais reposé(e)	vous étiez reposé(e)(s)
se reposait	se reposaient	s'était reposé(e)	s'étaient reposé(e)s
3 passé simple		10 passé antérieur	
me reposai	nous reposâmes	me fus reposé(e)	nous fûmes reposé(e)s
te reposas	vous reposâtes	te fus reposé(e)	vous fûtes reposé(e)(s)
se reposa	se reposèrent	se fut reposé(e)	se furent reposé(e)s
4 futur		11 futur antérieur	
me reposerai	nous reposerons	me serai reposé(e)	nous serons reposé(e)s
te reposeras	vous reposerez	te seras reposé(e)	vous serez reposé(e)(s)
se reposera	se reposeront	se sera reposé(e)	se seront reposé(e)s
5 conditionnel		12 conditionnel passé	
me reposerais	nous reposerions	me serais reposé(e)	nous serions reposé(e)s
te reposerais	vous reposeriez	te serais reposé(e)	vous seriez reposé(e)(s)
se reposerait	se reposeraient	se serait reposé(e)	se seraient reposé(e)s
6 présent du subjonctif		13 passé du subjonctif	
me repose	nous reposions	me sois reposé(e)	nous soyons reposé(e)s
te reposes	vous reposiez	te sois reposé(e)	vous soyez reposé(e)(s)
se repose	se reposent	se soit reposé(e)	se soient reposé(e)s
7 imparfait du subjonctif		14 plus-que-parfait du subjonctif	
me reposasse	nous reposassions	me fusse reposé(e)	nous fussions reposé(e)s
te reposasses	vous reposassiez	te fusses reposé(e)	vous fussiez reposé(e)(s)
se reposât	se reposassent	se fût reposé(e)	se fussent reposé(e)s

Impératif
repose-toi; ne te repose pas
reposons-nous; ne nous reposons pas
reposez-vous; ne vous reposez pas

---

reposer to put down again; **reposer la tête sur** to rest one's head on; **reposer sur** to be based on
le repos rest, repose; **Au repos!** At ease!
se reposer sur qqn, qqch to put one's trust in someone, something
un repose-pied footrest; **un repose-bras** armrest
Je suis fatigué; je vais me reposer. I'm tired; I'm going to rest.

Part. pr. **reprenant**	Part. passé **repris**	**reprendre**
Irregular verb	to take again, to take back, to recover, to resume	

The Seven Simple Tenses		The Seven Compound Tenses	
Singular	Plural	Singular	Plural
1 présent de l'indicatif		**8 passé composé**	
reprends	reprenons	ai repris	avons repris
reprends	reprenez	as repris	avez repris
reprend	reprennent	a repris	ont repris
2 imparfait de l'indicatif		**9 plus-que-parfait de l'indicatif**	
reprenais	reprenions	avais repris	avions repris
reprenais	repreniez	avais repris	aviez repris
reprenait	reprenaient	avait repris	avaient repris
3 passé simple		**10 passé antérieur**	
repris	reprîmes	eus repris	eûmes repris
repris	reprîtes	eus repris	eûtes repris
reprit	reprirent	eut repris	eurent repris
4 futur		**11 futur antérieur**	
reprendrai	reprendrons	aurai repris	aurons repris
reprendras	reprendrez	auras repris	aurez repris
reprendra	reprendront	aura repris	auront repris
5 conditionnel		**12 conditionnel passé**	
reprendrais	reprendrions	aurais repris	aurions repris
reprendrais	reprendriez	aurais repris	auriez repris
reprendrait	reprendraient	aurait repris	auraient repris
6 présent du subjonctif		**13 passé du subjonctif**	
reprenne	reprenions	aie repris	ayons repris
reprennes	repreniez	aies repris	ayez repris
reprenne	reprennent	ait repris	aient repris
7 imparfait du subjonctif		**14 plus-que-parfait du subjonctif**	
reprisse	reprissions	eusse repris	eussions repris
reprisses	reprissiez	eusses repris	eussiez repris
reprît	reprissent	eût repris	eussent repris

	Impératif
	reprends
	reprenons
	reprenez

reprendre froid   to catch cold again
reprendre ses esprits   to recover one's senses
reprendre le dessus   to regain the upper hand
reprendre ses forces   to recover one's strength
se reprendre   to take hold of oneself, to recover oneself
une reprise   resumption, renewal, repetition
à maintes reprises   over and over again

See also **apprendre**, **comprendre**, and **prendre**.

résoudre	Part. pr. **résolvant**	Part. passé **résolu (résous)**

to resolve, to solve   Irregular verb

The Seven Simple Tenses		The Seven Compound Tenses	
Singular	Plural	Singular	Plural
1 présent de l'indicatif		**8 passé composé**	
résous	résolvons	ai résolu	avons résolu
résous	résolvez	as résolu	avez résolu
résout	résolvent	a résolu	ont résolu
2 imparfait de l'indicatif		**9 plus-que-parfait de l'indicatif**	
résolvais	résolvions	avais résolu	avions résolu
résolvais	résolviez	avais résolu	aviez résolu
résolvait	résolvaient	avait résolu	avaient résolu
3 passé simple		**10 passé antérieur**	
résolus	résolûmes	eus résolu	eûmes résolu
résolus	résolûtes	eus résolu	eûtes résolu
résolut	résolurent	eut résolu	eurent résolu
4 futur		**11 futur antérieur**	
résoudrai	résoudrons	aurai résolu	aurons résolu
résoudras	résoudrez	auras résolu	aurez résolu
résoudra	résoudront	aura résolu	auront résolu
5 conditionnel		**12 conditionnel passé**	
résoudrais	résoudrions	aurais résolu	aurions résolu
résoudrais	résoudriez	aurais résolu	auriez résolu
résoudrait	résoudraient	aurait résolu	auraient résolu
6 présent du subjonctif		**13 passé du subjonctif**	
résolve	résolvions	aie résolu	ayons résolu
résolves	résolviez	aies résolu	ayez résolu
résolve	résolvent	ait résolu	aient résolu
7 imparfait du subjonctif		**14 plus-que-parfait du subjonctif**	
résolusse	résolussions	eusse résolu	eussions résolu
résolusses	résolussiez	eusses résolu	eussiez résolu
résolût	résolussent	eût résolu	eussent résolu

	Impératif
	résous
	résolvons
	résolvez

se résoudre à to make up one's mind to
résoudre qqn à faire qqch to induce someone to do something
résoudre un problème mathématique to solve a math problem
une résolution resolution
être résolu(e) à faire qqch to be resolved to doing something
Le feu a résous le bois en cendres. The fire has changed the wood into ashes.
(The past part. **résous** is used for things that have undergone a physical change.)
André a résolu le problème avant tous les autres élèves. Andrew solved the
problem before all the other students.

Part. pr. **ressemblant**	Part. passé **ressemblé**	**ressembler**

Regular -er verb · to resemble, to be like, to look like

The Seven Simple Tenses		The Seven Compound Tenses	
Singular	Plural	Singular	Plural
1 présent de l'indicatif		8 passé composé	
ressemble	ressemblons	ai ressemblé	avons ressemblé
ressembles	ressemblez	as ressemblé	avez ressemblé
ressemble	ressemblent	a ressemblé	ont ressemblé
2 imparfait de l'indicatif		9 plus-que-parfait de l'indicatif	
ressemblais	ressemblions	avais ressemblé	avions ressemblé
ressemblais	ressembliez	avais ressemblé	aviez ressemblé
ressemblait	ressemblaient	avait ressemblé	avaient ressemblé
3 passé simple		10 passé antérieur	
ressemblai	ressemblâmes	eus ressemblé	eûmes ressemblé
ressemblas	ressemblâtes	eus ressemblé	eûtes ressemblé
ressembla	ressemblèrent	eut ressemblé	eurent ressemblé
4 futur		11 futur antérieur	
ressemblerai	ressemblerons	aurai ressemblé	aurons ressemblé
ressembleras	ressemblerez	auras ressemblé	aurez ressemblé
ressemblera	ressembleront	aura ressemblé	auront ressemblé
5 conditionnel		12 conditionnel passé	
ressemblerais	ressemblerions	aurais ressemblé	aurions ressemblé
ressemblerais	ressembleriez	aurais ressemblé	auriez ressemblé
ressemblerait	ressembleraient	aurait ressemblé	auraient ressemblé
6 présent du subjonctif		13 passé du subjonctif	
ressemble	ressemblions	aie ressemblé	ayons ressemblé
ressembles	ressembliez	aies ressemblé	ayez ressemblé
ressemble	ressemblent	ait ressemblé	aient ressemblé
7 imparfait du subjonctif		14 plus-que-parfait du subjonctif	
ressemblasse	ressemblassions	eusse ressemblé	eussions ressemblé
ressemblasses	ressemblassiez	eusses ressemblé	eussiez ressemblé
ressemblât	ressemblassent	eût ressemblé	eussent ressemblé

Impératif
ressemble
ressemblons
ressemblez

---

ressembler à qqn   to resemble someone
Paulette ressemble beaucoup à sa mère.   Paulette looks very much like her mother.
se ressembler   to resemble each other, to look alike
Qui se ressemble s'assemble.   Birds of a feather flock together.
sembler   to seem, to appear
une ressemblance   resemblance
Ils se ressemblent comme deux gouttes d'eau.   They are as alike as two peas in
    a pod. (Literally: two drops of water.)

rester	Part. pr. **restant**	Part. passé **resté(e)(s)**

to remain, to stay; to be left (over)   Regular -er verb

The Seven Simple Tenses		The Seven Compound Tenses	

Singular	Plural	Singular	Plural
1 présent de l'indicatif		8 passé composé	
reste	**restons**	**suis resté(e)**	**sommes resté(e)s**
restes	**restez**	**es resté(e)**	**êtes resté(e)(s)**
reste	**restent**	**est resté(e)**	**sont resté(e)s**
2 imparfait de l'indicatif		9 plus-que-parfait de l'indicatif	
restais	**restions**	**étais resté(e)**	**étions resté(e)s**
restais	**restiez**	**étais resté(e)**	**étiez resté(e)(s)**
restait	**restaient**	**était resté(e)**	**étaient resté(e)s**
3 passé simple		10 passé antérieur	
restai	**restâmes**	**fus resté(e)**	**fûmes resté(e)s**
restas	**restâtes**	**fus resté(e)**	**fûtes resté(e)(s)**
resta	**restèrent**	**fut resté(e)**	**furent resté(e)s**
4 futur		11 futur antérieur	
resterai	**resterons**	**serai resté(e)**	**serons resté(e)s**
resteras	**resterez**	**seras resté(e)**	**serez resté(e)(s)**
restera	**resteront**	**sera resté(e)**	**seront resté(e)s**
5 conditionnel		12 conditionnel passé	
resterais	**resterions**	**serais resté(e)**	**serions resté(e)s**
resterais	**resteriez**	**serais resté(e)**	**seriez resté(e)(s)**
resterait	**resteraient**	**serait resté(e)**	**seraient resté(e)s**
6 présent du subjonctif		13 passé du subjonctif	
reste	**restions**	**sois resté(e)**	**soyons resté(e)s**
restes	**restiez**	**sois resté(e)**	**soyez resté(e)(s)**
reste	**restent**	**soit resté(e)**	**soient resté(e)s**
7 imparfait du subjonctif		14 plus-que-parfait du subjonctif	
restasse	**restassions**	**fusse resté(e)**	**fussions resté(e)s**
restasses	**restassiez**	**fusses resté(e)**	**fussiez resté(e)(s)**
restât	**restassent**	**fût resté(e)**	**fussent resté(e)s**

Impératif
reste
restons
restez

Combien d'argent vous reste-t-il?   How much money do you have left (over)?
Il me reste deux cents euros.   I have two hundred euros left.
rester au lit   to stay in bed
les restes   leftovers
le reste du temps   the rest of the time
Restez là; je reviens tout de suite.   Stay there; I'll be right back.
Simone est restée au lit toute la journée.   Simone stayed in bed all day.

Do not confuse **rester** with **se reposer**.

Regular -er verb   to return, to go back, to turn again

The Seven Simple Tenses		The Seven Compound Tenses	
Singular	Plural	Singular	Plural
1 présent de l'indicatif		8 passé composé	
retourne	**retournons**	**suis retourné(e)**	**sommes retourné(e)s**
retournes	**retournez**	**es retourné(e)**	**êtes retourné(e)(s)**
retourne	**retournent**	**est retourné(e)**	**sont retourné(e)s**
2 imparfait de l'indicatif		9 plus-que-parfait de l'indicatif	
retournais	**retournions**	**étais retourné(e)**	**étions retourné(e)s**
retournais	**retourniez**	**étais retourné(e)**	**étiez retourné(e)(s)**
retournait	**retournaient**	**était retourné(e)**	**étaient retourné(e)s**
3 passé simple		10 passé antérieur	
retournai	**retournâmes**	**fus retourné(e)**	**fûmes retourné(e)s**
retournas	**retournâtes**	**fus retourné(e)**	**fûtes retourné(e)(s)**
retourna	**retournèrent**	**fut retourné(e)**	**furent retourné(e)s**
4 futur		11 futur antérieur	
retournerai	**retournerons**	**serai retourné(e)**	**serons retourné(e)s**
retourneras	**retournerez**	**seras retourné(e)**	**serez retourné(e)(s)**
retournera	**retourneront**	**sera retourné(e)**	**seront retourné(e)s**
5 conditionnel		12 conditionnel passé	
retournerais	**retournerions**	**serais retourné(e)**	**serions retourné(e)s**
retournerais	**retourneriez**	**serais retourné(e)**	**seriez retourné(e)(s)**
retournerait	**retourneraient**	**serait retourné(e)**	**seraient retourné(e)s**
6 présent du subjonctif		13 passé du subjonctif	
retourne	**retournions**	**sois retourné(e)**	**soyons retourné(e)s**
retournes	**retourniez**	**sois retourné(e)**	**soyez retourné(e)(s)**
retourne	**retournent**	**soit retourné(e)**	**soient retourné(e)s**
7 imparfait du subjonctif		14 plus-que-parfait du subjonctif	
retournasse	**retournassions**	**fusse retourné(e)**	**fussions retourné(e)s**
retournasses	**retournassiez**	**fusses retourné(e)**	**fussiez retourné(e)(s)**
retournât	**retournassent**	**fût retourné(e)**	**fussent retourné(e)s**

Impératif
retourne
retournons
retournez

---

retourner une chaussette to turn a sock inside out
retourner un matelas to turn over a mattress
se retourner to turn around; **se retourner sur le dos** to turn over on one's back
un retour return; **un (billet) aller-retour** a round-trip ticket
être de retour to be back; **Madame Dupin sera de retour demain.**

Note: Use **avoir** as the helping verb when **retourner** takes a direct object:
Jeanne a retourné la carte pour lire ce qui était écrit sur l'envers.
Jean turned the card over to read what was written on the back.

See also **tourner**.

réussir	Part. pr. **réussissant**	Part. passé **réussi**

to succeed, to result

Regular **-ir** verb

The Seven Simple Tenses	The Seven Compound Tenses

Singular	Plural	Singular	Plural
1 présent de l'indicatif		8 passé composé	
réussis	**réussissons**	**ai réussi**	**avons réussi**
réussis	**réussissez**	**as réussi**	**avez réussi**
réussit	**réussissent**	**a réussi**	**ont réussi**
2 imparfait de l'indicatif		9 plus-que-parfait de l'indicatif	
réussissais	**réussissions**	**avais réussi**	**avions réussi**
réussissais	**réussissiez**	**avais réussi**	**aviez réussi**
réussissait	**réussissaient**	**avait réussi**	**avaient réussi**
3 passé simple		10 passé antérieur	
réussis	**réussîmes**	**eus réussi**	**eûmes réussi**
réussis	**réussîtes**	**eus réussi**	**eûtes réussi**
réussit	**réussirent**	**eut réussi**	**eurent réussi**
4 futur		11 futur antérieur	
réussirai	**réussirons**	**aurai réussi**	**aurons réussi**
réussiras	**réussirez**	**auras réussi**	**aurez réussi**
réussira	**réussiront**	**aura réussi**	**auront réussi**
5 conditionnel		12 conditionnel passé	
réussirais	**réussirions**	**aurais réussi**	**aurions réussi**
réussirais	**réussiriez**	**aurais réussi**	**auriez réussi**
réussirait	**réussiraient**	**aurait réussi**	**auraient réussi**
6 présent du subjonctif		13 passé du subjonctif	
réussisse	**réussissions**	**aie réussi**	**ayons réussi**
réussisses	**réussissiez**	**aies réussi**	**ayez réussi**
réussisse	**réussissent**	**ait réussi**	**aient réussi**
7 imparfait du subjonctif		14 plus-que-parfait du subjonctif	
réussisse	**réussissions**	**eusse réussi**	**eussions réussi**
réussisses	**réussissiez**	**eusses réussi**	**eussiez réussi**
réussît	**réussissent**	**eût réussi**	**eussent réussi**

Impératif
réussis
réussissons
réussissez

---

réussir à qqch   to succeed in something
réussir à un examen   to pass an exam
une réussite   success; **une réussite sociale**   social success
réussir   to result; **Le projet a mal réussi.**   The plan turned out badly; **Le projet a bien réussi.**   The plan turned out well.
une soirée réussie   a successful evening
réussir dans la vie   to succeed in life
Les fritures ne me réussissent pas.   Fried food doesn't agree with me.

Part. pr. **se réveillant**   Part. passé **réveillé(e)(s)**   **se réveiller**

Reflexive regular -er verb   to wake up

The Seven Simple Tenses		The Seven Compound Tenses	
Singular	Plural	Singular	Plural
1 présent de l'indicatif		8 passé composé	
me réveille	nous réveillons	me suis réveillé(e)	nous sommes réveillé(e)s
te réveilles	vous réveillez	t'es réveillé(e)	vous êtes réveillé(e)(s)
se réveille	se réveillent	s'est réveillé(e)	se sont réveillé(e)s
2 imparfait de l'indicatif		9 plus-que-parfait de l'indicatif	
me réveillais	nous réveillions	m'étais réveillé(e)	nous étions réveillé(e)s
te réveillais	vous réveilliez	t'étais réveillé(e)	vous étiez réveillé(e)(s)
se réveillait	se réveillaient	s'était réveillé(e)	s'étaient réveillé(e)s
3 passé simple		10 passé antérieur	
me réveillai	nous réveillâmes	me fus réveillé(e)	nous fûmes réveillé(e)s
te réveillas	vous réveillâtes	te fus réveillé(e)	vous fûtes réveillé(e)(s)
se réveilla	se réveillèrent	se fut réveillé(e)	se furent réveillé(e)s
4 futur		11 futur antérieur	
me réveillerai	nous réveillerons	me serai réveillé(e)	nous serons réveillé(e)s
te réveilleras	vous réveillerez	te seras réveillé(e)	vous serez réveillé(e)(s)
se réveillera	se réveilleront	se sera réveillé(e)	se seront réveillé(e)s
5 conditionnel		12 conditionnel passé	
me réveillerais	nous réveillerions	me serais réveillé(e)	nous serions réveillé(e)s
te réveillerais	vous réveilleriez	te serais réveillé(e)	vous seriez réveillé(e)(s)
se réveillerait	se réveilleraient	se serait réveillé(e)	se seraient réveillé(e)s
6 présent du subjonctif		13 passé du subjonctif	
me réveille	nous réveillions	me sois réveillé(e)	nous soyons réveillé(e)s
te réveilles	vous réveilliez	te sois réveillé(e)	vous soyez réveillé(e)(s)
se réveille	se réveillent	se soit réveillé(e)	se soient réveillé(e)s
7 imparfait du subjonctif		14 plus-que-parfait du subjonctif	
me réveillasse	nous réveillassions	me fusse réveillé(e)	nous fussions réveillé(e)s
te réveillasses	vous réveillassiez	te fusses réveillé(e)	vous fussiez réveillé(e)(s)
se réveillât	se réveillassent	se fût réveillé(e)	se fussent réveillé(e)s

Impératif
réveille-toi; ne te réveille pas
réveillons-nous; ne nous réveillons pas
réveillez-vous; ne vous réveillez pas

le réveillon   Christmas or New Year's Eve party
faire réveillon   to see the New Year in, to see Christmas in on Christmas Eve
un réveille-matin, un réveil   alarm clock
éveiller (réveiller) qqn   to wake up, awaken someone; éveiller   implies to awaken
   or wake up gently; réveiller   suggests with some effort
veiller   to stay awake; veiller à   to look after
veiller sur   to watch over; surveiller   to keep an eye on
la veille de Noël   Christmas Eve
Marie s'est réveillée à six heures.   Mary woke up at six o'clock.

revenir	Part. pr. **revenant**	Part. passé **revenu(e)(s)**

to come back

Irregular verb

The Seven Simple Tenses		The Seven Compound Tenses	
Singular	Plural	Singular	Plural
1 présent de l'indicatif		8 passé composé	
reviens	**revenons**	**suis revenu(e)**	**sommes revenu(e)s**
reviens	**revenez**	**es revenu(e)**	**êtes revenu(e)(s)**
revient	**reviennent**	**est revenu(e)**	**sont revenu(e)s**
2 imparfait de l'indicatif		9 plus-que-parfait de l'indicatif	
revenais	**revenions**	**étais revenu(e)**	**étions revenu(e)s**
revenais	**reveniez**	**étais revenu(e)**	**étiez revenu(e)(s)**
revenait	**revenaient**	**était revenu(e)**	**étaient revenu(e)s**
3 passé simple		10 passé antérieur	
revins	**revînmes**	**fus revenu(e)**	**fûmes revenu(e)s**
revins	**revîntes**	**fus revenu(e)**	**fûtes revenu(e)(s)**
revint	**revinrent**	**fut revenu(e)**	**furent revenu(e)s**
4 futur		11 futur antérieur	
reviendrai	**reviendrons**	**serai revenu(e)**	**serons revenu(e)s**
reviendras	**reviendrez**	**seras revenu(e)**	**serez revenu(e)(s)**
reviendra	**reviendront**	**sera revenu(e)**	**seront revenu(e)s**
5 conditionnel		12 conditionnel passé	
reviendrais	**reviendrions**	**serais revenu(e)**	**serions revenu(e)s**
reviendrais	**reviendriez**	**serais revenu(e)**	**seriez revenu(e)(s)**
reviendrait	**reviendraient**	**serait revenu(e)**	**seraient revenu(e)s**
6 présent du subjonctif		13 passé du subjonctif	
revienne	**revenions**	**sois revenu(e)**	**soyons revenu(e)s**
reviennes	**reveniez**	**sois revenu(e)**	**soyez revenu(e)(s)**
revienne	**reviennent**	**soit revenu(e)**	**soient revenu(e)s**
7 imparfait du subjonctif		14 plus-que-parfait du subjonctif	
revinsse	**revinssions**	**fusse revenu(e)**	**fussions revenu(e)s**
revinsses	**revinssiez**	**fusses revenu(e)**	**fussiez revenu(e)(s)**
revînt	**revinssent**	**fût revenu(e)**	**fussent revenu(e)s**

Impératif
reviens
revenons
revenez

le revenu revenue, income
à revenu fixe on fixed interest
revenir d'une erreur to realize one's mistake
revenir au même to amount to the same thing
revenir sur ses pas to retrace one's steps
revenir sur le sujet to get back to the subject
revenir sur sa parole to go back on one's word
Tout revient à ceci . . . It all boils down to this . . .

See also devenir, se souvenir, and venir.

Irregular verb   to see again, to see once more

The Seven Simple Tenses		The Seven Compound Tenses	
Singular	Plural	Singular	Plural
1 présent de l'indicatif		**8 passé composé**	
revois	**revoyons**	**ai revu**	**avons revu**
revois	**revoyez**	**as revu**	**avez revu**
revoit	**revoient**	**a revu**	**ont revu**
2 imparfait de l'indicatif		**9 plus-que-parfait de l'indicatif**	
revoyais	**revoyions**	**avais revu**	**avions revu**
revoyais	**revoyiez**	**avais revu**	**aviez revu**
revoyait	**revoyaient**	**avait revu**	**avaient revu**
3 passé simple		**10 passé antérieur**	
revis	**revîmes**	**eus revu**	**eûmes revu**
revis	**revîtes**	**eus revu**	**eûtes revu**
revit	**revirent**	**eut revu**	**eurent revu**
4 futur		**11 futur antérieur**	
reverrai	**reverrons**	**aurai revu**	**aurons revu**
reverras	**reverrez**	**auras revu**	**aurez revu**
reverra	**reverront**	**aura revu**	**auront revu**
5 conditionnel		**12 conditionnel passé**	
reverrais	**reverrions**	**aurais revu**	**aurions revu**
reverrais	**reverriez**	**aurais revu**	**auriez revu**
reverrait	**reverraient**	**aurait revu**	**auraient revu**
6 présent du subjonctif		**13 passé du subjonctif**	
revoie	**revoyions**	**aie revu**	**ayons revu**
revoies	**revoyiez**	**aies revu**	**ayez revu**
revoie	**revoient**	**ait revu**	**aient revu**
7 imparfait du subjonctif		**14 plus-que-parfait du subjonctif**	
revisse	**revissions**	**eusse revu**	**eussions revu**
revisses	**revissiez**	**eusses revu**	**eussiez revu**
revît	**revissent**	**eût revu**	**eussent revu**
		Impératif	
		revois	
		revoyons	
		revoyez	

au revoir   good-bye, see you again, until we meet again
se revoir   to see each other again
une revue   review, magazine
un, une revuiste   a writer of reviews
une révision   revision; **à revoir**   to be revised
passer en revue   to review, look through

See also **voir**.

rire	Part. pr. **riant**	Part. passé **ri**

to laugh   Irregular verb

The Seven Simple Tenses		The Seven Compound Tenses	
Singular	Plural	Singular	Plural
1 présent de l'indicatif		8 passé composé	
ris	**rions**	**ai ri**	**avons ri**
ris	**riez**	**as ri**	**avez ri**
rit	**rient**	**a ri**	**ont ri**
2 imparfait de l'indicatif		9 plus-que-parfait de l'indicatif	
riais	**riions**	**avais ri**	**avions ri**
riais	**riiez**	**avais ri**	**aviez ri**
riait	**riaient**	**avait ri**	**avaient ri**
3 passé simple		10 passé antérieur	
ris	**rîmes**	**eus ri**	**eûmes ri**
ris	**rîtes**	**eus ri**	**eûtes ri**
rit	**rirent**	**eut ri**	**eurent ri**
4 futur		11 futur antérieur	
rirai	**rirons**	**aurai ri**	**aurons ri**
riras	**rirez**	**auras ri**	**aurez ri**
rira	**riront**	**aura ri**	**auront ri**
5 conditionnel		12 conditionnel passé	
rirais	**ririons**	**aurais ri**	**aurions ri**
rirais	**ririez**	**aurais ri**	**auriez ri**
rirait	**riraient**	**aurait ri**	**auraient ri**
6 présent du subjonctif		13 passé du subjonctif	
rie	**riions**	**aie ri**	**ayons ri**
ries	**riiez**	**aies ri**	**ayez ri**
rie	**rient**	**ait ri**	**aient ri**
7 imparfait du subjonctif		14 plus-que-parfait du subjonctif	
risse	**rissions**	**eusse ri**	**eussions ri**
risses	**rissiez**	**eusses ri**	**eussiez ri**
rît	**rissent**	**eût ri**	**eussent ri**
		Impératif	
		ris	
		rions	
		riez	

éclater de rire to burst out laughing; **rire de** to laugh at
dire qqch pour rire to say something just for a laugh
rire au nez de qqn to laugh in someone's face
rire de bon coeur to laugh heartily
le rire laughter; **un sourire** smile; **risible** laughable
le fou rire fit of laughter, giggles
le rire franc a hearty laugh, an open laugh
Rira bien qui rira le dernier. Whoever laughs last laughs best.

See also **sourire**.

Regular -re verb endings: spelling change:	to break, to burst,
3rd person sing. of Tense No. 1 adds **t**.	to shatter, to break off

The Seven Simple Tenses		The Seven Compound Tenses	
Singular	Plural	Singular	Plural
1 présent de l'indicatif		**8 passé composé**	
romps	rompons	ai rompu	avons rompu
romps	rompez	as rompu	avez rompu
rompt	rompent	a rompu	ont rompu
2 imparfait de l'indicatif		**9 plus-que-parfait de l'indicatif**	
rompais	rompions	avais rompu	avions rompu
rompais	rompiez	avais rompu	aviez rompu
rompait	rompaient	avait rompu	avaient rompu
3 passé simple		**10 passé antérieur**	
rompis	rompîmes	eus rompu	eûmes rompu
rompis	rompîtes	eus rompu	eûtes rompu
rompit	rompirent	eut rompu	eurent rompu
4 futur		**11 futur antérieur**	
romprai	romprons	aurai rompu	aurons rompu
rompras	romprez	auras rompu	aurez rompu
rompra	rompront	aura rompu	auront rompu
5 conditionnel		**12 conditionnel passé**	
romprais	romprions	aurais rompu	aurions rompu
romprais	rompriez	aurais rompu	auriez rompu
romprait	rompraient	aurait rompu	auraient rompu
6 présent du subjonctif		**13 passé du subjonctif**	
rompe	rompions	aie rompu	ayons rompu
rompes	rompiez	aies rompu	ayez rompu
rompe	rompent	ait rompu	aient rompu
7 imparfait du subjonctif		**14 plus-que-parfait du subjonctif**	
rompisse	rompissions	eusse rompu	eussions rompu
rompisses	rompissiez	eusses rompu	eussiez rompu
rompît	rompissent	eût rompu	eussent rompu
		Impératif	
		romps	
		rompons	
		rompez	

rompu de fatigue worn out	corrompre to corrupt
rompu aux affaires experienced in business	interrompre to interrupt
se rompre à to get used to	une rupture rupture, bursting
se rompre la tête to rack one's brains	un rupteur circuit breaker
une rupture de contrat breach of	rompre avec qqn to have a falling
contract	out with someone

to seize, to grasp, to comprehend   Regular -ir verb

The Seven Simple Tenses		The Seven Compound Tenses	
Singular	Plural	Singular	Plural
1 présent de l'indicatif		**8 passé composé**	
saisis	saisissons	ai saisi	avons saisi
saisis	saisissez	as saisi	avez saisi
saisit	saisissent	a saisi	ont saisi
2 imparfait de l'indicatif		**9 plus-que-parfait de l'indicatif**	
saisissais	saisissions	avais saisi	avions saisi
saisissais	saisissiez	avais saisi	aviez saisi
saisissait	saisissaient	avait saisi	avaient saisi
3 passé simple		**10 passé antérieur**	
saisis	saisîmes	eus saisi	eûmes saisi
saisis	saisîtes	eus saisi	eûtes saisi
saisit	saisirent	eut saisi	eurent saisi
4 futur		**11 futur antérieur**	
saisirai	saisirons	aurai saisi	aurons saisi
saisiras	saisirez	auras saisi	aurez saisi
saisira	saisiront	aura saisi	auront saisi
5 conditionnel		**12 conditionnel passé**	
saisirais	saisirions	aurais saisi	aurions saisi
saisirais	saisiriez	aurais saisi	auriez saisi
saisirait	saisiraient	aurait saisi	auraient saisi
6 présent du subjonctif		**13 passé du subjonctif**	
saisisse	saisissions	aie saisi	ayons saisi
saisisses	saisissiez	aies saisi	ayez saisi
saisisse	saisissent	ait saisi	aient saisi
7 imparfait du subjonctif		**14 plus-que-parfait du subjonctif**	
saisisse	saisissions	eusse saisi	eussions saisi
saisisses	saisissiez	eusses saisi	eussiez saisi
saisît	saisissent	eût saisi	eussent saisi
		Impératif	
		saisis	
		saisissons	
		saisissez	

un saisissement   shock
saisissable   seizable
saisissant, saisissante   thrilling, piercing
une saisie   seizure
se saisir de   to take possession of
saisir l'occasion   to seize the
   opportunity

saisir la signification de qqch .   to
   grasp the meaning of something
saisi de joie   overcome with joy
insaisissable   elusive
saisir des données   to input data
   (comp.)
la saisie de données   data input
   (comp.)

Regular **-ir** verb   to soil, to dirty

The Seven Simple Tenses		The Seven Compound Tenses	
Singular	Plural	Singular	Plural
1 présent de l'indicatif		8 passé composé	
salis	**salissons**	**ai sali**	**avons sali**
salis	**salissez**	**as sali**	**avez sali**
salit	**salissent**	**a sali**	**ont sali**
2 imparfait de l'indicatif		9 plus-que-parfait de l'indicatif	
salissais	**salissions**	**avais sali**	**avions sali**
salissais	**salissiez**	**avais sali**	**aviez sali**
salissait	**salissaient**	**avait sali**	**avaient sali**
3 passé simple		10 passé antérieur	
salis	**salîmes**	**eus sali**	**eûmes sali**
salis	**salîtes**	**eus sali**	**eûtes sali**
salit	**salirent**	**eut sali**	**eurent sali**
4 futur		11 futur antérieur	
salirai	**salirons**	**aurai sali**	**aurons sali**
saliras	**salirez**	**auras sali**	**aurez sali**
salira	**saliront**	**aura sali**	**auront sali**
5 conditionnel		12 conditionnel passé	
salirais	**salirions**	**aurais sali**	**aurions sali**
salirais	**saliriez**	**aurais sali**	**auriez sali**
salirait	**saliraient**	**aurait sali**	**auraient sali**
6 présent du subjonctif		13 passé du subjonctif	
salisse	**salissions**	**aie sali**	**ayons sali**
salisses	**salissiez**	**aies sali**	**ayez sali**
salisse	**salissent**	**ait sali**	**aient sali**
7 imparfait du subjonctif		14 plus-que-parfait du subjonctif	
salisse	**salissions**	**eusse sali**	**eussions sali**
salisses	**salissiez**	**eusses sali**	**eussiez sali**
salît	**salissent**	**eût sali**	**eussent sali**
		Impératif	
		salis	
		salissons	
		salissez	

---

sale dirty, soiled	**se salir** to get dirty
salement disgustingly	**les mains sales** soiled hands
la saleté filth	
dire des saletés to use filthy language	

Avez-vous jamais lu ou vu la pièce de théâtre *Les mains sales* **de Jean-Paul Sartre?**
Have you ever read or seen the play *Dirty Hands* by Jean-Paul Sartre?

sauter	Part. pr. **sautant**	Part. passé **sauté**
to jump, to leap		Regular -er verb

The Seven Simple Tenses		The Seven Compound Tenses	
Singular	Plural	Singular	Plural
1 présent de l'indicatif		8 passé composé	
saute	sautons	ai sauté	avons sauté
sautes	sautez	as sauté	avez sauté
saute	sautent	a sauté	ont sauté
2 imparfait de l'indicatif		9 plus-que-parfait de l'indicatif	
sautais	sautions	avais sauté	avions sauté
sautais	sautiez	avais sauté	aviez sauté
sautait	sautaient	avait sauté	avaient sauté
3 passé simple		10 passé antérieur	
sautai	sautâmes	eus sauté	eûmes sauté
sautas	sautâtes	eus sauté	eûtes sauté
sauta	sautèrent	eut sauté	eurent sauté
4 futur		11 futur antérieur	
sauterai	sauterons	aurai sauté	aurons sauté
sauteras	sauterez	auras sauté	aurez sauté
sautera	sauteront	aura sauté	auront sauté
5 conditionnel		12 conditionnel passé	
sauterais	sauterions	aurais sauté	aurions sauté
sauterais	sauteriez	aurais sauté	auriez sauté
sauterait	sauteraient	aurait sauté	auraient sauté
6 présent du subjonctif		13 passé du subjonctif	
saute	sautions	aie sauté	ayons sauté
sautes	sautiez	aies sauté	ayez sauté
saute	sautent	ait sauté	aient sauté
7 imparfait du subjonctif		14 plus-que-parfait du subjonctif	
sautasse	sautassions	eusse sauté	eussions sauté
sautasses	sautassiez	eusses sauté	eussiez sauté
sautât	sautassent	eût sauté	eussent sauté

Impératif
saute
sautons
sautez

un saut leap, jump	sauter au bas du lit to jump out of bed
une sauterelle grasshopper	faire sauter une crêpe to toss a pancake
sautiller to skip, to hop	Cela saute aux yeux. That's obvious.
sauter à la corde to jump (skip) rope	sursauter to jump, to start

Regular **-er** verb

to rescue, to save

The Seven Simple Tenses		The Seven Compound Tenses	
Singular	Plural	Singular	Plural
1 présent de l'indicatif		8 passé composé	
sauve	sauvons	ai sauvé	avons sauvé
sauves	sauvez	as sauvé	avez sauvé
sauve	sauvent	a sauvé	ont sauvé
2 imparfait de l'indicatif		9 plus-que-parfait de l'indicatif	
sauvais	sauvions	avais sauvé	avions sauvé
sauvais	sauviez	avais sauvé	aviez sauvé
sauvait	sauvaient	avait sauvé	avaient sauvé
3 passé simple		10 passé antérieur	
sauvai	sauvâmes	eus sauvé	eûmes sauvé
sauvas	sauvâtes	eus sauvé	eûtes sauvé
sauva	sauvèrent	eut sauvé	eurent sauvé
4 futur		11 futur antérieur	
sauverai	sauverons	aurai sauvé	aurons sauvé
sauveras	sauverez	auras sauvé	aurez sauvé
sauvera	sauveront	aura sauvé	auront sauvé
5 conditionnel		12 conditionnel passé	
sauverais	sauverions	aurais sauvé	aurions sauvé
sauverais	sauveriez	aurais sauvé	auriez sauvé
sauverait	sauveraient	aurait sauvé	auraient sauvé
6 présent du subjonctif		13 passé du subjonctif	
sauve	sauvions	aie sauvé	ayons sauvé
sauves	sauviez	aies sauvé	ayez sauvé
sauve	sauvent	ait sauvé	aient sauvé
7 imparfait du subjonctif		14 plus-que-parfait du subjonctif	
sauvasse	sauvassions	eusse sauvé	eussions sauvé
sauvasses	sauvassiez	eusses sauvé	eussiez sauvé
sauvât	sauvassent	eût sauvé	eussent sauvé

Impératif
sauve
sauvons
sauvez

---

sauvegarder to safeguard
le sauvetage life-saving, rescue
Sauve qui peut! Run for your life!
sauver les apparences to preserve
  appearances

se sauver to run away, to escape,
  to rush off
sauver la vie à qqn to save someone's life
une échelle de sauvetage fire escape,
  escape ladder
un gilet de sauvetage a life jacket

See also **se sauver**.

se sauver	Part. pr. **se sauvant**	Part. passé **sauvé(e)(s)**

to run away, to rush off, to escape   Reflexive regular -er verb

The Seven Simple Tenses		The Seven Compound Tenses	
Singular	Plural	Singular	Plural
1 présent de l'indicatif		**8 passé composé**	
me sauve	nous sauvons	me suis sauvé(e)	nous sommes sauvé(e)s
te sauves	vous sauvez	t'es sauvé(e)	vous êtes sauvé(e)(s)
se sauve	se sauvent	s'est sauvé(e)	se sont sauvé(e)s
2 imparfait de l'indicatif		**9 plus-que-parfait de l'indicatif**	
me sauvais	nous sauvions	m'étais sauvé(e)	nous étions sauvé(e)s
te sauvais	vous sauviez	t'étais sauvé(e)	vous étiez sauvé(e)(s)
se sauvait	se sauvaient	s'était sauvé(e)	s'étaient sauvé(e)s
3 passé simple		**10 passé antérieur**	
me sauvai	nous sauvâmes	me fus sauvé(e)	nous fûmes sauvé(e)s
te sauvas	vous sauvâtes	te fus sauvé(e)	vous fûtes sauvé(e)(s)
se sauva	se sauvèrent	se fut sauvé(e)	se furent sauvé(e)s
4 futur		**11 futur antérieur**	
me sauverai	nous sauverons	me serai sauvé(e)	nous serons sauvé(e)s
te sauveras	vous sauverez	te seras sauvé(e)	vous serez sauvé(e)(s)
se sauvera	se sauveront	se sera sauvé(e)	se seront sauvé(e)s
5 conditionnel		**12 conditionnel passé**	
me sauverais	nous sauverions	me serais sauvé(e)	nous serions sauvé(e)s
te sauverais	vous sauveriez	te serais sauvé(e)	vous seriez sauvé(e)(s)
se sauverait	se sauveraient	se serait sauvé(e)	se seraient sauvé(e)s
6 présent du subjonctif		**13 passé du subjonctif**	
me sauve	nous sauvions	me sois sauvé(e)	nous soyons sauvé(e)s
te sauves	vous sauviez	te sois sauvé(e)	vous soyez sauvé(e)(s)
se sauve	se sauvent	se soit sauvé(e)	se soient sauvé(e)s
7 imparfait du subjonctif		**14 plus-que-parfait du subjonctif**	
me sauvasse	nous sauvassions	me fusse sauvé(e)	nous fussions sauvé(e)s
te sauvasses	vous sauvassiez	te fusses sauvé(e)	vous fussiez sauvé(e)(s)
se sauvât	se sauvassent	se fût sauvé(e)	se fussent sauvé(e)s

Impératif
sauve-toi; ne te sauve pas
sauvons-nous; ne nous sauvons pas
sauvez-vous; ne vous sauvez pas

---

se sauver de prison   to escape from prison
sauvegarder   to safeguard
le sauvetage   life-saving, rescue
le sauve-qui-peut   panic

sauver   to rescue, to save
sauver la vie à qqn   to save
    someone's life
Je me sauve!   I'm out of here!

Irregular verb   to know (how)

The Seven Simple Tenses		The Seven Compound Tenses	
Singular	Plural	Singular	Plural
1 présent de l'indicatif		**8 passé composé**	
sais	savons	ai su	avons su
sais	savez	as su	avez su
sait	savent	a su	ont su
2 imparfait de l'indicatif		**9 plus-que-parfait de l'indicatif**	
savais	savions	avais su	avions su
savais	saviez	avais su	aviez su
savait	savaient	avait su	avaient su
3 passé simple		**10 passé antérieur**	
sus	sûmes	eus su	eûmes su
sus	sûtes	eus su	eûtes su
sut	surent	eut su	eurent su
4 futur		**11 futur antérieur**	
saurai	saurons	aurai su	aurons su
sauras	saurez	auras su	aurez su
saura	sauront	aura su	auront su
5 conditionnel		**12 conditionnel passé**	
saurais	saurions	aurais su	aurions su
saurais	sauriez	aurais su	auriez su
saurait	sauraient	aurait su	auraient su
6 présent du subjonctif		**13 passé du subjonctif**	
sache	sachions	aie su	ayons su
saches	sachiez	aies su	ayez su
sache	sachent	ait su	aient su
7 imparfait du subjonctif		**14 plus-que-parfait du subjonctif**	
susse	sussions	eusse su	eussions su
susses	sussiez	eusses su	eussiez su
sût	sussent	eût su	eussent su

Impératif
sache
sachons
sachez

---

le savoir   knowledge
le savoir-faire   know-how, tact, ability
avoir le savoir-vivre   to be well-mannered, well-bred
faire savoir   to inform
Pas que je sache.   Not to my knowledge.

savoir faire qqch   to know how to do something; **Savez-vous jouer du piano?**   Do you know how to play the piano?
Autant que je sache . . .
   As far as I know . . .
C'est à savoir.   That remains to be seen.

Note: Be careful! If you're talking about knowing a person, use **connaître**:
Je le connais.   I know him.

sembler	Part. pr. —	Part. passé **semblé**

to seem	Impersonal verb (See note.)

The Seven Simple Tenses	The Seven Compound Tenses

Singular	Singular
1 présent de l'indicatif **il semble**	8 passé composé **il a semblé**
2 imparfait de l'indicatif **il semblait**	9 plus-que-parfait de l'indicatif **il avait semblé**
3 passé simple **il sembla**	10 passé antérieur **il eut semblé**
4 futur **il semblera**	11 futur antérieur **il aura semblé**
5 conditionnel **il semblerait**	12 conditionnel passé **il aurait semblé**
6 présent du subjonctif **qu'il semble**	13 passé du subjonctif **qu'il ait semblé**
7 imparfait du subjonctif **qu'il semblât**	14 plus-que-parfait du subjonctif **qu'il eût semblé**

Impératif
—

Note: This verb has regular forms in all the tenses (like **ressembler** among the 301 verbs in this book) but much of the time it is used impersonally in the forms given above with **il** (it) as the subject.

Il me semble difficile.
  It seems difficult to me.

C'est ce qui me semble.
  That's what it looks like to me.

Irregular verb   to feel, to smell, to perceive

The Seven Simple Tenses		The Seven Compound Tenses	
Singular	Plural	Singular	Plural
1 présent de l'indicatif		8 passé composé	
sens	sentons	ai senti	avons senti
sens	sentez	as senti	avez senti
sent	sentent	a senti	ont senti
2 imparfait de l'indicatif		9 plus-que-parfait de l'indicatif	
sentais	sentions	avais senti	avions senti
sentais	sentiez	avais senti	aviez senti
sentait	sentaient	avait senti	avaient senti
3 passé simple		10 passé antérieur	
sentis	sentîmes	eus senti	eûmes senti
sentis	sentîtes	eus senti	eûtes senti
sentit	sentirent	eut senti	eurent senti
4 futur		11 futur antérieur	
sentirai	sentirons	aurai senti	aurons senti
sentiras	sentirez	auras senti	aurez senti
sentira	sentiront	aura senti	auront senti
5 conditionnel		12 conditionnel passé	
sentirais	sentirions	aurais senti	aurions senti
sentirais	sentiriez	aurais senti	auriez senti
sentirait	sentiraient	aurait senti	auraient senti
6 présent du subjonctif		13 passé du subjonctif	
sente	sentions	aie senti	ayons senti
sentes	sentiez	aies senti	ayez senti
sente	sentent	ait senti	aient senti
7 imparfait du subjonctif		14 plus-que-parfait du subjonctif	
sentisse	sentissions	eusse senti	eussions senti
sentisses	sentissiez	eusses senti	eussiez senti
sentît	sentissent	eût senti	eussent senti

Impératif
sens
sentons
sentez

---

un sentiment   feeling, sense, impression
sentimental, sentimentale   sentimental
la sentimentalité   sentimentality
sentir le chagrin   to feel sorrow
se sentir + adj.   to feel + adj.;
    Je me sens malade.   I feel sick.
sentir bon   to smell good
sentir mauvais   to smell bad
faire sentir qqch à qqn   to make
    someone feel something

se faire sentir   to make itself felt
ne se sentir pas bien   not to feel well; Je
    ne me sens pas bien.   I don't feel well.
un sentiment d'appartenance   feeling
    of membership, belonging
Ouvre la fenêtre, Claire. Ça sent le
    renfermé ici!   Open the window,
    Claire. It smells stuffy here!

servir	Part. pr. **servant**	Part. passé **servi**

to serve, to be useful

Irregular verb

The Seven Simple Tenses		The Seven Compound Tenses	
Singular	Plural	Singular	Plural
1 présent de l'indicatif		8 passé composé	
sers	servons	ai servi	avons servi
sers	servez	as servi	avez servi
sert	servent	a servi	ont servi
2 imparfait de l'indicatif		9 plus-que-parfait de l'indicatif	
servais	servions	avais servi	avions servi
servais	serviez	avais servi	aviez servi
servait	servaient	avait servi	avaient servi
3 passé simple		10 passé antérieur	
servis	servîmes	eus servi	eûmes servi
servis	servîtes	eus servi	eûtes servi
servit	servirent	eut servi	eurent servi
4 futur		11 futur antérieur	
servirai	servirons	aurai servi	aurons servi
serviras	servirez	auras servi	aurez servi
servira	serviront	aura servi	auront servi
5 conditionnel		12 conditionnel passé	
servirais	servirions	aurais servi	aurions servi
servirais	serviriez	aurais servi	auriez servi
servirait	serviraient	aurait servi	auraient servi
6 présent du subjonctif		13 passé du subjonctif	
serve	servions	aie servi	ayons servi
serves	serviez	aies servi	ayez servi
serve	servent	ait servi	aient servi
7 imparfait du subjonctif		14 plus-que-parfait du subjonctif	
servisse	servissions	eusse servi	eussions servi
servisses	servissiez	eusses servi	eussiez servi
servît	servissent	eût servi	eussent servi

Impératif
sers
servons
servez

---

le serveur   waiter
la serveuse   waitress
le service   service
une serviette   napkin
un serviteur   servant
la servitude   servitude
desservir   to clear off the table
un serveur   server (computer)

See also se servir.

se servir   to serve oneself, to help oneself
se servir de qqch   to use something, to
  avail oneself of something, to
  make use of something
servir à qqch   to be of some use
servir à rien   to be of no use; Cela
  ne sert à rien.   That serves no purpose.

Reflexive irregular verb   to serve oneself, to help oneself (to food and drink)

The Seven Simple Tenses		The Seven Compound Tenses	
Singular	Plural	Singular	Plural
1 présent de l'indicatif		**8 passé composé**	
me sers	nous servons	me suis servi(e)	nous sommes servi(e)s
te sers	vous servez	t'es servi(e)	vous êtes servi(e)(s)
se sert	se servent	s'est servi(e)	se sont servi(e)s
2 imparfait de l'indicatif		**9 plus-que-parfait de l'indicatif**	
me servais	nous servions	m'étais servi(e)	nous étions servi(e)s
te servais	vous serviez	t'étais servi(e)	vous étiez servi(e)(s)
se servait	se servaient	s'était servi(e)	s'étaient servi(e)s
3 passé simple		**10 passé antérieur**	
me servis	nous servîmes	me fus servi(e)	nous fûmes servi(e)s
te servis	vous servîtes	te fus servi(e)	vous fûtes servi(e)(s)
se servit	se servirent	se fut servi(e)	se furent servi(e)s
4 futur		**11 futur antérieur**	
me servirai	nous servirons	me serai servi(e)	nous serons servi(e)s
te serviras	vous servirez	te seras servi(e)	vous serez servi(e)(s)
se servira	se serviront	se sera servi(e)	se seront servi(e)s
5 conditionnel		**12 conditionnel passé**	
me servirais	nous servirions	me serais servi(e)	nous serions servi(e)s
te servirais	vous serviriez	te serais servi(e)	vous seriez servi(e)(s)
se servirait	se serviraient	se serait servi(e)	se seraient servi(e)s
6 présent du subjonctif		**13 passé du subjonctif**	
me serve	nous servions	me sois servi(e)	nous soyons servi(e)s
te serves	vous serviez	te sois servi(e)	vous soyez servi(e)(s)
se serve	se servent	se soit servi(e)	se soient servi(e)s
7 imparfait du subjonctif		**14 plus-que-parfait du subjonctif**	
me servisse	nous servissions	me fusse servi(e)	nous fussions servi(e)s
te servisses	vous servissiez	te fusses servi(e)	vous fussiez servi(e)(s)
se servît	se servissent	se fût servi(e)	se fussent servi(e)s

Impératif
sers-toi; ne te sers pas
servons-nous; ne nous servons pas
servez-vous; ne vous servez pas

---

un serviteur servant	se servir de qqch to use something, to
la servitude servitude	make use of something
le serveur waiter	se servir to serve oneself, to help
la serveuse waitress	oneself; Servez-vous, je vous en
le service service	prie! Help yourself, please!
une serviette napkin	Est-ce qu'on se sert seul dans ce restaurant?
	—Oui, c'est un restaurant self-service.

See also servir.

songer	Part. pr. songeant	Part. passé songé
to dream, to think		Regular -er verb endings: spelling change: retain the ge before a or o to keep the soft g sound of the verb.

The Seven Simple Tenses		The Seven Compound Tenses	
Singular	Plural	Singular	Plural
1 présent de l'indicatif		**8 passé composé**	
songe	songeons	ai songé	avons songé
songes	songez	as songé	avez songé
songe	songent	a songé	ont songé
2 imparfait de l'indicatif		**9 plus-que-parfait de l'indicatif**	
songeais	songions	avais songé	avions songé
songeais	songiez	avais songé	aviez songé
songeait	songeaient	avait songé	avaient songé
3 passé simple		**10 passé antérieur**	
songeai	songeâmes	eus songé	eûmes songé
songeas	songeâtes	eus songé	eûtes songé
songea	songèrent	eut songé	eurent songé
4 futur		**11 futur antérieur**	
songerai	songerons	aurai songé	aurons songé
songeras	songerez	auras songé	aurez songé
songera	songeront	aura songé	auront songé
5 conditionnel		**12 conditionnel passé**	
songerais	songerions	aurais songé	aurions songé
songerais	songeriez	aurais songé	auriez songé
songerait	songeraient	aurait songé	auraient songé
6 présent du subjonctif		**13 passé du subjonctif**	
songe	songions	aie songé	ayons songé
songes	songiez	aies songé	ayez songé
songe	songent	ait songé	aient songé
7 imparfait du subjonctif		**14 plus-que-parfait du subjonctif**	
songeasse	songeassions	eusse songé	eussions songé
songeasses	songeassiez	eusses songé	eussiez songé
songeât	songeassent	eût songé	eussent songé

	Impératif
	songe
	songeons
	songez

---

un songe   dream
un songeur, une songeuse   dreamer
songer à l'avenir   to think of the future
faire un songe   to have a dream
songer à faire qqch   to contemplate
  doing something

songer à   to think of something, to
  give thought to something
Songez-y bien!   Think it over carefully!

Regular -er verb   **to ring**

The Seven Simple Tenses		The Seven Compound Tenses	
Singular	Plural	Singular	Plural
1 présent de l'indicatif		8 passé composé	
sonne	sonnons	ai sonné	avons sonné
sonnes	sonnez	as sonné	avez sonné
sonne	sonnent	a sonné	ont sonné
2 imparfait de l'indicatif		9 plus-que-parfait de l'indicatif	
sonnais	sonnions	avais sonné	avions sonné
sonnais	sonniez	avais sonné	aviez sonné
sonnait	sonnaient	avait sonné	avaient sonné
3 passé simple		10 passé antérieur	
sonnai	sonnâmes	eus sonné	eûmes sonné
sonnas	sonnâtes	eus sonné	eûtes sonné
sonna	sonnèrent	eut sonné	eurent sonné
4 futur		11 futur antérieur	
sonnerai	sonnerons	aurai sonné	aurons sonné
sonneras	sonnerez	auras sonné	aurez sonné
sonnera	sonneront	aura sonné	auront sonné
5 conditionnel		12 conditionnel passé	
sonnerais	sonnerions	aurais sonné	aurions sonné
sonnerais	sonneriez	aurais sonné	auriez sonné
sonnerait	sonneraient	aurait sonné	auraient sonné
6 présent du subjonctif		13 passé du subjonctif	
sonne	sonnions	aie sonné	ayons sonné
sonnes	sonniez	aies sonné	ayez sonné
sonne	sonnent	ait sonné	aient sonné
7 imparfait du subjonctif		14 plus-que-parfait du subjonctif	
sonnasse	sonnassions	eusse sonné	eussions sonné
sonnasses	sonnassiez	eusses sonné	eussiez sonné
sonnât	sonnassent	eût sonné	eussent sonné

Impératif
sonne
sonnons
sonnez

une sonnerie ringing, chiming	sonner creux to sound hollow
une sonnette house bell, hand bell	une sonnerie d'alarme alarm bell
une sonnette électrique electric bell	faire sonner un mot to emphasize a word
le son sound, ringing	
une sonnette de nuit night bell	
la sonnerie du téléphone the ringing	
of the telephone	

sortir	Part. pr. **sortant**	Part. passé **sorti(e)(s)**

to go out, to leave   Irregular verb

The Seven Simple Tenses		The Seven Compound Tenses	
Singular	Plural	Singular	Plural
1 présent de l'indicatif		8 passé composé	
sors	sortons	suis sorti(e)	sommes sorti(e)s
sors	sortez	es sorti(e)	êtes sorti(e)(s)
sort	sortent	est sorti(e)	sont sorti(e)s
2 imparfait de l'indicatif		9 plus-que-parfait de l'indicatif	
sortais	sortions	étais sorti(e)	étions sorti(e)s
sortais	sortiez	étais sorti(e)	étiez sorti(e)(s)
sortait	sortaient	était sorti(e)	étaient sorti(e)s
3 passé simple		10 passé antérieur	
sortis	sortîmes	fus sorti(e)	fûmes sorti(e)s
sortis	sortîtes	fus sorti(e)	fûtes sorti(e)(s)
sortit	sortirent	fut sorti(e)	furent sorti(e)s
4 futur		11 futur antérieur	
sortirai	sortirons	serai sorti(e)	serons sorti(e)s
sortiras	sortirez	seras sorti(e)	serez sorti(e)(s)
sortira	sortiront	sera sorti(e)	seront sorti(e)s
5 conditionnel		12 conditionnel passé	
sortirais	sortirions	serais sorti(e)	serions sorti(e)s
sortirais	sortiriez	serais sorti(e)	seriez sorti(e)(s)
sortirait	sortiraient	serait sorti(e)	seraient sorti(e)s
6 présent du subjonctif		13 passé du subjonctif	
sorte	sortions	sois sorti(e)	soyons sorti(e)s
sortes	sortiez	sois sorti(e)	soyez sorti(e)(s)
sorte	sortent	soit sorti(e)	soient sorti(e)s
7 imparfait du subjonctif		14 plus-que-parfait du subjonctif	
sortisse	sortissions	fusse sorti(e)	fussions sorti(e)s
sortisses	sortissiez	fusses sorti(e)	fussiez sorti(e)(s)
sortît	sortissent	fût sorti(e)	fussent sorti(e)s

Impératif
sors
sortons
sortez

This verb is conjugated with **avoir** when it has a direct object.

Example: **Elle a sorti son mouchoir.**   She took out her handkerchief.
BUT: **Elle est sortie hier soir.**   She went out last night.

ressortir to go out again
(Note: **Ressortir** à means "to pertain to."
In this usage **ressortir** is conjugated
like a regular -ir verb.)
une sortie exit; **une sortie de secours**
emergency exit

sortir du lit to get out of bed
se sortir d'une situation to get oneself
out of a situation
**Le magicien a sorti un lapin de son
chapeau haut-de-forme.** The
magician took a rabbit out of his top hat.

Regular -er verb   to blow, to pant, to prompt (an actor/actress with a cue)

The Seven Simple Tenses		The Seven Compound Tenses	
Singular	Plural	Singular	Plural
1 présent de l'indicatif		8 passé composé	
souffle	soufflons	ai soufflé	avons soufflé
souffles	soufflez	as soufflé	avez soufflé
souffle	soufflent	a soufflé	ont soufflé
2 imparfait de l'indicatif		9 plus-que-parfait de l'indicatif	
soufflais	soufflions	avais soufflé	avions soufflé
soufflais	souffliez	avais soufflé	aviez soufflé
soufflait	soufflaient	avait soufflé	avaient soufflé
3 passé simple		10 passé antérieur	
soufflai	soufflâmes	eus soufflé	eûmes soufflé
soufflas	soufflâtes	eus soufflé	eûtes soufflé
souffla	soufflèrent	eut soufflé	eurent soufflé
4 futur		11 futur antérieur	
soufflerai	soufflerons	aurai soufflé	aurons soufflé
souffleras	soufflerez	auras soufflé	aurez soufflé
soufflera	souffleront	aura soufflé	auront soufflé
5 conditionnel		12 conditionnel passé	
soufflerais	soufflerions	aurais soufflé	aurions soufflé
soufflerais	souffleriez	aurais soufflé	auriez soufflé
soufflerait	souffleraient	aurait soufflé	auraient soufflé
6 présent du subjonctif		13 passé du subjonctif	
souffle	soufflions	aie soufflé	ayons soufflé
souffles	souffliez	aies soufflé	ayez soufflé
souffle	soufflent	ait soufflé	aient soufflé
7 imparfait du subjonctif		14 plus-que-parfait du subjonctif	
soufflasse	soufflassions	eusse soufflé	eussions soufflé
soufflasses	soufflassiez	eusses soufflé	eussiez soufflé
soufflât	soufflassent	eût soufflé	eussent soufflé

Impératif
souffle
soufflons
soufflez

---

le souffle   breath, breathing
à bout de souffle   out of breath
retenir son souffle   to hold one's breath
couper le souffle à qqn   to take someone's breath away
un soufflé au fromage   cheese soufflé
souffler le verre   to blow glass
le souffle cardiaque   heart murmur
une souffleuse   snow blower

souffrir   Part. pr. **souffrant**   Part. passé **souffert**

to suffer, to endure   Irregular verb

The Seven Simple Tenses		The Seven Compound Tenses	
Singular	Plural	Singular	Plural
1 présent de l'indicatif		8 passé composé	
souffre	**souffrons**	**ai souffert**	**avons souffert**
souffres	**souffrez**	**as souffert**	**avez souffert**
souffre	**souffrent**	**a souffert**	**ont souffert**
2 imparfait de l'indicatif		9 plus-que-parfait de l'indicatif	
souffrais	**souffrions**	**avais souffert**	**avions souffert**
souffrais	**souffriez**	**avais souffert**	**aviez souffert**
souffrait	**souffraient**	**avait souffert**	**avaient souffert**
3 passé simple		10 passé antérieur	
souffris	**souffrîmes**	**eus souffert**	**eûmes souffert**
souffris	**souffrîtes**	**eus souffert**	**eûtes souffert**
souffrit	**souffrirent**	**eut souffert**	**eurent souffert**
4 futur		11 futur antérieur	
souffrirai	**souffrirons**	**aurai souffert**	**aurons souffert**
souffriras	**souffrirez**	**auras souffert**	**aurez souffert**
souffrira	**souffriront**	**aura souffert**	**auront souffert**
5 conditionnel		12 conditionnel passé	
souffrirais	**souffririons**	**aurais souffert**	**aurions souffert**
souffrirais	**souffririez**	**aurais souffert**	**auriez souffert**
souffrirait	**souffriraient**	**aurait souffert**	**auraient souffert**
6 présent du subjonctif		13 passé du subjonctif	
souffre	**souffrions**	**aie souffert**	**ayons souffert**
souffres	**souffriez**	**aies souffert**	**ayez souffert**
souffre	**souffrent**	**ait souffert**	**aient souffert**
7 imparfait du subjonctif		14 plus-que-parfait du subjonctif	
souffrisse	**souffrissions**	**eusse souffert**	**eussions souffert**
souffrisses	**souffrissiez**	**eusses souffert**	**eussiez souffert**
souffrît	**souffrissent**	**eût souffert**	**eussent souffert**
		Impératif	
		souffre	
		souffrons	
		souffrez	

la souffrance suffering
souffrant, souffrante ailing, sick
souffreteux, souffreteuse sickly, feeble
souffrir le froid to withstand (endure) the cold
Cela me fait souffrir. That hurts me.

souffrir du froid to suffer from the cold
souffrir de la chaleur to suffer from the heat

Regular -er verb

to wish

The Seven Simple Tenses		The Seven Compound Tenses	
Singular	Plural	Singular	Plural
1 présent de l'indicatif		8 passé composé	
souhaite	**souhaitons**	**ai souhaité**	**avons souhaité**
souhaites	**souhaitez**	**as souhaité**	**avez souhaité**
souhaite	**souhaitent**	**a souhaité**	**ont souhaité**
2 imparfait de l'indicatif		9 plus-que-parfait de l'indicatif	
souhaitais	**souhaitions**	**avais souhaité**	**avions souhaité**
souhaitais	**souhaitiez**	**avais souhaité**	**aviez souhaité**
souhaitait	**souhaitaient**	**avait souhaité**	**avaient souhaité**
3 passé simple		10 passé antérieur	
souhaitai	**souhaitâmes**	**eus souhaité**	**eûmes souhaité**
souhaitas	**souhaitâtes**	**eus souhaité**	**eûtes souhaité**
souhaita	**souhaitèrent**	**eut souhaité**	**eurent souhaité**
4 futur		11 futur antérieur	
souhaiterai	**souhaiterons**	**aurai souhaité**	**aurons souhaité**
souhaiteras	**souhaiterez**	**auras souhaité**	**aurez souhaité**
souhaitera	**souhaiteront**	**aura souhaité**	**auront souhaité**
5 conditionnel		12 conditionnel passé	
souhaiterais	**souhaiterions**	**aurais souhaité**	**aurions souhaité**
souhaiterais	**souhaiteriez**	**aurais souhaité**	**auriez souhaité**
souhaiterait	**souhaiteraient**	**aurait souhaité**	**auraient souhaité**
6 présent du subjonctif		13 passé du subjonctif	
souhaite	**souhaitions**	**aie souhaité**	**ayons souhaité**
souhaites	**souhaitiez**	**aies souhaité**	**ayez souhaité**
souhaite	**souhaitent**	**ait souhaité**	**aient souhaité**
7 imparfait du subjonctif		14 plus-que-parfait du subjonctif	
souhaitasse	**souhaitassions**	**eusse souhaité**	**eussions souhaité**
souhaitasses	**souhaitassiez**	**eusses souhaité**	**eussiez souhaité**
souhaitât	**souhaitassent**	**eût souhaité**	**eussent souhaité**

Impératif
souhaite
souhaitons
souhaitez

---

un souhait   a wish
à souhait   to one's liking
souhaits de bonne année   New Year's
  greetings
souhaiter bon voyage à qqn   to wish
  someone a good trip

souhaiter la bienvenue à qqn   to
  welcome someone
souhaiter le bonjour à qqn   to greet
  someone
souhaitable   desirable

soumettre	Part. pr. soumettant	Part. passé soumis

to submit

Irregular verb

The Seven Simple Tenses		The Seven Compound Tenses	
Singular	Plural	Singular	Plural
1 présent de l'indicatif		8 passé composé	
soumets	**soumettons**	**ai soumis**	**avons soumis**
soumets	**soumettez**	**as soumis**	**avez soumis**
soumet	**soumettent**	**a soumis**	**ont soumis**
2 imparfait de l'indicatif		9 plus-que-parfait de l'indicatif	
soumettais	**soumettions**	**avais soumis**	**avions soumis**
soumettais	**soumettiez**	**avais soumis**	**aviez soumis**
soumettait	**soumettaient**	**avait soumis**	**avaient soumis**
3 passé simple		10 passé antérieur	
soumis	**soumîmes**	**eus soumis**	**eûmes soumis**
soumis	**soumîtes**	**eus soumis**	**eûtes soumis**
soumit	**soumirent**	**eut soumis**	**eurent soumis**
4 futur		11 futur antérieur	
soumettrai	**soumettrons**	**aurai soumis**	**aurons soumis**
soumettras	**soumettrez**	**auras soumis**	**aurez soumis**
soumettra	**soumettront**	**aura soumis**	**auront soumis**
5 conditionnel		12 conditionnel passé	
soumettrais	**soumettrions**	**aurais soumis**	**aurions soumis**
soumettrais	**soumettriez**	**aurais soumis**	**auriez soumis**
soumettrait	**soumettraient**	**aurait soumis**	**auraient soumis**
6 présent du subjonctif		13 passé du subjonctif	
soumette	**soumettions**	**aie soumis**	**ayons soumis**
soumettes	**soumettiez**	**aies soumis**	**ayez soumis**
soumette	**soumettent**	**ait soumis**	**aient soumis**
7 imparfait du subjonctif		14 plus-que-parfait du subjonctif	
soumisse	**soumissions**	**eusse soumis**	**eussions soumis**
soumisses	**soumissiez**	**eusses soumis**	**eussiez soumis**
soumît	**soumissent**	**eût soumis**	**eussent soumis**

	Impératif
	soumets
	soumettons
	soumettez

se soumettre à   to give in to, to comply with
se soumettre à une décision   to comply with a decision
la soumission   submission

See also **admettre**, **mettre**, **permettre**, **promettre**, and **remettre**.

Irregular verb   to smile

The Seven Simple Tenses		The Seven Compound Tenses	
Singular	Plural	Singular	Plural
1 présent de l'indicatif		**8 passé composé**	
souris	**sourions**	**ai souri**	**avons souri**
souris	**souriez**	**as souri**	**avez souri**
sourit	**sourient**	**a souri**	**ont souri**
2 imparfait de l'indicatif		**9 plus-que-parfait de l'indicatif**	
souriais	**souriions**	**avais souri**	**avions souri**
souriais	**souriiez**	**avais souri**	**aviez souri**
souriait	**souriaient**	**avait souri**	**avaient souri**
3 passé simple		**10 passé antérieur**	
souris	**sourîmes**	**eus souri**	**eûmes souri**
souris	**sourîtes**	**eus souri**	**eûtes souri**
sourit	**sourirent**	**eut souri**	**eurent souri**
4 futur		**11 futur antérieur**	
sourirai	**sourirons**	**aurai souri**	**aurons souri**
souriras	**sourirez**	**auras souri**	**aurez souri**
sourira	**souriront**	**aura souri**	**auront souri**
5 conditionnel		**12 conditionnel passé**	
sourirais	**souririons**	**aurais souri**	**aurions souri**
sourirais	**souririez**	**aurais souri**	**auriez souri**
sourirait	**souriraient**	**aurait souri**	**auraient souri**
6 présent du subjonctif		**13 passé du subjonctif**	
sourie	**souriions**	**aie souri**	**ayons souri**
souries	**souriiez**	**aies souri**	**ayez souri**
sourie	**sourient**	**ait souri**	**aient souri**
7 imparfait du subjonctif		**14 plus-que-parfait du subjonctif**	
sourisse	**sourissions**	**eusse souri**	**eussions souri**
sourisses	**sourissiez**	**eusses souri**	**eussiez souri**
sourît	**sourissent**	**eût souri**	**eussent souri**

Impératif
souris
sourions
souriez

---

un sourire   a smile
Gardez le sourire!   Keep smiling!
un large sourire   a broad smile
le rire   laughter
sourire à   to favor, to be favorable to,
   to smile on; Claudine est heureuse;
   la vie lui sourit.

See also **rire**.

faire un sourire à qqn   to give
   someone a smile (to smile at
   someone)
Souris à la vie, et la vie te sourira.
   Smile at life, and life will smile at
   you.

se souvenir	Part. pr. se souvenant	Part. passé souvenu(e)(s)

to remember, to recall   Irregular verb

The Seven Simple Tenses		The Seven Compound Tenses	

Singular	Plural	Singular	Plural

1 présent de l'indicatif

me souviens	nous souvenons
te souviens	vous souvenez
se souvient	se souviennent

8 passé composé

me suis	nous sommes	
t'es	vous êtes	+ souvenu(e)(s)
s'est	se sont	

2 imparfait de l'indicatif

me souvenais	nous souvenions
te souvenais	vous souveniez
se souvenait	se souvenaient

9 plus-que-parfait de l'indicatif

m'étais	nous étions	
t'étais	vous étiez	+ souvenu(e)(s)
s'était	s'étaient	

3 passé simple

me souvins	nous souvînmes
te souvins	vous souvîntes
se souvint	se souvinrent

10 passé antérieur

me fus	nous fûmes	
te fus	vous fûtes	+ souvenu(e)(s)
se fut	se furent	

4 futur

me souviendrai	nous souviendrons
te souviendras	vous souviendrez
se souviendra	se souviendront

11 futur antérieur

me serai	nous serons	
te seras	vous serez	+ souvenu(e)(s)
se sera	se seront	

5 conditionnel

me souviendrais	nous souviendrions
te souviendrais	vous souviendriez
se souviendrait	se souviendraient

12 conditionnel passé

me serais	nous serions	
te serais	vous seriez	+ souvenu(e)(s)
se serait	se seraient	

6 présent du subjonctif

me souvienne	nous souvenions
te souviennes	vous souveniez
se souvienne	se souviennent

13 passé du subjonctif

me sois	nous soyons	
te sois	vous soyez	+ souvenu(e)(s)
se soit	se soient	

7 imparfait du subjonctif

me souvinsse	nous souvinssions
te souvinsses	vous souvinssiez
se souvînt	se souvinssent

14 plus-que-parfait du subjonctif

me fusse	nous fussions	
te fusses	vous fussiez +	souvenu(e)(s)
se fût	se fussent	

Impératif
souviens-toi; ne te souviens pas
souvenons-nous; ne nous souvenons pas
souvenez-vous; ne vous souvenez pas

un souvenir   souvenir, remembrance
Je m'en souviendrai!   I'll remember that! I won't forget that!
se souvenir de qqn ou de qqch   to remember someone or something
en souvenir de   in remembrance of
Je me souviens.   I remember. (Motto of the Province of Québec, Canada)

See also **devenir**, **revenir**, and **venir**.

Impersonal verb	to suffice, to be sufficient, to be enough
The Seven Simple Tenses	The Seven Compound Tenses

Singular	Singular
1 présent de l'indicatif **il suffit**	8 passé composé **il a suffi**
2 imparfait de l'indicatif **il suffisait**	9 plus-que-parfait de l'indicatif **il avait suffi**
3 passé simple **il suffit**	10 passé antérieur **il eut suffi**
4 futur **il suffira**	11 futur antérieur **il aura suffi**
5 conditionnel **il suffirait**	12 conditionnel passé **il aurait suffi**
6 présent du subjonctif **qu'il suffise**	13 passé du subjonctif **qu'il ait suffi**
7 imparfait du subjonctif **qu'il suffit**	14 plus-que-parfait du subjonctif **qu'il eût suffi**

Impératif
Qu'il suffise!   (Enough!)

---

la suffisance   sufficiency
suffisamment   sufficiently
Cela suffit!   That's quite enough!
Suffit!   Enough! Stop it!
Ça ne te suffit pas?   That's not enough
   for you?
Y a-t-il suffisamment à manger?
   Is there enough to eat?

Ma famille suffit à mon bonheur.
   My family is enough for my happiness.

suivre	Part. pr. **suivant**	Part. passé **suivi**
to follow		Irregular verb

The Seven Simple Tenses		The Seven Compound Tenses	
Singular	Plural	Singular	Plural

1 présent de l'indicatif		8 passé composé	
suis	suivons	ai suivi	avons suivi
suis	suivez	as suivi	avez suivi
suit	suivent	a suivi	ont suivi

2 imparfait de l'indicatif		9 plus-que-parfait de l'indicatif	
suivais	suivions	avais suivi	avions suivi
suivais	suiviez	avais suivi	aviez suivi
suivait	suivaient	avait suivi	avaient suivi

3 passé simple		10 passé antérieur	
suivis	suivîmes	eus suivi	eûmes suivi
suivis	suivîtes	eus suivi	eûtes suivi
suivit	suivirent	eut suivi	eurent suivi

4 futur		11 futur antérieur	
suivrai	suivrons	aurai suivi	aurons suivi
suivras	suivrez	auras suivi	aurez suivi
suivra	suivront	aura suivi	auront suivi

5 conditionnel		12 conditionnel passé	
suivrais	suivrions	aurais suivi	aurions suivi
suivrais	suivriez	aurais suivi	auriez suivi
suivrait	suivraient	aurait suivi	auraient suivi

6 présent du subjonctif		13 passé du subjonctif	
suive	suivions	aie suivi	ayons suivi
suives	suiviez	aies suivi	ayez suivi
suive	suivent	ait suivi	aient suivi

7 imparfait du subjonctif		14 plus-que-parfait du subjonctif	
suivisse	suivissions	eusse suivi	eussions suivi
suivisses	suivissiez	eusses suivi	eussiez suivi
suivît	suivissent	eût suivi	eussent suivi

Impératif
suis
suivons
suivez

suivant according to
suivant que... according as...
la suite continuation
à la suite de coming after
de suite in succession, right away
à suivre to be continued
Je vais suivre un cours de français
cet été. I'm going to take a course
in French this summer.

le jour suivant on the following day
les questions suivantes the following
questions
tout de suite immediately
suivre un cours to take a course
suivre un régime to be on a diet

278

Reflexive irregular verb   to be silent, to be quiet, not to speak

The Seven Simple Tenses		The Seven Compound Tenses	
Singular	Plural	Singular	Plural
1 présent de l'indicatif		**8 passé composé**	
me tais	nous taisons	me suis tu(e)	nous sommes tu(e)s
te tais	vous taisez	t'es tu(e)	vous êtes tu(e)(s)
se tait	se taisent	s'est tu(e)	se sont tu(e)s
2 imparfait de l'indicatif		**9 plus-que-parfait de l'indicatif**	
me taisais	nous taisions	m'étais tu(e)	nous étions tu(e)s
te taisais	vous taisiez	t'étais tu(e)	vous étiez tu(e)(s)
se taisait	se taisaient	s'était tu(e)	s'étaient tu(e)s
3 passé simple		**10 passé antérieur**	
me tus	nous tûmes	me fus tu(e)	nous fûmes tu(e)s
te tus	vous tûtes	te fus tu(e)	vous fûtes tu(e)(s)
se tut	se turent	se fut tu(e)	se furent tu(e)s
4 futur		**11 futur antérieur**	
me tairai	nous tairons	me serai tu(e)	nous serons tu(e)s
te tairas	vous tairez	te seras tu(e)	vous serez tu(e)(s)
se taira	se tairont	se sera tu(e)	se seront tu(e)s
5 conditionnel		**12 conditionnel passé**	
me tairais	nous tairions	me serais tu(e)	nous serions tu(e)s
te tairais	vous tairiez	te serais tu(e)	vous seriez tu(e)(s)
se tairait	se tairaient	se serait tu(e)	se seraient tu(e)s
6 présent du subjonctif		**13 passé du subjonctif**	
me taise	nous taisions	me sois tu(e)	nous soyons tu(e)s
te taises	vous taisiez	te sois tu(e)	vous soyez tu(e)(s)
se taise	se taisent	se soit tu(e)	se soient tu(e)s
7 imparfait du subjonctif		**14 plus-que-parfait du subjonctif**	
me tusse	nous tussions	me fusse tu(e)	nous fussions tu(e)s
te tusses	vous tussiez	te fusses tu(e)	vous fussiez tu(e)(s)
se tût	se tussent	se fût tu(e)	se fussent tu(e)s

Impératif
tais-toi; ne te tais pas
taisons-nous; ne nous taisons pas
taisez-vous; ne vous taisez pas

Marie, tais-toi! Tu es trop bavarde.   Marie, be quiet! You're too talkative.
Taisez-vous!   Be quiet!
Il est bon de parler et meilleur de se taire.   Speech is silver, silence is golden.

téléphoner	Part. pr. téléphonant	Part. passé téléphoné

to telephone   Regular -er verb

The Seven Simple Tenses		The Seven Compound Tenses	
Singular	Plural	Singular	Plural

1 présent de l'indicatif

téléphone	téléphonons
téléphones	téléphonez
téléphone	téléphonent

8 passé composé

ai téléphoné	avons téléphoné
as téléphoné	avez téléphoné
a téléphoné	ont téléphoné

2 imparfait de l'indicatif

téléphonais	téléphonions
téléphonais	téléphoniez
téléphonait	téléphonaient

9 plus-que-parfait de l'indicatif

avais téléphoné	avions téléphoné
avais téléphoné	aviez téléphoné
avait téléphoné	avaient téléphoné

3 passé simple

téléphonai	téléphonâmes
téléphonas	téléphonâtes
téléphona	téléphonèrent

10 passé antérieur

eus téléphoné	eûmes téléphoné
eus téléphoné	eûtes téléphoné
eut téléphoné	eurent téléphoné

4 futur

téléphonerai	téléphonerons
téléphoneras	téléphonerez
téléphonera	téléphoneront

11 futur antérieur

aurai téléphoné	aurons téléphoné
auras téléphoné	aurez téléphoné
aura téléphoné	auront téléphoné

5 conditionnel

téléphonerais	téléphonerions
téléphonerais	téléphoneriez
téléphonerait	téléphoneraient

12 conditionnel passé

aurais téléphoné	aurions téléphoné
aurais téléphoné	auriez téléphoné
aurait téléphoné	auraient téléphoné

6 présent du subjonctif

téléphone	téléphonions
téléphones	téléphoniez
téléphone	téléphonent

13 passé du subjonctif

aie téléphoné	ayons téléphoné
aies téléphoné	ayez téléphoné
ait téléphoné	aient téléphoné

7 imparfait du subjonctif

téléphonasse	téléphonassions
téléphonasses	téléphonassiez
téléphonât	téléphonassent

14 plus-que-parfait du subjonctif

eusse téléphoné	eussions téléphoné
eusses téléphoné	eussiez téléphoné
eût téléphoné	eussent téléphoné

Impératif
téléphone
téléphonons
téléphonez

---

le téléphone telephone
téléphonique telephonic
téléphoniquement telephonically
  (by telephone)
un, une téléphoniste telephone operator
téléphoner à qqn to telephone someone
Marie? Je lui ai téléphoné hier.
  Mary? I telephoned her yesterday.

le téléphone rouge hotline
un téléphone cellulaire, un téléphone
  portable, un portable cell phone
  (Note: Un portable can also refer to
  a laptop computer.)
faire un appel téléphonique
  to make a telephone call

Irregular verb   to hold, to grasp

The Seven Simple Tenses		The Seven Compound Tenses	
Singular	Plural	Singular	Plural
1 présent de l'indicatif		**8 passé composé**	
tiens	tenons	ai tenu	avons tenu
tiens	tenez	as tenu	avez tenu
tient	tiennent	a tenu	ont tenu
2 imparfait de l'indicatif		**9 plus-que-parfait de l'indicatif**	
tenais	tenions	avais tenu	avions tenu
tenais	teniez	avais tenu	aviez tenu
tenait	tenaient	avait tenu	avaient tenu
3 passé simple		**10 passé antérieur**	
tins	tînmes	eus tenu	eûmes tenu
tins	tîntes	eus tenu	eûtes tenu
tint	tinrent	eut tenu	eurent tenu
4 futur		**11 futur antérieur**	
tiendrai	tiendrons	aurai tenu	aurons tenu
tiendras	tiendrez	auras tenu	aurez tenu
tiendra	tiendront	aura tenu	auront tenu
5 conditionnel		**12 conditionnel passé**	
tiendrais	tiendrions	aurais tenu	aurions tenu
tiendrais	tiendriez	aurais tenu	auriez tenu
tiendrait	tiendraient	aurait tenu	auraient tenu
6 présent du subjonctif		**13 passé du subjonctif**	
tienne	tenions	aie tenu	ayons tenu
tiennes	teniez	aies tenu	ayez tenu
tienne	tiennent	ait tenu	aient tenu
7 imparfait du subjonctif		**14 plus-que-parfait du subjonctif**	
tinsse	tinssions	eusse tenu	eussions tenu
tinsses	tinssiez	eusses tenu	eussiez tenu
tînt	tinssent	eût tenu	eussent tenu

Impératif
tiens
tenons
tenez

---

tenir de qqn   to take after (to favor) someone; tenir le pari   to take on the bet
   Robert tient de son père.   Robert takes Tiens! Voilà Bob!
   after his father.   Look! There's Bob!
tenir de bonne source   to have on good authority
tenir à qqch   to cherish something
Ma nouvelle voiture a une excellente tenue de route.
   My new car holds the road (handles) very well.
Tenez votre droite.   Keep to your right.

Proverb: **Il vaut mieux "je tiens" que "je tiendrai."**   A bird in the hand is worth
   two in the bush. (It's better to say "I hold" than "I will hold.")

terminer　　　　　Part. pr. **terminant**　　　　Part. passé **terminé**

to terminate, to finish, to end

Regular -er verb

The Seven Simple Tenses		The Seven Compound Tenses	
Singular	Plural	Singular	Plural
1　présent de l'indicatif		8　passé composé	
termine	**terminons**	**ai terminé**	**avons teminé**
termines	**terminez**	**as terminé**	**avez terminé**
termine	**terminent**	**a terminé**	**ont terminé**
2　imparfait de l'indicatif		9　plus-que-parfait de l'indicatif	
terminais	**terminions**	**avais terminé**	**avions terminé**
terminais	**terminiez**	**avais terminé**	**aviez terminé**
terminait	**terminaient**	**avait terminé**	**avaient terminé**
3　passé simple		10　passé antérieur	
terminai	**terminâmes**	**eus terminé**	**eûmes terminé**
terminas	**terminâtes**	**eus terminé**	**eûtes terminé**
termina	**terminèrent**	**eut terminé**	**eurent terminé**
4　futur		11　futur antérieur	
terminerai	**terminerons**	**aurai terminé**	**aurons terminé**
termineras	**terminerez**	**auras terminé**	**aurez terminé**
terminera	**termineront**	**aura terminé**	**auront terminé**
5　conditionnel		12　conditionnel passé	
terminerais	**terminerions**	**aurais terminé**	**aurions terminé**
terminerais	**termineriez**	**aurais terminé**	**auriez terminé**
terminerait	**termineraient**	**aurait terminé**	**auraient terminé**
6　présent du subjonctif		13　passé du subjonctif	
termine	**terminions**	**aie terminé**	**ayons terminé**
termines	**terminiez**	**aies terminé**	**ayez terminé**
termine	**terminent**	**ait terminé**	**aient terminé**
7　imparfait du subjonctif		14　plus-que-parfait du subjonctif	
terminasse	**terminassions**	**eusse terminé**	**eussions terminé**
terminasses	**terminassiez**	**eusses terminé**	**eussiez terminé**
terminât	**terminassent**	**eût terminé**	**eussent terminé**

	Impératif
	termine
	terminons
	terminez

---

terminal, terminale terminal
la terminaison ending, termination
terminable terminable
interminable interminable, endless
exterminer to exterminate
se terminer to end (itself)
se terminer en to end in; un verbe qui se termine en *er . . .* a verb that ends in *er . . .*

terminer une session to log off (computer)
J'attends qu'elle termine le travail. I'm waiting for her to finish the work.
Les vacances d'été se terminent demain. Summer vacation ends tomorrow.

Regular -er verb   to fall

The Seven Simple Tenses		The Seven Compound Tenses	
Singular	Plural	Singular	Plural
1 présent de l'indicatif		8 passé composé	
tombe	tombons	suis tombé(e)	sommes tombé(e)s
tombes	tombez	es tombé(e)	êtes tombé(e)(s)
tombe	tombent	est tombé(e)	sont tombé(e)s
2 imparfait de l'indicatif		9 plus-que-parfait de l'indicatif	
tombais	tombions	étais tombé(e)	étions tombé(e)s
tombais	tombiez	étais tombé(e)	étiez tombé(e)(s)
tombait	tombaient	était tombé(e)	étaient tombé(e)s
3 passé simple		10 passé antérieur	
tombai	tombâmes	fus tombé(e)	fûmes tombé(e)s
tombas	tombâtes	fus tombé(e)	fûtes tombé(e)(s)
tomba	tombèrent	fut tombé(e)	furent tombé(e)s
4 futur		11 futur antérieur	
tomberai	tomberons	serai tombé(e)	serons tombé(e)s
tomberas	tomberez	seras tombé(e)	serez tombé(e)(s)
tombera	tomberont	sera tombé(e)	seront tombé(e)s
5 conditionnel		12 conditionnel passé	
tomberais	tomberions	serais tombé(e)	serions tombé(e)s
tomberais	tomberiez	serais tombé(e)	seriez tombé(e)(s)
tomberait	tomberaient	serait tombé(e)	seraient tombé(e)s
6 présent du subjonctif		13 passé du subjonctif	
tombe	tombions	sois tombé(e)	soyons tombé(e)s
tombes	tombiez	sois tombé(e)	soyez tombé(e)(s)
tombe	tombent	soit tombé(e)	soient tombé(e)s
7 imparfait du subjonctif		14 plus-que-parfait du subjonctif	
tombasse	tombassions	fusse tombé(e)	fussions tombé(e)s
tombasses	tombassiez	fusses tombé(e)	fussiez tombé(e)(s)
tombât	tombassent	fût tombé(e)	fussent tombé(e)s

	Impératif
	tombe
	tombons
	tombez

---

tomber amoureux (amoureuse) de qqn
   to fall in love with someone
tomber sur   to run into, to come across
laisser tomber   to drop
tomber malade   to fall sick
faire tomber   to knock down
retomber   to fall again
tomber en panne   to break down, to
   crash (computer)

tomber dans les pommes   to pass out,
   to faint
**David est tombé de l'échelle et il s'est
   cassé le bras.**   David fell from the
   ladder and broke his arm.
Cela tombe bien.   That's fortunate.
Il tombe des clous.   It's raining cats and
   dogs. (Nails are falling.)

toucher

Part. pr. **touchant**   Part. passé **touché**

to touch, to affect

Regular -er verb

The Seven Simple Tenses		The Seven Compound Tenses	
Singular	Plural	Singular	Plural
1 présent de l'indicatif		8 passé composé	
touche	touchons	ai touché	avons touché
touches	touchez	as touché	avez touché
touche	touchent	a touché	ont touché
2 imparfait de l'indicatif		9 plus-que-parfait de l'indicatif	
touchais	touchions	avais touché	avions touché
touchais	touchiez	avais touché	aviez touché
touchait	touchaient	avait touché	avaient touché
3 passé simple		10 passé antérieur	
touchai	touchâmes	eus touché	eûmes touché
touchas	touchâtes	eus touché	eûtes touché
toucha	touchèrent	eut touché	eurent touché
4 futur		11 futur antérieur	
toucherai	toucherons	aurai touché	aurons touché
toucheras	toucherez	auras touché	aurez touché
touchera	toucheront	aura touché	auront touché
5 conditionnel		12 conditionnel passé	
toucherais	toucherions	aurais touché	aurions touché
toucherais	toucheriez	aurais touché	auriez touché
toucherait	toucheraient	aurait touché	auraient touché
6 présent du subjonctif		13 passé du subjonctif	
touche	touchions	aie touché	ayons touché
touches	touchiez	aies touché	ayez touché
touche	touchent	ait touché	aient touché
7 imparfait du subjonctif		14 plus-que-parfait du subjonctif	
touchasse	touchassions	eusse touché	eussions touché
touchasses	touchassiez	eusses touché	eussiez touché
touchât	touchassent	eût touché	eussent touché
		Impératif	
		touche	
		touchons	
		touchez	

une personne qui touche à tout
  a meddlesome person
Touchez là! Put it there! Shake!
toucher à qqch to touch something
N'y touchez pas! Don't touch!
retoucher to touch up
toucher un chèque to cash a check
un, une touche-à-tout a meddler

le toucher touch, feeling, sense of touch
toucher de l'argent to get some money
Cela me touche profondément.
  That touches me deeply.

Regular -er verb　　　　　　　　　　　　　　　　　　　　　　to turn

The Seven Simple Tenses　　　　　|　The Seven Compound Tenses

Singular	Plural	Singular	Plural
1 présent de l'indicatif		**8 passé composé**	
tourne	**tournons**	**ai tourné**	**avons tourné**
tournes	**tournez**	**as tourné**	**avez tourné**
tourne	**tournent**	**a tourné**	**ont tourné**
2 imparfait de l'indicatif		**9 plus-que-parfait de l'indicatif**	
tournais	**tournions**	**avais tourné**	**avions tourné**
tournais	**tourniez**	**avais tourné**	**aviez tourné**
tournait	**tournaient**	**avait tourné**	**avaient tourné**
3 passé simple		**10 passé antérieur**	
tournai	**tournâmes**	**eus tourné**	**eûmes tourné**
tournas	**tournâtes**	**eus tourné**	**eûtes tourné**
tourna	**tournèrent**	**eut tourné**	**eurent tourné**
4 futur		**11 futur antérieur**	
tournerai	**tournerons**	**aurai tourné**	**aurons tourné**
tourneras	**tournerez**	**auras tourné**	**aurez tourné**
tournera	**tourneront**	**aura tourné**	**auront tourné**
5 conditionnel		**12 conditionnel passé**	
tournerais	**tournerions**	**aurais tourné**	**aurions tourné**
tournerais	**tourneriez**	**aurais tourné**	**auriez tourné**
tournerait	**tourneraient**	**aurait tourné**	**auraient tourné**
6 présent du subjonctif		**13 passé du subjonctif**	
tourne	**tournions**	**aie tourné**	**ayons tourné**
tournes	**tourniez**	**aies tourné**	**ayez tourné**
tourne	**tournent**	**ait tourné**	**aient tourné**
7 imparfait du subjonctif		**14 plus-que-parfait du subjonctif**	
tournasse	**tournassions**	**eusse tourné**	**eussions tourné**
tournasses	**tournassiez**	**eusses tourné**	**eussiez tourné**
tournât	**tournassent**	**eût tourné**	**eussent tourné**

Impératif
tourne
tournons
tournez

se tourner to turn around	**retourner** to return
tourner qqn en ridicule to ridicule someone	**tourner l'estomac à qqn** to turn someone's stomach
un tourne-disque record player (**des tourne-disques**)	**faire une tournée** to go on a tour
un tournevis screwdriver	**tourner autour du pot** to beat around the bush

See also **retourner**.

traduire   Part. pr. **traduisant**   Part. passé **traduit**

to translate   Irregular verb

The Seven Simple Tenses		The Seven Compound Tenses	
Singular	Plural	Singular	Plural
1 présent de l'indicatif		8 passé composé	
traduis	traduisons	ai traduit	avons traduit
traduis	traduisez	as traduit	avez traduit
traduit	traduisent	a traduit	ont traduit
2 imparfait de l'indicatif		9 plus-que-parfait de l'indicatif	
traduisais	traduisions	avais traduit	avions traduit
traduisais	traduisiez	avais traduit	aviez traduit
traduisait	traduisaient	avait traduit	avaient traduit
3 passé simple		10 passé antérieur	
traduisis	traduisîmes	eus traduit	eûmes traduit
traduisis	traduisîtes	eus traduit	eûtes traduit
traduisit	traduisirent	eut traduit	eurent traduit
4 futur		11 futur antérieur	
traduirai	traduirons	aurai traduit	aurons traduit
traduiras	traduirez	auras traduit	aurez traduit
traduira	traduiront	aura traduit	auront traduit
5 conditionnel		12 conditionnel passé	
traduirais	traduirions	aurais traduit	aurions traduit
traduirais	traduiriez	aurais traduit	auriez traduit
traduirait	traduiraient	aurait traduit	auraient traduit
6 présent du subjonctif		13 passé du subjonctif	
traduise	traduisions	aie traduit	ayons traduit
traduises	traduisiez	aies traduit	ayez traduit
traduise	traduisent	ait traduit	aient traduit
7 imparfait du subjonctif		14 plus-que-parfait du subjonctif	
traduisisse	traduisissions	eusse traduit	eussions traduit
traduisisses	traduisissiez	eusses traduit	eussiez traduit
traduisît	traduisissent	eût traduit	eussent traduit

Impératif
traduis
traduisons
traduisez

---

un **traducteur,** une **traductrice**
  translator
une **traduction** a translation
traduisible translatable
une **traduction littérale** a literal
  translation
une **traduction libre** a free translation

se **traduire** to be translated; Cette
  phrase se traduit facilement.
  This sentence is easily translated.
une **traduction fidèle** a faithful
  translation
traduire du français en anglais
  to translate from French to English
traduire de l'anglais en français
  to translate from English to French

Regular -er verb   to work

The Seven Simple Tenses		The Seven Compound Tenses	
Singular	Plural	Singular	Plural

1 présent de l'indicatif

travaille	travaillons		
travailles	travaillez		
travaille	travaillent		

8 passé composé

ai travaillé	avons travaillé
as travaillé	avez travaillé
a travaillé	ont travaillé

2 imparfait de l'indicatif

travaillais	travaillions
travaillais	travailliez
travaillait	travaillaient

9 plus-que-parfait de l'indicatif

avais travaillé	avions travaillé
avais travaillé	aviez travaillé
avait travaillé	avaient travaillé

3 passé simple

travaillai	travaillâmes
travaillas	travaillâtes
travailla	travaillèrent

10 passé antérieur

eus travaillé	eûmes travaillé
eus travaillé	eûtes travaillé
eut travaillé	eurent travaillé

4 futur

travaillerai	travaillerons
travailleras	travaillerez
travaillera	travailleront

11 futur antérieur

aurai travaillé	aurons travaillé
auras travaillé	aurez travaillé
aura travaillé	auront travaillé

5 conditionnel

travaillerais	travaillerions
travaillerais	travailleriez
travaillerait	travailleraient

12 conditionnel passé

aurais travaillé	aurions travaillé
aurais travaillé	auriez travaillé
aurait travaillé	auraient travaillé

6 présent du subjonctif

travaille	travaillions
travailles	travailliez
travaille	travaillent

13 passé du subjonctif

aie travaillé	ayons travaillé
aies travaillé	ayez travaillé
ait travaillé	aient travaillé

7 imparfait du subjonctif

travaillasse	travaillassions
travaillasses	travaillassiez
travaillât	travaillassent

14 plus-que-parfait du subjonctif

eusse travaillé	eussions travaillé
eusses travaillé	eussiez travaillé
eût travaillé	eussent travaillé

Impératif
travaille
travaillons
travaillez

---

travailleur, travailleuse   industrious;
  worker
être sans travail   to be out of work
faire travailler son argent   to put one's
  money to work (to earn interest)
Madame Reed fait travailler ses élèves dans la classe de français.
  Mrs. Reed makes her students work in French class.

le travail   work, labor,
  travail (les travaux)
les travaux publics   public works
les vêtements de travail   work clothes

Proverb: **Choisissez un travail que vous aimez et vous n'aurez pas à travailler
  un seul jour de votre vie.**   Choose a job you love and you will never have
  to work a day in your life. (Confucius)

traverser	Part. pr. traversant	Part. passé traversé

to traverse, to cross   Regular -er verb

The Seven Simple Tenses		The Seven Compound Tenses	
Singular	Plural	Singular	Plural
1 présent de l'indicatif		**8 passé composé**	
traverse	traversons	ai traversé	avons traversé
traverses	traversez	as traversé	avez traversé
traverse	traversent	a traversé	ont traversé
2 imparfait de l'indicatif		**9 plus-que-parfait de l'indicatif**	
traversais	traversions	avais traversé	avions traversé
traversais	traversiez	avais traversé	aviez traversé
traversait	traversaient	avait traversé	avaient traversé
3 passé simple		**10 passé antérieur**	
traversai	traversâmes	eus traversé	eûmes traversé
traversas	traversâtes	eus traversé	eûtes traversé
traversa	traversèrent	eut traversé	eurent traversé
4 futur		**11 futur antérieur**	
traverserai	traverserons	aurai traversé	aurons traversé
traverseras	traverserez	auras traversé	aurez traversé
traversera	traverseront	aura traversé	auront traversé
5 conditionnel		**12 conditionnel passé**	
traverserais	traverserions	aurais traversé	aurions traversé
traverserais	traverseriez	aurais traversé	auriez traversé
traverserait	traverseraient	aurait traversé	auraient traversé
6 présent du subjonctif		**13 passé du subjonctif**	
traverse	traversions	aie traversé	ayons traversé
traverses	traversiez	aies traversé	ayez traversé
traverse	traversent	ait traversé	aient traversé
7 imparfait du subjonctif		**14 plus-que-parfait du subjonctif**	
traversasse	traversassions	eusse traversé	eussions traversé
traversasses	traversassiez	eusses traversé	eussiez traversé
traversât	traversassent	eût traversé	eussent traversé
		Impératif	
		traverse	
		traversons	
		traversez	

la traversée the crossing	une traversée de voie railroad crossing
à travers through	traverser la foule to make one's way
de travers askew, awry, crooked	through the crowd
marcher de travers to stagger	

Part. pr. trouvant	Part. passé trouvé		trouver
Regular -er verb			to find

The Seven Simple Tenses		The Seven Compound Tenses	
Singular	Plural	Singular	Plural

1 présent de l'indicatif		8 passé composé	
trouve	trouvons	ai trouvé	avons trouvé
trouves	trouvez	as trouvé	avez trouvé
trouve	trouvent	a trouvé	ont trouvé

2 imparfait de l'indicatif		9 plus-que-parfait de l'indicatif	
trouvais	trouvions	avais trouvé	avions trouvé
trouvais	trouviez	avais trouvé	aviez trouvé
trouvait	trouvaient	avait trouvé	avaient trouvé

3 passé simple		10 passé antérieur	
trouvai	trouvâmes	eus trouvé	eûmes trouvé
trouvas	trouvâtes	eus trouvé	eûtes trouvé
trouva	trouvèrent	eut trouvé	eurent trouvé

4 futur		11 futur antérieur	
trouverai	trouverons	aurai trouvé	aurons trouvé
trouveras	trouverez	auras trouvé	aurez trouvé
trouvera	trouveront	aura trouvé	auront trouvé

5 conditionnel		12 conditionnel passé	
trouverais	trouverions	aurais trouvé	aurions trouvé
trouverais	trouveriez	aurais trouvé	auriez trouvé
trouverait	trouveraient	aurait trouvé	auraient trouvé

6 présent du subjonctif		13 passé du subjonctif	
trouve	trouvions	aie trouvé	ayons trouvé
trouves	trouviez	aies trouvé	ayez trouvé
trouve	trouvent	ait trouvé	aient trouvé

7 imparfait du subjonctif		14 plus-que-parfait du subjonctif	
trouvasse	trouvassions	eusse trouvé	eussions trouvé
trouvasses	trouvassiez	eusses trouvé	eussiez trouvé
trouvât	trouvassent	eût trouvé	eussent trouvé

	Impératif
	trouve
	trouvons
	trouvez

J'ai une nouvelle voiture; comment la trouvez-vous?
    I have a new car; how do you like it?
trouver un emploi   to find a job
trouver bon de faire qqch   to think fit to do something
retrouver   to find again, to recover, to retrieve
trouver porte close, trouver visage de bois   not to find anyone answering the
    door after knocking
le bureau d'objets trouvés   lost and found

See also se trouver.

se trouver   Part. pr. **se trouvant**   Part. passé **trouvé(e)(s)**

to be located, to be situated   Reflexive regular -er verb

The Seven Simple Tenses		The Seven Compound Tenses	
Singular	Plural	Singular	Plural
1 présent de l'indicatif		8 passé composé	
me trouve	nous trouvons	me suis trouvé(e)	nous sommes trouvé(e)s
te trouves	vous trouvez	t'es trouvé(e)	vous êtes trouvé(e)(s)
se trouve	se trouvent	s'est trouvé(e)	se sont trouvé(e)s
2 imparfait de l'indicatif		9 plus-que-parfait de l'indicatif	
me trouvais	nous trouvions	m'étais trouvé(e)	nous étions trouvé(e)s
te trouvais	vous trouviez	t'étais trouvé(e)	vous étiez trouvé(e)(s)
se trouvait	se trouvaient	s'était trouvé(e)	s'étaient trouvé(e)s
3 passé simple		10 passé antérieur	
me trouvai	nous trouvâmes	me fus trouvé(e)	nous fûmes trouvé(e)s
te trouvas	vous trouvâtes	te fus trouvé(e)	vous fûtes trouvé(e)(s)
se trouva	se trouvèrent	se fut trouvé(e)	se furent trouvé(e)s
4 futur		11 futur antérieur	
me trouverai	nous trouverons	me serai trouvé(e)	nous serons trouvé(e)s
te trouveras	vous trouverez	te seras trouvé(e)	vous serez trouvé(e)(s)
se trouvera	se trouveront	se sera trouvé(e)	se seront trouvé(e)s
5 conditionnel		12 conditionnel passé	
me trouverais	nous trouverions	me serais trouvé(e)	nous serions trouvé(e)s
te trouverais	vous trouveriez	te serais trouvé(e)	vous seriez trouvé(e)(s)
se trouverait	se trouveraient	se serait trouvé(e)	se seraient trouvé(e)s
6 présent du subjonctif		13 passé du subjonctif	
me trouve	nous trouvions	me sois trouvé(e)	nous soyons trouvé(e)s
te trouves	vous trouviez	te sois trouvé(e)	vous soyez trouvé(e)(s)
se trouve	se trouvent	se soit trouvé(e)	se soient trouvé(e)s
7 imparfait du subjonctif		14 plus-que-parfait du subjonctif	
me trouvasse	nous trouvassions	me fusse trouvé(e)	nous fussions trouvé(e)s
te trouvasses	vous trouvassiez	te fusses trouvé(e)	vous fussiez trouvé(e)(s)
se trouvât	se trouvassent	se fût trouvé(e)	se fussent trouvé(e)s

Impératif
trouve-toi; ne te trouve pas
trouvons-nous; ne nous trouvons pas
trouvez-vous; ne vous trouvez pas

Où se trouve le bureau de poste?   Where is the post office located?

Trouve-toi dans ce café à huit heures ce soir.   Be in this café at 8 o'clock tonight.

Vous avez été malade; allez-vous mieux maintenant? —Oui, je me trouve mieux, merci!   You have been sick; are you feeling better now? —Yes, I'm feeling better, thank you!

Pouvez-vous me dire où se trouvent les toilettes?   Can you tell me where the restrooms are located?

See also trouver.

Regular -ir verb		to unite, to join

The Seven Simple Tenses		The Seven Compound Tenses	
Singular	Plural	Singular	Plural
1 présent de l'indicatif		**8 passé composé**	
unis	unissons	ai uni	avons uni
unis	unissez	as uni	avez uni
unit	unissent	a uni	ont uni
2 imparfait de l'indicatif		**9 plus-que-parfait de l'indicatif**	
unissais	unissions	avais uni	avions uni
unissais	unissiez	avais uni	aviez uni
unissait	unissaient	avait uni	avaient uni
3 passé simple		**10 passé antérieur**	
unis	unîmes	eus uni	eûmes uni
unis	unîtes	eus uni	eûtes uni
unit	unirent	eut uni	eurent uni
4 futur		**11 futur antérieur**	
unirai	unirons	aurai uni	aurons uni
uniras	unirez	auras uni	aurez uni
unira	uniront	aura uni	auront uni
5 conditionnel		**12 conditionnel passé**	
unirais	unirions	aurais uni	aurions uni
unirais	uniriez	aurais uni	auriez uni
unirait	uniraient	aurait uni	auraient uni
6 présent du subjonctif		**13 passé du subjonctif**	
unisse	unissions	aie uni	ayons uni
unisses	unissiez	aies uni	ayez uni
unisse	unissent	ait uni	aient uni
7 imparfait du subjonctif		**14 plus-que-parfait du subjonctif**	
unisse	unissions	eusse uni	eussions uni
unisses	unissiez	eusses uni	eussiez uni
unît	unissent	eût uni	eussent uni

	Impératif
	unis
	unissons
	unissez

---

s'unir   to join together, to marry
réunir   to reunite; se réunir   to meet together
les Etats-Unis   the United States
les Nations-Unies (l'ONU)   the United Nations
une union   union, alliance

un trait d'union   hyphen
unir ses forces   to combine one's forces
chanter à l'unisson   to sing in unison
unir en mariage   to join in marriage
Elle unit l'intelligence au courage.
   She combines intelligence with courage.

vaincre		Part. pr. vainquant	Part. passé vaincu

to vanquish, to conquer Irregular verb

The Seven Simple Tenses		The Seven Compound Tenses	
Singular	Plural	Singular	Plural
1 présent de l'indicatif		8 passé composé	
vaincs	vainquons	ai vaincu	avons vaincu
vaincs	vainquez	as vaincu	avez vaincu
vainc	vainquent	a vaincu	ont vaincu
2 imparfait de l'indicatif		9 plus-que-parfait de l'indicatif	
vainquais	vainquions	avais vaincu	avions vaincu
vainquais	vainquiez	avais vaincu	aviez vaincu
vainquait	vainquaient	avait vaincu	avaient vaincu
3 passé simple		10 passé antérieur	
vainquis	vainquîmes	eus vaincu	eûmes vaincu
vainquis	vainquîtes	eus vaincu	eûtes vaincu
vainquit	vainquirent	eut vaincu	eurent vaincu
4 futur		11 futur antérieur	
vaincrai	vaincrons	aurai vaincu	aurons vaincu
vaincras	vaincrez	auras vaincu	aurez vaincu
vaincra	vaincront	aura vaincu	auront vaincu
5 conditionnel		12 conditionnel passé	
vaincrais	vaincrions	aurais vaincu	aurions vaincu
vaincrais	vaincriez	aurais vaincu	auriez vaincu
vaincrait	vaincraient	aurait vaincu	auraient vaincu
6 présent du subjonctif		13 passé du subjonctif	
vainque	vainquions	aie vaincu	ayons vaincu
vainques	vainquiez	aies vaincu	ayez vaincu
vainque	vainquent	ait vaincu	aient vaincu
7 imparfait du subjonctif		14 plus-que-parfait du subjonctif	
vainquisse	vainquissions	eusse vaincu	eussions vaincu
vainquisses	vainquissiez	eusses vaincu	eussiez vaincu
vainquît	vainquissent	eût vaincu	eussent vaincu

Impératif
vaincs
vainquons
vainquez

---

convaincre qqn de qqch   to convince, to persuade someone of something
vainqueur   victor, victorious; conqueror, conquering
convaincant, convaincante   convincing
les vaincus   the defeated, the vanquished
s'avouer vaincu   to admit defeat
Nous vaincrons.   We shall conquer; we shall overcome.

Irregular verb   to be worth, to be as good as, to deserve, to merit, to be equal to

The Seven Simple Tenses		The Seven Compound Tenses	
Singular	Plural	Singular	Plural
1 présent de l'indicatif		8 passé composé	
vaux	valons	ai valu	avons valu
vaux	valez	as valu	avez valu
vaut	valent	a valu	ont valu
2 imparfait de l'indicatif		9 plus-que-parfait de l'indicatif	
valais	valions	avais valu	avions valu
valais	valiez	avais valu	aviez valu
valait	valaient	avait valu	avaient valu
3 passé simple		10 passé antérieur	
valus	valûmes	eus valu	eûmes valu
valus	valûtes	eus valu	eûtes valu
valut	valurent	eut valu	eurent valu
4 futur		11 futur antérieur	
vaudrai	vaudrons	aurai valu	aurons valu
vaudras	vaudrez	auras valu	aurez valu
vaudra	vaudront	aura valu	auront valu
5 conditionnel		12 conditionnel passé	
vaudrais	vaudrions	aurais valu	aurions valu
vaudrais	vaudriez	aurais valu	auriez valu
vaudrait	vaudraient	aurait valu	auraient valu
6 présent du subjonctif		13 passé du subjonctif	
vaille	valions	aie valu	ayons valu
vailles	valiez	aies valu	ayez valu
vaille	vaillent	ait valu	aient valu
7 imparfait du subjonctif		14 plus-que-parfait du subjonctif	
valusse	valussions	eusse valu	eussions valu
valusses	valussiez	eusses valu	eussiez valu
valût	valussent	eût valu	eussent valu
		Impératif	
		vaux	
		valons	
		valez	

---

la valeur   value
valeureusement   valorously
valeureux, valeureuse   valorous
la validation   validation
valide   valid
Mieux vaut tard que jamais.   Better late than never.
valoir cher   to be worth a lot
valoir de l'argent   to be worth money

Cela vaut la peine.
   It's worth the trouble.
faire valoir   to make the most of,
   to invest one's money

vendre	Part. pr. **vendant**	Part. passé **vendu**

to sell

Regular **-re** verb

The Seven Simple Tenses		The Seven Compound Tenses	
Singular	Plural	Singular	Plural
1 présent de l'indicatif		8 passé composé	
vends	vendons	ai vendu	avons vendu
vends	vendez	as vendu	avez vendu
vend	vendent	a vendu	ont vendu
2 imparfait de l'indicatif		9 plus-que-parfait de l'indicatif	
vendais	vendions	avais vendu	avions vendu
vendais	vendiez	avais vendu	aviez vendu
vendait	vendaient	avait vendu	avaient vendu
3 passé simple		10 passé antérieur	
vendis	vendîmes	eus vendu	eûmes vendu
vendis	vendîtes	eus vendu	eûtes vendu
vendit	vendirent	eut vendu	eurent vendu
4 futur		11 futur antérieur	
vendrai	vendrons	aurai vendu	aurons vendu
vendras	vendrez	auras vendu	aurez vendu
vendra	vendront	aura vendu	auront vendu
5 conditionnel		12 conditionnel passé	
vendrais	vendrions	aurais vendu	aurions vendu
vendrais	vendriez	aurais vendu	auriez vendu
vendrait	vendraient	aurait vendu	auraient vendu
6 présent du subjonctif		13 passé du subjonctif	
vende	vendions	aie vendu	ayons vendu
vendes	vendiez	aies vendu	ayez vendu
vende	vendent	ait vendu	aient vendu
7 imparfait du subjonctif		14 plus-que-parfait du subjonctif	
vendisse	vendissions	eusse vendu	eussions vendu
vendisses	vendissiez	eusses vendu	eussiez vendu
vendît	vendissent	eût vendu	eussent vendu
		Impératif	
		vends	
		vendons	
		vendez	

un vendeur, une vendeuse salesperson	vendre à bon marché to sell at
une vente a sale	a reasonably low price (a good buy)
maison à vendre house for sale	une vente aux enchères auction
revendre to resell	vendre au rabais to sell at a discount
en vente on sale	On vend des livres ici. Books are
une salle des ventes sales room	sold here.

Proverb: **Il ne faut pas vendre la peau de l'ours avant de l'avoir tué.** Don't count
   your chickens before they're hatched. (Literally: Don't sell the bear's pelt before
   you've killed it.)

Part. pr. **venant**	Part. passé **venu(e)(s)**		**venir**

Irregular verb   to come

The Seven Simple Tenses		The Seven Compound Tenses	
Singular	Plural	Singular	Plural
1 présent de l'indicatif		**8 passé composé**	
viens	**venons**	**suis venu(e)**	**sommes venu(e)s**
viens	**venez**	**es venu(e)**	**êtes venu(e)(s)**
vient	**viennent**	**est venu(e)**	**sont venu(e)s**
2 imparfait de l'indicatif		**9 plus-que-parfait de l'indicatif**	
venais	**venions**	**étais venu(e)**	**étions venu(e)s**
venais	**veniez**	**étais venu(e)**	**étiez venu(e)(s)**
venait	**venaient**	**était venu(e)**	**étaient venu(e)s**
3 passé simple		**10 passé antérieur**	
vins	**vînmes**	**fus venu(e)**	**fûmes venu(e)s**
vins	**vîntes**	**fus venu(e)**	**fûtes venu(e)(s)**
vint	**vinrent**	**fut venu(e)**	**furent venu(e)s**
4 futur		**11 futur antérieur**	
viendrai	**viendrons**	**serai venu(e)**	**serons venu(e)s**
viendras	**viendrez**	**seras venu(e)**	**serez venu(e)(s)**
viendra	**viendront**	**sera venu(e)**	**seront venu(e)s**
5 conditionnel		**12 conditionnel passé**	
viendrais	**viendrions**	**serais venu(e)**	**serions venu(e)s**
viendrais	**viendriez**	**serais venu(e)**	**seriez venu(e)(s)**
viendrait	**viendraient**	**serait venu(e)**	**seraient venu(e)s**
6 présent du subjonctif		**13 passé du subjonctif**	
vienne	**venions**	**sois venu(e)**	**soyons venu(e)s**
viennes	**veniez**	**sois venu(e)**	**soyez venu(e)(s)**
vienne	**viennent**	**soit venu(e)**	**soient venu(e)s**
7 imparfait du subjonctif		**14 plus-que-parfait du subjonctif**	
vinsse	**vinssions**	**fusse venu(e)**	**fussions venu(e)s**
vinsses	**vinssiez**	**fusses venu(e)**	**fussiez venu(e)(s)**
vînt	**vinssent**	**fût venu(e)**	**fussent venu(e)s**

Impératif
viens
venons
venez

---

venir de faire qqch   to have just done
  something
Je viens de manger.   I have just eaten.
venir à + inf.   to happen to;   **Si je viens
  à devenir riche ...**   If I happen to
  become rich ...

faire venir   to send for
Tu viens avec moi?   Are you coming
  with me?
le va et vient   coming and going
  (of people, cars, etc.)

L'appétit vient en mangeant.   The more you have, the more you want.
(Literally: Appetite comes while eating.)

See also **devenir**, **revenir**, and **se souvenir**.

visiter	Part. pr. visitant	Part. passé visité
to visit		Regular -er verb

The Seven Simple Tenses		The Seven Compound Tenses	
Singular	Plural	Singular	Plural

1 présent de l'indicatif		8 passé composé	
visite	visitons	ai visité	avons visité
visites	visitez	as visité	avez visité
visite	visitent	a visité	ont visité

2 imparfait de l'indicatif		9 plus-que-parfait de l'indicatif	
visitais	visitions	avais visité	avions visité
visitais	visitiez	avais visité	aviez visité
visitait	visitaient	avait visité	avaient visité

3 passé simple		10 passé antérieur	
visitai	visitâmes	eus visité	eûmes visité
visitas	visitâtes	eus visité	eûtes visité
visita	visitèrent	eut visité	eurent visité

4 futur		11 futur antérieur	
visiterai	visiterons	aurai visité	aurons visité
visiteras	visiterez	auras visité	aurez visité
visitera	visiteront	aura visité	auront visité

5 conditionnel		12 conditionnel passé	
visiterais	visiterions	aurais visité	aurions visité
visiterais	visiteriez	aurais visité	auriez visité
visiterait	visiteraient	aurait visité	auraient visité

6 présent du subjonctif		13 passé du subjonctif	
visite	visitions	aie visité	ayons visité
visites	visitiez	aies visité	ayez visité
visite	visitent	ait visité	aient visité

7 imparfait du subjonctif		14 plus-que-parfait du subjonctif	
visitasse	visitassions	eusse visité	eussions visité
visitasses	visitassiez	eusses visité	eussiez visité
visitât	visitassent	eût visité	eussent visité

Impératif
visite
visitons
visitez

---

rendre visite à qqn   to visit someone, to pay a call
un visiteur, une visiteuse   visitor, caller
une visite de douane   customs inspection
une visite à domicile   a house call
passer à la visite médicale   to have a physical exam

rendre une visite à qqn   to return a visit
les heures de visite   visiting hours
une visitation   visitation
une visite guidée   a guided tour

Irregular verb   to live

The Seven Simple Tenses		The Seven Compound Tenses	
Singular	Plural	Singular	Plural
1 présent de l'indicatif		**8 passé composé**	
vis	vivons	ai vécu	avons vécu
vis	vivez	as vécu	avez vécu
vit	vivent	a vécu	ont vécu
2 imparfait de l'indicatif		**9 plus-que-parfait de l'indicatif**	
vivais	vivions	avais vécu	avions vécu
vivais	viviez	avais vécu	aviez vécu
vivait	vivaient	avait vécu	avaient vécu
3 passé simple		**10 passé antérieur**	
vécus	vécûmes	eus vécu	eûmes vécu
vécus	vécûtes	eus vécu	eûtes vécu
vécut	vécurent	eut vécu	eurent vécu
4 futur		**11 futur antérieur**	
vivrai	vivrons	aurai vécu	aurons vécu
vivras	vivrez	auras vécu	aurez vécu
vivra	vivront	aura vécu	auront vécu
5 conditionnel		**12 conditionnel passé**	
vivrais	vivrions	aurais vécu	aurions vécu
vivrais	vivriez	aurais vécu	auriez vécu
vivrait	vivraient	aurait vécu	auraient vécu
6 présent du subjonctif		**13 passé du subjonctif**	
vive	vivions	aie vécu	ayons vécu
vives	viviez	aies vécu	ayez vécu
vive	vivent	ait vécu	aient vécu
7 imparfait du subjonctif		**14 plus-que-parfait du subjonctif**	
vécusse	vécussions	eusse vécu	eussions vécu
vécusses	vécussiez	eusses vécu	eussiez vécu
vécût	vécussent	eût vécu	eussent vécu
		Impératif	
		vis	
		vivons	
		vivez	

---

revivre to relive, to revive
survivre à to survive
Vive la France! Long live France!
avoir de quoi vivre to have enough
  to live on
vivre de to subsist on
la joie de vivre the joy of living

avoir du savoir-vivre to be
  well-mannered
Vivent les Etats-Unis! Long live the
  United States!
le vivre et le couvert room and board
la vie life; j'aime la vie. I love life.
C'est la vie! That's life!
Qui vivra verra. Time will tell.

voir	Part. pr. voyant	Part. passé vu

to see   Irregular verb

The Seven Simple Tenses		The Seven Compound Tenses	
Singular	Plural	Singular	Plural

1 présent de l'indicatif		8 passé composé	
vois	voyons	ai vu	avons vu
vois	voyez	as vu	avez vu
voit	voient	a vu	ont vu

2 imparfait de l'indicatif		9 plus-que-parfait de l'indicatif	
voyais	voyions	avais vu	avions vu
voyais	voyiez	avais vu	aviez vu
voyait	voyaient	avait vu	avaient vu

3 passé simple		10 passé antérieur	
vis	vîmes	eus vu	eûmes vu
vis	vîtes	eus vu	eûtes vu
vit	virent	eut vu	eurent vu

4 futur		11 futur antérieur	
verrai	verrons	aurai vu	aurons vu
verras	verrez	auras vu	aurez vu
verra	verront	aura vu	auront vu

5 conditionnel		12 conditionnel passé	
verrais	verrions	aurais vu	aurions vu
verrais	verriez	aurais vu	auriez vu
verrait	verraient	aurait vu	auraient vu

6 présent du subjonctif		13 passé du subjonctif	
voie	voyions	aie vu	ayons vu
voies	voyiez	aies vu	ayez vu
voie	voient	ait vu	aient vu

7 imparfait du subjonctif		14 plus-que-parfait du subjonctif	
visse	vissions	eusse vu	eussions vu
visses	vissiez	eusses vu	eussiez vu
vît	vissent	eût vu	eussent vu

Impératif
vois
voyons
voyez

---

revoir   to see again
faire voir   to show
voir la vie en rose   to see the bright
   side of life, to see life through
   rose-colored glasses
Voyez vous-même!   See for yourself!
entrevoir   to catch a glimpse, to glimpse
C'est à voir.   It remains to be seen.
Cela se voit.   That's obvious.

Voyons!   See here now!
Voir c'est croire.   Seeing is believing.
Édith a tendance à voir la vie en rose.
   Edith tends to see life through rose-
   colored glasses.
Qu'est-ce que tu caches dans ton sac-à-
   dos? Fais voir.   What are you hiding
   in your backpack? Show me.

Regular -er verb

to fly, to steal

The Seven Simple Tenses		The Seven Compound Tenses	
Singular	Plural	Singular	Plural
1 présent de l'indicatif		**8 passé composé**	
vole	volons	ai volé	avons volé
voles	volez	as volé	avez volé
vole	volent	a volé	ont volé
2 imparfait de l'indicatif		**9 plus-que-parfait de l'indicatif**	
volais	volions	avais volé	avions volé
volais	voliez	avais volé	aviez volé
volait	volaient	avait volé	avaient volé
3 passé simple		**10 passé antérieur**	
volai	volâmes	eus volé	eûmes volé
volas	volâtes	eus volé	eûtes volé
vola	volèrent	eut volé	eurent volé
4 futur		**11 futur antérieur**	
volerai	volerons	aurai volé	aurons volé
voleras	volerez	auras volé	aurez volé
volera	voleront	aura volé	auront volé
5 conditionnel		**12 conditionnel passé**	
volerais	volerions	aurais volé	aurions volé
volerais	voleriez	aurais volé	auriez volé
volerait	voleraient	aurait volé	auraient volé
6 présent du subjonctif		**13 passé du subjonctif**	
vole	volions	aie volé	ayons volé
voles	voliez	aies volé	ayez volé
vole	volent	ait volé	aient volé
7 imparfait du subjonctif		**14 plus-que-parfait du subjonctif**	
volasse	volassions	eusse volé	eussions volé
volasses	volassiez	eusses volé	eussiez volé
volât	volassent	eût volé	eussent volé

Impératif
vole
volons
volez

---

un vol flight, theft	survoler to fly over
le voleur thief	le volant steering wheel
à vol d'oiseau as the crow flies	se mettre au volant to take the (steering)
un vol de nuit night flying (airplane),	wheel
night flight	Au voleur! Stop, thief!
New York à vol d'oiseau	s'envoler to take off, to fly away
a bird's eye view of New York	

vouloir	Part. pr. **voulant**	Part. passé **voulu**

to want — Irregular verb

The Seven Simple Tenses		The Seven Compound Tenses	
Singular	Plural	Singular	Plural
1 présent de l'indicatif		**8 passé composé**	
veux	voulons	ai voulu	avons voulu
veux	voulez	as voulu	avez voulu
veut	veulent	a voulu	ont voulu
2 imparfait de l'indicatif		**9 plus-que-parfait de l'indicatif**	
voulais	voulions	avais voulu	avions voulu
voulais	vouliez	avais voulu	aviez voulu
voulait	voulaient	avait voulu	avaient voulu
3 passé simple		**10 passé antérieur**	
voulus	voulûmes	eus voulu	eûmes voulu
voulus	voulûtes	eus voulu	eûtes voulu
voulut	voulurent	eut voulu	eurent voulu
4 futur		**11 futur antérieur**	
voudrai	voudrons	aurai voulu	aurons voulu
voudras	voudrez	auras voulu	aurez voulu
voudra	voudront	aura voulu	auront voulu
5 conditionnel		**12 conditionnel passé**	
voudrais	voudrions	aurais voulu	aurions voulu
voudrais	voudriez	aurais voulu	auriez voulu
voudrait	voudraient	aurait voulu	auraient voulu
6 présent du subjonctif		**13 passé du subjonctif**	
veuille	voulions	aie voulu	ayons voulu
veuilles	vouliez	aies voulu	ayez voulu
veuille	veuillent	ait voulu	aient voulu
7 imparfait du subjonctif		**14 plus-que-parfait du subjonctif**	
voulusse	voulussions	eusse voulu	eussions voulu
voulusses	voulussiez	eusses voulu	eussiez voulu
voulût	voulussent	eût voulu	eussent voulu

Impératif
veuille
veuillons
veuillez

---

un voeu   a wish
meilleurs voeux   best wishes
Vouloir c'est pouvoir.   Where there's a will there's a way.
vouloir dire   to mean; Qu'est-ce que cela veut dire?   What does that mean?
vouloir bien faire qqch   to be willing to do something

sans le vouloir   without meaning to, unintentionally
en temps voulu   in due time
en vouloir à qqn   to bear a grudge against someone
Que voulez-vous dire par là?   What do you mean by that remark?
Veuillez éteindre vos téléphones cellulaires/vos portables.   Please turn off your cell phones.

Regular **-er** verb endings: spelling change: retain the   to travel
ge before **a** or **o** to keep the soft **g** sound of the verb.

The Seven Simple Tenses		The Seven Compound Tenses	
Singular	Plural	Singular	Plural
1 présent de l'indicatif		8 passé composé	
voyage	voyageons	ai voyagé	avons voyagé
voyages	voyagez	as voyagé	avez voyagé
voyage	voyagent	a voyagé	ont voyagé
2 imparfait de l'indicatif		9 plus-que-parfait de l'indicatif	
voyageais	voyagions	avais voyagé	avions voyagé
voyageais	voyagiez	avais voyagé	aviez voyagé
voyageait	voyageaient	avait voyagé	avaient voyagé
3 passé simple		10 passé antérieur	
voyageai	voyageâmes	eus voyagé	eûmes voyagé
voyageas	voyageâtes	eus voyagé	eûtes voyagé
voyagea	voyagèrent	eut voyagé	eurent voyagé
4 futur		11 futur antérieur	
voyagerai	voyagerons	aurai voyagé	aurons voyagé
voyageras	voyagerez	auras voyagé	aurez voyagé
voyagera	voyageront	aura voyagé	auront voyagé
5 conditionnel		12 conditionnel passé	
voyagerais	voyagerions	aurais voyagé	aurions voyagé
voyagerais	voyageriez	aurais voyagé	auriez voyagé
voyagerait	voyageraient	aurait voyagé	auraient voyagé
6 présent du subjonctif		13 passé du subjonctif	
voyage	voyagions	aie voyagé	ayons voyagé
voyages	voyagiez	aies voyagé	ayez voyagé
voyage	voyagent	ait voyagé	aient voyagé
7 imparfait du subjonctif		14 plus-que-parfait du subjonctif	
voyageasse	voyageassions	eusse voyagé	eussions voyagé
voyageasses	voyageassiez	eusses voyagé	eussiez voyagé
voyageât	voyageassent	eût voyagé	eussent voyagé
		Impératif	
		voyage	
		voyageons	
		voyagez	

---

un voyage   a trip
faire un voyage   to take a trip
un voyageur, une voyageuse   traveler
une agence de voyages   travel agency
Bon voyage!   Have a good trip!
Bon voyage et bon retour!   Have a good trip and a safe return!
J'aime le roman *Voyage au centre de la Terre* **de Jules Verne.**
   I like the novel *Journey to the Center of the Earth* by Jules Verne.

English-French Verb Index

The purpose of this index is to give you instantly the French verb for the English verb you have in mind to use. This saves you time if you do not have at your fingertips a standard English-French word dictionary.

If the French verb you want is reflexive (e.g., **s'appeler** or **se lever**), you will find it alphabetically among the verbs under the first letter of the verb and not under the reflexive pronoun *s'* or *se*.

When you find the French verb you need through the English verb, look up its verb forms in this book, where all the verbs are listed alphabetically at the top of each page. If it is not listed among the 301 verbs in this book, consult the list of over 1,000 French verbs conjugated like model verbs among the 301 that begins on page 312. If it is not listed there, consult our more comprehensive book, *501 French Verbs,* Sixth Edition, with new features.

A

able, be **pouvoir**, 217
accept **accepter**, 1
accompany **accompagner**, 2
acquainted with, be **connaître**, 61
act (in a play) **jouer**, 155
add **ajouter**, 11
admire **admirer**, 6
admit **admettre**, 5
adore **adorer**, 7
advance **avancer**, 30
afraid, be **craindre**, 71
aid **aider**, 9
allow **laisser**, 156; **permettre**, 208
amaze **étonner**, 118
amuse **amuser**, 15; **égayer**, 100
amuse oneself **s'amuser**, 16
angry, become **se fâcher**, 124
annoy **ennuyer**, 107
answer **répondre**, 245
apologize **s'excuser**, 121
appear **paraître**, 193
arrange **arranger**, 21
arrest **arrêter**, 22
arrive **arriver**, 24
ascend **monter**, 173

ask (for) **demander**, 81
assist **aider**, 9
assist (at) **assister**, 26
assure oneself **s'assurer**, 27
astonish **étonner**, 118
attend **assister**, 26

B

babble **bavarder**, 36
be **être**, 119
be a matter of **s'agir**, 8
be a question of **s'agir**, 8
be able **pouvoir**, 217
be acquainted with **connaître**, 61
be afraid **craindre**, 71
be as good as **valoir**, 293
be born **naître**, 179
be busy **s'occuper**, 188
be enough **suffire**, 277
be like **ressembler**, 249
be located **se trouver**, 290
be named **s'appeler**, 18
be necessary **falloir**, 127
be present (at) **assister**, 26
be quiet **se taire**, 279

be silent **se taire**, 279
be situated **se trouver**, 290
be sufficient **suffire**, 277
be the matter **s'agir**, 8
be worth **valoir**, 293
beat **battre**, 34
become **devenir**, 90
become angry **se fâcher**, 124
begin **commencer**, 57; **se mettre**, 172
believe **croire**, 73
beware **se méfier**, 168
bite **mordre**, 175
blow **souffler**, 271
bore **ennuyer**, 107
born, be **naître**, 179
borrow **emprunter**, 105
break **casser**, 45; **se casser**, 46; **rompre**, 257
bring **amener**, 14; **apporter**, 19
bring down **descendre**, 86
bring up (take up) **monter**, 173
brush **brosser**, 40
brush oneself **se brosser**, 41
build **bâtir**, 33; **construire**, 62
burden **charger**, 52
burn **brûler**, 42
burst **rompre**, 257
busy, be **s'occuper**, 188
buy **acheter**, 4

C

call **appeler**, 17
call again **rappeler**, 231
call back **rappeler**, 231
call oneself **s'appeler**, 18
can **pouvoir**, 217
carry **porter**, 215
carry away **enlever**, 106
cast **jeter**, 153
catch **attraper**, 29
cause **causer**, 47
cease **cesser**, 49

change **changer**, 50
charge **charger**, 52
chase **chasser**, 53
chat **bavarder**, 36; **causer**, 47
chatter **bavarder**, 36
cheer up **égayer**, 100
chide **gronder**, 142
choose **choisir**, 55
clean **nettoyer**, 181
close **fermer**, 128
come **venir**, 295
come back **revenir**, 254
come in **entrer**, 110
command **commander**, 56
commence **commencer**, 57
commit sin **pécher**, 201
complain **se plaindre**, 211
complete **finir**, 130
conduct **conduire**, 60
conquer **vaincre**, 292
construct **construire**, 62; **bâtir**, 33
continue **continuer**, 64
cook **cuire**, 75
correct **corriger**, 65
cost **coûter**, 69
count **compter**, 59
cover **couvrir**, 70
cross **traverser**, 288
cry **pleurer**, 213
cry out **crier**, 72
cure **guérir**, 143
cut **couper**, 67

D

damage **gâter**, 138
dance **danser**, 76
defend **défendre**, 79
demand **exiger**, 122
depart **partir**, 196
derange **déranger**, 85
descend **descendre**, 86
describe **décrire**, 78
deserve **valoir**, 293

desire **désirer**, 87
destroy **détruire**, 89
detest **détester**, 88
die **mourir**, 176; **périr**, 207
dine **dîner**, 92
dirty **salir**, 259
discover **découvrir**, 77
dislike **détester**, 88
display **montrer**, 174
distrust **se méfier**, 168
disturb **déranger**, 85
do **faire**, 126
doubt **douter**, 96
dream **songer**, 268
dress oneself **s'habiller**, 144
drink **boire**, 39
drive (a car) **conduire**, 60
drive out **chasser**, 53
dwell (in) **habiter**, 145

E

earn **gagner**, 136
eat **manger**, 165
embrace **embrasser**, 101
employ **employer**, 104
end **finir**, 130; **terminer**, 282
enjoy oneself **s'amuser**, 16
enliven **égayer**, 100
enough, be **suffire**, 277
enter **entrer**, 110
entertain **amuser**, 15; **égayer**, 100
excuse oneself **s'excuser**, 121
exhibit **montrer**, 174
explain **expliquer**, 123
extinguish **éteindre**, 116

F

fail **faillir**, 125
fall **tomber**, 283
fear **craindre**, 71
feed **nourrir**, 182

feel **sentir**, 265
fight **se battre**, 35
fill **remplir**, 240
find **trouver**, 289
finish **finir**, 130; **terminer**, 282
fish **pêcher**, 202
flee **fuir**, 134
fly **fuir**, 134; **voler**, 299
follow **suivre**, 278
forbid **défendre**, 79;
   interdire, 149
force **forcer**, 131
forget **oublier**, 191
forgive **pardonner**, 194
freeze **geler**, 139
frighten **effrayer**, 99
fry **frire**, 133

G

gain **gagner**, 136
gather **cueillir**, 74
get **obtenir**, 186; **recevoir**, 233
get angry **se fâcher**, 124
get dressed **s'habiller**, 144
get up **se lever**, 161
give **donner**, 94
give back **remettre**, 238;
   rendre, 242
go **aller**, 12
go away **s'en aller**, 13
go back **retourner**, 251
go down **descendre**, 86
go forward **avancer**, 30
go in **entrer**, 110
go out **sortir**, 270
go to bed **se coucher**, 66
go up **monter**, 173
gossip **bavarder**, 36
grasp **saisir**, 258
greet **accueillir**, 3
grow (up, grow taller) **grandir**, 141
grow thin **maigrir**, 164
guard **garder**, 137

H

happen **se passer**, 198;
  arriver, 24
harm **blesser**, 37; **nuire**, 183
hasten **se dépêcher**, 83
hate **haïr**, 146
have **avoir**, 31
have (hold) **tenir**, 281
have a good time **s'amuser**, 16
have a snack **goûter**, 140
have dinner **dîner**, 92
have lunch **déjeuner**, 80
have to **devoir**, 91
hear **entendre**, 109
help **aider**, 9
help oneself (to food and drink)
  se servir, 267
hide **cacher**, 43
hide oneself **se cacher**, 44
hinder **empêcher**, 103; **nuire**,
  183
hit **battre**, 34; **frapper**, 132
hold **tenir**, 281
hope **espérer**, 113
hunt **chasser**, 53
hurl **lancer**, 157
hurry **se dépêcher**, 83
hurt **blesser**, 37
hurt oneself **se blesser**, 38

I

increase **grandir**, 141
inhabit **habiter**, 145
injure **blesser**, 37
injure oneself **se blesser**, 38
insist **insister**, 147
instruct **instruire**, 148
insure oneself **s'assurer**, 27
intend **compter**, 59
interrupt **interrompre**, 150
introduce **introduire**, 151
invite **inviter**, 152

J

join **joindre**, 154
jump **sauter**, 260

K

keep **garder**, 137
keep oneself busy **s'occuper**, 188
kiss **embrasser**, 101
knock **frapper**, 132
know **connaître**, 61
know (how) **savoir**, 263

L

lack **manquer**, 166
lament **se plaindre**, 211
laugh **rire**, 256
launch **lancer**, 157
lead **amener**, 14; **conduire**, 60;
  mener, 169
lead away **emmener**, 102
leap **sauter**, 260
learn **apprendre**, 20
leave **laisser**, 156; **partir**, 196;
  quitter, 229; **sortir**, 270
lend **prêter**, 221
let **laisser**, 156; **permettre**, 208
lie down **s'étendre**, 117;
  se coucher, 66
lie, tell a **mentir**, 170
lift **lever**, 160
like **aimer**, 10
listen (to) **écouter**, 97
live **vivre**, 297
live (reside) **demeurer**, 82
live (in) **habiter**, 145
load **charger**, 52
located, be **se trouver**, 290
look (at) **regarder**, 236
look for **chercher**, 54
look like **ressembler**, 249

R

rain **pleuvoir**, 214
raise (lift) **lever**, 160
read **lire**, 162
recall **rappeler**, 231; **se rappeler**, 232; **se souvenir**, 276
receive **recevoir**, 233
recollect **se rappeler**, 232
recover **reprendre**, 247
reduce (one's weight) **maigrir**, 164
reflect **réfléchir**, 234
refuse **refuser**, 235
relate **conter**, 63; **raconter**, 230
remain **rester**, 250; **demeurer**, 82
remember **se rappeler**, 232; **se souvenir**, 276
remind **rappeler**, 231
remove **enlever**, 106
render **rendre**, 242
repeat **répéter**, 244
replace **remettre**, 238; **remplacer**, 239
reply **répondre**, 245
reprimand **gronder**, 142
request **demander**, 81
require **exiger**, 122
rescue **sauver**, 261
resemble **ressembler**, 249
reside **demeurer**, 82
resolve **résoudre**, 248
rest **se reposer**, 246
resume **reprendre**, 247
retain **garder**, 137
return **rentrer**, 243; **retourner**, 251
return (something) **rendre**, 242
ring **sonner**, 269
run **courir**, 68
run away **se sauver**, 262

S

save (rescue) **sauver**, 261
say **dire**, 93
scold **gronder**, 142
search **chercher**, 54
see **voir**, 298
see again **revoir**, 255
see once more **revoir**, 255
seem **paraître**, 193; **sembler**, 264
seize **saisir**, 258
select **choisir**, 55
sell **vendre**, 294
send **envoyer**, 111
serve **servir**, 266
serve oneself **se servir**, 267
shatter **rompre**, 257
shine **luire**, 163
should **devoir**, 91
shout **crier**, 72
show **montrer**, 174
show in **introduire**, 151
silent, be **se taire**, 279
sin **pécher**, 201
sing **chanter**, 51
sit down **s'asseoir**, 25
skate (on ice) **patiner**, 199
sleep **dormir**, 95
smell **sentir**, 265
smile **sourire**, 275
smoke **fumer**, 135
snow **neiger**, 180
soil **salir**, 259
solve **résoudre**, 248
speak **parler**, 195
speak, not to **se taire**, 279
spend (money) **dépenser**, 84
spend (time) **passer**, 197
spoil **gâter**, 138
start **commencer**, 57; **se mettre**, 172
stay **rester**, 250; **demeurer**, 82
steal **voler**, 299
stink **puer**, 227

Index of Common Irregular French Verb Forms Identified by Infinitive

The purpose of this index is to help you identify those verb forms that cannot be readily identified because they are irregular in some way. For example, if you come across the verb form *fut* (which is very common) in your French readings, this index will tell you that *fut* is a form of être. Then you look up être in this book and you will find that verb form on the page where all the forms of être are given.

Verb forms whose first three or four letters are the same as the infinitive have not been included because they can easily be identified by referring to the alphabetical listing of the 301 verbs in this book.

été **être**
êtes **être**
étiez **être**
eu **avoir**
eûmes **avoir**
eurent **avoir**
eus **avoir**
eusse, *etc.* **avoir**
eut, eût **avoir**
eûtes **avoir**

F

faille **faillir, falloir**
fais, *etc.* **faire**
fasse, *etc.* **faire**
faudra **faillir, falloir**
faudrait **faillir, falloir**
faut **faillir, falloir**
faux **faillir**
ferai, *etc.* **faire**
fîmes **faire**
firent **faire**
fis, *etc.* **faire**
font **faire**
fûmes **être**
furent **être**
fus, *etc.* **être**
fut, fût **être**
fuyais, *etc.* **fuir**

I

ira, irai, iras, *etc.* **aller**

L

lis, *etc.* **lire**
lu **lire**
lus, *etc.* **lire**

M

meure, *etc.* **mourir**
meus, *etc.* **mouvoir**
mîmes **mettre**
mirent **mettre**
mis **mettre**
misses, *etc.* **mettre**
mit **mettre**
mort **mourir**
mû, mue **mouvoir**
mussent **mouvoir**
mut **mouvoir**

N

naquîmes, *etc.* **naître**
né **naître**

O

omis **omettre**
ont **avoir**

P

pars **partir**
paru **paraître**
peignis, *etc.* **peindre**
peuvent **pouvoir**
peux, *etc.* **pouvoir**
plu **plaire, pleuvoir**
plurent **plaire**
plut, plût **plaire, pleuvoir**
plûtes **plaire**
pourrai, *etc.* **pouvoir**
prîmes **prendre**
prirent **prendre**
pris **prendre**
prisse, *etc.* **prendre**
pu **pouvoir**

puis **pouvoir**
puisse, *etc*. **pouvoir**
pûmes, *etc*. **pouvoir**
purent **pouvoir**
pus **pouvoir**
pusse **pouvoir**
put, pût **pouvoir**

R

reçois, *etc*. **recevoir**
reçûmes, *etc*. **recevoir**
reviens, *etc*. **revenir**
revins, *etc*. **revenir**
riiez **rire**
ris, *etc*. **rire**

S

sache, *etc*. **savoir**
sais, *etc*. **savoir**
saurai, *etc*. **savoir**
serai, *etc*. **être**
sers, *etc*. **servir**
sois, *etc*. **être**
sommes **être**
sont **être**
sors, *etc*. **sortir**
soyez **être**
soyons **être**
su **savoir**
suis **être**, **suivre**
suit **suivre**
sûmes **savoir**
surent **savoir**
susse, *etc*. **savoir**
sut, sût **savoir**

T

tiendrai, *etc*. **tenir**
tienne, *etc*. **tenir**

tînmes **tenir**
tins, *etc*. **tenir**
tu **taire**
tûmes **taire**
turent **taire**
tus **taire**
tusse, *etc*. **taire**
tut, tût **taire**

V

va **aller**
vaille **valoir**
vais **aller**
vas **aller**
vaudrai, *etc*. **valoir**
vaux, *etc*. **valoir**
vécu **vivre**
vécûmes, *etc*. **vivre**
verrai, *etc*. **voir**
veuille, *etc*. **vouloir**
veulent **vouloir**
veux, *etc*. **vouloir**
viendrai, *etc*. **venir**
vienne, *etc*. **venir**
viens, *etc*. **venir**
vîmes **voir**
vînmes **venir**
vinrent **venir**
vins, *etc*. **venir**
virent **voir**
vis **vivre**, **voir**
visse, *etc*. **voir**
vit **vivre**, **voir**
vît **voir**
vîtes **voir**
vont **aller**
voudrai, *etc*. **vouloir**
voyais, *etc*. **voir**
vu **voir**

Over 1,000 French Verbs Conjugated Like Model Verbs Among the 301

The number after each verb is the page number in this book where a model verb is shown fully conjugated. At times there are two page references; for example, **abréger** is conjugated like **céder** on page 48 because é changes to è and like **manger** on page 165 because **abréger** and **manger** are both -ger type verbs.

If the French verb you want is reflexive (*e.g.,* s'appeler or se lever), you will find it listed alphabetically under the first letter of the verb and not under the reflexive pronoun *s'* or *se*.

F

fabriquer 123
fabuler 42
faciliter 145
façonner 94
faiblir 240
se faire 126
  (with *être*)
falsifier 120
farcir 55
farder 137
se farder 44
fatiguer 237
se fatiguer 66
favoriser 15
feindre 204
féliciter 145
fendre 242
filer 10
filmer 128
filtrer 174
fixer 1
flâner 269
flanquer 166
flatter 45
flirter 260
flotter 40
foncer 225
fonder 142
fondre 242
former 128
fouetter 273
fouiller 287
fournir 291
franchir 55
frémir 228
fréquenter 97
fricasser 45
friser 47
frissonner 94
frotter 40
fuser 15
fusiller 287

G

gâcher 43
gambader 9
garantir 130
gargouiller 287
garnir 130
gaspiller 287
gazouiller 287
gémir 130
gêner 10
glisser 37
gonfler 271
gratter 45
grêler 10
grelotter 40
grimacer 209
grimper 67
grincer 57
gripper 132
grogner 2
grossir 164
grouper 67
guider 9

H

NOTE: The mark • in front of
the letter *h* denotes that it is
aspirate; make no liaison and
use *je* instead of *j'*.

habiliter 145
habiller 145
s'habituer 16
•haleter 4
•hanter 51
•harasser 45
•harceler 4
•hasarder 137
•hâter 138
se •hâter 38, 138
•hausser 53
hériter 145
hésiter 145

V

W

U

Z

Indispensable for Students . . .
Handy for Travelers

Here is a series to help the foreign language student successfully approach verbs and all their details. Complete conjugations of the verbs are arranged one verb to a page in alphabetical order. Verb forms are printed in boldface type in two columns, and common idioms using the applicable verbs are listed at the bottom of the page in each volume. Some titles include a CD-ROM.

501 Verb Series

501 Arabic Verbs
978-0-7641-3622-1, $18.99, *Can$22.99*

501 English Verbs, 2nd, with CD-ROM
978-0-7641-7985-3, $18.99, *Can$22.99*

501 French Verbs, 6th, with CD-ROM
978-0-7641-7983-9, $16.99, *Can$19.99*

501 German Verbs, 4th, with CD-ROM
978-0-7641-9393-4, $18.99, *Can$22.99*

501 Hebrew Verbs, 2nd
978-0-7641-3748-8, $18.99, *Can$22.99*

501 Italian Verbs, 3rd, with CD-ROM
978-0-7641-7982-2, $16.99, *Can$19.99*

501 Japanese Verbs, 3rd
978-0-7641-3749-5, $18.99, *Can$22.99*

501 Latin Verbs, 2nd
978-0-7641-3742-6, $18.99, *Can$22.99*

501 Portuguese Verbs, 2nd
978-0-7641-2916-2, $18.99, *Can$22.99*

501 Russian Verbs, 3rd
978-0-7641-3743-3, $18.99, *Can$22.99*

501 Spanish Verbs, 7th, with CD-ROM and Audio CD
978-0-7641-9797-0, $16.99, *Can$19.99*

To order visit
www.barronseduc.com
or your local book store

Barron's Educational Series, Inc.
250 Wireless Blvd.
Hauppauge, N.Y. 11788
Order toll-free: 1-800-645-3476
Order by fax: 1-631-434-3217

Prices subject to change without notice.

In Canada:
Georgetown Book Warehouse
34 Armstrong Ave.
Georgetown, Ontario L7G 4R9
Canadian orders: 1-800-247-7160
Order by fax: 1-800-887-1594

(#200) R5/10

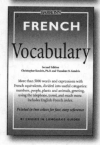